Soldiers, Peasants, and Bureaucrats

Published under the auspices of the
Center for International and Strategic Affairs,
University of California, Los Angeles.

Soldiers, Peasants, and Bureaucrats

Civil–Military Relations in Communist and Modernizing Societies

Edited by
Roman Kolkowicz and Andrzej Korbonski
Center for International and Strategic Affairs,
University of California

London
GEORGE ALLEN & UNWIN
Boston   Sydney

George Allen & Unwin (Publishers) Ltd,
40 Museum Street, London WC1A 1LU, UK

George Allen & Unwin (Publishers) Ltd,
Park Lane, Hemel Hempstead, Herts HP2 4TE, UK

Allen & Unwin Inc.,
9 Winchester Terrace, Winchester, Mass. 01890, USA

George Allen & Unwin Australia Pty Ltd,
8 Napier Street, North Sydney, NSW 2060, Australia

First published in 1982

British Library Catologuing in Publication Data

Soldiers, peasants and bureaucrats.
1. Armed forces — Political activity
2. Socialism
I. Kolkowicz, Roman   II. Korbonski, Andrzej
322'.5   JC507
ISBN 0-04-322007-X

Library of Congress Cataloging in Publication Data

Soldiers, peasants, and bureaucrats.
Includes index.
1. Civil supremacy over the military — Addresses,
essays, lectures. 2. Civil supremacy over the military
— Near East — Addresses, essays, lectures. 3. Civil
supremacy over the military — Communist countries —
Addresses, essays, lectures. I. Kolkowicz, Roman.
II. Korbonski, Andrzej.
JF195.C5S63   322'.5   81-17584
ISBN 0-04-322007-X   AACR2

Set in 10 on 11 point Times by Alan Sutton Publishing Ltd,
Gloucester
and printed in Great Britain
by Mackays of Chatham

Contents

Introduction Civil–Military Studies: Fragmentation and
Integration *by Roman Kolkowicz*   *page* 1

PART ONE   CIVIL–MILITARY RELATIONS IN THE MIDDLE
EAST

1 The Study of Civil–Military Relations in Modernizing
   Societies in the Middle East: A Critical Assessment
   by Fuad I. Khuri   9
2 Egypt and Turkey: The Military in the Background
   by Richard H. Dekmejian
3 The Syrian Armed Forces in National Politics: The Role   28
   of the Geographic and Ethnic Periphery *by Alasdair
   Drysdale*   52
4 The Israel Defense Forces: A Civilianized Military in a
   Partially Militarized Society *by Dan Horowitz*   77

PART TWO   CIVIL–MILITARY RELATIONS IN SOCIALIST
SOCIETIES

5 Military Intervention in the Soviet Union: Scenario for
   Post-Hegemonial Synthesis *by Roman Kolkowicz*   109
6 The Military as a Political Actor in China *by Ellis Joffe*   139
7 The Military as a Political Actor in Poland *by Andrzej
   Korbonski and Sarah M. Terry*   159
8 The Role of the Military in Yugoslavia: An Historical
   Sketch *by A. Ross Johnson*   181
9 Party–Military Relations in Eastern Europe: The Case
   of Romania *by Alex Alexiev*   199

PART THREE   SYSTEMIC CHANGE AND THE ROLE OF
THE MILITARY: MODERNIZATION, DEVELOPMENT,
AND CIVIL–MILITARY RELATIONS

10 Toward a Theory of Civil–Military Relations in
    Communist (Hegemonial) Systems *by Roman
    Kilkowicz*   231
11 The Praetorian Army: Insecurity, Venality, and
    Impotence *by David C. Rapoport*   252
12 The Morphology of Military Regimes *by Samuel E. Finer*   281
13 Civil–Military Relations in Socialist Authoritarian and
    Praetorian States: Prospects and Retrospects
    by Amos Perlmutter   310

Notes on the Editors and Contributors   332

Index   335

Introduction

Civil–Military Studies: Fragmentation and Integration

ROMAN KOLKOWICZ

In *The Structure of Scientific Revolutions*, Thomas Kuhn observed:[1]

Close historical investigation of a given speciality at a given time discloses a set of recurrent and quasi-standard illustrations of various theories in their conceptual, observational, and instrumental applications. These are the community's paradigms, revealed in its textbooks, lectures, and laboratory exercises. By studying them and by practicing with them, the members of the corresponding community learn their trade.

Kuhn refers here to the 'normal science' arena which is dominated by the prevailing paradigms. However, outside this 'normal science' Kuhn also perceives 'a penumbral area occupied by achievements whose status is still in doubt'. These observations are applicable to our enterprise. Our concern here, in planning the conference and in preparing this volume, has been with problems and stresses between the mainline 'normal science' of the dominant paradigms and the penumbral areas in the study of civil and military institutions and the dynamics of their interactions.

In his book on *The Soviet Union and Social Science Theory*, Jerry Hough[2] challenged those 'leading figures in the social sciences [who] have condemned area studies and have demanded that area specialists become main-line social scientists.' While this in itself is clearly a commendable idea, Hough finds that, in practice, these social scientists have shown little interest in bringing such studies 'into the discipline.' In one particular instance (Soviet studies) he asserts that social scientists were clearly uninterested in seriously understanding the object of analysis, but instead tended to analyze it 'in black and white, ideal type terms that emphasize its distinctive character both empirically and normatively . . .' Misperceiving its peculiarities and heterodoxies, they generally used it 'for little more than a foil against which to highlight the virtues of Western political systems or non-Communistic models of development,' thus effectively confining such area studies 'to a ghetto within the social sciences.'

A primary objective of this conference was to dismantle, at least in part, the walls of the disciplinary ghettos in the field of civil–military studies. We hoped to encourage confrontations and appreciations across boundaries of the several specialized areas of the field – a process that would ameliorate certain disciplinary hubris as well as parochialisms. A sense of open-endedness was intended, in the spirit of Kuhn's clear-headed observation that 'philosophers of science have repeatedly demonstrated that more than one theoretical construction can always be placed upon a given collection of data,'[3] and also in the spirit of Max Weber's wise admonition to social scientists that their sciences (or as he preferred to call them 'cultural sciences') can only proceed by means of a 'perpetual process of reconstruction of those concepts in terms of which we seek to lay hold of reality.'[4]

Western research on civil–military relations may be divided into three broad areas of concentration in the developed, developing, and communist countries. Each research area contains its specific conceptual focus, analytical method, dominant assumptions and prescriptive norms. Each research area appears to contain a dominant orientation influenced by its major exponents. Thus, the study of the military in the *developed* countries was initially influenced by sociologists, with inputs from political science and history.[5] The study of the military in the *developing* areas was initially dominated by experts from the fields of comparative politics and sociology.[6] The writings on the military in the *socialist* countries have come largely from nonacademic sources, mainly from research institutes, governmental agencies, and from Sovietologists and Sinologists.[7]

The strong influence of the dominant group in each area of research has resulted in a not-unexpected conceptual, methodological, and attitudinal preference congenial to each particular group. Thus, the *sociologists* tended to emphasize the importance of internal structures, social origins and composition of officer corps, and the value systems prevalent in the military in developed countries. The *comparativists* tended toward paradigmatic approaches to military organizations and their role in the developing countries, emphasizing such analytical criteria as development, intervention, maintenance, integration, and performance. The *Sovietologists* tended toward approaches premised in threat perception, capability studies, strategic doctrines, weapons technologies, and elite tensions.

More specifically, the scholars and analysts in the three areas of research asked significantly different questions in order to arrive at a better understanding of their subjects. The analysts of the military in the *developed* countries inquired into the social composition of the military, the degree of its professionalization, and its congruity with democratic or anti-democratic traditions and forms of government; the military's role as an interest group and its influence on political decisions and social priorities within the country; the impacts of modern technology on the military ethos, on managerial functions within a bureaucratized military establishment.

The literature on the military in the *developing* countries has grown in recent years to such an extent that it was viewed as being 'a sure sign of the explosion of interest in the subject.' The primary concerns of the analysts in this field are with such problems as: Is the military a modernizing force in developing societies or is it retrogressive? Is the military a more efficient organization than civilian regimes for political development, economic management, social stability, and national integration? Is the military more interested in its own power rather than in national development and modernization? Under what circumstances does the military tend to intervene in the political process and civilian regimes, and what are some of the means and consequences of military intervention?

Now while the study of the military in the developed and developing countries has received serious and rather extensive scholarly attention in the West, this cannot be said about the military in the *socialist* countries. It is rather ironic that while the socialist countries comprise more than a third of the world's population and include military organizations in countries ranging from 'developed' to clearly 'underdeveloped', they have nevertheless received but scant attention from academic researchers and scholars. There may be various explanations for this lacuna: absence of reliable data; poor access to institutions or members of the military; virtual ignorance about the social composition and institutional procedures. This situational complexity was further exacerbated by the research focus of most Western analysts studying the military in socialist countries. Starting from the premise that these countries and their governments were our adversaries, and perceiving a direct threat from the military in the socialist countries to our own vital interests and very survival, analysts in the West concentrated largely on assessing their 'threat potential'. They asked, therefore, the following kinds of questions: How destructive and efficient are their weapons and military technologies? What kinds of strategies motivate socialist defense policies? What proportion of the GNP, of the manpower pools, of scientific/ technical communities goes to the military and defense sectors? Little effort was made to study the military in socialist countries in terms of its social composition, social roles, institutional values and interests, or its larger role in society. It is quickly apparent that Western research on the military in the three parts of the world differs significantly in terms of conceptual approaches, analytic methods, and normative prescriptions. These differences were further accentuated by certain cognitive biases and certain assumptions regarding the political context of the three types of military organizations.

The analysts in their three respective areas of research differed also in their perceptions regarding the level or scope of change or modernization in the developed, developing, and socialist countries. Thus, it was generally assumed these areas contain respectively: societies undergoing gradual, *evolutionary change* (developed); societies undergoing rapid, almost *revolutionary change,* or societies where conditions for such change are assumed to be imminent (developing); and societies that remain politically *static,* while technologically and economically modernizing at a fairly rapid rate (socialist). Correspondingly, the military in the developed countries was not considered to be an important instrument of change; in the developing countries it is considered to be an important actual or potential source of change; and in the socialist countries the military's capabilities or willingness to effect change was rarely considered.

It would appear, therefore, that Western studies of the military institutions and their role within society are characterized by a certain unevenness, by a set of historically idiosyncratic circumstances and by a certain parochialism. It is rather unfortunate that the isolation of the respective parts of the field have made it difficult, if not impossible, to transfer certain insights from a more 'developed' research area to one that is still rather 'underdeveloped'. Moreover, the inadequate participation of scholars and analysts from the regions under consideration may have introduced certain ethnocentricities into the research products in these fields.

It is with these considerations in mind that the organizers of the Santa Barbara Conference on Civil–Military Relations began to plan for a meeting of scholars from a variety of disciplines as well as from the various countries and respective regions of study. It was our intention to bring together a group of scholars for a serious examination of the dominant theoretical, methodological, and empirical approaches to the study of the military in all three areas of concentration: moreover, to concentrate the major research concerns at the conference upon the role of the military in the modernizing political systems in both the socialist countries and the broad Middle Eastern region. While such an arbitrary focus does leave out a number of research-worthy regions of the world, we nevertheless became convinced that in the interest of economy of effort, and in the light of the sponsoring organizations' primary research focus (Europe and the Middle East), such a program would serve to innovate the field.

The thirty-six scholars who gathered in Santa Barbara in May 1979 were: Kamel S. Abu-Jaber (University of Jordan); Alex Alexiev (RAND Corporation); Gabriel Almond (Stanford University); Vernon Aspaturian (Pennsylvania State University); Anton Bebler (University of Ljubljana); Henry Bienen (Princeton University); Alexander Dallin (Stanford University); Robert Dean (RAND Corporation); Michael Deane (University of Miami); Richard H. Dekmejian (State University of New York, Albany); Ali Dessouki (University of Cairo); Alasdair Drysdale (University of New Hampshire); Paul Godwin (Air Force University); Dale R. Herspring (US Department of State); Arnold Horelick (Central Intelligence Agency); Dan Horowitz (Hebrew University, Jerusalem); Ellis Joffe (Hebrew University, Jerusalem); A. Ross Johnson (RAND Corporation); Kenneth Jowitt (University of California, Berkeley); Ibrahim Karawan (University of Cairo); Malcolm Kerr (University of California, Los Angeles); Fuad Khuri (American University, Beirut); Roman Kolkowicz (University of California, Los Angeles); Andrzej Korbonski (University of California, Los Angeles); Moshe Ma'oz (Hebrew University, Jerusalem); Amos Perlmutter (American University); Jonathan Pollock (RAND Corporation); Itamar Rabinovitch (Tel Aviv University); David Rapoport (University of California, Los Angeles); Robin Remington (University of Missouri); Sarah M. Terry (Tufts University); Jan Triska (Stanford University); Jiri Valenta (Naval Postgraduate School); Edward L. Warner III (US Air Force); Jerzy Wiatr

(University of Warsaw). The conference was made possible by the co-operative efforts and financial support of the Joint Committee on Eastern Europe of the American Council of Learned Societies and the Social Science Research Council, International Communications Agency, International Research and Exchanges Board, University of California Center for Russian and East European Studies and University of California Center for International and Strategic Affairs. One additional essay by Samuel E. Finer of All Souls College, Oxford, broadened the scope of ideas presented and discussed at the conference. Donna Beltz, Lori Gronich, Randy Haddock, Gerri Page, William Potter and Pedro Ramet also provided invaluable assistance in organizing the conference and preparing this manuscript for publication.

The deliberations of the conference underlined the problems of disciplinary parochialism and the burden of past neglect among the three dominant analytical schools in the study of military institutions. The conference, nonetheless, contributed to a better understanding of this problem, and provided a congenial forum for presentation of papers and for vigorous discussion. It is important that this process, a sustained dialogue across disciplinary and field boundaries, should continue. The Santa Barbara Conference on Civil–Military Relations in Socialist and Modernizing Societies is but a single, though important, step in that direction.

NOTES

1 Thomas S. Kuhn, *The Structure of Scientific Revolutions*, 2nd edn, enlarged (Chicago: University of Chicago Press, 1970), p. 43.
2 Jerry F. Hough, *The Soviet Union and Social Science Theory* (Cambridge, Mass.: Harvard University Press, 1977) p. 1.
3 Kuhn, op. cit., p. 43.
4 Max Weber, 'Objectivity in social science and social policy,' in E. Shils (ed.), *The Methodology of the Social Sciences* (Glencoe, Ill.: The Free Press, 1949), p. 105.
5 See Richard K. Betts, *Soldiers, Statesmen and Cold War Crises* (Cambridge, Mass.: Harvard University Press, 1977); Samuel P. Huntington, *Soldier and the State: The Theory and Politics of Civil–Military Relations* (Cambridge, Mass.: Harvard University Press, 1957); Morris Janowitz, *The Professional Soldier: A Social and Political Portrait* (New York: The Free Press, 1960); Malham Wakin (ed.), *War, Morality and the Military Profession* (Boulder, Colo.: Westview Press, 1979); Samuel P. Huntington, *The Common Defense* (New York: Columbia University Press, 1961); Michael Howard, 'Civil–military relations in Great Britain and the United States, 1945–1958', *Political Science Quarterly* (March 1960); Bruce Russett and Alfred Stepan (eds), *Military Force and American Society* (New York: Harper & Row, 1973); Samuel P. Huntington *et al.*, *Civil–Military Relations* (Washington, DC: American Enterprise Institute for Public Policy Research, 1977); James Clotfelter, *Military in American Politics* (New York: Harper & Row, 1973); Quincy Wright, *A Study of War* (Chicago: University of Chicago Press, 1965); John Kenneth Galbraith, *How to Control the Military* (New York: New American Library, 1969); Alfred Vagts, *A History of Militarism* (New York: Meridian, 1967); Ernest R. May (ed.), *The Ultimate Decision* (New York: Braziller, 1960); and Richard J. Barnet, *Roots of War* (New York: Atheneum, 1972).
6 See Samuel E. Finer, *The Man on Horseback: The Role of the Military in Politics* (Baltimore, Md: Penguin, 1975); Samuel P. Huntington (ed.), *Changing Patterns of Military Politics* (New York: The Free Press, 1962); Morris Janowitz, *Military Institu-*

tions and Coercion in the Developing Nations (Chicago: University of Chicago Press, 1977); Eric Nordlinger, *Soldiers in Politics* (Englewood Cliffs, NJ: Prentice-Hall, 1977); Amos Perlmutter, *The Military in Modern Times: On Professionals, Praetorians and Revolutionary Soldiers* (New Haven, Conn.: Yale University Press, 1977); Claude Welch and Arthur Smith, *Military Role and Rule* (North Scituate, Mass. – Belmont, Calif.: Duxbury Press, 1974); Edward Feit, *The Armed Bureaucrats* (New York, Boston, Mass.: Houghton Mifflin, 1973); Stephen Hoadley, *The Military in the Politics of Southeast Asia* (Harmondsworth: Penguin, 1975); Samuel P. Huntington, *Political Order in Changing Societies* (New Haven, Conn.: Yale University Press, 1968); Morris Janowitz and Jacques Van Doorn (eds), *On Military Intervention* (Rotterdam: Rotterdam University Press, 1971); Philippe C. Schmitter (ed.), *Military Rule in Latin America* (Beverly Hills, Calif.: Sage, 1973); Alfred Stepan, *The Military in Politics* (Princeton, NJ: Princeton University Press, 1971); Claude E. Welch, *Soldier and State in Africa: A Comparative Analysis of Military Intervention and Political Change* (Evanston, Ill.: Northwestern University Press, 1970); Ernest W. Lefever, *Spear and Sceptor: Army, Police and Politics in Tropical Africa* (Washington, DC: Brookings Institution, 1970); Claude E. Welch (ed.), *Civilian Right and Military Might: Government Control of the Armed Forces in Developing Countries* (Albany, NY: State University of New York Press, 1976).

7   See Dale R. Herspring, *East German Civil–Military Relations: The Impact of Technology, 1949–1972* (New York: Irvington, 1973); Dale R. Herspring and Ivan Volgyes (eds), *Civil–Military Relations in Communist Systems* (Boulder, Colo.: Westview Press, 1978); Ellis Joffe, *Party and Army: Professionalism and Political Control in the Chinese Officer Corps 1949–1963* (Cambridge, Mass.: Harvard University Press, 1965); A. Ross Johnson, *The Transformation of Communist Ideology: The Yugoslav Case, 1945–1953* (Cambridge, Mass.: MIT, 1972); Roman Kolkowicz, *The Soviet Military and the Communist Party* (Princeton, NJ: Princeton University Press, 1967); William W. Whitson and Huang Chen-hsian, *The Chinese High Command: A History of Communist Military Politics, 1927–1971* (New York: Praeger, 1973); Harvey W. Nelsen, *The Chinese Military System: An Organizational Study of the Chinese People's Liberation Army* (Boulder and London: Westview Press and Thorton Cox Publishers, 1977); Herbert Goldhamer, *The Soviet Soldier* (New York: Crane Russak, 1975); Raymond Garthoff, *Soviet Military Policy* (New York: Praeger, 1966); Jerry F. Hough and Merle Fainson, *How the Soviet Union Is Governed* (Cambridge, Mass.: Harvard University Press, 1979); Timothy J. Colton, *Commissars, Commanders and Civilian Authority: The Structure of Soviet Military Politics* (Cambridge, Mass.: Harvard University Press, 1979); William E. Odom, *The Soviet Volunteers* (Princeton, NJ: Princeton University Press, 1973); Ivan Volgyes, 'The political and professional perspectives of the Hungarian armed forces,' *Journal of Political and Military Sociology*, (Autumn 1977), pp. 275–94; Ithiel de Sola Pool, *et al.*, *Satellite Generals: A Study in Military Elites in the Soviet Sphere* (Stanford, Calif.: Stanford University Press, 1955); and Jorge I. Dominguez, 'The civic soldier in Cuba', in Catherine Kelleher (ed.) *Political–Military Systems: Comparative Perspectives*, (Beverly Hills, Calif.: Sage, 1974), pp. 209–39.

Part One

Civil–Military Relations in the Middle East

1 The Study of Civil–Military Relations in Modernizing Societies in the Middle East: A Critical Assessment

FUAD I. KHURI

This chapter focuses on four points: (1) a brief and general assessment of the Arabic and English literature on the military in the Middle East, (2) the prototypes of military models, (3) performances and ideological commitments of military regimes, and (4) the continuation of peasant, community-based practices in military organizations, which limit their capacities for modernization. While military institutions enhance mobility in peasant society, peasant society, in turn, modifies the structure of relationships within military organizations.

Three themes emerge in the discussion. First, the distinction between civil and military institutions in the Middle East is valid when applied to top government operations, the formal state structure, and does not involve different normative, value systems at the popular level. In other words, the military has not yet developed a clearly distinct code or honor that sets them apart from civilian behavioral expectations. This lack of distinction can be better understood if military models, the prototypes of military organizations laid down in the 1920s, are adequately analyzed as parts of total state structures. It is assumed here that the performance of the military, or the way it links to society, have been fashioned by these prototypes.

Second, military regimes seem to have affected the performance and ideological commitments of elites in high office without visibly altering or transforming local community power structures. The modernizing effects of military regimes are mostly felt in broad and monolithic social, political, and economic projects that have the elements of greatness and grandeur, but which do not seem to have contributed to the development of an infrastructure continuously adjusting to the technological and industrial requirements of the age. The army in military governments is not more effective as an instrument of change than the army in civilian governments.

Third, these discrepancies between official policies and commitments at the top and the realities of social life at the graft emerge from the peasant character of society and from military organization and technology. The gap between the center and the periphery, the elites and the masses, which characterize peasant society continue in new form; officers becoming a distinct social class sometimes replacing landed aristocracy and traditional elites.

A BRIEF NOTE ON THE LITERATURE

The literature on military regimes in the Middle East focuses on (1) the regimes' performances irrespective of their military character, and on (2) group dynamics and elementary social relationships within the ruling military juntas. Military regimes are dealt with as if they simply represent a continuous line of successive governments – emphasis is placed upon the performance of regimes, military or otherwise, in economics, education, agriculture, foreign policy, social and public works. Militarism in military regimes is ignored. This observation is illustrated in the writings of the Lacoutures (1958), *Egypt in Transition*; Vatikiotis (1961b), *The Egyptian Army in Politics*; Little (1958), *Egypt*; Abdel Malek (1968), *Egypt: Military Society*; Kerr (1965), *The Arab Cold War 1958–1964*; Wheelock (1960), *Nasser's New Egypt*; and a host of other works in Arabic.[1] Some of the works in Arabic include the following titles: 'Nasser and the Developmental Revolution,' 'Development and the Arab Nasserite Generation,' 'The Sun of Nasser Rises Over the Universe,' 'The Historical Roots for Nasserite Ideology,' 'Nasserism and Arab Unity,' which clearly speak of Nasser's performance in relation to broad ideological issues rather than to his military orientation. In these works no relationship is drawn between Middle Eastern militarism and the performance of military regimes in government. Militarism as a social system, an organizational format, a skill structure, an ideology, or a system of values, which are referred to in the work of Khuri and Obermeyer (1974, p. 79) as 'military ethnography', are the least studied in the Middle East.

Instead, the literature abounds in the details on personal networks and cliques, the social, ethnic and sectarian backgrounds, and career histories of individual army officers. The social origin of officers is rather well documented especially for Turkey, Syria, Egypt, and Iraq;[2] so are the tribal, ethnic or sectarian divisions within the army,[3] or the actual executions of military coups.[4] The actual executions of military coups, the internal composition of military cliques, the making of plots and intrigues, and other material related to the operation of top government offices, seem to receive considerable attention especially in the Arabic literature on the military. Most of this literature is written by, or about, army officers in power or by, and about, those who were ousted from office. The first type tends to be written mostly about Nasser and Sadat of Egypt, sometimes by Sadat himself; the second on various coups and military officers in Syria at the time the military Baᶜth took over government.[5] In Syria the most prolific writers were the military officers ousted from office in the coups of 1963, 1966 and 1970. Interestingly, the Arabic literature on the military increases immediately after coups, counter coups, or change of regimes, and slackens in times of stability. Very little is written between 1973 and 1978 which has relatively been a period of stability.

No doubt, the literature on the performance of high office or on group dynamics within military juntas is informative and useful if one seeks to understand the politics of a nation, or the tactics and maneuvers politicians use to further their immediate goals. It is useful if a person or a country seek to pursue its interests through the manipulation of factionalism and political rivalry within high office or in another country's government. This literature would be of utmost interest should the analyst focus on tactics and maneuvers in order to draw a generalized theory of political action as Fredrick Bailey (1969), for example, did in his work on *Strategems and Spoils,* whereby he compared the tactics and maneuvers used by Swat Pathans leaders in Pakistan with those used by De Gaulle in France, Wilson in England, and Cosa Nostra in Chicago. The literature on military intrigues, plots or cliques within government seems to lose its significance once the actors disappear from the political scene, which does not speak very strongly for its lasting theoretical value. Perhaps it is in this vein that Janowitz complained:

> In preparing my *The Military in the Political Development of New Nations,* I found the greatest difficulty in assembling materials on the Middle East. I would also claim that this part of the analysis is the weakest. In the years since the completion of this essay new monographic literature bearing on armed forces and society has appeared but, again, compared with other areas, such as Africa and Latin America, even the descriptive study materials still lag very much behind. (1975, p. 148)

However, the Middle Eastern military experiences are too diverse to be summarized in a single, monolithic theoretical orientation. True, certain elements – such as the lack of a tradition that separates between civilian and military authority (Halpern, 1962, p. 277; Vatikiotis, 1961a, p. 99; Khadduri, 1953), or the hinterland, lower-middle class or bureaucratic occupational origins of the military (Janowitz, 1975, p. 157) – are common to almost all armies in the Middle East, but these commonalities do not explain the differences in military performance. They do not explain, for example, why the Turkish military, although continuously intervening in the conduct of government, has so far hesitated to take it over without seeking legitimacy through civilian institutions. Whereas the Iraqi military, which has almost the same social origins as the Turkish, took over government and wiped out the formal civil institutions associated with legitimate authority. Besides, commonalities tell us little about the concentration of military coups in Egypt, Syria and Iraq, and not in Saudi Arabia, Oman, Jordan or Algeria, even though they all belong to the same cultural tradition. Nor do they tell us why the frequency of attempted coups or countercoups has been higher in Syria or Iraq than in Egypt, even though they all have been governed by military regimes for a longer period of time.

Some of these puzzling issues, I thought, can be answered if we focus, instead, on the formative period, the time military models were institutionalized within modern state structures and the way they related, then, to society at large. In this procedure the emphasis is placed more upon the socio-cultural context of civil-military relations than top government performances.

THE FORMATIVE PERIOD: THE PROTOTYPES

The performance of the military in war and their interference in politics are modified by the extent to which civil and military institutions and values are formally and socially distinguished from each other.[6] In turn, the distinction between civil and military structures varies with the cultural background, bureaucratic organization, historical experiences, and the technological order of society. Thus, the military models (I use 'model' to refer to military organization and the way it links to society) in the Middle East, which were borne out of a colonial situation, an imperial (Ottoman) bureaucracy, and of peasant social structure and economy, do not, and should not be expected to, conform to those in Europe. There (in Europe) they emerged amidst series of nationalistic wars, political struggles for the democratization of government, the rise of industrialization and urbanization, and the weakening of peasant society and economy.

Military professionalism in Europe, which according to Huntington first appeared in Prussia in the early part of the nineteenth century (1967, p. 39), acquired a sharply differentiated code and developed standardized personality traits. Concerning personality traits, European militarism placed emphasis on discipline, logic, scientific knowledge, and lack of intuitiveness and emotionality (Huntington, 1967, p. 60). At the interpersonal and organizational levels, military honor meant that officers be gentlemen and the military a cohesive brotherhood having the right to self-regulation.[7] One of the basic elements of professionalism was that the soldier be 'above politics' in domestic affairs, which, according to Janowitz (1960, p. 388), was historically achieved in American society through a two-way struggle between generals and politicians. Just as the military opposed the appointment of political generals, the politicians opposed the use of the military as a device for reputation building in politics.

Compared to Europe, military experience in the Middle East has had an entirely different history of development. Except for Egypt, Morocco, Turkey, and Iran, which had a longer history of professional militarism, armed forces, as specialized institutions, came up only after World War I when many of the countries of the Middle East were made separate states under colonial tutelage or protection.[8] Establishing an army or a police force then was part of an effort to build state institutions: parliaments, courts of justice, civil bureaucracy, municipal organizations, service departments and offices. The 1920s era witnessed the transfer of European state and government models into the Middle East; this was irrespective of whether or not a country was subject to colonial rule or influence. The countries which were not subject to direct colonial rule, such as Turkey and Iran, came under Western influence and adopted European models. Turkey did so through the modernizing efforts of Kamal Ataturk, and Iran through the efforts of Rida Shah Pahlavi.

The transfer of European government and state models into a Middle Eastern cultural setting meant that these models were adopted in response to external stimuli rather than to the emergence of new local circumstances. Therefore, the aims served by these models, including the formal distinction between military and civil institutions, were likewise external to the local scene. This is the reason that this distinction remained valid only in respect to high office, the formal state structure, and never developed into a specialized military subculture. In reviewing the last ten issues of a Syrian military journal, called *Jaish al-Sha^{c}b* (The People's Army), I found that the value-orientations of the military do not seem to differ from the adult male behavioral expectations. Manliness *(rujūla)*, honor *(sharaf)*, dignity *(karāma)*, generosity *(karam)*, self-respect *(ihtirām al-dhāt)*, toughness *(qaswa)*, austerity *(qasāwa)*, revenge-fulness *(al-tha'ir)*, anger *(ghadab)*, bitterness *(marārā)*, supporting the weak *(nisrat al-da^c-if)*, which are treated in the journal as military values are cultural ones, indeed. The stereotypes that center around the personality of soldiers in the West – namely, discipline, rigidity, lack of emotionality and intuitiveness – which set them apart from civilians, have no parallel at the cultural level in the Middle East.

Deriving his typology from top government functions, Janowitz (1964, pp. 10–11) classified 'civil–military models' in the Middle East, and for that matter in all new nations, into five types: authoritarian-personal control, authoritarian mass party, democratic-competitive and semi-competitive systems, civil–military coalition, and military oligarchy. According to him, Pakistan, Egypt, Iraq and Yemen have a military-oligarchy model; Turkey, Algeria, Syria and Jordan a civil–military coalition model; Morocco, Tunisia, Israel and Lebanon a democratic-competitive model; Saudi Arabia an authoritarian-personal control model. If we focus, on the other hand, on the initial formation of military institutions and the way they related to society then, a different typology and, therefore, a different set of classification would emerge. In this respect, four types of military experiences can be discerned: (1) the nation-building model, (2) the struggle-for-independence model, (3) the peasant and minorities-dominated model, and (4) the tribally based model. These models and the classification derived from them must not be treated as fixed compartments; they are dynamic processes that change with changing circumstances and policies. A country may adopt one model at a time and change to another later on, following changes in policies, revolutions, or socio-economic transformations. The Egyptian military, for example, was formed initially as a minorities-dominated model, but changed into a nation-building type after the revolution of 1952 and the series of wars with Israel and the 'reactionary' regime of Northern Yemen. By the same token, the Algerian and Israeli armies were formed in the process of independence struggles, but turned gradually into a nation-building model after the achievement of self-rule.

The nation-building model implies the participation of a large part of society in the military experience, which necessarily brings to the front the most dominant social group. This arrangement may take place under two conditions: (1) when the old imperial or colonial order begins to collapse, and (2) when the national forces begin to formulate a new policy with as little external interference as possible. This is what happened in Iran and Turkey after World War I and the collapse of the Ottoman Empire, and in Algeria and Israel after the waning of French and British colonialism in these two countries respectively.

The association between national struggle for independence and the pre-eminence of the dominant social group in this struggle creates pride in military service and dispels negative images and stereotypes about soldiery. Here the soldier is not thought of as a destitute or a social outcast searching for a living in military service for lack of opportunity elsewhere. Military service becomes a source of social respect and personal pride, which attracts to the profession the more intelligent youth, especially if the army acquires sophisticated technology as in Iran, Turkey, or Israel. In Israel the continuous threat of war has blurred the boundary lines between military and civilian subcultures. Not only is Israel a 'nation in arms,' as Ben Halpern put it (1962, p. 350), but 'the army is an army of civilians.'

The identification of the military with national pride and honor creates a sort of political aloofness on their part, based on the conviction that politics is beneath military honor. They stand for consensus; politics implies competition, rivalry, and conflict between interest groups. They symbolize the interest of the whole nation; politics seeks the interests of particular groups within the nation. In these environments, the military interferes in domestic politics, when they do, in order to reestablish consensus and social unity rather than to transform the socio-economic bases of society and revolutionize social life. Their interference tends to be conservative and free of modernizing ideological commitments. In this sense, it can be argued that military intervention in Algeria under Boumedian put an end to the revolutionary ideologies of Ben Bella; it led to the bureaucratization of the military and the stabilization of the social system and political life.

Unlike the nation-building model which seems to emerge from national struggle for independence, the minorities-dominated model is typically (1) a colonial situation or (2) an index of the continuation of a ruling dynasty from the pre-World War I era to the present day. A good example of the first type is located in the military experiences of Syria, Lebanon, and to a much lesser extent, Iraq, where minorities of hinterland origins – Alawites, Maronites, Druzes, Kurds, Assyrians – have at different times dominated in the military. The second is found in Morocco where the Berber element still constitutes the backbone of military organization. Built upon minority culture, the military looks forward for a political career and only reluctantly does it refrain from political intervention. It is built as a 'party' and acts in accordance with its structure.

The military appetite for power in minorities-dominated models is strengthened if the political institutions and civil bureaucracy are controlled by the dominant social group, as the case has been in Syria where civil political institutions and bureaucracy fell in the hands of the Sunni Muslims. In Lebanon the confessional balance in government and the army, which militated against military intervention, simultaneously weakened both government and army alike.

The capacity of the minorities-dominated military to mobilize the populace for a common, national cause is limited. It is doubtful whether the successive military regimes in Syria have ever been more able to mobilize support against Israel than the civilian governments before 1949. The Lebanese army crumbled when it was put to the test during the two-year war of 1975–7; as a collective body it was never able to fight a war internally or externally. I say 'as a collective body' because the Lebanese army did fight in the war, but only after it split into two opposing factions following the abortive military coup of Colonel Ahdab in March 1976.

Morocco presents a different case. The colonial attempts to drive a wedge between Arab and Berber have failed (Micaud, 1972, pp. 433–8), which meant that the Berber-dominated military was never socially alienated from the dominant Islamic patterns. In Morocco, Islam seems to enhance social cohesion irrespective of ethnic variations, which cannot be said about ethnic and sectarian variations in the Arab East.

The tribally based military models came up first in Jordan following the political disturbances in the 1930s in Palestine (Glubb, 1948 and 1957; A. Murad, 1973; Vatikiotis, 1967), and in Arabia and the Gulf after the development of oil and the building of state institutions. In the context of Jordan, Arabia and the Gulf, tribe is no longer a whole, self-sufficient system as it has until recently been among Arab nomads. Following the development of oil and the foundation of state institutions and civil bureaucracies, tribe had become a form of social organization within which kinship principles are used to regulate marriage, social interaction and the distribution of power, wealth and benefits. It is a social category where individual behavior is subject to collective means of control, and alliances between groups are drawn on the bases of traditionally accepted genealogies. Defined this way, tribe is a 'part-society' that coexists simultaneously with peasant or urban populations, which is well evidenced in the social structure of Jordan, the oasis of mainland Arabia, the commercial urban centers of Hijaz, or in the trading and fishing centers spread around the Gulf.

With the rise of state institutions, the tribal segment of the population who claim historical rights to land and other natural resources, including oil, came to dominate the power-force-oriented offices: defense, security, courts of justice, governorship of provinces, and sometimes emigration, labor affairs, or education, as these relate to the power base in one way or another. Offices related to development, industry, finance, economics, public works, etc. are allocated to technocrats of peasant or urban origin. In the context of Bahrain, where I carried out fieldwork in 1974–5, people of tribal origin *(cabīlī)* were never treated as if they were a single bloc, party or a social category, opposing others of peasant or urban origin, collectively called *khdairī*, as they are today following the development of oil and the transformation of the socio-economic order.[9]

The tribally based army, like the minorities-dominated model, has a 'party' structure, but unlike this model, it is socially an extension of government and, therefore, competes for it against other socio-political groupings. Religious and sectarian minorities in the Middle East have always been rebellious groups and continue to be so when they find themselves in control of military institutions. In the tribally based military, the authority of the tribe is not entirely destroyed, which weakens the professionalization process within the military, but lessens the probability of military intervention in domestic politics. Thus far, military regimes in the Middle East have arisen in peasant-oriented societies with a feudalistic tradition, such as Syria, Egypt and Iraq, rather than in tribally based societies, as in Arabia and the Gulf.[10] No wonder that in these peasant-based societies, military regimes have championed socialism which they largely identify with land reforms.

The continuation of tribal authority in the army is expected to weaken its capacity for military action. The tribally based military models have not yet been put to the test in external warfare; they seem to perform well internally as instruments of government intervention. Whether they perform likewise in external wars remains to be seen; theoretically, it is doubtful that the tribally based armies, being built upon an intricate system of balance and primary social loyalties, will sustain prolonged external military confrontation. The performance of the Jordanian army in the Arab–Israeli War of 1967, I believe, is highly exaggerated. It emerged from the war almost intact, which suggests that it could not have fought as hard as it was reputed to have done.

Military professionalization and tribal loyalties are structurally contradictory phenomena. The dual military organizations, national guards and regularized army units, which spread in tribally oriented societies,[11] are meant to reconcile these inherent contradictions. These two military, or semi-military, organizations differ in recruitment, socialization, and military technology. The national guard is recruited on the bases of tribal levies, which is a very ancient practice in Arabia, and the regular army is recruited from people of peasant, urban, or sometimes foreign origins. Tribal levies are paid through their tribal chiefs who, in turn, receive revenues from the central government; the regular army is an extension of national defense subject to the direct authority of the central government. In Saudi Arabia, for example, the regular army is built to be strongest in the air force, whereas the national guard is strongest in ground troops. The cynics have it that it is much more difficult to stage a military coup using the air force alone; ground troops are necessary as evidenced in the many successful coups in Syria, Egypt or Iraq. The only coup staged by the air force was Shawwaf's attempted coup in Iraq, in the early 1960s, which was ruthlessly crushed.

This brief, broad account of military prototypes in the Middle East is intended to raise a point rather than to work out a detailed formula for military–civil relations. It shows that the distinction between military and civilian subcultures and subsequently military interference in domestic politics are in many ways dependent upon the initial models upon which the military organizations are built sociologically. There are gradations in military intervention. Finer distinctions between four types – influence, pressures or blackmail, displacement and supplantment – ranging from the appeal to reason, as in the case of influence, to taking over government, as in the case of supplantment (1962, pp. 86–7). With regard to the Middle East, it appears as if the prototype built upon the countryside, minorities-dominated model has exercised the highest stage – the supplantment level – of military intervention; the rest seem to have practiced a combination of other gradations.

Countryside or hinterland origins mixed with minority–cultural settings render the military most receptive to new and modern nationalistic or socialistic ideologies. The phrase 'minority-cultural setting' refers to the situation where the military is either dominated by minority groups, as in Syria, or operates in a minority-fragmented society, as in Iraq. The military regimes in Syria and Iraq have generally been more ideologically bound than those in Egypt; the latter being less heterogeneous socially, ethnically, and religiously. Arab nationalism, as a modern ideology, has established deeper roots among the Iraqi and Syrian officers than the Egyptians; likewise, it seems to have greater appeal to peasant minorities than to the urban Sunni Muslims who constitute the dominant religious group in the urban centers of the Arab world (al-Razzaz, 1967, pp. 158–9). The urban Sunni Muslims tend to be recruited into religious organizations at a much higher rate than in Arab nationalistic or socialistic movements, which suggests that the 'masses' have not yet responded favorably to the modern ideological commitments of military regimes. In general, the ideological commitments of military regimes affect the performance of high office rather than the lower substructures of society.

PERFORMANCE AND IDEOLOGICAL COMMITMENTS OF MILITARY REGIMES

I am concerned here with performances and ideological commitments that are unique to military regimes, which can be considered a product of militarism as opposed to civilian ways. One of the most striking aspects of military regimes is the emphasis they place upon comprehensively monolithic political and economic projects. Military regimes in Syria, Egypt, Iraq and more recently Libya have invariably fostered Arab nationalistic movements, socialism, land reforms, Islamic socialism, national single-party systems, cultural revolutions, programs of political mobilization, powerful radio stations, peoples' armies. Additionally, they built dams (the Aswan in Egypt and the Euphrates in Syria), enlarged armies, enhanced armament, waged wars, and nationalized oil companies. Not that civilian regimes have failed to sponsor such huge projects – they did especially in Turkey, Tunisia, Saudi Arabia, and Iran; but the combination of these in a single syndrome uniquely characterizes military performance. A new political language focusing on the big, the magnificent, the visible socially and politically, seem to always mark the ascendancy of the military to power. The style of the military in government is replete with slogans such as 'the rights of the masses,' 'the victories and gains of the people,' 'the inevitability of progress,' 'national liberation and steadfastness,' 'establishing cultural and social harmony,' 'eliminating social fragmentation,' 'molding social variations,' and other expressions of this order. The military mind focuses on two broad directions, (1) commitment to grand-scale processes of change and (2) standardization and uniformity of actions, attitudes, outlooks, and behaviors.

The modernizing tendencies of military regimes are one aspect of civil–military relations that have received considerable attention in the literature on the military, especially in the early 1960s when a large part of the Third World achieved self-rule. Most of this literature was favorable to military rule which it saw as an instrument of social change and modernity. Edward Shils's statement, 'the ascendancy of the military in the domestic life of these [new] states has been a response to the difficulties which the new states have encountered in their efforts to establish themselves as modern sovereignties' (1962, p. 8) speaks for a large part of this literature. M. Halpern (1962), Vatikiotis (1961a) and Berger (1966) make similar arguments about the Middle East. Halpern writes, 'the army is the principal political actor and instrument of a new middle class' (1962, pp. 278–9); Vatikiotis argues 'the army is the instrument of political change and the manipulator of political ideology' (1961a, p. xii); Berger states 'of all the native elite groups, the army probably has held the most rationally calculating, secular and unromantic approach to the problems which Egypt had faced' (1966, p. 21).

Many of the arguments about the modernizing capacities of the military relate to the social and occupational origins of army officers; the assumption being that hinterland, lower-middle-class origins mixed with bureaucratic occupational careers predispose the officer corps to be responsive to social change. 'What is novel today in the Middle East is not control by army officers,' declares Halpern, 'what is new are the groups for which the army speaks and the interests it represents' (1962, p. 278). He argues that 'as the army officer corps came to represent the interests and views of the middle class, it became the most powerful instrument of that class' (1963, p. 258).

It is difficult to deny the impact of class origin on the officers' reaction, acceptance, or rejection, to particular programs of change, but 'class' alone is only one of many variables that operate in these situations. Hurewitz (1969, p. 104) and Janowitz (1975, pp. 155–62) have already demonstrated how ethnicities, communal solidarities, bureaucratic institutions, religious sects, regional affinities, tribal, peasant, or urban origins, which cut across classes, modify military recruitment and intervene in the class structure of military organization. Besides, class in the Middle East seems to operate more as a modifier of individual behaviors – manners of speech, dress, housing, personal possessions, patterns of marriage, etc. – than as a determinant of collective action.[12] When the military, or part of it, take over government or when they carry on wholistic programs of change, their action is not necessarily precipitated by the uniformity of class origin.

The value of social origins, whatever they are, must not be exaggerated. The military is not less or more modernistic than structurally similar groups in society – elementary and secondary school teachers, skilled technicians, university students, clerks, salaried labor, civil employees, political parties, labor unions or what the late Colonel Umran of Syria called 'the abstract classes' (n.d., p. 59). Among the military there is the conservative and the liberal, the religionist and the progressivist, the rightist and the leftist, the zealot and the indifferent, combined together into a single-authority system. The Revolutionary Council of 1952 in Egypt housed a wide spectrum of political inclinations ranging from communism to Muslim brotherhood. Like other formal institutions in new states – civil bureaucracy, parliaments, cabinets, courts of justice, and other specialized offices – the military is an outlet for the making of new elites. Unlike these institutions, however, the military is built upon a wholistic authority system which makes it possible for a few, key officers to politically engage the total organization. It is here in military organization and authority that the capacity of the military to *deal with change* actually lies. The literature on the actual execution of coups, cited earlier, clearly demonstrates how a little, tiny but active fraction of the officer corps acts to engage the whole organization politically. Ironically it is the policy of 'above politics' that makes military organization vulnerable to the whims of the few but politically active officers. The policy of building 'ideologized armies' in Syria and Iraq is intended to put an end to further coups through politicization of the army, thus making it a partisan to the ruling Ba^{c}th parties.

The capacity of the military to deal with change is fashioned by military values, organization and authority which stand for national grandeur and honor, discipline and standardization and the wholistic approach to human problems – together constituting the military gestalt. The military is a wholistic, self-regulating organization. Their preference for grand-scale, wholistic ideologies or programs of change – nationalism, land reforms, confiscation of large landholdings, nationalization of economic resources, building of dams, and large armies, is an extension of this military gestalt. In his insightful account of the contradictions between the civilian and military factions within the Ba^{c}th party in Syria following the coups of 1963, Munif al-Razzaz, a prominent Ba^{c}th writer, says: 'the army used the Ba^{c}th ideologies and programs of change as a symbolic means for its comprehensive, coercive control of society' (1967, p. 208). To what extent land reforms, confiscation of large landholdings, or nationalization of banking and industry, were instruments of control and coercion is a question that can only be answered by further research. This is an area about which very little is known or written. Logically, however, it follows that these grand-scale projects allow the military to interfere in the processes of redistribution, thus tightening their political hold on government and society.

In the final analysis, the question is whether or not society will lend itself to the same means of control as military organization. The military answer to this question has always been the adoption of a monolithic political ideology which they consider to be an appropriate means for the control of civilians. It is interesting to note in this regard that many military juntas adopt this policy some time after they sieze power. However, the Egyptian, Syrian, and Iraqi experiences with wholistic and monolithic ideologies of change seem to have failed thus far.[13]

By adopting wholistic ideologies of change, the military alienates itself from the cultural value-orientations and political convictions and alignments of the populace. There develops an ideological elitism that deepens the gap between the military elites and the masses. The ideologies of Turkicization in Turkey carried out by Ataturk and his followers, Persianization in Iran adopted by Rida Shah Pahlavi and his successors, and Arab nationalism in Egypt adopted by Nasser and in Syria and Iraq by the Ba^cth Party – these have not yet successfully superseded the religious-folk base. One of the first things Jafar Imami's Cabinet did when it came to power in Iran after a month of disturbances, August 1978, was to announce the reinstitution of the Islamic calendar instead of the Persian calendar, which was obviously a symbolic gesture appeasing the Shi^ca Muslim discontentment with the Shah's rule. Following an interview with high officials in revolutionary Iraq and South Yemen, Hudson relates, 'Each said that their government were frustrated because they were compelled to accommodate a religious mentality and organized religious influence at the grass-roots level' (1977, p. 230). In his work on Egypt, Iliya Harik (1974, ch. 5) similarly demonstrates how in the village of Shubra al-Jadida political factionalism based in grand family coalitions have, interestingly contradictorily, adopted the emblems of the Egyptian revolutionary regime, remained in power and continued to compete against each other in the same way as they did before the revolution. He shows how revolutionary symbols have locally become controversial issues dividing the community into what in reality have been traditional feudal–family alliances. He concludes:

> Nasser's single party is highly centralized; delegated authority is concentrated in the hands of appointed leaders who advocate the transformation of society by revolutionary means. However, this model breaks down at subnational levels of Egyptian party organization, where leaders are representative, power is diffuse among various groups, concern with ideology is limited, and political mobilization is carried out with moderation. In effect, Egypt's single party regime reflects the characteristics of the revolutionary-centralized pattern at the top level and those of the pragmatic-pluralistic pattern at subnational levels. (Harik, 1974, p. 64)

In spite of many decades of elitist indoctrination in Turkey, Iran, Egypt, Syria, and Iraq, traditional religious organizations – reading circles, guilds, sufi orders, funeral houses *(ma'ātim)*, and ceremonial flagellations among the Shi^ca – plus a wide variety of community-based political alliances, still remain the basic instruments of collective action at the popular level.

The gap between military elitist ideology at the top and the continuation of religious and community-based organisations at the graft is a source of tension to military regimes who, by virtue of their professional training, are intolerant of deviation and discord. Military political thought abounds in concepts that call for conformity to a single national model and uniformity of actions, attitudes, outlooks and behaviors. These concepts are well exemplified in phrases such as 'the national mold,' 'the oneness of the nation,' 'the unity of people,' 'the elimination of social fragmentation,' 'the search for social and national consensus,' which recur in the mass media under military direction. Writing about armed struggle, Colonel Tallas, who is Minister of Defense in Syria at present, urges that 'armed struggle is the war of socially and politically united masses led by an organized ideology, and that such wars have historical roots in the consensus of the community during the holy wars of early Islam' (1967, pp. 116–17). In the same vein, the late Colonel Umran of Syria sees 'social fragmentation' *(al-tashardhum)* as the main barrier to progress (n.d., pp. 52, 99, 188).

The military insistence on conformity and uniformity produces a series of corollary measures – indoctrination through mass media, treating news as if it were an editorial, suppression of youth fashions and fads such as growing long hair by males and wearing unisex jeans by girls, standardization of scholastic achievements and academic awards, and above all, the use of force and coercion, the creation of militia-like task forces, and a complex network of intelligence. Admittedly, some civilian regimes use some of these tactics, but no military regime has yet failed to do so. Opposing these measures and tactics, the skilled, entrepreneurial and professional classes tend to emigrate whenever the opportunity allows, which necessarily slows down the process of development and change. Indeed, there is evidence to believe that the army in a civilian-controlled government is not less effective as an instrument of modernization and change than the army in a military-controlled government. This lack of difference pertains directly to the peasant structure of society and to military organization and technology.

PEASANT SOCIETY AND MILITARY ORGANIZATION AND TECHNOLOGY

As a state institution, the army provides an instance of mobility and modernization irrespective of whether government is controlled by the military or civilians. Peasants who live on subsistence find in military careers an 'occupational heaven' characterized by stability of employment, fixed salaries, promotions and guaranteed pension and retirement policies.[14] The same observation can be generalized to the officer corps. Recruited mostly from provincial towns and capitals from the sons of small landholders, merchants, middle-level civil servants, village notables and army officers,[15] the officer corps acquire through military service, social aggressiveness and a sense of aloofness accentuated by college training. In his book *Syria . . . A Pioneer of Struggle,* Sami al-Jundi, a civilian Ba^cth leader who was discredited by the military Ba^cth coup of 1966, describes the Ba^cth officer thus: 'We were scared of him coming into our meetings uninvited to lecture, to threaten, swear, scold and warn . . .' Military service marks a change of status for both soldier and officer alike, and here lies the bureaucratic aspect of the military.

The bureaucratic dimension of military organization in the peasant societies of the Middle East is felt in the material rewards, economic securities and the stability of employment it provides. To say that the 'military is a bureaucratic group' (Janowitz, 1975, p. 160) must not be construed to mean that the military possesses the same authority system or behavioral expectations as civil bureaucracy. It means that military and civil-bureaucracy services operate as outlets for social mobility and instances of modernization. Literacy, travel, service outside one's own immediate community, contacts with outsiders, knowledge of some technical skills, which are prestige-investments in peasant society are simultaneously requirements for recruitment in military and bureaucratic employment. While performing their jobs, officers and civil bureaucrats acquire leadership qualities – contacts with influential men, exercise of authority, management of people's affairs, recipients of mediation.

Although they provide channels for mobility and modernization, civil-bureaucracy and military organizations do not alter or transform the peasant structure of society, neither socially nor technologically. It is, at best, a two-way process: while they enhance mobility in peasant society, peasant society, in turn, modifies the structure of relationships within bureaucratic and military organizations. Plenty of peasant, community-based practices continue to operate in military organizations; these include the internal composition of military factions and ruling juntas, the sharp distinction between social classes, and the gap between the military elite and the masses. Several military regimes and 'loci of influence' within the army are built upon kinship, marriage, sectarian, or community of origin ties. The strong men in the ruling military regime in Iraq come from the same town, Tikrit; the Syrian officers who managed the coup against the United Arab Republic in 1961 were all from Damascus sharing descent and in-law ties. The coups of 1963, 1966 and 1970 in Syria, which were engineered by different factions of the Ba^cth officers, were all built into a syndrome of community-derived ties: sect, region, village of origin, traditional family coalitions.[16] What al-Jundi (1969*b*, pp. 160–1) refers to as 'the wings of the party,' meaning the competing factions within the military Ba^cth, are in reality continuations of traditional cleavages in society. In the daily press of Beirut today, there are recurrent references to Sadat of Egypt and his brothers-in-law in government and business, together forming a close-knit fabric of relations reminiscent of preindustrial society.[17]

More important than the continuation of these community-derived ties is the emergence of the military elite as a distinct social class enjoying, on the one hand, a multitude of privileges that set them apart from soldiers and the masses, thus replacing, on the other hand, the traditional political elites. There are gaps and differences in all armies of the world, but these differences in armies built upon technologically sophisticated weaponry relate directly to a specialized system of military authority, and are not automatically translated into a class system at the societal level. Janowitz and Little argue that sophisticated military technology has changed military authority from being based on 'domination', which is derived from traditional and ascriptive criteria, to 'a wider utilization of manipulation' based on achievement (1965, p. 43). In peasant societies with less-developed technology, the differences between soldier and officer are translated into a class system with distinct behavioral expectations. The salaries of officers in the Middle East have a range from three to six times more than soldiers; officers are entitled to housing allowances, teaching facilities for children, domestic maids, cars, drivers, and cooks. Some high-ranking officers retain these privileges after retirement; others are employed in high government posts as in Turkey and Iran, or in diplomatic services as in Syria, Egypt, and Iraq.

The privileges and status symbols officers acquire through military careers are translated into social power. Officers become leaders, linking local and relatively isolated peasant communities with the central administration and government. They interfere to further the interests of their kin and kith, provide them with protection, and help settle their disputes. In this connection, al-Jundi (1969*a*, p. 88) contends that the nationalization of industry and banking in Syria allowed the successive military juntas to interfere in the process of employment, which, according to him, led to an unprecedented influx of rural people to the city of Damascus where industry is located. Given the peasant, hinterland origins of officers and their emergence as community leaders, it is expected that their coming to power in the city would increase rural-to-urban migration.

The class distinction between officers and soldiers is accentuated by military organization and technology. In peasant-based economies, like those of the Middle East, infantry divisions constitute the backbone of military organization with a high ratio of soldier to officer. It is estimated, roughly, that the ratio in the Middle East ranges between one officer to fifteen and sometimes fifty soldiers, depending upon the military technology at hand. The more sophisticated the technology the lower the ratio.[18] The high ratio of soldier to officer, coupled by concentration on infantry units, exaggerate the status of military officers; officership in these circumstances becoming a scarce commodity. The more so if the state adopts a policy of compulsory military training, or when it acquires massive amounts of less-sophisticated weaponry. Looked at this way, compulsory training and armament are not only instances of war and international tension; they are, additionally, instances of social mobility and political power. War, armaments and compulsory training render the position of military officers a scarcity and, therefore, a social desirability. No wonder that the military, once in power, launch on different programs to build the army, prepare for war, enforce compulsory military training, and indulge in the armament race.

The irony of it is that the officer corps who seem to be more receptive to wholistic ideologies of development, combined with strong nationalistic tendencies,[19] seem to simultaneously and contradictorily embark on projects – armaments, wars, compulsory training – that undermine both development and independence. Not only do these projects chop off a large part, reaching at times about 70 per cent, of the national budget, but they also allow the arms-export country to continuously interfere in the internal and external affairs of the import-country.[20]

Besides, the acquisition of imported arms, however sophisticated, is not automatically translated into an industrial-technological input in society. The contention that the military forms 'the technical college of society' (Z. Murad, 1966, p. 46) is at best a questionable assumption. Upon release from active service most soldiers tend to become shop-keepers or taxi drivers in urban Lebanon, or return to the simple tribal life of the Western Desert in the case of the Bedouin of Egypt.[21] Vatikiotis (1967, p. 87) notes that two-thirds of the Bedouin in Jordan who left a regiment after a five-year enlistment returned to their tribes. The same observation can be made about officers who after retirement or expulsion from office tend to become technocrats, 'doctors', heads of departments, diplomats or civil administrators (Abdel-Malek, 1968, p. 177). Obviously, the technological standards of peasant society are incapable of absorbing the technical skills acquired in military careers, nor does the imported military technology generate corollary sophisticated technical knowledge in society. The industrial-technological output of society depends more on capital, scientific knowledge, raw materials, markets, values, systems of education, manpower, concentration of skills, than simply driving tanks or airplanes.

The lack of distinction between civil and military subcultures, the continuation of peasant, community-based ties and values within military organization, the emergence of the military elites as a bureaucratic group, the class distinctions between officers and the peasant masses, the limited capacity of the military to generate technical skills in society – all these lead us to reverse the question. Instead of asking how does the military modernize society, we should ask how does society modernize the military?

NOTES

1 See, for example, *Publications of Development Studies*, no. 17; Matar (1975); al-Hakim (1971); *(Arab) Unity Thought*, no. 5.
2 See Be'eri (1970) on Egypt; al-Qazzaz (1971) on Iraq; Umran (n.d.) on Syria; and Frey (1965) on Turkey.
3 Hurewitz's work (1969) is a good source on this subject.
4 The Arabic literature is very rich in these details. See, for example, Umran (n.d.); Zahr al-Din (1966); Mustapha (1969); Ammash (1967); Khattab (1969); and al-Barawy (1952). See also the works of Carleton (1950) and Badeau (1955).
5 See the works of Husain (1973), al-Aqqad (1970), Matar (1975) and Badeau (1955) on Nasser; and those of Sadat (1958 and 1972) and Lutfi (1972) on Sadat. On Syria, see the works of former officers such as Umran (n.d.) and Zahr al-Din (1966), or Ba'th party leaders such as al-Razzaz (1967) and al-Jundi (n.d., 1969a, 1969b).
6 Many of the theories that pertain to this assumption are detailed in Smith and Welch Jr (1974, pp. 10–49).
7 For more details, see Janowitz (1960, pp. 215–20).
8 This is with the exception of Algeria and Israel whose armies were born out of a national struggle for independence after World War II.
9 For more details, see Khuri's work on *Tribe and State in Bahrain*, (Chicago: University of Chicago Press, 1980), ch. 9.

10 See Khuri and Obermeyer (1974, p. 67).
11 This is true especially of Saudi Arabia and, to a lesser extent, Jordan. See Hurewitz (1969, pp. 233–73) for details.
12 On this point see Khuri (1975).
13 Reference here is made to the single-party system of the Baᶜth in Syria and Iraq, and to the National Unionist Party in Egypt.
14 This phrase is taken from Vatikiotis (1967, p. 139). See also, Antoun (1972, p. 33); Khuri (1969); Abdel-Malek (1968); and Glubb (1948).
15 See the works of al-Qazzaz (1971), Be'eri (1970), and Frey (1965) on Iraq, Egypt, and Turkey respectively.
16 See Zahr al-Din (1966, pp. 52, 134, 302, 362, 419); Umran (n.d., pp. 28, 51, 99, 188, 194); al-Jundi (1969b, pp. 143–4); al-Razzaz (1967, pp. 63, 140, 159, 262, 263); al-Sayyid (1973, p. 210); Haikal (n.d.).
17 Most of these writings appeared in *as-Safir*, nos 1,546, 1,552, 1,558, 1,567, 1,568, 1,569 (all 1978).
18 After an oral interview with Captain K. Jalbout in the Lebanese army.
19 The nationalistic tendencies of the military in the Middle East has been alluded to by many writers on the subject. See Caractacus (1959, p. 124); Janowitz (1975, p. 161); Berger (1966, p. 24); Vatikiotis (1961a, p. 107).
20 See the work of Khalid (1978) on this subject.
21 See Khuri (1975, p. 95) on Lebanon and Obermeyer (1969) on the Western Desert.

BIBLIOGRAPHY

Abdel-Malek, Anouar (1968), *Egypt: Military Society* (New York: Vintage Books).
Ammash, Salih M. (1967), *al-Wahda al-ᶜAskariyah: al-Madmūn al-ᶜAskari lil-Wahda al-ᶜArabiyah* (The Military Unity: The Military Meaning for Arab Unity) (Beirut: Dar al-Taliᶜa).
Antoun, Richard (1972), *Arab Village* (Bloomington, Ind.: University of Indiana Press).
al-Aqqad, Amir (1970), *Jamal Abdel-Nassir, Hayātuhu wa Jihāduhu* (Jamal Abdel-Nassir, His Life History and Struggle) (Cairo: al-Shaᶜb Press).
Badeau, John S. (1955), 'A role in search of a hero. A brief study of the Egyptian revolution,' *Middle East Journal*, vol. 9, pp. 373–84.
Bailey, G.F. (1969), *Stratagems and Spoils* (New York: Schocken Books).
al-Barawy, Rashed (1952), *The Military Coup in Egypt* (Cairo: The Renaissance Press).
Be'eri, Eliezer (1970), *Army Officers in Arab Politics and Society* (New York: Praeger).
Berger, Morroe (1966), *Military Elite and Social Change: Egypt Since Napoleon* (Princeton, NJ: Princeton University Press).
Caractacus (pseud.) (1959), *Revolution in Iraq* (London: Gollancz).
Carleton, Alford (1950), 'The Syrian coup d'état of 1949,' *Middle East Journal*, vol. 4, pp. 1–11.
Finer, S. E. (1962), *The Man on Horseback. The Role of the Military in Politics* (New York: Praeger).
Frey, Frederick W. (1965), *The Turkish Political Elite* (Cambridge, Mass.: Harvard University Press).
Glubb, John B. (1948), *The Story of the Arab Legion* (London: Hodder & Stoughton).
Glubb, John B. (1957), *A Soldier with the Arabs* (London: Hodder & Stoughton).
Haikal, Hasanain M. (n.d.), *Mā al-Ladhi Jara fi Sūriyah* (What Happened in Syria) (Cairo: al-Oawmiyah Press).
al-Hakim, Mustapha M. (1971), *Abdel-Nassir: Qadāya wa Mawāqif* (Abdel-Nassir: Issues and Stands) (Beirut: Sawt al-Urūba Press).
Halpern, Ben (1962), 'The role of the military in Israel,' in John J. Johnson (ed.), *The Role of the Military in Underdeveloped Countries* (Princeton, NJ: Princeton University Press).
Halpern, Manfred (1962), 'Middle Eastern armies and the new middle class,' in John J. Johnson (ed.), *The Role of the Military in Underdeveloped Countries* (Princeton, NJ: Princeton University Press).
Halpern, Manfred (1963), *The Politics of Social Change in the Middle East and North Africa* (Princeton, NJ: Princeton University Press).

Harik, Iliya (1974), *The Political Mobilization of Peasants* (Bloomington, Ind.: Indiana University Press).

Hudson, Michael C. (1977), *Arab Politics* (New Haven, Conn.: Yale University Press).

Huntington, Samuel P. (1957), *The Soldier and the State* (Cambridge, Mass.: The Belknap Press).

Hurewitz, J.C. (1969), *Middle East Politics: The Military Dimension* (New York: Praeger).

Husain, Ahmad (1973), *Kaifa ʿAraft Abdel-Nassir wa ʿIsht 'Ayyāma Hayātih* (How I Knew Abdel-Nassir and Lived During His Life Time) (Cairo: Ahrar Press).

Janowitz, Morris (1960), *The Professional Soldier. A Social and Political Portrait* (Glencoe, Ill.: The Free Press).

Janowitz, Morris (1964), *The Military in the Political Development of New Nations* (Chicago: University of Chicago Press).

Janowitz, Morris (1975), *Military Conflict* (Beverly Hills, Calif.: Sage).

Janowitz, M. and Little, Roger W. (1965), *Sociology and the Military Establishment* (New York: Russell Sage Foundation).

al-Jundi, Sami (n.d.), *Sūriyah Rā'idat Kifāh* (Syria . . . A Pioneer of Struggle) (Beirut: Abi Akar Press).

al-Jundi, Sami (1969a), *Sadīqī 'Ilyās* (My Friend Elyas) (Beirut: al-Nahar Press).

al-Jundi, Sami (1969b), *al-Baʿth* (The Baʿth Party) (Beirut: al-Nahar Press).

Kerr, Malcolm (1965), *The Arab Cold War 1958–1964* (London: Oxford University Press).

Khadduri, Majid (1953), 'The role of the military in Middle East politics,' *American Political Science Review*, vol. 47, pp. 511–24.

Khalid, Abdullah M. (1978), *Takdīs al-'Asliha wa al-Siyāsa al-'Impiriyāliyah fi al-Khalīj* (Piling of Arms and the Imperial Policy in the Gulf) (Beirut: al-Karmel Press).

Khattab, Mahmud (1969), *al-Wahda al-ʿAskariyah al-ʿArabiyah* (The Military Arab Unity) (Beirut: al-Irshad Press).

Khuri, Fuad I. (1969), 'The changing class structure in Lebanon,' *Middle East Journal*, vol. 23, no. 1, pp. 29–44.

Khuri, Fuad I. (1975), *From Village to Suburb* (Chicago: University of Chicago Press).

Khuri, Fuad I. (1980), *Tribe and State in Bahrain* (Chicago: University of Chicago Press).

Khuri, Fuad and Obermeyer, Gerald (1974), 'The social bases for military intervention in the Middle East,' in Catherine McArdle Kelleher (ed.), *Political Military Systems* (Beverly Hills, Calif.: Sage).

Lacouture, J. and S. (1958), *Egypt in Transition* (New York: Criterion Books).

Little, Tom (1958), *Egypt* (London: Ernest Benn).

Lutfi, Hamdi (1972), *Anwar al-Sadat* (Cairo: Dar al-Hilal).

Matar, Fuad (1975), *Bi-Sarāha ʿAn Abdel-Nassir* (About Abdel-Nassir with Frankness) (Beirut: Dar al-Cadaya).

Micaud, Charles (1972), 'Conclusion' in Ernest Gellner and Charles Micaud (eds), *Arabs and Berbers* (Lexington, Mass.: D.C. Heath (Lexington Books)).

Murad, Abbass (1973), *al-Dawr al-Siyāsī lil-Jaīsh al-'Urdunī* (The Political Role of the Jordanian Army) (Beirut: Research Center of Palestinian Liberation Organization).

Murad, Ziki (1966), 'Hawl 'Imkānāt al-Thawra lil-Juyūsh' (Around the revolutionary possibilities of the military), *al-Talʿa*, vol. 2, pp. 40–8.

Mustapha, Khalil (1969), *Suqūt al-Jālān* (The Fall of Gollan) (Amman: Dar al-Yaqin).

Obermeyer, Gerald (1969), 'Structure and Authority in a Bedouin Tribe', PhD dissertation, Indiana University. *Publications of Development Studies*, no. 17.

al-Qazzaz, Ayad (1971), 'The changing pattern of the politics of the Iraqi army', in Morris Janowitz and Jacques Doorn (eds), *On Military Intervention* (Rotterdam: University of Rotterdam Press).

al-Razzaz, Munif (1967), *al-Tajriba al-Murra* (The Bitter Experience) (Beirut: Dar Ghandur).

Sadat, Anwar (1958), *Yā Waladi . . . Hādha ʿAmmuka Jamāl* (Oh, My Son, This is Your Uncle Jamal) (Cairo: al-Urfan Press).

Sadat, Anwar (1972), *Tarīq Jamāl Abdel-Nassir* (The Path of Jamal Abdel-Nassir) (Cairo: al-Urfan Press).

al-Sayyid, Jalal (1973), *Hizb al-Baʿth al-ʿArabi* (The Arab Baʿth Party) (Beirut: al-Nahar Press).

Shils, Edward (1962), 'The military in the political development of the new states,' in John J. Johnson (ed.), *The Role of the Military in Underdeveloped Countries*, (Princeton, NJ: Princeton University Press).

Smith, Arthur K. and Welch, Claude E. Jr (1974), *Military Role and Rule* (North Scituate, Mass. – Belmont, Calif.: Duxbury Press).

Tallas, Mustapha (1967), *al-Kifāh al-Musallah* (The Armed Resistance) (Beirut: Taliᶜa Press).

Umran, Muhammad (n.d.), *Tajribatī fī al-Thawra* (My Experience in The Revolution) (No place of publication or publisher).

(Arab) Unity Thought, no. 5.

Vatikiotis, P. J. (1961*a*), 'Dilemmas of political leadership in the Arab Middle East,' *American Political Science Review*, vol. 55, pp. 103–11.

Vatikiotis, P. J. (1961*b*), *The Egyptian Army in Politics* (Bloomington, Ind.: Indiana University Press).

Vatikiotis, P. J. (1967), *Politics and the Military in Jordan* (London: Cass).

Wheelock, Keith (1960), *Nasser's New Egypt* (New York: Praeger).

Zahr al-Din, Abdel-Karim (1966), *Mudhakkarātī ᶜAn Fatrat al-'Infisāl fī Sūriyah* (My Memoirs on the Period of Syria's Session from the UAR) (Beirut: no publisher).

2 Egypt and Turkey: The Military in the Background

RICHARD H. DEKMEJIAN

The comparative study of civilian–military relations in Egypt and Turkey reveals important similarities and differences in the military's dynamic role — i.e. the patterns of intervention, the processes of civilianization, corporate identity and professionalism, the elements of civilian and military control, and the respective socio-political milieux of political activity. This chapter will analyze the dynamics of the civilian–military interaction in the two countries by using an eclectic conceptual scheme derived from the theoretical contributions of Huntington, Perlmutter, Welch and Rapoport. A brief comparative analysis will complete the study.

(1) A DYNAMIC CONTINUUM

Because of the generally low level of institutionalization and systemic/elite legitimacy in Third World countries, civilian–military relations are usually in constant flux. This phenomenon necessitates a dynamic model for the analysis of civilian–military relationships in a comparative context. Such a model can be developed through a fusion of the approaches proposed by Claude Welch and Amos Perlmutter.

A substantially revised version of Welch's basic schema[1] is presented in Figure 2.1, where 'civilian rule' and 'military rule' are seen as the two opposite ends of the spectrum of civilian–military relations. In neither case can these be regarded as 'pure' types since there is always some degree of military influence in civilian regimes and vice versa. Thus, moving toward the center of the continuum there would be two intermediate categories of civilian–military 'partnership', where either the civilians or the military might be predominant.

In order to sharpen conceptually the nature of the military's roles in Welch's schema, it is useful to consider Perlmutter's three-fold classification of military officers, based on their differing orientations toward civilian authority. Perlmutter's 'professional soldier', possessing a strong sense of corporatism and clientship considers himself subservient to civilian authority, and thereby characterizes civilian–military relations in the left-of-center categories of the continuum. The opposite is the case with the 'praetorian soldier' who seeks to identify the military's corporate

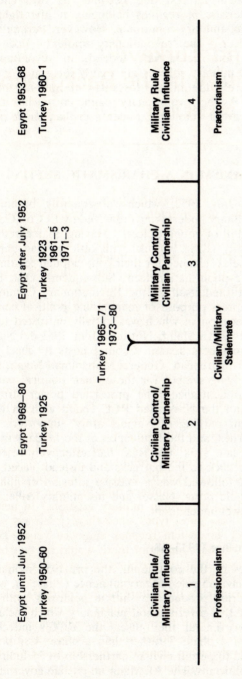

Figure 2.1 *The Civilian–Military Continuum*

aspirations with the national interest and becomes its own client.[2] Praetorian rule is characteristic of regimes belonging to the right-of-center sectors of the civilian–military continuum. However, Perlmutter's third type of military officer – the 'revolutionary soldier' – does not readily fit into Welch's four categories. Indeed, in revolutionary situations, the civilian and military spheres are tightly integrated into a single vanguard party, whereby the military loses its corporate autonomy and professional integrity. As the revolutionary regime entrenches itself, the military may regain partial autonomy under a civilian single-party system.

(2) EGYPT: PRAETORIANISM IN A CHARISMATIC SETTING

The coup d'état of 23 July 1952, which subsequently became a revolution, was a purely military undertaking organized by Lt Col. Gamal Abd al-Nasser and a handful of young officers.[3] Having engineered the overthrow of royal authority (King Farouk) with little civilian participation, the officers nevertheless claimed for their coup popular legitimacy expressed in terms of Egyptian nationalism. Subsequently, the Free Officers Executive reconstituted itself as the Revolutionary Command Council (RCC) for the express purpose of maintaining political control and setting policy, the execution of which was initially entrusted to an all-civilian Cabinet headed by Ali Mahir. Not until June 1953 did Nasser and other leading RCC members assume Cabinet posts to check the growing popularity of their figurehead, General Muhammad Nagib, who as President became a rallying symbol for the civilian political parties which the RCC aimed to neutralize. The protracted power struggle between General Nagib and the Nasser-led RCC ended with an RCC victory and the consequent purging of Nagib's army supporters, the suppression of political parties, and the liquidation of the fundamentalist Muslim Brotherhood. By late 1954, the RCC had effectively rejected General Nagib's call to go back to the barracks and instead placed him under house arrest. What followed was a massive infusion of military officers into key bureaucratic posts. Nasser and his military colleagues had decided to stay in power indefinitely.

Military Rule/Civilian Influence (1953–68)

In terms of the categories of the continuum, the pre-1952 monarchy exemplified a situation of civilian rule/military influence (Phase 1), while the early revolutionary period produced a shift in polarities, with the military in firm control of the governmental machinery which included civilian participation. However, at the outset, the RCC's indecisive behavior was suggestive of a phase 3 rather than a phase 4 situation, where the officers appeared to permit civilian partnership by including in the Cabinet well-known politicians. The Ali Mahir all-civilian government instituted by the RCC symbolized the developing military–civilian partnership. The civilian component of the partnership was diluted, when

General Nagib became Prime Minister at the head of the two successive civilian Cabinets in September and December 1952, which were more amenable to implementing the RCC's Agrarian Reform Law designed to break up large landholdings by redistributing lands to the peasants.[4] The appearance of four RCC officers – Nasser, Baghadi, Amir and S. Salim – in top Cabinet posts in June 1953, further diluted the civilian presence at the top[5] signaling the formal onset of praetorianism.[6] During the ensuing Nasser–Nagib power struggles in 1953–4, the military component of the Cabinet continued to increase from 26·3 percent in June 1953, to 40·9 percent in the reshuffled October 1953 Cabinet. A further increase to 45·8 percent in the April 1954 Cabinet reflected the Nasserite consolidation of power against Nagib and his civilian supporters outside the government. By September 1954 the military's presence reached a peak of 52·1 percent when for the first time the number of officers exceeded that of civilians.[7] Simultaneously there had been a basic qualitative transformation in the civilian component. Increasingly, civilian politicians were replaced by highly educated technocrats. Consequently what had been a phase 3 military–civilian partnership was rapidly becoming a situation of maximal military control over nonpolitical civilian technocrats, who were no longer the 'partners' of the military, but its docile servants. Two and a half years after the coup d'état, Egypt had developed into a full-blown praetorian regime (phase 4).[8]

In subsequent years, variations in the military v. civilian Cabinet lineup appeared to be related to the incidence of major events and crises. In the June 1956 Cabinet the military presence dipped to a low of 36·3 percent; however, the consummation of the Syrian–Egyptian Union (UAR) dramatically raised the number of officers, reaching 51·5 percent in August 1961.[9] Having recovered from the shock of Syria's breakaway, a new phase of partial civilianization was started as the regime initiated a drive for comprehensive control over the economy under its new program of Arab socialism. The subsequent wholesale nationalization of large- and medium-size enterprizes manifested the elite's commitment to étatism and rapid industrialization which could not be achieved without greater reliance on civilian expertise; hence the progressive decline of the military component in the Cabinet to 47 percent in September 1962 and 36·3 percent in March 1964.[10]

Despite its declining overall presence at the Cabinet level, the military elite did not materially foresake its overwhelming control over the main sectors of Egyptian life. For example, in the September 1962 two-level Cabinet structure, the Presidential Council (supreme policy-making group) was 83 percent military, in contrast to 29 percent officer representation of the Executive Council. Also in the multilevel Cabinet of March 1964, the officers scored 41·5 percent at the deputy prime minister level, but only 22·2 percent at the ministerial level.[11]

Consequently, the RCC core contingent of revolutionary officers constituted only the visible head of the pro-Nasser faction of the Egyptian military. This 'praetorian directorate' maintained its power through the allegiance of approximately fifty second- and third-string Free Officers who were placed in key positions in the governmental machinery to assure control. After years of such apprenticeship, these officers gradually emerged during the late 1950s and early 1960s to assume top positions in the Nasserite elite.[12]

In terms of the military's overall 'presence' in the system, clearly there was predominance at the highest and intermediary levels. At the zenith of the power structure, out of an aggregate of 186 Cabinet-rank leaders, who served between 1952 and 1973, 60 or 32 percent had been military officers of various types in contrast to 126, or 67·7 percent, who had a civilian background.[13] However, one should not be misled by the two-to-one civilian majority. While it clearly illustrates the regime's reliance on civilians, especially in technical areas, it is not to be regarded as a valid index of their relative power. Most of these civilians were the tools of the RCC and subsequently of Nasser himself. Since the civilians lacked an independent power base, none of the 126 emerged as a political leader in his own right in the Nasserite period, not even during the postwar turmoil of 1967–9. Coupled with Nasser's persistence in placing ex-officers in key ministries, this made the military the virtual master of the system. Only after Nasser's death did two civilians become Prime Minister – Mahmud Fawzi and Aziz Sidqi.

To be sure, one peculiarity of recent Egyptian political life has been the appalling lack of backbone among the civilian leadership. Though men of great intelligence, efficiency, and expertise, they were also singularly depoliticized, devoid of political and ideological consciousness, and therefore unable or unwilling to present a counterweight to the military. In the various power contests at the top, the civilians tended to side with different factions headed by former officers; yet as far as one can discern no civilian actually led a factional power struggle. The few who have dared to stand up to the military have been purged; the vast majority, more interested in high office than principles, complied with the military's wishes.

The best index of the officers' position within the leadership was their control of strategic posts. All of Egypt's Presidents – Nagib, Nasser and Sadat – were once officers, as were all of its Vice-Presidents. The five Premiers during the Nasserite period – Nagib, Nasser, Sabri, Muhyi al-Din and Sulayman – were also ex-officers. In addition, several key ministries – Defense, Local Administration, Military Production, and the Ministry of State (for Intelligence) – were headed by officers from the very outset. Certain other ministries alternated between ex-officers and civilians, that is, Foreign Affairs, Industry, Power, High Dam, Information, Scientific Research, Communications, Agrarian Reform, Supply, Youth, Labor, Education, Social Affairs, Planning, Waqfs, Culture, and National Guidance. The highly sensitive Interior Ministry became the preserve of ex-officers such as Muhyi al-Din and Guma'a, with the single exception of Abd al-Azim Fahmi, a police officer. Ministries with uninterrupted civilian heads included Justice, Public Works, Housing and Utilities, Irrigation, Commerce, Agriculture, Treasury, and Higher Education. These were highly technical areas, generally unsuitable for individuals of military background. Yet, in the final analysis, various means were devised to assure military control over these 'civilian' ministries as well. Nor was the Arab Socialist Union spared the effects of praetorianism; no less than half the members of its Supreme Executive Committee were ex-officers.[14]

Basically, there have been three control strategies since the military's direct involvement in government beginning in 1953. The first and crudest strategy was the outright takeover of key ministries by leading RCC members, who employed civilians in second-level slots as sources of expert advice. In later years, as vice-presidents and deputy premiers in charge of clusters of ministries, or sectors, the leading officers continued to exercise direct supervisory functions over the subordinate ministries, which civilians often headed. Baghdadi, Shafi'i, Muhyi al-Din, Husayn, Rif'at, Abbas Rudwan, Abu al-Nur and Hatim, all headed such super-ministries. The second strategy was to maintain a military presence in the civilian-led ministries by placing officers in the number two positions.

The military's most ingenious method of control was through the appointment of a new breed of officers identified here as officer-technocrats (off-techs). Most of these men began to appear in leading positions in the late 1950s and soon achieved Cabinet or higher status, often displacing civilians and other nontechnical military men.

Virtually all of the 23 (12·5 percent) off-techs have been military men who went on to receive nonmilitary degrees in diverse fields – engineering, physics, medicine, political science, law, history, and journalism. In essence, the rise of the off-techs was the military's answer to its civilian critics, since it now had its own trained experts to cope with the new and diverse complexities of an industrializing society. Through these men the military could extend its scope of effective control, simultaneously reducing its reliance on the civilian experts. Given the perceptions and needs of the leadership, the off-techs were bound to succeed; they combined and enjoyed the best of two worlds.[15] In retrospect the off-techs constituted the military's most refined method for its role expansion. Prior to the 1967 War, the Egyptian army's role expansion included such diverse tasks as running the Cairo public transport system, Marshal Amir's abortive involvement in the regime's scheme 'to liquidate feudalism' in the mid-1960s, and the frequent use of the army intelligence apparatus for internal security.

A multitude of economic and political problems converged in the mid-1960s – the Yemeni War, the economy, internal unrest – to produce a protracted crisis situation culminating in the 1967 War. The immediate effect of this turmoil was to produce an upswing in the military component of the Muhyi al-Din government and continued to rise to an unprecedented 55·2 percent in the Sulayman government of September 1966. In the aftermath of the June War, the military presence in the Cabinet reached 65·4 percent. This peak came at a time of great internal instability accentuated by Marshal Amir's attempted coup. It appeared that in Nasser's perception a military-dominated leadership could more effectively control internal unrest and neutralize further insurrectionist activity by the demoralized military establishment.

Popular reaction against the military after the 1967 defeat, coupled with the student–worker riots of February 1968, prompted Nasser to begin a farreaching reorganization of political and economic life (30 March Program). The civilian component of the Cabinet was doubled, with a concomitant sharp decrease in the military component to 39·4 percent; a similar reduction occurred in the army's role in the civilian sectors of Egyptian society. The civilizing trend begun in 1968 continued into the Sadat period.[16]

Praetorianism under Challenge: The June 1967 War

Following the defeat, Nasser took over direct command of the armed forces in addition to holding the posts of president, prime minister, and party chief. Greater control was exercised through a new law requiring presidential approval on promotions to the rank of colonel or above. In view of the army's preoccupation with the enemy across the Suez, the security organization and the police emerged as the key tools of internal control. It was essential to keep the army involved with the enemy both to increase its remaining military effectiveness and to neutralize its possible use against the ruling elite. After 1967 the emphasis shifted from praetorianism to professionalism.

The most dangerous dilemma confronting the leadership was the irrepressible public criticism of the military's performance in the war. As a people who had bestowed special privileges and perquisites upon its officer corps since 1952, the Egyptians demanded not only punishment but also explanation. Yet realism dictated the immediate shoring up of the army's morale in the continuing military confrontation with Israel – morale that had been shattered by the recent defeat, the widespread purge of its leadership, and the biting criticism at home. Also a protracted press campaign against the military could conceivably turn it against the regime itself. Despite the delicacy of the matter, press criticism of the military was extensive and vigorous, especially in late 1967. During 1968 the debate continued, but along more constructive and less emotional lines.

The fiercest attacks came from the ASU, an organization generally more militant and leftist than the army or the government. The criticism centered on the military leadership's reluctance to permit the ASU's political vanguard horizontal access to the armed forces.[17] This provided official confirmation of what certain observers had suspected since the birth of the ASU. The precise relationship of the ASU to the military organization had never been clarified; it had been simply 'left to the Supreme Executive Committee' during the mid-1960s. Clearly Marshal Amir had successfully kept the armed forces isolated from the ASU organizationally and ideologically. Whatever the merits of the Soviet *zampolit* system in terms of ideological indoctrination and party control, it never existed in the Egyptian army. In the immediate postwar period the left demanded the immediate politicization of the military ranks by ASU cadres as the only way to assure victory in a future war.[18] Prescriptions for change ranged from total reform to specific remedies. The pressure for comprehensive change came most frequently, but not exclusively, from the left. In essence, they wanted the liquidation of the 'exclusiveness' of the officer corps, the infusion of revolutionary ideology into the armed forces, and the 'cementing' of the military to the 'popular forces'. However, as time passed the leftist prescription to forge a revolutionary army was shelved and the Egyptian military was able to retain its corporate identity.

A most intriguing revelation was the strained relationship between Nasser and Amir, his long-time friend. Amir and his military associates had succeeded in diluting presidential control over the armed forces which the marshal ran as his personal fief. Indeed, the situation prior to the 1967 War reflected a certain anomaly. The praetorian elite around Nasser had been in power for over a decade during which they had shed their uniforms and experienced some degree of civilianization. Yet they had permitted one of their own – Marshal Amir – to take control of the army, one of the main props of the praetorian regime. Consequently, there was a corporate separatism between the ruling elite and the military establishment. As a ruling class, the ex-officers and civilian technocrats around Nasser could not regard the army as their primary client; they now had larger popular constituencies to satisfy, in addition to their own self-clientship – the imperative of surviving as a corporate political elite.

Political survival depends not only on the possession of power (i.e. the army) but also the acquisition of legitimacy. While the army provided the primary prop for Nasserite control in the early years of the revolution, gradually the regime amassed a significant degree of popular legitimacy, uncommon to most praetorian situations. The legitimacy was of the charismatic type which Nasser almost singlehandedly derived from his foreign confrontations and exploits after the mid-1950s.[19] Nasser's charismatic popularity set him apart and above his colleagues in the government, the army, and the Socialist Union. Thus charisma engendered alienation between Nasser and his top associates; it also tended to protect Nasser from possible challenges from his colleagues who may have entertained hopes of replacing him by the use of force. To the extent that the head of Egypt's praetorian leadership succeeded in garnering popular self-legitimization, it would be necessary to modify Perlmutter's classification of Egyptian praetorianism.

Sadat's Presidency: Military–Civilian Partnership

Anwar el-Sadat's assumption of Egypt's presidency initially did not signify any major change in the patterns of civilian–military relationships established after Marshal Amir's departure. The reorganization of the armed forces instituted under Nasser substantially depoliticized the professional military and brought to the top better-educated younger officers whose main preoccupation became the war of attrition against Israel (1968–70). However, from the outset, Sadat's ascendancy faced major challenges from a coalition of powerful leaders including Party Secretary Ali Sabri; Interior Minister Sharawi Guma'a; and Minister of War, General Muhammad Fawzi. During May 1971 Sadat was able to purge his enemies with one brilliant stroke without directly involving the military in the power struggle. General Fawzi was readily replaced as

Minister of War by General Muhammad Sadiq – who had thrown the army's support behind Sadat during the power struggles with the Sabri faction. Perhaps the key to Sadat's success was the loyalty of the Presidential Guard (*al-huras al-Gumhuri*) under General Al-Laithi Nassif, which had been originally organized by Nasser as a counterweight to the army after Marshal Amir's unsuccessful coup in August 1967. Under Sadat this practice has been substantially expanded.

The pattern of civilian–military relations established after the 1967 War indicated a clear and continuous movement toward the 'civilian' sector of Figure 2.1. While the military could not be ignored as a political actor after the purge of Amir's circle, it was pushed into a background role by Nasser. Increasingly, the situation in the late Nasser and early Sadat periods was one of civilian control/military partnership. In other words, the remaining praetorians and their civilian technocrat allies exercised effective control over the military which could be regarded as a hidden partner of the regime. Sadat's phenomenal success in disciplining and neutralizing potential military adversaries might indicate evolution toward a structure of civilian control/military influence (Figure 2.1, phase 1).

Until the October 1973 War, Sadat's relations with the military were closely intertwined with his need to end Israeli occupation of Arab land and the nature of Egyptian clientship vis-à-vis the Soviet Union. Despite Sadat's victory over the Sabri faction, it was imperative that he should produce some movement with respect to Israel, to shore up his tenuous legitimacy. Suddenly on 18 July 1972, Sadat ordered the withdrawal of Soviet forces from Egypt stationed there since the war of attrition. A combination of domestic and foreign factors had pushed Sadat to risk a rupture with the USSR, thereby increasing Egypt's vulnerability from Israel. The Soviet unwillingness to accord Egypt all-out military support to engage Israel in a large-scale war was criticized by Sadat, as well as the army leadership. Both Sadat and the military found the Soviets 'crude, even rude', and lacking confidence in the Egyptian army's ability to wage successful wars against Israel.[20] The anti-Soviet orientation of General Sadiq may have been decisive in prompting Sadat to oust the Soviets – an action greeted by signs of mass relief and a concomitant increase in Sadat's popularity. The Egyptian expectation was that the Soviet expulsion would generate a favorable American and Israeli response. Yet, the Nixon administration's preoccupation with Vietnam and the electoral campaign of 1972 precluded a US peace initiative toward Israel and the Arabs. Consequently in October 1972, Sadat moved to the left moderately healing the breach with the USSR and reopening its pipeline of advanced weaponry to the armed forces. Simultaneously, Sadat dismissed General Sadiq along with 100 officers, in a move reminiscent of Khrushchev's purge of Marshal Zukov, his former ally. The general who had supported Sadat against the Sabri faction in May 1971 and had been instrumental in inducing the Soviet exodus was now considered the odd man out. Having assured new supplies of advanced Soviet weaponry, Sadat moved in one stroke to ameliorate the army's hurt feelings, redirect its attention toward the forthcoming war against Israel, and at the same time purge the anti-Soviet general with relative impunity. The Sadiq affair demonstrated Sadat's ability to sustain a phase 2 relationship – civilian control/military partnership.

Civilian–Military Relations after the October War

The October 1973 War was bound to have an impact on civilian–military relations in Egypt. Despite the Israeli breakthrough to the Canal's West Bank, Egypt's army had performed beyond the expectations of most observers and analysts. In destroying the Bar-Lev line and inflicting substantial human and material losses on Israel, the army had shattered the sense of inferiority that Egyptians had come to manifest during centuries of foreign rule.

Therefore, both President Sadat and the army leadership stood to profit from the victory. Yet, in the end, Sadat acquired the upper hand by criticizing the army's Chief of Staff, General Sa'ad al-Din Shazli, for his failure to bloc the Israeli thrust into the West Bank. Now Sadat could take overall credit for the army's achievements, while simultaneously deflating its leadership by replacing specific officers. In January 1974, General Shazli was sent into diplomatic exile as ambassador to Britain and two major generals were purged. Clearly, Shazli possessed all the attributes of a possible threat to Sadat's primacy. The general enjoyed considerable popularity in the army like the late Marshal Amir who had become a threat to Nasser before 1967. Shazli was also liked by the public which in a future crisis may have sought a charismatic replacement to Sadat.

Sadat lacks the charisma of his predecessor; what he possesses in a large measure is a sense of timing and tactical balance both in his domestic and foreign policies. Less than a month after reducing the Shazli threat, he let out of prison six top army and intelligence officers in a move to placate the military. The amnesty covered none other than the former War Minister, General Muhammad Fawzi, who had been jailed for involvement with the Sabri group in May 1971. A second contingent of pardoned officers included Marshal Amir's old cronies – Defense Minister General Shams al-Din Badran, Major-General Ismail Labib, Air Vice-Marshall Sidqi Mahmud, and intelligence chief Salah Nasr and Abbas Rudwan. They had been found responsible for the 1967 defeat and incarcerated after their abortive moves against Nasser as a part of the Amir plot in August–September 1967.[21]

This balancing act was a stroke of genius, since it provided 'a cover' for Sadat to make concessions to Henry Kissinger and the Israelis as a prelude to disengagement on the Suez Front. To be sure, the army manifested opposition to 'thinning out' its concentrations at the Canal, and during March 1974 fighting erupted between Third Army soldiers and the police in Tahrir Square as the soldiers protested against Sadat's ceasefire agreement; the army, or a part of it, wanted 'a war to the finish.'[22]

The balancing act did not mean that Sadat was operating from a position of weakness. In fact, because of the October War he had become 'an uncrowned King'; it was precisely because of his popularity that he could switch suddenly from a policy of war, to peace, from a pro-Soviet stance to a pro-American position. Also, the steps taken by Nasser after the 1967 debacle had increased the professionalization and the technical competence of the officers' corps as increasing numbers of university graduates entered the army. Therefore given his new popularity and the depoliticized and self-confident state of the army, Sadat possessed substantial latitude for movement if he could count on his newly acquired American friends to bring about an Israeli withdrawal.

In analyzing civilian–military relations after October 1973, aside from Sadat's personal authority, there was insufficient institutionalization of the civilian sectors to pose a credible counterweight to the military should the latter decide to intervene in a future crisis. The great bureaucracies continued to be overwhelmingly in civilian hands (technocrats and some lawyers), and the People's Assembly still functioned, although at less than full steam. As to the Cabinet, the sharp reduction in the proportion of ex-officers begun by Nasser was not reversed. It is significant that Sadat has not reverted to Nasser's pre-1968 practice of enlarging the Cabinet's military component every time there was an external or internal crisis. Despite the student demonstrations and the October War itself, Sadat continued to keep the 'military' Cabinet contingent at about 30 percent. In the postwar Cabinet of September 1974, the military 'presence' reached an all-time low of 15 percent under a civilian Prime Minister, Abd al-Aziz al-Higazi.

Civilian–Military Relations (1975–9)

In reaction to the rioting of January and March 1975, Sadat appointed a new Cabinet headed not by a military officer, but by Interior Minister Mamduh Salim, a police general. Simultaneously the last of the original RCC officers, Husayn al-Shafi'i was dismissed as Vice-President. Significantly, his replacement was also recruited from the military in the person of Air Marshal Husni Mubarak who had been decorated for his performance in the October War. Sadat further stated that the military would be represented in the Central Committee and the Supreme Executive Council of a newly reorganized Arab Socialist Union.[23]

In mid-1975 Sadat's 'honeymoon' period after the October War appeared to be at an end. Sadat's policy of *infitah* provided an opening to the West ideologically and economically as well as a relaxation of the 'socialist' framework promoting the public sector. In the consequent inflationary milieu, several destabilizing factors manifested themselves including plots by Islamic fundamentalists, leftists and the armed forces. In June 1975, forty-three army officers were accused of plotting to oust the government.[24] During January 1976, a cleavage was reported between the military headed by Vice-President Mubarak and War Minister Abd al-Ghani al-Gamasi, and the civilian elite led by Assembly Speaker Sayyid Mar'i and Deputy Mahmud Abu Wafia, in the context of the regime's experiment of establishing 'platforms' representing various ASU factions.[25] In February and April 1976 there were additional signs of instability in the armed forces as a large number of officers were reported to have resigned in protest at the regime's economic policies.[26]

A number of factors have continued to produce increasing alienation between the military and the government in recent years. While the October War accorded the army a welcome feeling of pride and self-confidence, it also opened the way to an inflationary economy detrimental to government officials on fixed incomes. While the civilian bureaucrats could well supplement their shrinking incomes by 'moonlighting', the military was severely hampered in pursuing entrepreneural activities to supplement its salaries. No less significant were the January 1977 food riots which shook the government and necessitated a massive display of army might – a risky undertaking. It appeared that the army waited a long time before deploying in the streets, amid indications that it opposed the price increases as well as the repressive role of the Presidential Guard and the security apparatus. Indeed, the military revolutionaries of July 1952 had taken power in the name of the Egyptian people and pursued social and economic policies which benefitted the middle- and lower-middle classes from which they had originated. Now the military was being called upon to sustain a regime which was identified in the popular mind with upper- and upper-middle class interests. Consequently, the army's reluctance to fight its own people may well be compounded by the military's ultimate sympathy toward the rioters and their cause based upon their common economic difficulties and social origins.

Additional contradictions became manifest in President Sadat's relationship with the military during 1977 and 1978. The army that fought the October War was a new military machine that had been completely reorganized after the massive purges of Marshal Amir and the officer corps. In this sense the new army was Nasser's handiwork, in terms of its depoliticization and reindoctrination. Its motivational level was high by virtue of the clarity of its objective (i.e., to liberate the Sinai) and its professional imperative to perform to regain its lost dignity and honor. In the context of the Egyptian–American rapprochement of the mid-1970s, the 'attitudinal polarity' of the military had to be reversed. The army that had been sent to support Lumumba in 1960, was dispatched to aid the pro-Western Mobutu regime in 1977. As the Egyptian–Israeli peace-making efforts intensified in the context of the eroding American position in Afghanistan, Ethiopia, and Iran, Sadat declared his willingness to commit the Egyptian army to fight against destabilizing influences if the USA would bear the costs in weaponry and financial support.

There exists considerable evidence that the new 'anti-communist' role of the military was not well received by the high command as well as many lower echelon officers. In mid-1977 several top commanders were replaced as the regime crushed an attempted coup by naval officers. More serious were the developments of the summer and fall of 1978. On 19 June the former Chief of Staff, General Sa'ad al-Din al-Shazli was removed from his post as Ambassador to Portugal for denouncing Sadat as a dictator and calling for a military coup to remove him from office. On 24 July, Sadat ordered a major shakeup of the High Command and in August the regime jailed fourteen paratroop officers who had supported General Shazli.[27] Finally, during October 1978 the War Ministry was replaced by a Ministry of Defense, as its occupant General Abd al-Ghani al-Gamasi lost his Cabinet and military posts; the Chief of Staff, General Fahmi, was also replaced. It was significant that these changes coincided with the Camp David agreements between Egypt and Israel. While Gamasi reiterated the importance of the Eastern Front, Sadat increasingly came to view Libya as a threat. With Gamasi's departure, the only individual in the government who had possessed an independent power base left the political arena. Significantly, aside from Sadat, there was no single political leader of any note in the ranks of the elite save for the new Prime Minister, Mustafa Khalil, who had been Minister of Communications under Nasser. Most of the civilians in the Cabinet were technocrats with little grassroots legitimacy. Aside from the People's Assembly, the institutional vacuum has not been filled by Sadat since his virtual dismantling of the ASU. The existence of such a political vacuum and the consequent weakness of the civilian component, leaves the political system vulnerable to future praetorian takeovers.

Whatever the political wisdom of Sadat's policies toward the military after October 1973, they have been consistent with his reiteration that the army has no political role. Military men are not permitted to vote in elections, nor is the army considered as a corporate member of the Alliance of Popular Forces, as it was under Nasser. Moreover, the imposition of an ideological and strategic reorientation upon the army may further increase the apparent estrangement of the military from the regime. Also, a reduction of the army's size prompted by the easing of the Egyptian–Israeli confrontation will produce a major unemployment problem with massive destabilizing consequences. However, the army's restructuring, presumably under American guidance, could provide certain benefits for the officer's corps, thereby ameliorating anti-Sadat attitudes. These could include American supplies of highly sophisticated weapons systems, and increased pay scales, especially for the officer corps. Moreover, Sadat's pro-Western orientation could create opportunities for the army to fight in various small African or Middle Eastern conflicts which would further contribute to military salaries ('hazardous pay') and keep the army 'busy' away from the political home front. Such limited combat opportunities and the regime's stated plans to redeploy the armed forces to implement domestic civilian projects may well succeed in maintaining civilian supremacy over the military establishment.

(3)   TURKEY: POLITICS OF MILITARY GUARDIANSHIP

The important role which the military has played in contemporary Turkish politics can be traced back to the Ottoman period. The dominant position of the Yeni Çeri at the pinnacle of the imperial system was not broken until 1826, and it was only after this that Sultan Mahmut II was able to pursue his modernization program which included military reforms.

The Young Turk Revolution of 1908 once again demonstrated the military's propensity to intervene decisively in the political process. Despite its purely civilian origins, the Committee of Union and Progress

(Ittihad ve Terakki) was increasingly dominated by military men after the coup of 1913 who had been instrumental in leading the 1908 revolution and subsequently occupying key positions in the government. After the Turkish defeat in World War I, once again the military took the leading role in establishing the Republic in 1923 under Mustafa Kemal Paşa Atatürk.

Atatürk's Legacy

In terms of the military–civilian continuum (see Figure 2.1), Atatürk's single-party dictatorship represented a fusion of nationalist officers and bureaucrats who had manifested enough military strength to maintain control over Anatolia. The institutional framework of the military-bureaucratic elite was the Republican People's Party (RPP) (Halk Partisi) which came to symbolize Atatürk's radical reform program of etatism, secularization and modernization.[28]

Despite being the leader of the nationalist struggle, Atatürk was not immune to challenge from Islamic conservatives and Pan-Turkish officials of the previous regime. Equally serious was the recalcitrance of guerrilla leader Çerkes Edhem and of the generals Kiazim Karabekir and Ali Fuat Çebesoy who had distinguished themselves in the struggle for independence. All of these challenges were successfully defeated in the context of the one-party system which Atatürk controlled. Thus what had started as a military–civilian partnership (phase 3) with military dominance, became increasingly civilianized under Atatürk's constant prodding. As President of the Republic, Atatürk led the way toward civilianization, by resigning his military commission, thereby institutionalizing the formal separation between the military and political spheres that has been maintained with some exceptions until today.[29] Consequently, the early Atatürk period might be classified as a phase 2 situation of civilian control and military partnership which increasingly moved toward phase 1 during the 1930s. Despite the military background of Ismet Inönü, who assumed Atatürk's mantle after the latter's death in 1938, the process of civilianization continued as Turkey evolved toward a multi-party system after 1945. With the victory of the Democratic Party in 1950, the government came to be dominated by civilian politicians whose relationship with the military was of the phase 1 variety. Soon, however, a number of factors were instrumental in inducing military intervention.

Precisely because of Atatürk's distinguished military record during and after World War I, he became the embodiment of the *Ghazi* tradition prevalent in the early Ottoman state. As the victorious *Ghazi*, Atatürk was able to infuse the nascent republic with the legitimacy of his charisma which had been mainly derived from his military heroism. As his successor and close associate, General Inönü was well situated to carry on the legitimizing tradition of Atatürk's charisma which had become routinized in the RPP as well as the military itself. Indeed, more than any other institution, the military had been imbued with Atatürk's radical reforms to the extent that it considered itself the prime repository and ultimate guardian of the *Ghazi's* modernizing legacy.

In contrast to the RPP, the Democratic Party of Prime Minister Adnan Menderes lacked strong historical ties to the military and the legitimizing influence of Atatürk's charisma. Equally serious were the Democrats' increasing departure from the tenets of Atatürkism soon after their 1950 electoral victory.

During its ten-year tenure in power, the government of Prime Minister Menderes progressively restricted political freedom by purging judges and university professors, curtailing political parties, stifling the press, and using the police to suppress popular protest.[30] By pursuing policies of accommodation toward the religious conservatives, the landlords, and the rising capitalist classes, the Democrats amassed impressive victories against their opponents headed by Inönü. Significantly, the opposition consisted of the modernized sectors of Turkish society, which had been at the forefront of Atatürk's revolution – the intelligentsia, the civil service, and the officer class.[31] Moreover, Menderes had alienated the military by basing promotions on personal fidelity to his party. While he had pushed ahead with the rapid modernization of the military establishment, Menderes did little to ameliorate the officer's declining economic status as a result of inflation. Nor did the Democrats rely on the military as a source of recruitment of Cabinet members and lawmakers, as had been the case under RPP rule.[32]

The May 1960 Coup d'État

Interventionist sentiment began to develop in the mid-1950s, and in 1957 a number of military plotters were arrested. However, it was not until 27 May 1960 that thirty-eight army and air force officers took power in the name of a National Unity Committee (NUC) at a time when the Menderes regime was manifestly incapable of exercising control without help from the military, which had been ordered to quell the demonstrators. Having ended the First Republic, the NUC started building the Second Republic by appointing a committee of law professors to write a new constitution – a task subsequently delegated to a constituent assembly, with the NUC exercising decisive control over the framing of the document. Thus, the NUC became a legislative body as its chairman, General Çemal Gürsel, presided over a Cabinet of civilian technocrats and two officers, constituting a phase 4 situation of military rule/civilian influence.

Soon after the coup of 27 May, the classic pattern of junta disunity manifested itself in the NUC and the army command. The NUC was an oversized group of thirty-eight officers ranging from general to captain, thirty-six of which surrendered their military commissions following the pattern set by Atatürk. In November 1960, the NUC purged itself of fourteen officers led by Alpaslan Türkes, who advocated permanent military rule. Meanwhile, the NUC succeeded in retiring about 5,000 officers, but could not manage to solidify its hold on the top command of the military establishment. Increasingly, power flowed from the NUC to the Supreme Military Council (SMC), an advisory body consisting of the staff chief, his deputy, the commanders of the three services, the three army area chiefs, the prime minister, and the defense minister.[33]

In June 1961, the NUC–SMC conflict reached a showdown, in which the SMC prevailed in safeguarding the autonomy of the armed forces and reiterating the necessity of returning the country to civilian rule. Consequently, the split in the military as well as the tradition of civilian rule were instrumental in aborting any attempt to establish a military dictatorship. During the next few months, the SMC took the lead in negotiating with General Gürsel and the civilian politicians a set of guidelines under which a return to civilian rule would be effected. The elections of 15 October 1961 resulted in a victory for the RPP, closely seconded by the Justice Party, which was the purged Democratic Party in disguise. Under pressure from the SMC, the two rival parties formed a coalition government headed by ex-President Ismet Inönü, as General Gürsel was elected to the presidency of the Republic. This pattern of SMC intervention repeated itself in June 1962 and January 1964 when it was necessary to heal breakdowns in succeeding coalition governments. The problem that confounded SMC civilianization efforts centered on the RPP decline at the polls, accompanied by a significant resurgence of Justice Party strength. Yet the SMC was not prepared to sacrifice the aims of the 27 May Revolution by returning to power the partisans of Menderes as represented by the Justice Party. Not until 1965 did the SMC reluctantly approve the formation of a fourth coalition government without Inönü's RPP, consisting of the Justice Party and three smaller parties. Significantly, the new Cabinet was headed by an independent senator, Suat Hayri Ürgüplü, with the Justice Party leader Suleiman Demirel as Deputy Premier.[34] In October 1965, the Justice Party won an absolute majority and formed a new government without SMC intervention. Meanwhile, the SMC continued to maintain its 'guardianship' over Turkish politics as well as the army itself. Two attempted military coups led by Colonel Talat Aydemir[35] (February 1962 and May 1963) were foiled and the Demirel government promised to uphold the principles of the 1960 revolution. Moreover, the SMC succeeded in inducing Parliament to elect Chief of Staff, General Çevdet Sünay as President in March 1966, to succeed the ailing General Gürsel. As to the armed forces' role, the SMU manifested little inclination to permit a return to full civilian control.[36] Under the circumstances, Turkish politics of the mid and late 1960s could be characterized as a 'silent partnership' in which the military maintained its full autonomy from the government while keeping a watchful eye over the parameters of civilian political life. In view of the progressive increase in the strength of the ruling Justice Party in the 1965 and 1969 elections in the midst of improving economic conditions, the incentive for military intervention decreased. In terms of the military–civilian relations, the regime increasingly moved to the center of the continuum in the context of an uneasy partnership. The two elements coexisted within a single political system and continued to operate in their respective spheres of responsibility. The Demirel government was not predisposed to question the military's independent position or its muted guardianship function; not was the military interested in challenging the electoral legitimacy of Justice Party rule. Demirel was careful not to repeat Menderes's errors. He maintained good relations with the military elite and routinely consulted with high-ranking officers; he also worked to improve the economic position of the officer corps.[37]

In retrospect, it appears that during the 1960s the Turkish army increasingly assumed a new and unprecedented role in the political process which ran counter to the Atatürk model. In fact its self-delegated role of neutral guardianship evolved into that of partisan protector of the Demirel regime against its many opponents. Indeed, the 'silent partnership' was based on mutually beneficial tradeoffs. The High Command hoped that Demirel's significant electoral support could be translated into stability; hence the army's support of the status quo which by the mid-1960s had been singularly hospitable to the social, economic and political aspirations of the officer corps. In addition to higher pay scales, the officers were given better housing and a consequent improvement in their social status. After retirement, they were recruited into the upper realms of the bureaucracy or into private and governmental enterprises; and top commanders were given prestigious ambassadorships. Equally significant was the creation of the Army Mutual Assistance Association (Ordu Yardimlasma Kurumu) which became one of the largest business conglomerates of Turkey.[38] In sum, the top echelons of the officer corps had become a privileged part of the establishment – Turkey's own military–industrial complex.

Intervention by Ultimatum: March 1971

It was not until the internal weakening of the Justice Party and the manifestation of growing domestic turmoil that the military once again resorted to interventionism in March 1971. The factors promoting instability were manifold. At the most basic level there was an ominous convergence of class conflict and ethnic conflict, leading to a progressive decline of elite legitimacy. Atatürk's nationalist ideology could no longer provide social cohesion among the diverse elements of the population now split both ideologically and ethnically, which often became mutually reinforcing. The internally split Demirel government was unable to cope with the growing campus warfare, labor union strikes, ethnic clashes and violent manifestations of anti-Americanism.[39] Under the threat of a military takeover Prime Minister Demirel resigned. Significantly, however, the army refrained from an outright assumption of power, but permitted the establishment of a succession of non-partisan Cabinets to impose martial law, suppress the newspapers, outlaw strikes, arrest hundreds of leftists and dissolve the leftist Turkish Workers' Party and the rightwing of the Turkish National Order Party.

Unlike the 1960 takeover, the military's intervention of 1971 was not led by a mix of lower- and higher-ranking officers but by the top brass. The timing of the army's move was not determined by the civil strife which had been going on for some time, but by certain critical developments inside the officer corps. The National Security Council,[40] an organ dominated by the military, was increasingly challenged by a rising tide of interventionism coming from younger generals and colonels who were pushing for Demirel's ouster. Under the circumstances, the decision to dismiss Demirel was taken by the Chief of the General Staff, Memduh Tağmaç, in order to pre-empt a coup d'état by younger officers. Thus, the situation after March 1971 constituted a move to the right of center in the civilian–military continuum characterized by military control/civilian partnership (phase 3). However, the army's position of supremacy proved less than viable, precisely because of its internal instability.[41] Between August 1970 and August 1971 hundreds of generals and colonels were retired or arrested for their advocacy of direct military rule. Nor was it clear that the army possessed sufficient potential after March 1971 to bend the politicians to its will, as illustrated by the refusal of the two major parties to accept the candidacy of the Chief of Staff General Gürler to succeed President Sünay in 1973.[42]

The constitutional crisis eased with the choice of a retired naval commander in chief, Admiral Fahri Korutürk, an elderly nonpolitical senator. Martial law was ended by September 1973, as the new chief of staff, General Semih Sançar retired nearly 200 top officers for engaging in political activities. Meanwhile, the RPP had won a major victory under the leadership of Bülent Eçevit who had moved the party to the left to capture support from the outlawed Turkish Labor Party. As Prime Minister, Eçevit presided over an unholy coalition with the Islamic Traditionalist National Salvation Party.

The Turkish invasion of Cyprus in mid-1974 provided Eçevit with an emotional cause to rally the Turkish masses and evoke grassroots support for his regime. In September 1974, Eçevit resigned hoping to increase RPP's strength in the Assembly in the electoral contest. Instead, an interim government was formed in March 1975 and Demirel returned at the head of a four-party coalition including the Justice Party, the Pan-Turkist National Action Party, the Islamic National Salvation Party and the National Reliance Party. Having aborted Eçevit's strategem, the Demirel government proved even more ineffective in dealing with the street violence, the deteriorating economy and the Cyprus conflict. Early elections were held in June 1977 which gave Eçevit 213 seats in Parliament, but not a majority. His consequent failure to form a majority government by coalition once again brought Demirel to the prime ministry as leader of a conservative three-party government.

Throughout the mid-1970s the military's stance toward successive civilian governments was deeply critical due to the politicians' manifest inability to promote stability. On a number of occasions, the military leaders issued outright threats to intervene forcefully. For example, in January 1975, Chief of Staff General Semih Sançar warned that 'the Army will not stay away from the nation's problems.'[43] Also instructive was the 'letter of protest' sent to Prime Minister Demirel by Turkey's youngest general, Irfan Ozaydinli charging the government with 'mismanagement'.[44] Yet an outright military takeover did not occur, despite the protracted stalemate in political life and the persistence of violence which in 1979 claimed over 1,000 lives.

To explain the army's reluctance to assume power in the mid-1970s, the traditional explanations are clearly insufficient. Atatürk's legacy of civilian government, no less than the continuing strength of the political parties militated against army takeover. More instructive, however, were the lessons of May 1960 and March 1971, where not only the military found itself unable to deal with large-scale conflict, but also realized its institutional weakness to unite itself as a praetorian ruling elite. By the late 1970s the level of conflict, both ideological and ethnic, was incomparably higher than that of 1960 or 1971, as were the cleavages within the armed forces. It appeared that more forceful army intervention was aborted because the various interventionalist factions worked to neutralize each other; no one faction could marshall enough support to effect a takeover. Moreover, the higher echelons of the military had become a part of the Turkish establishment since the coup d'état of 1960.[45] Thus, the officers' class interests dictated a continuation of the status quo within a stable framework, rather than the assumption of direct military rule. Indeed, it was safer for the military to stay in the background and permit the civilian politicians to carry out its wishes and be blamed for the consequences. This conservative orientation of the military elite was in sharp contrast to the reformist sentiments of the Turkish military in previous decades. By the mid-1970s, not even their ideological conservatism could unite the top military elites, much less the lower ranks. Periodically, there were reports of incipient coups including one on 2 March 1975 by junior officers (majors and colonels) which was suppressed by the general staff. More serious was the premature retirement of the Land Forces Commander, General Nameh Kemal Ersun on 3 June 1977, two days prior to the general elections, who was reported to have planned a coup to install a rightwing government, under Alpaslan Turkeş.[46]

The retirement of General Ersun opened the way for a struggle of succession among the high-ranking generals, which was exacerbated by President Korutürk and Prime Minister Demirel who were supporting opposing military factions. On 31 December 1977 Demirel resigned as Prime Minister as Bülent Eçevit returned to office and won a vote of confidence on 17 January 1978, vowing to reestablish law and order. By the year's end, however, Eçevit had failed to check the ongoing violence; neither was he able to arrest Turkey's drift toward economic bankruptcy. Eçevit's most notable success was to negotiate the lifting of the American congressional ban on military aid to Turkey in mid-1978, although his government was too weak to make the necessary concessions to resolve the Cyprus dilemma. Such concessions would be opposed by extreme rightist parties and the military itself. Finally, in the face of electoral losses in October 1979, the Eçevit government resigned in the midst of continuing political violence and economic chaos.

Prospects for Intervention

The ebb and flow of civilian–military relations in Turkey during the late 1970s tended toward the center of the civilian–military spectrum, as the two internally unstable centers of power carried on their uneasy coexistence. The antagonistic civilian coalitions under Eçevit and Demirel agreed on little except the imperative of preventing direct military rule.[47] The civilian camp was further split along ideological lines as was the military itself – a factor that tended to reduce its effectiveness as an instrument of praetorian intervention. Despite the top military elite's explicit commitment to Atatürk's ideals, there has been some erosion of Kemalist ideology[48] in the officer corps which has been partly replaced by at least three competing ideological tendencies – Pan-Islamism, Pan-Turkism and socialism – in addition to its affliction with embourgeoisment. In the context of civilian–military relations, there is considerable evidence of linkages between the military factions and their civilian ideological counterparts within and outside the recognized political parties. Consequently, the historical RPP–army linkage has weakened despite its temporary renewal in the Cyprus crisis. Increasingly, there appears to be substantial collusion between rightist army officers and the Pan-Turkist National Action Party of ex-Vice Premier Alpaslan Turkeş. As the modern-day exponent of the Turanism of the Young Turks, Turkeş preaches the doctrine of Turkish superiority and irredentism to establish a 'Greater Turkey'. His private army of 'Grey Wolves' has been active in promoting urban violence and sectarian/ethnic conflict, too often without interference from the military. The National Action Party has become Turkey's fastest growing party and its cadres are reported to have infiltrated the security services and the army itself.[49] The protracted crisis milieu of the late 1980s may provide an ideal breeding ground for a takeover of power by ex-Colonel Turkeş, in alliance with Pan-Turkist officers.

The army's cohesiveness is further threatened by the tendency toward 'Bonapartism', among certain non-ideological officers. In such cases, intervention may be initiated by officers seeking power not primarily in the name of specific groups or ideologies, but because of personal ambition. A more serious problem, however, is the threat of ethnic separatism in the officer corps and the soldiery. While it is difficult to ascertain the precise ethnic components of the officer corps and the noncommissioned ranks, it is possible that the ongoing inter-ethnic conflicts at the mass level may affect the military itself. These ethnic cleavages are primarily along linguistic and sectarian lines, involving the Turks, the Kurds, the Laz and the Alevi. The first three groups are predominantly Sunni Muslim, while the Alevis are a branch of the Shi'ite sect, who are especially fearful of the Sunni Turks.[50]

The exacerbation of the conflictual milieu has been due to the reinforcement of ethnic cleavages by class divisions as well as restrictive governmental policies toward ethnic groups which date back to the Ottoman period. With the establishment of the Republic, the Laz were able to accommodate themselves to Turkish predominance both culturally and politically and went on to assume important positions in the political, military and economic elite. In sharp contrast, the Kurdish minority resisted the efforts of Turkification due to their traditional orientation and tribal communal structure, no less than their persecution under Atatürk during the mid-1920s. Consequently, the Kurds were unable to achieve sufficient upward mobility in political and economic life to become coopted by the system. The Kurdish revolts in Iran and Iraq further sharpened the Kurds' feelings of a separatism in the Turkish context.

Given the ethnic and class polarization of the mass base, the military's potential as a coercive instrument may be somewhat impaired. While ethnic Turkish and Laz officers are still dominant in the higher military ranks, significant numbers of Kurdish and Alevi officers may be found among lower officers and non-commissioned ranks. In such a situation, the military may find it difficult to suppress Kurdish insurrectionist attempts in the eastern provinces. In a future environment of protracted crisis, the pull of ethnic and ideological loyalties could well destroy the Turkish military's utility as a fighting force and as a political actor capable of assuming a direct, or an indirect, role in government.

(4) MILITARY–CIVILIAN RELATIONS IN EGYPT AND TURKEY: A COMPARATIVE ANALYSIS

The foregoing analysis of civilian–military relations in Egypt and Turkey reveal sharp differences as well as some similarities which are summarized as follows:

(a) The personalities of the two main leaders – Atatürk and Nasser – and the anatomy of their respective revolutions, were decisive in defining the nature of civilian–military relations in the two countries. Atatürk's revolutionary elite included a genuine civilian component which militated against full-scale praetorianism. In sharp contrast, the Nasserite Revolution of 1952 was almost purely a military affair. Both leaders, however, were reluctant to permit (Nasser more than Atatürk) full-scale civilian multiparty political life.

(b) As a consequence of the different legacies of the two leaders, the status of the civilian components was dissimilar. Gradually, the civilians under Atatürk functioned as politicians; under Nasser and Sadat the civilian component remained basically technocratic. Moreover, less than a decade after Atatürk's death, a multiparty system emerged mostly led by civilian politicians. No such evolution occurred in Egypt, although Sadat's new initiatives on the home front (April 1979) contain the promise of evolution toward civilian party government.

(c) In retrospect, both Atatürk and Nasser were not fully successful in routinizing their charisma – to legitimize and institutionalize their reform programs over the long run, except in a limited way in the military establishment. In both countries, large sectors of civilian elites were instrumental in eroding Atatürk's and Nasser's revolutionary legacies. Also, as Ottoman successor states, both Turkey and Egypt shared a common Islamic heritage and traditions. Atatürk's precedent was significant in influencing Nasser, Sadat and their colleagues. Moreover, the two revolutions were initiated by middle-class army officers whose primary preoccupation was national independence. Both military regimes came to rely on bureaucratic systems and attempted to rule through single-party systems. Finally, both regimes initiated etatist political economies, but increasingly moved toward mixed capitalist systems.

(d) Despite the greater strength of the civilian sectors in Turkey, frequent army intervention was not prevented. Thus a strong ex-military leader like Sadat may prove more able than Turkey's politicians to keep the military from forceful intervention in politics. Nevertheless, the Turkish army was destined to wait twenty-two years after Atatürk to intervene directly (May 1960). In the Egyptian case, President Sadat's departure from the presidency might well trigger an early military takeover due to the weakness of civilian institutions and the propensity for ideological conflict between the rightists and leftists compounded by Islamic revivalism.

(e) Other variables being equal, in the long range the Egyptian military is more likely to operate as a cohesive interventionist force than the Turkish military due to the virtual absence of ethnic cleavages and a lower level of ideological polarization, than appears to be the case in the Turkish army.

(f) The two armies have experienced diametrically opposed evolutions. A victorious Turkish army under Atatürk was initially divorced from politics until 1960, when increasing political involvement may have reduced its effectiveness as a fighting force. In contrast, a defeated Egyptian army (1948) took power in 1952 and continued to erode its professionalism through political involvement, until after the 1967 War, when its relative separation from political life seems to have contributed to its credible performance in the October 1973 War.

(g) The most outstanding similarity between the Egyptian and Turkish military establishments is their 'behind-the-scenes' role in the political process. While ex-officers still occupy prominent positions in the civilianized political structure, the officer corps remains institutionally separate from the government, although there is an institutionalized 'consultative' linkage at the top in both countries between the government and the military establishment. In both situations, the presidency (occupied by two ex-officers) provides the crucial tie between the military and civilian sectors. However, the nature of the linkages is dissimilar. The Egyptian President deals with his military establishment from a position of relative strength somewhat akin to the Atatürk model. In sharp contrast, the Turkish President and the main civilian politicians often function at the sufferance of the military, and sometimes as its virtual agents.

NOTES

1   Claude E. Welch Jr (ed.), *Civilian Control of the Military*, (Albany, NY: State University of New York Press, 1976), pp. 2–6.
2   Amos Perlmutter, *The Military and Politics in Modern Times*, (New Haven, Conn. and London: Yale University Press, 1977), pp. 11–13.
3   For an extended discussion see P. J. Vatikiotis, *The Egyptian Army in Politics*, (Bloomington, Ind.: Indiana University Press, 1961), pp. 44–68.
4   ibid., pp. 75–6.
5   A detailed analysis of military component of the Egyptian elite is presented in R. Dekmejian, *Patterns of Political Leadership*, (Albany, NY: State University of New York Press, 1975), pp. 176–224.

6   For a most comprehensive analysis of Egyptian praetorianism, see Amos Perlmutter, *Egypt: The Praetorian State*, (New Brunswick, NJ: Transaction Books, 1974).
7   Dekmejian, *Patterns of Political Leadership*, pp. 188–91.
8   Perlmutter states that praetorianism was institutionalized in 1956. See Perlmutter, *Egypt*, p. 200.
9   Dekmejian, *Patterns of Political Leadership*, p. 191.
10 ibid.
11 ibid.
12 ibid., p. 178.
13 ibid., p. 185.
14 R. Hrair Dekmejian, *Egypt under Nasir*, (London: University of London Press, 1972), pp. 278–81.
15 Dekmejian, *Patterns of Political Leadership*, pp. 185–9.
16 ibid., p. 197. For an attack on role expansion before 1967, see Muhammad Hasanayn Haikal, *Al-Ahram*, (21 June 1968).
17 An interesting analysis is presented by Ahmad Hamrush, 'Man Yahmi al-Thawrah' (Who defends the revolution), *Ruz al-Yusif* (31 July 1967), pp. 6–7.
18 Ahmad Hamrush, 'Min Ajl Himayat al-Thawrah' (In order to defend the revolution), *Ruz al-Yusif* (7 August 1967), p. 7.
19 Dekmejian, *Egypt under Nasir*, pp. 37–63, 244–310.
20 Anwar el-Sadat, *In Search of Identity* (New York: Harper & Row, 1978), pp. 225, 284.
21 Dekmejian, *Egypt under Nasir*, p. 252.
22 See article by Ihsan Abd al-Quddus in *Akhbar al-Yawm* (2 February 1974).
23 *Arab Report and Record* (1–15 April 1975), p. 215.
24 *Al-Safir* (29 July 1975).
25 *Inter-Press Service* (6 January 1976).
26 *Arab Report and Record* (1–15 February 1976), p. 70.
27 *Arab Report and Record* (1–15 August 1976). The possibility of a military coup was discussed by Sadat and Abd al-Azim Ramadan, see *Ruz al-Yusif* (10 July 1978).
28 Joseph S. Szyliowicz, 'Elites and modernization in Turkey', in Frank Tauchau (ed.), *Political Elites and Political Development in the Middle East* (Cambridge, Mass.: Schenkman, 1975), p. 32.
29 ibid., pp. 32–3. For an extensive discussion, see Robert E. Ward and Dankwart A. Rustow (eds), *Political Modernization – Japan and Turkey*, (Princeton, NJ: Princeton University Press, 1964), pp. 352–88.
30 C. H. Dodd, *Politics and Government in Turkey* (Berkeley, Calif.: University of California Press, 1969), pp. 26–8.
31 ibid., p. 28.
32 J. C. Hurewitz, *Middle East Politics: The Military Dimension* (New York: Praeger, 1969), pp. 214–15. For a detailed analysis see George S. Harris, 'The causes of the 1960 revolution in Turkey,' *Middle East Journal*, vol. 24, no. 4 (Autumn 1970), pp. 438–54.
33 ibid., p. 220.
34 Dodd, op. cit., pp. 97–103.
35 ibid., pp. 77–80.
36 Hurewitz, op. cit., pp. 226–7.
37 Michael P. Hyland, 'Crisis at the polls: Turkey's 1969 elections,' *Middle East Journal*, vol. 24, no. 1 (Winter 1970), p. 14; Szyliowicz, op. cit., p. 55.
38 Feroz Ahmad, *The Turkish Experiment in Democracy 1950–1975*, (Boulder, Colo.: Westview Press, 1977), p. 194.
39 On the growing anti-Americanism, see A. Haluk Ulman and R.H. Dekmejian, 'Changing patterns in Turkish foreign policy, 1959–1967,' *Orbis*, vol. 11 (Fall 1967), p. 780–1.
40 On the role of the National Security Council, *T. C. Devlet Teşkilati Rehberi* (Ankara, 1968), pp. 124–5.
41 Ahmad, op. cit., p. 202.
42 For a detailed study of these elections, see Roger P. Nye, 'Civil–military confrontation in Turkey: the 1973 presidential elections,' *International Journal of Middle East Studies*, vol. 8, no. 2 (April 1977), pp. 209–28. Also, Ahmad, op. cit., pp. 308–9.
43 *Keesing's Contemporary Archives*, (1 January 1975).
44 *Facts on File* (26 February 1977).

45 About 80,000 officers belonged to OYAK which by 1978 had assets of L89 million. See *New Statesman*, (11 August 1978), p. 177.
46 *Keesing's Contemporary Archives*, (15 June 1977).
47 C. L. Sulzberger, 'The Turks and their army,' *New York Times* (3 May 1975).
48 The ideology of Ataturkism has acquired many meanings and interpretations. See Metin Tamkoç, 'Stable instability of the Turkish polity,' *Middle East Journal*, vol. 27, no. 3 (Summer 1973), pp. 335–7.
49 *New Statesman* (6 April 1979), p. 478.
50 For an analysis of ethnic conflicts, see *New Statesman*, (6 April 1979), pp. 477–8.

3 The Syrian Armed Forces in National Politics: The Role of the Geographic and Ethnic Periphery

ALASDAIR DRYSDALE

Syria's twentieth-century nation-building experience has been profoundly affected by repeated military intervention in political life. In no other Middle Eastern country have the armed forces consistently played so dominant a political role. The results have been mixed: the military has variously protected an antiquated status quo and initiated radical reforms; it has been both a destabilizing and stabilizing force; and it has been both a symbol of national disunity and a vehicle for national integration.

Whatever the numerous causes and consequences of this extensive involvement in national politics, however, civil–military relations have been greatly complicated by the perception among many Syrians that the armed forces have been geographically and ethnically unrepresentative for most of their existence. By design or default, a disproportionate number of soldiers have come from the country's spatial margins and from religious or linguistic minority communities. Because of this, the periphery has occasionally played a conspicuous, and not always popular, role in Syrian politics. Thus, during the French mandate between the two world wars the colonial power relied heavily on minority soldiers to suppress a nationalist uprising. In the early post-independence years, minority officers had a leading part in several coups d'état. The role of the periphery has been especially evident, however, since a coup installed the pan-Arab, socialist, secularist Ba'th Party in power in 1963. A striking number of the regime's leading military figures have been from the minority Alawi Shi'a Muslim splinter sect. Few issues have been more sensitive in this heterogeneous and still weakly integrated country. This chapter examines the changing role of the periphery in the armed forces and the ways in which civil–military relations have been affected by ethnic factors.

COLONIAL FOUNDATIONS

The European penchant for creating ethnically and geographically unbalanced armed forces in their colonies has been widely noted.[1] The French made no exception in Syria: during their mandate between 1920 and 1946 they exhibited a blatant preference for recruits who were not from the majority Sunni Muslim Arab community. To some extent this bias laid foundations for the role that the geographic and ethnic periphery has played in contemporary national politics, because the modern Syrian military is a direct descendant of the various forces created by the colonial power.

Data on the composition of the so-called *Troupes Auxiliaires* between 1924–8 confirm, but understate, the unrepresentativeness of the Syrian military during its formative years.[2] Among the most clearly favored groups were the Alawis and Christians, who together accounted for approximately 46 percent of all soldiers, considerably more than their share of the total population. Moreover, although Sunni Muslims accounted for only about one-half of all troops, a disproportionate number of these spoke Kurdish and Circassian rather than Arabic (see Figure 3.1).

Statistics on the *Troupes Auxiliaires* reveal little about the geographic origins of soldiers or about the composition of particular ranks, however. As the French themselves admitted, initially nonofficer ranks 'were almost exclusively made up of Muslims and Alawis [sic],' while 'the majority of officers were Christian.'[3] According to data painstakingly

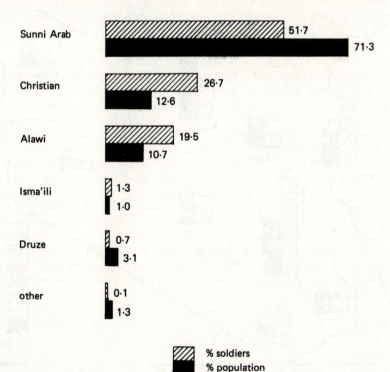

Figure 3.1 *Composition of the Troupes Auxiliaires, 1924–8. (Prepared from data in République Francaise, Ministère des Affaires Etrangères,* Rapport sur la situation de la Syrie et du Liban, 1924–1928.)

gathered by Van Dusen, some 250 officers graduated from the Military Academy at Hims before control passed out of French hands.[4] Over 50 percent of these, however, came from the largely Alawi peripheral province of al-Ladhiqiyah or from Damascus. Sunni Arabs accounted for less than one-half of all graduates. By contrast, minorities – especially Druzes, Circassians, and Armenians – were overrepresented. This imbalance was evident even at the regional level: a majority of officers from the predominantly Sunni Arab province of Aleppo were from minority communities, and most graduates from the overwhelmingly Sunni Arab Dar'a region were Circassian. Significantly, Alawis, although notably overrepresented in the armed forces as a whole, were underrepresented in the officer corps. This is to be expected given the appalling poverty and educational deprivation of the Alawi region at the time. Nevertheless, it disproves the widespread belief that even at this stage Alawis played a leading role in the officer corps. Clearly, the present composition of the officer corps is not simply a legacy of colonial rule (see Figures 3.1 and 3.2).[5]

The unrepresentativeness of the armed forces during the mandate is

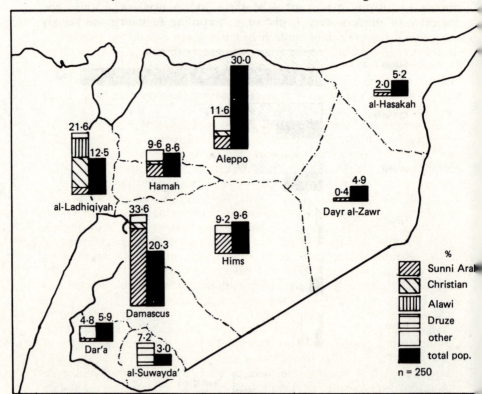

Figure 3.2 *Origins of Pre-1946 Military Academy Graduates. (Prepared from data in Michael H. Van Dusen, Intra- and Inter-Generational Conflict in the Syrian Army' (PhD dissertation, Johns Hopkins University, 1971), apps. 1–3, pp. 375–90. Note: for comparative purposes present administrative divisions have been used wherever possible.)*

best explained by France's divide-and-rule strategy in the Levant. A military within which minorities played a dominant role was both a reflection of this strategy and an instrument of it. From the start, the French exploited ethnic differences at every turn and favored rural and peripheral populations against urban and central ones.[6] Nowhere was this more apparent than in the creation of Alawi and Druze micro-states. These absurd entities, apart from validating and giving political geographic expression to ethnic differences, confirmed and extended the power of traditional elites, who developed a vested interest in perpetuating the status quo. By co-option, the French hoped to compartmentalize and contain opposition to their rule as well as mobilize the periphery against the nationalists before the nationalists mobilized it against them. They considered peripheral minority groups best qualified for this task because peoples like the Alawis and Druzes 'appeared to resemble the Berber tribes of Morocco and Algeria in their traditional opposition to the central authorities.'[7]

The French justification for the Balkanization of the Levant – that this was necessary to separate peoples given to communal strife and was, in any case, in keeping with the principle of self-determination – was but hollow cant, the most cynical piousness. From the beginning, the French recognized that minorities could help them. Even before the mandate, a future French governor to the Alawi state wrote that the Alawis 'could be extremely useful, perhaps even indispensable. They are all armed and possess weapons and if they wished they could put up a stiff resistance to us . . . We have the greatest interest in gaining their good feelings . . and even in favoring them.'[8]

The strategy of weakening nationalist opposition by pitting the periphery against it and of dividing Syria by emphasizing ethnic differences was, of course, one of the principal reasons for the heavy recruitment of minorities into the military.[9] France's callous use of minority troops – especially Circassian and Armenian – to quell nationalist demonstrations, break strikes, and put down the 1925–7 revolt was to be bitterly remembered; it left a residue of suspicion between majority and minority, center and periphery, and civilian and military that was slow to dissipate.

The French, like the British, had an unfortunate habit of categorizing ethnic groups under their control as either martial or nonmartial. Spurious stereotypes and distorted perceptions (which affected spatially peripheral groups in particular) both reinforced recruitment patterns and served as a convenient explanation of imbalances.

According to the French, 'taken as a whole, the Syrians were not a warlike people.'[10] But there were exceptions. A French High Commissioner commented once that 'there were two warlike peoples in Syria and the Lebanon, the Druzes and the Alawis.'[11] This view was ubiquitous and, it must be said, held by many Syrians. The Druzes were characterized, typically, as 'fanatic and bellicose mountaineers'[12] and as 'born soliders . . . fanatics in every sense of the term.'[13] The Alawis were portrayed in wholly similar fashion, for they were deemed to be 'savages and bandits.'[14] The Circassians, who incidentally also were 'soldiers by birth,'[15] stirred the French poetic imagination: these 'savage cavaliers' it seems were 'fierce like eagles, lithe and slender like spears.'[16] They were, in short, 'magnificently endowed for warfare.'[17] So also one must presume were the Isma'ilis, a heterodox Shi'a Muslim sect distantly related to the Alawis, for they were characterized as 'cruel warriors.'[18] Indeed, one wonders to whom the French referred when they observed that 'the Syrians are not a warlike people,' for like everyone else, the Kurds, in some mysterious way, produced a sufficiently pugnacious progeny to warrant being described as 'born fighters'.[19] Conspicuous by their absence, of course, were the truculent Sunni Arabs, whose particular war at the time – against the French – was not appreciated.

But martial skills were not enough: the ideal soldier had also to be noble. Thus the Druze had 'a sense of discipline and would give himself to the point of death to the leader of his choosing.'[20] Although 'dour, unfriendly to strangers and inclined to savagery, [he] was capable also of great loyalty and tough endurance.'[21] Honor and savagery seemed to be inexplicably and inextricably linked in the colonial mind. The Alawis, according to their first French Governor, were like 'perfect musketeers.'

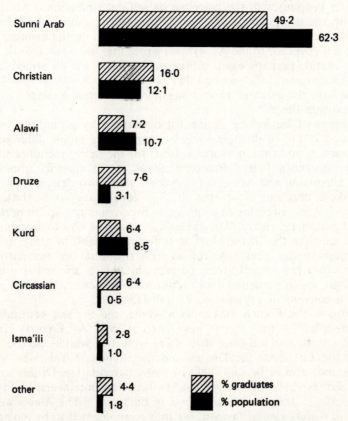

Figure 3.3 *Origins of Pre-1946 Military Academy Graduates. (Prepared from data in Van Dusen, 'Intra- and Inter-Generational Conflict,' apps. 1–3, pp. 375–90.)*

He asserted that 'even in their pillage and brigandage one finds among them a well-tempered soul, a virile character, something dignified.'[22]

French divide-and-rule policy and myths about particular ethnic groups' martial skills served as catalysts to the development of geographic and ethnic imbalances in the military. Ultimately minorities enlisted because they themselves found military service attractive. Heavy Alawi overrepresentation, in particular in nonofficer ranks was – and still is – a direct consequence of the acute poverty of the mountainous, Alawi-dominated interior portion of al-Ladhiqiyah. This region, with its poor stony soil, paltry per capita agricultural production, and overpopulation, has always been one of Syria's most underdeveloped areas. During the mandate an estimated 61 percent of all Alawis had trachoma, a rate two to three times higher than any other ethnic group within the al-Ladhiqiyah region. Endemic disease, malnutrition, and constant food shortages manifested themselves in tragic infant mortality rates: in many Alawi villages, two of every three children died before the age of 1.[23] Educationally, Alawis were similarly disadvantaged. Of students attending government schools in al-Ladhiqiyah in 1936, for example, only 27 percent were Alawi, although Alawis made up well over 60 percent of the province's population. Even this overstated their position, for few attended the far more numerous and better equipped nongovernment schools in which 68 percent of all Syrian and Lebanese students were enrolled. Only 13 percent of Alawis who received some form of education went to private schools.[24] Not unexpectedly, the Alawi region sustained a high rate of emigration Many of those who left the area formed a sort of underclass, becoming migrant agricultural laborers on plantations in Cilicia, shoe shiners and refuse collectors in Tripoli, or maidservants in Damascus and in other cities. To such a people, military service offered a chance of escape and emancipation. The wages Alawi soldiers earned 'made an important contribution to the economic life of the region.'[25] Moreover, this poverty, which did not abate with independence, led a disproportionate number of Alawi soldiers to support the socialist Ba'th Party, a marriage that had farreaching consequences in the 1960s.

THE ROLE OF THE PERIPHERY: FROM INDEPENDENCE TO UNION

Because of the magnitude of French-cultivated ethnic and geographical imbalances, minority officers played a conspicuous role in each of independent Syria's first three coups d'état, which all occurred in 1949. Their respective leaders – Husni al-Za'im, Sami Hinnawi, and Adib Shishakli – were Kurds or part-Kurdish, for example. At least 43 percent of the thirty officers on Za'im's High Command whose origins I could identify (there were thirty-nine officers altogether) were not Sunni Arab. The composition of Hinnawi's ephemeral ad hoc Supreme War Council is especially instructive: of its ten officers, only two were Sunni Arab (see Table 3.1).

Table 3.1 *Composition of the Supreme War Council*

Officer	Province	Community
Sami Hinnawi	Idlib	Kurd (Sunni)
Bahij Kallas	Hamah	Christian
Alam al-Din Qawwas	al-Ladhiqiyah	Alawi
Amin Abu Asaf	al-Suwayda'	Druze
Mahmud Rifa'i	Hims	Sunni Arab
Khalid Jada	Hims	Circassian (Sunni)
Hasan al-Hakim	al-Ladhiqiyah	Isma'ili
Muhammed Diyab	Hamah	Isma'ili
Muhammed Ma'aruf	al-Ladhiqiyah	Alawi
Isam Murawid	Damascus	Sunni Arab

Source: Compiled from data in Eliezer Be'eri, *Army Officers in Arab Politics and Society* (New York: Praeger, 1970), pp. 60–1 and Van Dusen, 'Intra- and inter-generational conflict,' p. 384.

However, this prominence was entirely a function of past recruitment patterns; in any coup d'état at this time minority officers would almost necessarily have been involved. With some notable exceptions, the minority ethnic identities of many top officers counted for little during these early years of military rule. They did not cause panic among the majority or promote ethnic cleavages within the armed forces.[26] Nor did the Sunni Arab majority have any cause to feel excluded from political decision-making since it played the leading part in the regimes these coups spawned. At this stage, the military was genuinely an agent of national integration in an otherwise fragmented society, a national symbol in a precarious republic.

Although Syria's 1949 coups differed in origin and purpose all were in some way inspired by the inability of those who led the country to independence to solve outstanding nationbuilding problems, to provide honest, competent leadership, or to address themselves adequately to the needs of a military impatient for modernization and expansion. The first and third coups, in particular, sought to strengthen the governmental center, whose weakness, corruption, fragmentation and unpopularity had been brought into sharp focus by the humiliating and traumatic defeat of Arab armies in their first direct confrontation with the newly born state of Israel.[27] The early years of military rule (which was increasingly authoritarian and unpopular) therefore saw a concerted effort to bridge divisions that had been exacerbated by the French. Za'im, for instance, sought to remove references to ethnic identity from Syrian passports and all government documents and statistics. Under Shishakli, minorities were 'inundated with decrees against their identity' and regional and ethnic clubs were proscribed.[28] In addition, institutionalized proportional parliamentary representation of the various sects, an inherently divisive system that still impedes neighbouring Lebanon's unity, was ended. Druze and Alawi autonomist tendencies were decisively undermined and checked.

The clustering of minority officers in upper echelon positions after independence was short-lived. Because colonial recruitment patterns were partly contingent upon external control and manipulation they did not continue unaltered into the post-independence era. Although enlistment patterns in nonofficer ranks resisted sudden modification, Syrian control of the Military Academy brought abrupt changes in both the number and composition of officer cadets.[29] Obviously this was intentional: nationalists had been profoundly critical of the way the French had made the military an instrument and embodiment of their divide-and-rule policies. In a somewhat artificial state where ethnic identities were often stronger than national ones, many recognized the risks of an unrepresentative military.

Whereas Sunni Arabs comprised under one-half of all pre-independence officer cadets, they accounted for 80 percent of all graduates in the first five post-independence classes, the only period for which complete and reliable published data exist. The percentage of Christians, Druzes, and Alawis fell correspondingly. Geographically, Damascus province still provided most cadets, although proportionately it sent no more to the academy than in pre-independence years. The most dramatic change was

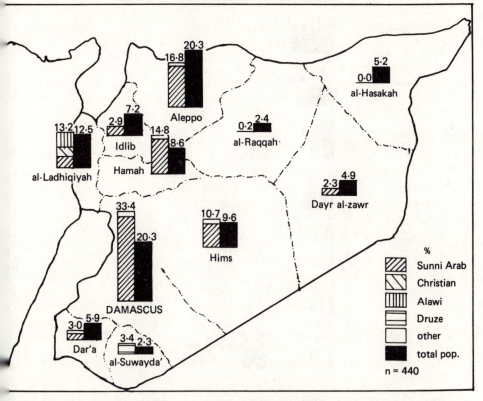

Figure 3.4 *Origins of Military Academy Graduates, 1947–51. (Prepared from data in Van Dusen, 'Intra- and Inter-Generational Conflict,' app. 4, pp. 391–413.)*

the increased representation of the largely Sunni provinces of Aleppo, Hims, and Hamah and the sharp fall in the percentage of cadets from the predominantly minority peripheral provinces of al-Ladhiqiyah and al-Suwayda'. To the extent that these data can be considered indicative of recruitment throughout the 1950s, and this is open to debate, they emphasize the limitations of simplistically explaining the composition of the current regime primarily in terms of uninterrupted and massive minority, and especially Alawi, overrepresentation in the officer corps since its birth (see Figures 3.4 and 3.5).

While this influx of Sunni Arabs was most instrumental in causing a proportional decrease in the number of minority officers, other factors also played a part. First, many of the highest-ranking minority officers paid a price for their early political activism, for while they led coups d'état they were also often their victims. Many were purged or dismissed by Shishakli especially, who promoted a younger cohort of Sunni Arab

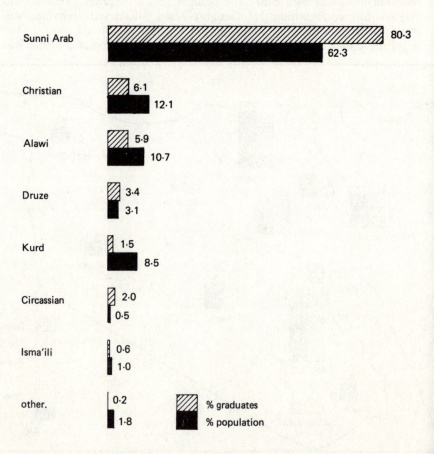

Figure 3.5   *Origins of Military Academy Graduates, 1947–51. (Prepared from data in Van Dusen, 'Intra- and Inter-Generational Conflict,' app. 4, pp. 391–413.)*

officers to key positions toward the end of his dictatorship in 1954. Secondly, in the mid-1950s a large number of minority officers were cashiered because of their membership of the fascist, secularist Syrian Social Nationalist Party, which was outlawed in 1955 after attempting to seize power and being implicated in the assassination of a popular Ba'thi officer. This party, a major competitor of the Ba'th for influence within the officer corps, drew most of its support from minority communities.[30]

Because of these compositional changes, minority officers were altogether less conspicuous between 1954, when the tyrannical Shishakli was overthrown, and 1958, when Syria united with Egypt. This is evident in the origins of seventeen of the most politically prominent officers in 1958. All but two were Sunni Arab, only two were Damascenes, and practically all graduated from the academy in 1947 or 1948 (see Table 3.2).

During the five years preceding union, the armed forces constantly cajoled and threatened the civilian politicians who ostensibly governed the country and who had been elected in Syria's freest elections ever in 1954. Though by no means cohesive, the officer corps was increasingly at loggerheads with the traditional ruling class, from which it differed in social composition and political ideology. The old civilian elite was comprised largely of conservative, well-established, urban-based land-owning and mercantile families. By and large, they 'despised the army as a profession' and bought their way out of compulsory service. They viewed the academy as a place for 'the lazy, the rebellious, the

Table 3.2 *Origins of Leading Syrian Officers, 1958*

Officer	Town	Community	Graduation
Afif Bizri	Damascus	Sunni Arab	1946?
Mustafa Hamdun	Hamah	Sunni Kurd	1948
Ahmad Abd al-Karim	Mutbin	Sunni Arab	1947
Ahmad al-Hinaydi	Dayr al-Zawr	Sunni Arab	1947
Tu'mah al-Awdatallah	Dar'a	Sunni Arab	1947
Husayn Hidda	Yabrud	Sunni Arab	1948
Abd al-Ghani Qannut	Hamah	Sunni Arab	1948
Muhammed al-Nasr	Kafr Harib	Sunni Arab	1948
Yasin Farjani	Tadmur	Sunni Arab	1948
Abdallah Jasuma	al-Bab	Sunni Arab	1948
Jadu Izz al-Din	al-Suwayda'	Druze	1947
Mustafa Ram Hamdani	Hims	Sunni Arab	1948
Akram Dayri	Damascus	Sunni Arab	1947
Jamal al-Sufi	Hims	Sunni Arab	1947
Amin Nafuri	Nabak	Sunni Arab	from ranks
Abd al-Hamid Sarraj	Hamah	Sunni Arab	1947
Jamal Faysal	Hims	Sunni Arab	?

Source: Prepared from data in Seale, *The Struggle for Syria*, p. 320, and Van Dusen, 'Intra- and Inter-Generational Conflict,' apps 3–4, pp. 382–96.

academically backward, or the socially undistinguished.'[31] However, poorer Syrians, those from rural areas and small provincial towns, viewed the officer corps as perhaps the single most attractive avenue of upward mobility.[32] Equally important, many saw it as the most likely instrument of political change and entered it for that very reason.[33] The growing number of such officers gradually radicalized and destabilized national politics and ultimately strengthened the position of the reformist Ba'th Party.

THE EMERGENCE OF THE PERIPHERY: 1958–63

By 1958 a large majority of Syrian officers were Sunni Arab. Aside from Alawi overrepresentation in nonofficer ranks, few significant vestiges of the military's French colonial parentage remained. Yet by the end of 1963, many Syrians were convinced that officers from the geographic and ethnic periphery, in the name of the Ba'th Party, dominated the armed forces and controlled the country. How did this dramatic change occur?

The mid-1950s were turbulent times for Syria. Internationally, the country's sense of embattled vulnerability was heightened by heavy-handed attempts to draw it into an Anglo-Iraqi-sponsored defense pact, by the joint invasion of Egypt by Britain, France, and Israel, by an Iraqi-backed coup attempt, by the landing of US marines in Lebanon and the Eisenhower doctrine, by the stationing of British troops in Jordan, and by Turkish military 'exercises' conducted at American behest near the Syrian border. But this was not all Syria had to contend with. Domestically, attempts to create any sort of political consensus and achieve a modicum of stability were crippled by a struggle for power between traditional and modernizing elites, between those who sought to prevent change and those for whom it was a paramount goal, between the regionally based conservative parties of the *ancien régime* (like the People's and National Parties) and the nationally based, reformist parties of the middle and lower-middle class (like the growing Ba'th), between those who favored union with Egypt and those who looked to Iraq, and between those who favored closer ties to the Eastern Bloc or a neutral stance in the Cold War and those who wanted Syria to align itself with the West.

Significantly, all of these conflicts and tensions were also present within the officer corps, since 'more than in other Arab countries, Syrian officers fell under the influence of their non-military friends and families.'[34] In Syria, the boundary between military and civilian sectors has always been blurred and permeable; political activism among officers has traditionally been the rule rather than the exception. By the time of the union the army was 'a jungle of intrigue' and its feuding factions had brought it 'to the verge of dismemberment.'[35] The chaos within the military was, in turn, both cause and consequence of Syria itself being almost on the point of 'disintegration as an organized political community.'[36] The Ba'thi-engineered union with Egypt, one of the few things upon which most Syrians agreed, was as much a desperate attempt to avert chaos as it was an expresison of Syria's inveterate commitment to pan-Arabism.[37]

Syria's merger with Egypt was an ignominious failure, however, and ended in 1961 when a group of predominantly Damascene officers, many of whom had close links with the business community, led a coup. The immediate cause of secession was the resentment that Nasser's national-ization and land reform measures had provoked among Syria's traditional ruling class. Nevertheless, few Syrians were not disillusioned by the unionist experiment. Egypt's tendency to treat Syria as a colony rather than as a partner, large-scale purges of over 1,100 Syrian officers and the transfer to Egypt of another 500, the appointment of Egyptians to most senior executive and administrative positions, and the voluntary dis-banding of the Ba'th Party and its resulting loss of influence within Syria all alienated many who originally backed the union.

The so-called secessionist regime from 1961–3 was an attempt by the traditional elite to stem a rising tide of radicalism within the country and reassert its power. Many of the socialist reforms introduced during the union were reversed, large numbers of officers were dismissed, and power was nominally restored to civilians. Elections produced a Parliament that closely resembled the one formed in 1954.

But with the exception of the traditional elite, few were prepared to go back almost a decade. If the legendary 'fifty families' were making a last bid for power, so also were a multifactioned and greatly diminished Ba'th Party and Nasserite groups still sympathetic to union with Egypt. Ba'this, Nasserites, and other radical nationalist groups all opposed the reactionary secessionist regime. The eighteen months between secession and the Ba'thi revolution were, as a result, among the most politically complex and chaotic that Syria has ever experienced. A number of mutually hostile groups waged war against one another within a thoroughly politicized and acutely divided officer corps.[38] In fact, the armed forces were so weakened and immobilized by factionalism and repeated coup attempts that in April 1962 a Military Congress was convened to decide how to restore order and discipline. The meeting was attended by forty-one top officers, who represented all major units and military regions. Significantly, almost all of them (36) were Sunni.[39]

These many divisions within the armed forces are crucial to under-standing how the geographic and ethnic periphery came to play so important a role in Syria. During the union, a group of Ba'thi officers stationed in Egypt formed a secret Military Committee. Their aim was to fashion a new Ba'th Party, to replace the aging urban bourgeois leader-ship, and ultimately to seize power. Of its five founding members three were Alawi (Salah Jadid, Muhammed Umran, and Hafiz al-Asad), and two were Isma'ili (Ahmad al-Mir and Abd al-Karim Jundi). Later, it was expanded to include additional officers from minority communities and from the periphery, especially Druzes (see Table 3.3).[40]

This strong ethnic minority coloration was not altogether coincidental. For several years the officer corps had been battered and buffeted and had barely managed to avoid disintegration. Discipline had almost completely collapsed. Constant purges and the promotion of politically reliable officers made a mockery of formal lines of authority, which were increasingly supplemented and even circumvented by patron–client net-

Table 3.3 *Composition of the Military Committee*

Officer	Province	Community
Muhammed Umran	Hamah	Alawi
Salah Jadid	al-Ladhiqiyah	Alawi
Hafiz al-Asad	al-Ladhiqiyah	Alawi
Abd al-Karim Jundi	Hamah	Isma'ili
Ahmad al-Mir	al-Ladhiqiyah'	Isma'ili
Salim Hatum	al-Suwayda'	Druze
Hamad Ubayd	al-Suwayda'	Druze
Muhammed Rabah al-Tawil	al-Ladhiqiyah	Sunni
Husayn Milhim	Aleppo	Sunni
Uthman Kan'an	al-Ladhiqiyah	Alawi
Sulayman Haddad	al-Ladhiqiyah	Alawi
Mustafa al-Hajj Ali	Dar'a	Sunni
Ahmad Suwaydani	Dar'a	Sunni
Musa al-Zu'bi	Dar'a	Sunni
Amin al-Hafiz	Aleppo	Sunni

works. Mistrust among officers was, for good reason, endemic. Repeated, flagrant violation of professional rules eroded any corporate integrity and morale which still remained. In these circumstances, officers of the Military Committee recognized that primordial ethnic and regional ties could cement their ideologically based alliance and give them a decisive advantage over the many other factions which could have led a coup at that time, given the near collapse of conventional chains of command.[41]

It must be emphasized that this solidarity was initially seen as a means to an end, Ba'thi rule. These officers, like disproportionate number of Syrians from ethnic minorities and from disadvantaged geographic regions, were attracted to the Ba'th precisely because it was secularist and socialist. Moreover, the ethnic complexion of the Military Committee reflected the presence of a growing number of minority officers in the military once again. Compositional changes came about, in part, because most of those purged in the late 1950s and early 1960s were Sunni Arab.[42] In addition, the tremendous post-independence expansion of secondary education in provinces like al-Ladhiqiyah effectively opened up the Military Academy to Alawis on a large scale for the first time. This would not be reflected in Van Dusen's data, which cover only the pre-1951 period. Since educated Alawis especially had few avenues of upward mobility in a society which still discriminated against them, they were understandably attracted to a profession with an explicitly national, secular ethos, one which confirmed and reified their Syrian, as opposed to minority, identity. They were manifestly overrepresented in nonofficer ranks, so it is entirely logical to expect that they would also become over-represented in the officer corps once the expansion of education made entrance to the Military Academy a realizable goal.

SYRIA UNDER THE BA'TH

The extremely complicated coup d'état that brought the Ba'th Party to power in 1963 was, ultimately, planned and executed by the Military Committee, even if non-Ba'thi officers initially played a major role. More to the point, the common ethnic minority and peripheral geographic origins of Military Committee officers played a crucial part in lubricating the Ba'th's climb to power and assisted greatly in bolstering the regime's position.

At the time of the coup the Ba'th Party was reputed to have fewer than 500 members in Syria. To consolidate its tenuous control over the country, it initiated a massive recruitment drive, relaxing entrance requirements to the party and relying extensively on primordial ties. By the party's later admission this frantic push resulted in the admission of what it called 'elements alien and strange to the party's mentality.'[43] However, according to a former secretary-general of the party's National Command, it also boosted party membership fivefold during the first year of Ba'thi rule.[44]

The party's weakness was especially serious in the armed forces. However, partly through careful and selective manipulation of ethnic, regional and familial ties, Ba'thi officers gained control of most key positions in the armed forces within a few months of the coup: they commanded the most important brigades, they headed the various intelligence agencies, and they made all the major decisions about appointments, promotions, transfers, and dismissals.[45] More important, the regime radically and abruptly transformed the composition, structure and function of the armed forces by attempting to create an 'ideological', which is to say Ba'thi, army. The fashioning of this 'ideological army' entailed ferocious purges and considerable organizational upheaval within the officer corps.

To underline how differently the Ba'th viewed the role of the armed forces from preceding regimes, it is worth quoting at length from a 1966 party document. An army, it said,

> is the shield which ruling organizations erect around themselves in order that they may be active in developing their achievements, that they may be protected against surprises, whether internal or external, and that they may even strike . . . all those who attempt to obstruct the functioning of their organization. In this sense the Army is a two-edged weapon: either it is a people's army representing the toiling classes and safeguarding their accomplishments or, if it is a professional or bourgeois army it is a sword drawn against the neck of those classes . . . Therefore, world imperialism and its agents make desperate efforts to maintain the bourgeois composition of the armies in the developing countries. They do so . . . by introducing a spirit of professionalism and blind obedience into military concepts and by excluding the army from politics . . . The replacement of the concept of the classical bourgeois 'professional army' by that of the 'ideological army' was the greatest blow aimed in modern times at world imperialist interests in the developing countries.[46]

According to the Ba'th 'the technical competence of a military man . . . becomes a secondary precondition to his ideological competence.'[47] (The consequences of this view were clearly demonstrated one year later during the 1967 Arab–Israeli War.) The Ba'th sought 'to tie the army organically to the party,' to give it the opportunity 'to participate in the process of socialist construction and transformation,' and 'to participate in elaborating the party's policies.'[48] The creation of the ideological army symbolized and embodied what Rabinovich aptly described as a 'symbiosis' between the Ba'th Party and the armed forces after the 1963 coup. It was an explicit, formal recognition and legitimization of the military as a political actor par excellence.

Efforts to consolidate the party's position within the armed forces substantially changed their geographic and ethnic composition. Critics of the regime repeatedly charged that urban Sunnis were systematically denied entrance to the Military Academy, transferred to unimportant posts, or pensioned off, while minorities and Sunnis from geographically peripheral, underdeveloped provinces were actively encouraged to enter the officer corps. Two brigades notorious for their participation in coups d'état, the 5th and 70th, became especially heavily minority-dominated.[49] Seymour claimed that by the mid-1960s the proportion of Alawi soldiers in individual divisions varied between 20 percent and 100 percent, although this last figure seems extremely unlikely.[50] Alawis and Druzes were soon alleged to control virtually all top positions within the armed forces: 'The posts in most divisions and brigades were divided among these two minorities. In case the commander would be an Alawi, his deputy would be a Druze, or the other way around.'[51]

It should be noted that the Ba'th Party itself underwent a significant and in some ways parallel transformation. During the union, party branches in the traditional peripheral Ba'thi stronghold provinces of al-Ladhiqiyah, Dar'a, al-Suwayda', and Dayr al-Zawr – the very ones from which most Military Committee officers came – defied the directions of party leaders to disband. The Ba'this who controlled these branches were younger and more radical than the party's veteran urban bourgeois leaders and were anxious to take over and rejuvenate the party after the union failed and the old Ba'th had been discredited.[52] The core of the Ba'thi regime was formed by a marriage between these radical civilian Ba'this from the periphery and officers of the Military Committee.

Although the Ba'thi revolution was engineered by the periphery and had a marked ethnic coloration, ultimately its most significant consequence has been the enormous strengthening and invigoration of the political center. Ma'oz believes that the Ba'th has provided the country with its first strong government in centuries, one

> which succeeded in overcoming the centrifugal and autonomous tendencies of various social groups and in gaining considerable authority over the population as a whole. Interregional fragmentations were abolished, class differences reduced . . . and the feeling of Syrian territorial identification amplified.[53]

This strengthening of the center has been reflected in unprecedented, though by no means complete, stability, especially since 1970.

Those who seized power in 1963 sought to transform Syria as well as to rule it. They realized, however, they could not hold power or make a revolution 'simply by seizing the political center.'[54] At the very least they had to eliminate the traditional landed and mercantile ruling class by demolishing its material base of power. Large-scale land expropriations and sweeping nationalization of industry and commerce in 1964 and 1965 largely accomplished this, although not without fierce opposition. These actions were, of course, consonant with the Ba'th's commitment to redistribute wealth. They also abruptly and dramatically increased the scope of government.

At the outset the Ba'th was committed to activist one-party rule and recognized the necessity of supplementing direction from above with mass-mobilized support from below if it was ever going to achieve its developmental goals. As part of its mobilization efforts, it created, co-opted, or took control of a variety of organizations, such as a people's militia, unions, syndicates, professional associations, and women's and student clubs. Peasant unions and agricultural cooperatives, which were introduced with land reform, have been particularly important. By 1977, these cooperatives numbered 3,432 and had a membership of 267,265.[55] According to the most generous and favorable interpretation, the regime's efforts to mobilize mass support have created 'a new political order in the countryside . . . a new network of political power linking the Ba'thist elite to a mass base.'[56] This rural base of support has been a source of stability and power. Today the party claims over 100,000 members and its apparatus is ubiquitous. Ba'thi organization has enabled the regime to widen political participation while at the same time closely controlling it. Moreover, it has helped to bridge old urban–rural cleavages and to 'directly and systematically tie political center and periphery together.'[57] The party's paramount role is even recognized in the 1973 constitution, whose preamble grandiloquently extolls the Ba'th as

> the first movement in the Arab nation which gave Arab unity its genuine revolutionary direction, established a nexus between the national struggle and the socialist struggle and represented the desire of the Arab nation and its aspirations for a future that could link it to its glorious past and enable it to fulfill its role in the victory of the cause of freedom of all the peoples.[58]

Article 8 stipulates that the Ba'th is 'the vanguard party in the society and the state.'

Since the revolution, the state has played a notably more active role in solving developmental problems both through the public sector, which has burgeoned to the point that few aspects of the economy are untouched by it, and through government planning agencies, which have proliferated and now greatly influence most major investment decisions. To some extent, this is suggested by government development expenditures, which totaled L. Sy. 561·8 million in 1964 but amounted to L. Sy. 10·6 billion in 1978, a massive increase even without adjusting for inflation. Similarly, projected allocations in the country's five-year plans leapt from L. Sy. 2·8 billion in the first (1960–5) to L. Sy. 54 billion in the unrealistic and overly ambitious fourth (1976–80).

Most of the regime's developmental energy has been geared to creating or improving the country's economic infrastructure, which was all but ignored throughout the 1950s as governments replaced one another in rapid succession. The gigantic Euphrates dam and related irrigation and power schemes, port expansion, road and railway construction, mineral (especially oil and phosphate) exploitation, and general agrarian improvement have therefore received most attention.

In the sphere of social development, gains have been impressive, at least on paper. Expenditures on education increased from L. Sy. 139 million in 1964 to L. Sy. 1·26 billion in 1977. During the same period the number of secondary school students increased from 138,742 to 485,873, the number of secondary teachers grew from 6,216 to 28,606, and the number of secondary schools rose from 407 to 1,150. In the area of health care, the number of doctors more than trebled in the decade and a half following the revolution and the average number of persons per doctor dropped from 5,105 to only 2,515.[59]

Although Syria has lived under Ba'thi rule for over seventeen years and has enjoyed unprecedented stability, there have been significant changes within the regime since the revolution. The 1963–6 period was one of regime consolidation and witnessed the destruction of Syria's traditional ruling class and many farreaching social and economic reforms. During these years also, there were a series of complex and protracted power struggles within the Ba'th. The most critical generally pitted the younger, more radical, *petit bourgeois* military and civilian Ba'this from the periphery against the party's aging civilian founders, most of whom were middle-class Damascene or Aleppan Sunnis. A coup d'état in 1966 marked the complete victory of the radical faction (sometimes called the neo-Ba'th) and removed the few remaining obstacles to the periphery's complete ascendance.

However, between 1966 and 1970 there were bitter disagreements within the regime about the position of the private sector in the national economy, relations with other Arab countries, the extent to which non-Ba'thi groups should participate in political decision-making, the degree of control that should be exercised over the Palestinian guerrillas, the best strategy to regain the Israeli-occupied Golan Heights, and, significantly, about the proper role of the military. These differences fueled a power struggle between two of the Alawi officers who founded the Military Committee, Salah Jadid and Hafiz al-Asad. The more impetuous, unpopular and radical Jadid and his predominantly civilian supporters sought more extensive political indoctrination and closer Ba'thi control of the military. The moderate, pragmatic Asad supported a more conventional role for the armed forces, especially after the 1967 Arab–Israeli War demonstrated that the ideological army was also a rather incompetent, ill-prepared, and badly equipped one on the battlefield. Sensitive to widespread criticism of the army's performance in the war and to charges that it 'had become no more than a party gendarmerie,'[60] Asad accused the Jadid faction of destroying the military through reckless political experimentation. In 1968 and 1969 there were a series of confrontations between Asad and Jadid. Because Asad's power base was in the armed forces and Jadid's rested on his control of the Ba'th Party's civilian apparatus, the former was in the stronger position. He steadily cut the civilian Ba'thi leadership off from the party's military organization, prohibiting members of the Regional Command and civilian party officials from direct contact with Ba'thi officers and vice versa.[61] This led the political leadership to issue a manifesto denouncing 'the army's revolt against the party.'[62] It should be emphasized that the conflict between the factions transcended ethnic lines; both Jadid and Asad had Alawi, Sunni, and other support.

Asad finally ousted Jadid and his followers altogether in a 1970 coup d'état. He quickly moved Syria sharply back to the center. Relations with Arab moderates, notably Jordan and Saudi Arabia, were restored and strengthened. Capitalists were encouraged to return and rules governing investment and profit were eased. Many more urban Sunnis were appointed to top offices. Political freedoms were widened. Non-Ba'thi socialist groups were given a nominal share of power through a so-called National Progressive Front. A new constitution was adopted and national elections to a People's Assembly held. Significantly, civilian tampering with the armed forces was greatly reduced, allowing a markedly more professional and cohesive officer corps to be created.[63]

Since 1970, power has been concentrated in the hands of Asad, who was elected President in 1971, and a small group of mostly Alawi officers. Parliament and Cabinets notwithstanding, Asad's regime is a military one and few major policy decisions are made without the participation of top officers. Indeed, the Ba'th Party's civilian organizational apparatus, although still intact, has become increasingly irrelevant to the regime's fortunes. The frantic mass-mobilization efforts of the Jadid years have been toned down considerably.

Given the indispensability of military support, the regime has done several things to guard against future coups d'état. First, it has maintained Ba'thi control over the armed forces, albeit more discreetly and without the organizationally disruptive ideological purism of the Jadid years. The charter of the Ba'thi-dominated National Progressive Front specifies that the Ba'th has the exclusive right to engage in political activity within the armed forces and educational institutions, which are described very appropriately as 'delicate' sections of the population.[64] But Asad has redefined the ideological role of the army in the broadest terms:

> The Syrian army is an ideological army believing in an ideology. Not all soldiers are necessarily party members, but they are imbued with an ideology which is characteristic of the goals of the party and the goals of the people and the workers, in accordance with the party platform . . . since the party stems from the people and works for the interest of the people.[65]

Ba'thi penetration of the armed forces must be considered reasonably thorough and successful. The regime has claimed that 80 percent of all army officers killed in the 1973 Arab–Israeli War were party members.[66]

Secondly, the regime has ensured that officers continue to occupy a privileged position in Syrian society. Officers are pampered: army cooperatives provide them with cost-price articles and with duty-free foreign imports not obtainable elsewhere in the country; interest-free loans allow them to buy villas and speculate in very lucrative real estate; and they receive generous salaries, free medical care, liberal travel allowances, and miscellaneous other fringe benefits.[67] Moreover, since Syria is a country at war with Israel, little effort has been spared to meet the military's persistent demands for large quantities of expensive, modern and sophisticated hardware. In recent years, defense expenditures have amounted to over 16 percent of the country's GNP, one of the highest proportions in the world. In 1979, defense outlays exceeded US $1 billion, well over one-quarter of the total budget.[68] For a country with only 8·4 million people, the costs of maintaining 227,500 men in uniform are enormous. If the armed forces do stage a coup d'état it will not be because their needs have been ignored.

Finally, the regime has sought to protect itself by reserving a disproportionate share of key positions within the armed forces and internal security and intelligence organizations for Alawis and trusted relatives. By one account, Alawis may hold as many as eighteen of the top twenty-five positions within the armed forces.[69] Special mention must also be made of Asad's infamous palace guard, the elite 20,000-man *saraya al-difa'*. This highly trained force is commanded by the President's younger brother, Rif'at, and is dominated by Alawi soldiers, many of whom come from the Asad family's home district of al-Qardahah. Stationed outside Damascus, it is one of the best-equipped forces in Syria and even has its own intelligence network. There is no question that any coup attempt emanating from outside Rif'at al-Asad's units would risk an extremely bloody confrontation. In effect, this palace guard has both reduced the internal policing role of the armed forces proper and removed some of their temptation to intervene.

Arguably, the most radical transformation of the Syrian army occurred not under Jadid but Asad, who fashioned it into something it had never, but always should have, been: a reasonably cohesive, disciplined, and effective instrument of war. Its performance during the 1973 Arab–Israeli War was, by most accounts, very creditable and did much to bolster corporate self-esteem. That Asad dared to expose 30,000 troops to the Lebanese civil war was a measure of his confidence in their new resilience and reliability: ten years earlier such an intervention would have been unthinkable.

The perceived power of Alawis has been one of the most sensitive issues within Syria since the 1963 coup, despite the fact that Alawis have fought, purged, jailed, exiled, and occasionally assassinated one another and have rarely acted in concert by virtue of common ethnic origin alone. Even the presence of many Sunnis from the periphery in top positions has often been dismissed by opponents as a blatant attempt to disguise the regime's narrow ethnic and geographic base. The Ba'th has, therefore, gone to great lengths to stress its commitment to creating a secular society, inveighing against sectarianism as a reactionary obstacle to national unity and socialism and as an imperialist plot against the revolution. Although the irony of such fulminations escapes few Syrians, many leading Ba'this, particularly in the regime's early years, genuinely hoped to initiate a nationbuilding revolution. Initially, they viewed the manipulation of primordial ties as a distasteful but necessary expedient.

The regime's ability to contain sectarian strife and stifle criticism of the Alawi community's disproportionate share of political power has been greatly undermined since 1975, however. Despite Asad's personal popularity and his early efforts to liberalize Ba'thi rule, the regime has steadily lost support. Party discipline and organization have deteriorated seriously. High-level corruption has become rampant, and the ostentatious display of wealth and open abuse of power by some elite members have caused considerable resentment against the regime in general. The fact that this corruption has gone essentially unchecked has only deepened the cynicism of the regime's opponents. It remains to be seen whether the creation in January 1980 of a new seventy-five member Ba'thi central committee and a separate 'control and inspection' committee to supervise an overhauled Regional Command will rejuvenate and strengthen the party. The elite, fearful of the retribution that would inevitably follow a coup d'état, is increasingly bound together by patron–client networks and intermarriage rather than by belief in a particular set of principles. Now that Ba'thi ideology seems hollow and the regime bereft of a sustaining vision and new ideas, the dominant position of Alawis is less acceptable to many Syrians.

Two events, in particular, have brought sectarian strife out into the open. First, Syria's intervention in the Lebanese civil war has been profoundly unpopular both in Syria and Lebanon. Initially, Syrian forces sided with the rightist Christian militias against leftist Muslim and Palestinian groups. The latter, traditionally reluctant to draw attention to sectarian divisions within Syria both for ideological reasons and because the regime usually supported them, responded by emphasizing the Alawi complexion of the Ba'thi regime. When Syrian forces tried to suppress the Christian militias they, too, attempted to exploit the issue of the regime's composition and publicized every hint of sectarian strife within Syria. The effects of this propaganda in Syria and on its soldiers serving in Lebanon are difficult to ascertain. However, there is no question that sectarian conflict in Lebanon brought similar tensions to the surface in Syria and placed the armed forces under a tremendous strain. This was inevitable because the historical, economic, cultural, and even familial links between Syria and Lebanon are extremely close. Many Syrians never accepted France's division of the region into two countries and still entertain irredentist thoughts.

A second development that has deeply affected intercommunal relations in Syria has been the resurgence of Islamic fundamentalism within the region. The Syrian regime is especially vulnerable for two reasons. First, because it professes to be among the most secular regimes in the Middle East, it is unusually open to charges of being insensitive to the depth of Muslim feeling in the country. From its inception the regime has been accused of being irreligious and atheistic by conservative Sunni Muslim leaders. Secondly, and more serious perhaps, many Sunni Muslims do not regard Alawis as Muslim at all. Intense religiosity has both emphasized the differences between ruler and ruled and served as a potent means of expressing opposition to the regime.

During the past three years there has been a wave of assassinations of prominent Alawis, including key officers, intelligence and internal security agents, Ba'th party officials, and even doctors, lawyers, and academics. By some estimates these have occurred at a rate of two or three each week. In June 1979, over sixty mostly Alawi military cadets were massacred by Muslim fundamentalist gunmen in Aleppo. This provoked heavy-handed repression of various rightwing religious groups, which, in turn, led to riots. The murder of two Alawi religious leaders in al-Ladhiqiyah in August 1979 led to the first large-scale clashes between Alawis and Sunnis since the periphery took power in 1963. Dozens were killed before 2,000 of Rif'at al-Asad's troops restored order. But the most serious challenge to the regime by far occurred in March 1980, when massive demonstrations and widespread strikes, particularly in Aleppo, briefly suggested the beginnings of an Iranian-style popular uprising. These events emphasized that the discontent, far from being confined to the Muslim Brotherhood, as the regime claimed, was deeply felt by a wide spectrum of Syrians. The bloody disturbances in Aleppo ended only after some 10,000 crack troops had been dispatched to the city and several hundred civilians had lost their lives. By mid-1980 the regime looked more precarious than at any previous time.

Still, some crucial questions remain unanswered. Has mounting opposition to what is increasingly perceived as monolithic Alawi control of the country spread to the armed forces in any significant degree? Is Alawi control of the military complete enough to ensure the regime's long-term survival? Can Asad broaden the ethnic base of the regime without losing control? Would a successful Sunni coup d'état lead to bloody reprisals against Alawis or even a resurgence of Alawi autonomist sentiment?

CONCLUSION

The role played by the periphery in national politics by virtue of its position within the armed forces has been extraordinarily complex and, most important, varied. While officers from minority communities have been highly visible, the origins, manifestations, and consequences of this conspicuousness during the mandate and since the Ba'thi revolution are unrelated and altogether dissimilar.

During the colonial period, the military was both an odious symbol and an instrument of ethnically and geographically divisive French policies. French recruitment policies favored the periphery since it was felt it could best counterbalance nationalist opposition. At this stage, the military widened rather than bridged the cleavages which separated Syrians. Many minorities continued to be viewed with suspicion and antipathy after independence because of their ambivalence toward the nationalist movement.

Radical changes accompanied Syrian control over the armed forces, however. The army, instead of being a symbol of foreign domination and national disunity, became a symbol of Syria's independence and one of its greatest national institutions. Within a few years colonially cultivated compositional imbalances, at least in the officer corps, had been considerably attenuated by an influx of Sunni Arabs, who dominated most coups d'état between the early 1950s and early 1960s. This turbulent interlude is important, because it emphasizes the sharp, almost complete discontinuity between the two eras within which minority officers played a leading role in the armed forces.

The roots of the periphery's ascendance under the Ba'th lie less in colonial, or even post-independence, recruitment patterns than in the increasing chaos within the officer corps with each coup d'état. Minority, and especially Alawi, officers emerged in force after 1963 both because they had especially strong links with the socialist, secularist Ba'th and because they manipulated ethnic ties to their advantage. It was after the revolution, not before it, that the periphery really exerted a controlling influence over the officer corps. This control was for the most part justified as being necessary to consolidate and protect the Ba'thi regime. Nevertheless, the periphery's role in national politics remains highly controversial and one of the regime's most obvious points of vulnerability. Almost all Syrians recognize that but for the armed forces, political power would not be in the hands of the periphery.

NOTES

1 See Morris Janowitz, *The Military in the Political Development of New Nations* (Chicago: University of Chicago Press, 1964), p. 52, and Ruth First, *Power in Africa: Political Power in Africa and the Coup d'État* (Harmondsworth: Penguin Books, 1971), pp. 77–8.

2 This is the only period for which complete published statistics covering all ranks are available. The nomenclature and organization of the colonial forces are somewhat confusing. Initially, the French created a force called La Légion Syrienne. This evolved into the Troupes Auxiliaires, which in 1930 merged with the emergency Troupes Supplétives to become the Troupes Spéciales du Levant. Control of the Troupes Spéciales passed to Syria only in 1946. Statistics on the Troupes Auxiliaires for 1924–8 underestimate the favored position of the periphery during the colonial era because the Troupes Supplétives, with which they eventually merged, were even more heavily dominated by minorities, and included 6 Druze, 8 Circassian, 3 Kurdish, and several Alawi units. The Troupes Supplétives, which were formed during the 1925–7 nationalist/Druze revolt, were intentionally unbalanced because the colonial power considered most minorities loyal during its hour of crisis. After the rebellion, conversely, many Sunni Arabs were reluctant to serve in what was clearly designed to be a malleable and repressive instrument of French rule.

3 République Française, Ministère des Affaires Etrangères, *Rapport sur la situation de la Syrie et du Liban, 1924* (Paris, 1925), p. 15.

4 Michael H. Van Dusen, 'Intra- and Inter-Generational Conflict in the Syrian Army,' PhD dissertation, Johns Hopkins University, 1971, apps 1–3, pp. 375–90. A few of these officers, in fact, graduated during Ottoman rule. The French established the

Military Academy in Damascus in 1920; in the early 1930s, it was moved to Hims, where it has remained until this day. Competition for entrance during the mandate was stiff; the ratio of accepted cadets to applicants was 12:124 in 1924, 7:59 in 1925, 12:30 in 1926 (reflecting feeling during the nationalist/Druze revolt), 22:100 in 1927, 26:147 in 1928, 17:225 in 1929, 13:191 in 1930, 15:171 in 1931, and up to 27:200 in 1936. This competitiveness made it very easy for the French to manipulate the army's ethnic composition.

5 It should be noted that the proportion of officers from particular regions and ethnic groups varied in each graduating class. The approach of independence coincided with an apparent French attempt to cram the officer corps with non-Sunnis and with persons from al-Ladhiqiyah province. In the 1945 class, for example, fourteen of the twenty-four graduates were from minority communities and in that of 1946, the last before independence, slightly under one-half of the nineteen graduates came from al-Ladhiqiyah.

6 This policy was inspired by the methods and goals of Lyautey's administration of Morocco between 1912 and 1925. Many of the first French officials in Syria were originally a part of Lyautey's entourage or served in Morocco. See Edmund Burke, 'A comparative view of French native policy in Morocco and Syria, 1912–1925,' *Middle Eastern Studies*, vol. 9 (1973), pp. 175–6, for an excellent, if incomplete, analysis of links between French policy-makers in Syria and Morocco.

7 ibid., pp. 182–3. Senior French officials admitted that Lyautey's strategy in Morocco was relevant to Syria. Bremond, for example, who served in Morocco and Syria, considered French policy in the latter to be 'a new application of the principles of . . . Lyautey: giving each ethnic group its autonomy, or even its independence, under our control' ('L'État Druse en 1930 et 1931,' *L'Asie française* (February 1932), p. 51.

8 J. de La Roche, 'Notes sur les débuts de notre occupation du Territoire des Alaouites,' *L'Asie française* (December 1931), p. 369.

9 Janowitz has noted similar recruitment policies in many colonies. European powers typically 'developed a strong ethnic imbalance in order to fashion what they believed to be a politically reliable organization . . . They recruited enlisted personnel and . . . officers from tribal groups remote from the central capital, from minority groups, and especially groups with limited independence aspirations. Frequently these groups came from economically less developed areas and they were, therefore, attracted by the opportunities in the army' (Janowitz, op. cit., p. 52). First has also observed that in most colonial armies 'men with an urban background were distrusted and kept out of the officer corps, for they were likely to be infected with nationalist sentiment' (First, op. cit., p. 77). The French strategy in Syria was not always understood by non-Syrians. A member of the League of Nations' Permanent Mandates Commission, for example, observed with a naiveté that would be hard to surpass that 'the population of the central part of the country, and of Damascus in particular, devoted themselves to politics and relied on the inhabitants of outlying districts to defend them' (*Minutes of the Thirty-Fifth Session*, 10th meeting, 28 October 1938, p. 89). At least, Syrian nationalists were not under similar illusions about who was defending whom.

10 League of Nations, Permanent Mandates Commission, *Minutes of the Eighth Session*, 15th meeting, 26 February 1926, p. 123.

11 idem, *Minutes of the Ninth Session*, 16th meeting, 17 June 1926, p. 112.

12 Commandant Hassler, 'Les insurrections Druses avant la guerre de 1914–1918,' *L'Asie française* (March 1926), p. 102.

13 'La répression des insurrections Druses,' *L'Asie française*, (March 1929), p. 87.

14 J. de La Roche, 'La religion des Ansariés,' *La Géographie*, vol. 38 (1922), p. 287.

15 Joseph Kessel, *En Syrie* (Paris: Les Éditions Kra, 1927), p. 79.

16 J. Zimmerman, 'Les escadrons tcherkesses en Syrie,' *L'Asie française* (May 1937), p. 117 and p. 150.

17 *Le Livre d'or des Troupes du Levant, 1918–1936* (Paris: Bureau Typographique des Troupes du Levant, 1937), p. 167.

18 Kessel, op. cit., p. 83.

19 Noel Maestracci, *La Syrie contemporaine* (Paris: Charles Lavanzelle, 1930), p.159.

20 Louis Jalalbert, *Syrie et Liban: Réussite française?* (Paris: Librairie Plon, 1934), p. 71.

21 S.H. Longrigg, *Syria and Lebanon under French Mandate* (London: Oxford University Press, 1958), p. 9.

22 J. de La Roche, 'Notes sur les débuts de notre occupation,' p. 369.
23 Jacques Weulersse, *Le Pays des Alaouites* (Tours: Arrault et Cie., 1940), pp. 77–8.
24 République Française, Ministère des Affaires Etrangères, *Rapport sur la situation de la Syrie et du Liban 1937* (Paris, 1937), p. 237.
25 Weulersse, op. cit., p. 326.
26 Za'im, it should be noted, caused some concern by relying increasingly on Kurdish and Circassian units toward the end of his very brief dictatorship.
27 For good accounts of these early coups and military regimes, see Patrick Seale, *The Struggle for Syria: A Study of Post-War Arab Politics, 1945–1958* (London: Oxford University Press, 1965), pp. 24–147, and Gordon H. Torrey, *Syrian Politics and the Military, 1945–58* (Columbus, Ohio: Ohio State University Press, 1964), pp. 121–264.
28 Seale, op. cit., p. 134. See also Moshe Ma'oz, 'Society and state in modern Syria,' in Menahem Milson (ed.), *Society and Political Structure in the Arab World,* (New York: Humanities Press, 1973), pp. 66–8.
29 Whereas the class of 1946 had only 19 officer graduates, the class of 1947 had 63. Za'im, immediately after taking power, ordered an expansion of the armed forces from 5,000 to 27,000 soldiers (Torrey, op. cit., p. 129).
30 Seale, op. cit., p. 71.
31 ibid., p. 37.
32 Torrey, op. cit., p. 45.
33 Michael H. Van Dusen, 'Political integration and regionalism in Syria,' *Middle East Journal,* vol. 26 (1972), p. 132.
34 Seale, op. cit., p. 244.
35 ibid., p. 246.
36 ibid., p. 307.
37 Not without reason did President Quwatli reputedly warn President Nasser of Egypt that 'you will find Syria a difficult country to govern. The Prophet himself travelled this far and turned back. Fifty percent of the Syrians consider themselves national leaders, twenty-five percent think they are prophets, and ten percent imagine they are gods' (cited in Malcolm Kerr, *The Arab Cold War, 1958–1967: A Study of Ideology in Politics*, 2nd edn (London: Oxford University Press, 1967), p. 29.
38 This period is described in Itamar Rabinovich, *Syria Under the Ba'th, 1963–1966: The Army–Party Symbiosis* (Jerusalem: Israel Universities Press, 1972), pp. 26–35, and in Eliezer Be'eri, *Army Officers in Arab Politics and Society* (New York: Praeger, 1970), pp. 141–50.
39 Nikolaos van Dam, *The Struggle for Power in Syria: Sectarianism, Regionalism and Tribalism in Politics, 1961–1978* (New York: St Martin's Press, 1979), p. 48.
40 Sami al-Jundi, *Al-Ba'th* (Beirut: Dar al-Nahar, 1969), p. 85, and Nikolaos van Dam, 'The struggle for power in Syria and the Ba'th Party, 1958–1966,' *Orient*, vol. 14 (1973), pp. 10, 20. It must be emphasized that the Military Committee itself was internally divided and virtually all of these officers except Hafiz al-Asad had been ousted by 1970.
41 For a more detailed discussion of this activation of ethnic ties, see Alasdair Drysdale, 'Ethnicity in the Syrian Officer Corps: a conceptualization,' *Civilisations*, vol. 29 (1979), pp. 359–74.
42 This point is argued by van Dam, 'The struggle for power in Syria,' p. 16. It could also be said that many Alawis entered the officer corps from the ranks rather than through the Military Academy.
43 Cited in Rabinovich, op. cit., p. 76.
44 ibid., p. 76.
45 Martin Seymour, 'The dynamics of power in Syria since the break with Egypt,' *Middle Eastern Studies*, vol. 6 (1970), p. 38; Tabitha Petran, *Syria* (New York: Praeger, 1972), p. 171; Rabinovich, op. cit., p. 57; and van Dam, 'The Struggle for Power in Syria,' p. 11.
46 Cited in van Dam, *The Struggle for Power in Syria*, p. 114.
47 ibid., p. 115.
48 ibid., pp. 122–3.
49 Munif al-Razzaz, *Al-Tajribah al-Murrah* (Beirut: Dar Ghandur, 1967), pp. 158–60 and Muta' Safadi, *Hizb al-Ba'th: Ma'sat al-Mawlid, Ma'sat al-Nihayah* (Beirut: Dar al-Adab, 1964), pp. 338–40.
50 Seymour, 'The dynamics of power in Syria,' p. 40.

51 Van Dam, 'The struggle for power in Syria,' p. 17.
52 For background, see Alasdair Drysdale, 'The Origins of the Syrian Ba'thi Regime and Some Geographical and Political Dimensions of Its Performance,' paper presented at the conference on 'Radical and Reformist Military Regimes,' Fredonia, New York, 1978; Avraham Ben-Tzur, 'The Neo Ba'th Party of Syria,' *Journal of Contemporary History*, vol. 3 (1968), pp. 161–81; and John F. Devlin, *The Ba'th Party; A History from its Origins to 1966* (Stanford, Calif.: Hoover Institution Press, 1976), pp. 187–209.
53 Ma'oz, 'Society and state in modern Syria,' p. 87. See also Moshe Ma'oz, 'Attempts at creating a political community in modern Syria,' *Middle East Journal*, vol. 26 (1972), pp. 389–404.
54 Raymond A. Hinnebusch, 'Local politics in Syria: organization and mobilization in four village cases,' *Middle East Journal*, vol. 30 (1976), p. 1.
55 Syrian Arab Republic, Central Bureau of Statistics, *Statistical Abstract, 1978* (Damascus, 1978), p. 623.
56 Hinnebusch, op. cit., p. 6.
57 ibid., p. 22.
58 'The permanent Syrian constitution of March 13, 1973,' *Middle East Journal*, vol. 28 (1974), p. 54.
59 These statistics are drawn from various editions of Syria's annual *Statistical Abstract*.
60 Petran, op. cit., p. 240.
61 Van Dam, *The Struggle for Power in Syria*, p. 85.
62 Petran, op. cit., p. 243.
63 For background on the Asad regime, see Malcolm H. Kerr, 'Hafiz Asad and the changing patterns of Syrian politics, *International Journal*, vol. 28 (1973), pp. 689–706.
64 A.I. Dawisha, 'Syria under Asad, 1970–8: The centres of power,' *Government and Opposition*, vol. 13 (1978), p. 342.
65 Moshe Ma'oz, 'Alawi military officers in Syrian politics, 1966–74,' in H.Z. Schiffrin (ed.), *The Military and State in Modern Asia* (Brunswick, NJ: Transaction Books, 1976), p. 289.
66 Dawisha, op. cit., p. 353.
67 Petran, op. cit., p. 235.
68 *Events* (23 February 1979), p. 6.
69 *Arab Report and Record* (1–15 July 1977), p. 559.

4 The Israel Defense Forces: A Civilianized Military in a Partially Militarized Society*

DAN HOROWITZ

(1) INTRODUCTION

Since the inception of the scholarly study of civil–military relations in Israel, it has been repeatedly emphasized that 'Israel is so exceptional among other countries of its class that it provides a check against hasty generalizations arising from a comparative study.'[1] Neither the results of scholarly research conducted since this observation was first made in the early 1960s nor developments in Israeli society itself made it necessary to modify it in any sense: the case of Israel is still unique in many respects but not irrelevant to the comparative study of civil–military relations.[2] Thus, the point of departure of this chapter is the assumption that, as in other studies of 'deviant' cases in comparative politics and sociology, the examination of factors which account for the unique features of an exceptional case facilitates the identification of variables applicable to the analysis of more 'common' cases.[3]

The most salient unique characteristic of civil–military relations in Israel is the rare combination of multiparty democratic politics, on the one hand, and centrality of military institutions, values, and elites due to involvement in an external, acute, and prolonged conflict, on the other.[4] The case of Israel does not support the proposition that growth in resource allocation to security or the salience of the security issue inevitably lead to a restriction of democratic principles relating to open criticism of government. The prevailing Israeli outlook on national security, which is based on a broad consensus that the rules of the games governing security will not be applied to other spheres, provides for both public recognition of the centrality of national security and mutual understanding between the military and civilian elites on the limits of the military's role expansion.

The differentiation between matters which relate to national security and issues of politics, economics, and welfare enables Israel to function as a democratic society. The perception of national security as a politically noncontroversial sphere of public policy is not conducive to the development of a full separation between civilian and military roles, groups performing these roles and values molding the mode of operation of these

* Based on a study of 'Influences of the IDF (Israel Defense Forces) and the Israeli Defense establishment on the Formulation of Foreign and Defense Policy', supported by a grant from the Leonard Davis Institute for International Relations, Jerusalem.

groups. On the other hand, the legitimacy rendered to political conflict in matters concerning distributive justice facilitates the preservation of democratic values and multi-party politics.

Consequently, students of civil–military relations dealing with the case of Israel tend \ to refer to two models which allow for both democratic politics and intense interaction between civilian and military institutions and elites – the 'garrison state' model and the 'nation-in-arms' model.[5] Both models are not free from normative connotations – negative in the case of the 'garrison state' and positive in the case of the 'nation in arms'. Thus, for example, a sociologist who maintains that in Israel 'society is the army and the army is society,'[6] concludes from it that Israel is a 'garrison state', while in Israel itself the popular phrase 'the Israeli Army is the people of Israel in uniform' is considered an argument for the immunity of Israeli society against the preponderance of military values.[7]

Confusion arises owing to the ambiguity in the distinction between a 'garrison state' and a 'nation in arms'. The concept of a 'militarized society' has been attached to the former, while the latter is regarded as a 'civilianized army'. One of the few attempts made at distinguishing between these ideal types focuses on the nature of the boundary between the military establishment and socio-political environment, which is termed 'integral' with respect to the 'garrison state', and 'fragmented' in a 'nation in arms'.[8] Ambiguity is not, however, entirely eliminated even with the introduction of the permeability of the variables of boundaries. While militarization of society 'in the case of the garrison state' relates to one variable, the relative scope and centrality of the functions performed by the military and civilian institutions – the 'civilianization of the military' in the case of a 'nation in arms' relates to another – the degree to which there is at all a clear-cut division of functions between the two subsystems of society. In this context the nature of the association between the two variables (which logically permit two additional hypothetical constructs), remains unclear as demonstrated by the inclusion of both Israel and Switzerland in the same category of 'nation in arms' in spite of profound differences between them in terms of the first variable.[9]

The permeability of the boundaries of the military institutions (with 'fragmented' boundaries as a middle category between 'integral' and 'permeable') may nevertheless serve as a useful conceptual tool for the analysis of the struggle for the maintenance of the uneasy balance between civic values and national security imperatives in democratically governed societies such as Israel facing an external military threat. Fragmented boundaries, unlike fully permeable or strictly integral boundaries, are compatible with rules of the game which permit military participation in certain spheres of public policy-making and not in others.

Harold Lasswell developed the 'garrison-state' model, or developmental construct in his own terminology, in the context of World War II and the consequent need to explain the phenomenon of a state ruled by 'experts in violence' not necessarily via formal military seizure of power nor the destruction of democratic institutions. Though Lasswell perceived 'the military' and 'the civilian' as two rival approaches contending for power in society, he neither presented the dilemma between 'civilianism' and 'militarism' as analogous to a zero-sum game nor assumed a total spillover of militaristic values into civilian social and political institutions. Civilianism in his view was 'the movement that *to a degree* we can say is developing counter to militarism . . .'[10] and the expected increased role of the military was not expected to eliminate domestic political conflict.

These qualifications notwithstanding, the 'garrison-state' construct has been widely accepted as purporting that the rise of centrality in national security issues leading to the expanding role of military elites entails a politically significant diminution in the role of civil institutions, and the penetration of authoritarian values into the political system.[11]

The potential conflicts between military and civilian in modern democratic societies involve: (1) the tension between military professionalism which is oriented toward segregation of the military from society and military participation in decision-making on issues pertaining to national security interests; (2) the rivalry over priorities in resource allocation between national security needs and domestic political demands; and (3) the incompatibility of military authoritarianism and of violence with the egalitarianism and pacifist tendencies prevalent in modern democratic societies.

The differences in this respect between the 'garrison state' and 'nation in arms' is to be distinguished in the way that conflict tendencies are expressed. Unlike in the case of the 'garrison state', in a 'nation in arms' there is no clearcut dichotomic distinction between 'civilianism' and 'militarism', nor is the control over the legitimate use of means of violence secured primarily by maintaining the formal demarcation between civil and military institutions.

The Israeli case fits this characterization. The Israeli pattern of civil–military relations is characterized by a partial penetration of 'civilian' values and modes of operation into the institutional realm of the military and vice versa and on a normative emphasis placed on the exceptional status of the sphere of national security rather than on the institutional distinctiveness of the military.[12]

Features of the Israeli case which render it incompatible with the 'garrison-state' model include the penetration of civilian values into the military sphere which offsets the impact of military values on civilian institutions and the consensus held by civilian and military elites on confining the partial fusion of civilian and military institutions to the sphere of national security. A point to be reckoned with is that the interests of a partially civilianized military do not clash with the interests and values of civilian elites and public opinion which are highly responsive to national security requirements under such conditions. The influence of democratic egalitarianism on the military provides a check against tendencies toward authoritarianism while civilian pacifism is mitigated and reduced under the impact of threat perceptions and a siege mentality. Moreover, the residue value conflict, which still exists, is expressed in terms other than direct confrontation between the civilian and military establishments and focuses on the legitimate boundary of the sphere of national security. Indeed, the military establishment itself is not directly involved in this ongoing public debate.[13] A broad or a narrow definition of national security interests is particularly relevant to issues such as the limits of censorship of the press[14] or in the replacement of striking laborers with army personnel in public services deemed as vital to the maintenance of national security.[15]

These issues relate to government misuse of the consensus surrounding national security rather than to abuses of authority by the military institutions exercising their national security 'prerogative'. In fact, the scope of this 'prerogative' itself has changed in recent years due to the impact of judgement errors and neglect as exposed in the mishaps of the first days of the October 1973 War. The most salient expression of this change is found in the considerable diminution of 'de facto' immunity accorded the defense establishment in general, and the IDF in particular, by public opinion with respect to criticism of prevailing concepts, modes of operation, and norms of behavior.[16] Recent tendencies toward public debate of national strategic issues and military organization has deprived the military of a previous almost-monolithic role in the conceptualization for strategic planning and the shaping of defense policy. Paradoxically, this diminution in autonomy of the military occurred simultaneously to its acquisition of a greater share of national resources. Hence, contrary to the premises of the 'garrison-state' model, in Israel the increased allocation of financial and manpower resources to the military, explained by an intensified threat perception created by the national security situation, did not result in the further militarization of Israeli society. Instead the permeability of the boundary between civilian and military elites and institutions has facilitated an increase of civilian input to the military sphere, counterbalancing the effects of the military's enhanced economic role.

The post-1973 War period in Israeli civil–military relations demonstrates the fallacy behind associating the degree of military preparedness directly with the preponderance of militaristic values in a society. The observation that 'Israel's exceedingly militaristic society is not militaristic' need not thus be presented as paradoxical. The premise that 'the ethos of militarism – the glorification of war and the celebration of martial values' and 'its correlate the corporate political control of society'[17] are necessary attributes of society at war is devoid of historical validity, as the example of ancient Athens suggests. Thus, it seems that a modern Athens, too, can preserve its civic ethos in the eventuality of war without experiencing the kind of metamorphosis which would transform her into a modern Sparta.

(2)   THE SOCIOLOGICAL PERSPECTIVE

The role of the military in Israeli society is largely determined by a defense posture based on broad popular participation whose strategic rationale is the need to offset the impact of population ratios in the Arab–Israeli balance of power. The compatibility of this defense posture with the underlying premises of the 'nation-in-arms' construct, is a consequence of a pattern of manpower mobilization which tends to blur the demarcation line between the military and civilian systems. The Israeli reserve system known as *miluim* implies that most of the Jewish male adult population of Israel (and a certain small percentage of the female population as well) possess a dual status of civilian and part-time soldier who is thus subject to military authority.[18] Hence the institutional permeability of the boundary between the military and civilian systems on the micro-sociological level is epitomized in a saying attributed to the former IDF Chief of Staff who designed the *miluim* system (later professor of archaeology and senior political figure), General Yigael Yadin, 'the civilian is a soldier on eleven months' annual leave.' This saying relates to the fact that according to the Israel Defense Service Law, every adult male resident of Israel is liable to be called for one month's annual military duty in the reserves until he reaches the age of 39, and then for a shorter period until the age of 54.[19]

Though the validity of Yadin's formula as an interpretation of the legal situation may be challenged, its broad popularity, as reflected in its repeated citation for a period of twenty-five years, points to its compatibility with the prevailing Israeli view on the individual's contribution required for maintaining the country's defense effort.

This contribution, or cost to the individual, is twofold. On the one hand, it can be measured in terms of commitment of time resources to the military service. On the other hand, it involved an infringement upon his autonomous civilian status by imposing on him the role of part-time soldier.

According to the Defense Law, a male resident of Israel on reaching the age of 18 is liable to serve three years in the regular army, after which he can be called up for thirty-one days of annual service in the reserves up to the age of 39, and fourteen days from the age of 40–55. This applies to privates; from the rank of corporal up, annual service in the reserves is seven days longer, i.e. thirty-eight days to the age of 39 and twenty-one days from the age of 40–55. In addition, all reservists may be called up for one day a month, and up to four such days may be made consecutive. Altogether, the amount of time which a resident of Israel may be called upon to serve in the army from the ages of 18 to 55 in terms of the Defense Service Law is from six to seven years, according to his rank in the reserves. In addition, during periods of war and postwar, people have been called up for longer periods by emergency mobilization orders.[20] The military service of women is shorter, and reaches two years of regular service in the army from the age of 18, and a shorter period of annual reserve service for childless women up to the age of 29.

This commitment of time which necessitates relinquishing of personal autonomy, adds up to a negative input for membership in the Israeli collectivity, in terms of the individual's balance of deprivations and rewards. Yet, the acceptance of this burden by the vast majority of the Israeli population, as reflected in political behavior, indicates the existence of positive inputs which compensate for the high personal costs.[21] The perception of an acute threat and the resultant high salience of national security transforms the notion of security and its psychological corollary – anxiety reduction – into an effective 'reward' in itself. Furthermore, in terms of the individual's perception of his role as a member of the collectivity, his deprivations consequential upon the requirements of national security are compensated by the rewards deriving from the evaluation of his performance as a participant in a collective endeavor.[22]

Participation as a reward facilitates the mobilization of individual commitment to the community for the attainment of collective goals. The integrative function of participation is particularly notable in Israeli society whose ethos reflects the Zionist collective and future-oriented values of a pioneering community of immigrants transformed into a nation.[23] Contributing to the national security effort thus remains inspired by the overwhelming commitment of the majority of the Jewish population of Israel to the normative precepts of Zionism and the collective identity associated with it.

The connection between the security problem and the value system which guided Jewish settlement in Palestine and the building of the Israeli nation stems from the foundation of Zionist ideology. The basic insecurity which characterized the physical survival of Jews in the diaspora was without a doubt among the factors which nourished the Zionist conception of a need to create a framework which would provide the Jews with a measure of security, not only as individuals but also as a collectivity.[24] Even those schools of Zionist thought which did not see the establishment of a Jewish state as a means of increasing the personal security of the individual Jew, lent priority status to military security as an expression of Jewish auto-emancipation.[25] The image of the emancipated Jew as one who is capable of defending himself and the national collectivity to which he belonged, was adopted by practically all Zionist streams of thought. Jewish sovereignty was also conceived as related to the security aspect of auto-emancipation.

There are three levels of security as perceived by Zionist ideology, the first consisted of individual security for each member of the Jewish collectivity. The second level comprised the notion of auto-emancipation based on the principle of self-reliance as prerequisite to collective security. The third constituted the rejection of the insecurity of diaspora existence by means of fostering a 'Judaism with muscles'.[26]

In addition to these perceptions of security, there is also the influence of the threat to national survival embodied in the Arab–Israeli conflict. The basic insecurity of Jewish existence in the diaspora, on the one hand, and the actual danger to Israel stemming from the Arab–Israeli conflict, on the other, strengthened the tendency to perceive Israel's security in terms of Jewish national identity.[27]

It is in the security sphere, more than any other, that the problem of defining the boundaries of the Israeli collectivity is manifested.[28] During the British Mandate, membership in the national community called the *yishuv* was determined on the basis of national cultural affiliation, plus Zionist ideological consciousness. The Declaration of Independence defined the State of Israel as the state of the Jewish people, while at the same time undertaking to maintain 'full equality of social and political rights for all citizens regardless of religion, race or sex.' This resulted in a twofold definition of the Israeli identity.

According to one definition, the Israeli nation includes all citizens of the state, whether Jews or non-Jews. It is on this definition, for example, that the elections to the Knesset are held. The law grants every citizen of Israel an equal right to participate in electing the representatives to the institution responsible for governing the country.[29] On the same principle, the law withheld the right to vote in the elections to the Knesset from Jews who were residents of Israel, but not citizens. On the other hand, the definition of Israeli identity on the basis of national-ethnic affiliation has been preserved not only in the law as the Law of Return,[30] which serves as a base for the granting of automatic citizenship rights to all Jews immigrating to Israel,[31] but also in the arrangements determining participation in the sphere of national security. The Defense Service Law allows for the conscription not only of citizens, but also of permanent residents who are not citizens. However, the law is enforced only in the case of those permanent residents who are Jews.[32]

In this way, the reward of participation in the national security effort relates to identification with the Jewish people rather than to citizenship in the State of Israel. Such participation defines the extent to which an individual is 'in' the social-evaluative system of Israel – a system whose boundaries are not identical to those of the formal political system. Israeli Arabs are 'in' with respect to the formal political system and 'out' with respect to the informal system which is clearly Jewish nationalism-oriented.[33]

The marginal position held by extreme Jewish orthodox groups – which reject Zionist ideology – is also emphasized by a de facto exemption of members of these groups from military service. The exemption of women is based on a regulation which states that a girl who declares religious commitment is exempted from military service.[34] Men who register as students in Yeshivot (traditional colleges of Biblical and Jewish studies) have their service postponed, in most cases indefinitely, because they are 'rabbinical scholars'.[35]

Differential participation in the national security effort may reflect the implicit assumption that participation in the security effort is rewarding as it involves: (1) the sense of possessing the ability to influence decision- and policy-making; (2) accessibility to restricted and classified infor-mation; (3) attachment to the common central goals through actual performance.

The rewards of participation – mediated by the central values and the perception of the country's military and political situation – seem to be so decisive that they offset the potentially dysfunctional effects of another characteristic of reserve service: the differential relinquishment of time resources by various individuals, which seems to be inconsistent with the demand for distributive justice for the individual. The length of reserve duty is not determined by consideration of the rights of the individual in society, but rather in accordance with the army's functional needs. Whoever the army needs more, sometimes because of accidental place-ment in a particular unit, is called upon to relinquish more of his time than is someone else, whose services, for one reason or another, are less in demand by the army.

Such acquiescence to the needs of the national collectivity conferred by the individual upon the sphere of national security does not concur with respect to other institutional frameworks.[36] It is, however, noteworthy that when the unequal burden became most salient as a result of extended emergency service by certain units, it did become a public issue.[37]

It is worth mentioning that the Israeli army, as opposed to many other armies, is organized in such a way as to reduce considerably the impact of social stratification outside the army on the military hierarchy and on prospects for mobility within the military framework. Israel has no military academy whose graduates are drafted as officers; there is no requirement of a high school education for promotion to an officer's rank, nor does education at university level ensure the attainment of an officer's rank (except in the case of physicians). Every draftee usually follows the same path which begins at the recruit's base and continues through various courses in order to become an officer. There is no tradition of recruitment of regular officers from a particular social stratum. This does not imply that the officer corps, or even the IDF as a whole, is a 'mirror of society'. Some social groups are overrepresented for various reasons (levels of education and motivation, and so on), while others are underrepresented.

On the other hand, the reservist's position in the military hierarchy gives him an additional status component which effects his position in the civilian social stratification system.

Participation of 'civilians' in the military effort implies some degree of 'militarization of society'. On the other hand, the same pattern of participation when looked upon from the viewpoint of the military sub-system itself constitutes a channel for 'civilianization of the military'. The two propositions are not necessarily irreconcilable. In terms of inputs to the military system from the civilian environment, the 'soldier on eleven months' annual leave' contributes to the introduction of civilian values and modes of operation into the military sphere. Reservists are not only a reservoir of manpower called to service in time of war, but are part of an organized disposition of standing units who rank from battalion and brigade to division commanders. Indeed, professional soldiers frequently find themselves serving under the command of reserve officers who are civilians in their daily lives.

The prevailing civilian nature of the officer corps prevented the development of a segregated military elite in Israel.[38] Moreover, in order to allow for the integration of civilian officers into the military organization, a large measure of flexibility is called for in organizational patterns and modes of operation. Hence the army tends to become less 'militaristic' while the civilian sphere remains highly involved in security matters, thereby mitigating military alienation from its civilian environment.[39]

The 'civilian' orientation of the military elite in Israel is reflected in the relatively low level of authoritarianism in the army, which is characterized by a lack of structurally rigid hierarchy of authority. This exemplified by the low level of ritualization and symbolization of differences in status, such that the Israeli Defense Forces fits the model of the 'popular' or 'democratic' army; in this respect the IDF has little in common with the disciplinary tradition of the British and German armies from which it derived its organizational structure. Indeed, the level of authoritarianism has never matched even that of the US military forces. Recurrent attempts at giving the IDF a more military image through imposing measures of external discipline and ritualizing rank hierarchy have not succeeded.[40] This lack of traditionalism has not always resulted in solidarity of comrades in arms. In certain cases the inability of officers to rely on deference to authority resulted in attempts to improve discipline by means that are not endorsed by military regulations. The absence of a traditional code of honor for the officer corps, combined with the effects of cultural group differentiation, led in extreme instances to the opposite, that is, as abuse of authority where certain junior officers resorted to arbitrary disciplinary measures.[41]

The controversy over 'internal discipline' based on 'personal example' and more strict measures of external discipline has never been resolved and each chief of staff tries, in most cases unsuccessfully, to impose his own style of leadership and discipline on the lower echelons of command.[42]

For instance, during the 1950s, certain officers who had previously served in the British army felt that the use of insignia would improve discipline in the IDF. Efforts to build an army which would shine on the parade ground as well as the battlefield were shortly abandoned, however, when the tone of the IDF began to be set by the paratroopers who reverted to the style of the War of Independence. The title of 'fighter' was preferred to that of 'soldier'. In their disregard for ritual expressions of discipline, external appearance and insignia, the para-troopers continued the tradition of the *Palmah,* the striking force of the *Haganah* underground organization which formed the nucleus of the IDF. The *Palmah,* which has been described as a 'youth movement in arms,'[43] continued to influence the IDF by means of many high- and middle-ranking officers who had received their military training in its framework. During the 1960s and 1970s, a difference emerged in the IDF between patterns of discipline in the paratroop corps and the armored corps, with the latter placing greater emphasis on formal discipline.

This issue was aroused again in the wake of the report prepared by the Commission of Inquiry that investigated the reasons for the IDF's low level of preparedness for the October 1973 War.[44] One of the report's conclusions cited the loose patterns of discipline as an IDF shortcoming which the Arab surprise attack brought to light. Yet this statement was only partially accepted by the IDF command. Among those unwilling to impose farreaching external forms of discipline was the Chief of General Staff whose view was that the problem was not lack of discipline, but rather the tendency of some officers to avoid assuming responsibility when not directly covered by orders from their superiors. The problem faced by the 'disciplinarian' school has been the need to counteract the egalitarian ethos of a society which still retains certain features of a pioneering frontier community, and in addition the following factors: the small size of the country which minimizes the physical and social distance between soldiers and their civilian environment; the absence of barracks-style living due to the reserve-duty nature of service in the field and the general proximity of the field to the soldiers' home. above all, is the difficulty entailed in the need to cope with the civilianized outlook of reservists. In this regard, it must be stressed that the daily-life functions of the soldier take place outside the military system, and the reservist, the soldier in the regular army, and even the professional soldier continue to maintain close attachments not only to their families, but also to different social groups, some of which perform the function of reference groups. A striking example of this is the attachment of soldiers from *kibbutzim* and *moshavim* to their settlements. As members of settlements, they are in fact committed at one and the same time to both frameworks.[45] Urban soldiers, too, spend a considerable amount of time in their civilian milieu.

Paradoxically, the absorption of retired officers into civilian elites which has often been cited as a channel for the penetration of military values into the political sphere,[46] has in fact contributed more to the civilianization of the army in which they continue to serve as reservists.

The common phenomenon of former military officers occupying civilian elite functions is a consequence of two basic features of the Israeli military organization: (1) the 'three-tier' structure, and (2) the 'early-retirement' system.

The three-tier structure is the organizational design which facilitated the development of a modern army in accordance with the 'nation-in-arms' model. The three-tier structure pattern of the IDF is composed of: (1) a core of professional military personnel, often referred to as the 'skeleton' of the IDF; (2) the conscripts force, on which the peacetime defense posture of Israel is based; and (3) the reserve force which constitutes the main component of strength in the Israeli army during war. Since the professional 'tier' includes the higher command echelon for the entire conscript force, parts of the reserve force and permanent technical personnel for the IDF as a whole, it is composed of officers and of noncommissioned officers in roles which require a high level of proficiency. Officers, particularly higher-ranking officers, are over-represented in the professional 'tier'. Moreover, almost all higher-ranking officers, including higher-ranking reserve officers, have served some period in the capacity of professional officers and many of them served long enough to justify labeling them 'career officers' in the Israeli sense of the term.

The meaning of 'career officer' in Israel differs from that in other countries as a consequence of the IDF's early-retirement system. Israeli officers, with few exceptions, retire before reaching the age of 50 (many even earlier), and are expected to start a second career after retirement from professional military service.[47]

The early-retirement scheme was initiated during the mid-1950s by the then Chief of Staff of the IDF Moshe Dayan as a measure against the aging of the professional officer corps and the resultant clogging of the channels of mobility for younger officers. It reflected a preference for fighting morale and innovative spirit over experience in professional service.[48] At the same time, it facilitated the building of exclusively reservist units by creating a pool of reserve officers. The second-career prospects made professional officers more inclined to retain the professional self-image of a 'citizen in uniform' and to foster social links with members of other elite groups.[49] In this respect, the military elite remained one of several major group components in a relatively integrated network of elites, in a framework in which 'everyone knows everyone.'[50] The common social milieu, shared by the various Israeli elites, also facilitates the absorption of retired senior officers into civilian elite groups. This relatively easy absorption process is indicative of a broader feature of Israeli society: military status tends to be transformed into civilian status. This phenomenon is a consequence of the centrality assigned to military roles within the context of the values prevailing in Israeli society.

In this respect, the Israeli version of the nation-in-arms model is linked to the profound features of the nation-building process in Israel.[51]

Since Israel is a new society still undergoing the process of crystallization, location on the center–periphery continuum constitutes a basis for social status. The significance of the center–periphery continuum is reflected in the varying degrees of participation of different groups in spheres of social activity defined as central according to the prevailing social values.

In the period preceding the establishment of the state, this phenomenon was especially conspicuous in activities defined as 'pioneering', especially that of agricultural settlement. After independence, the sphere of security became the most significant, and differential participation in this sphere has come to reflect location on the center–periphery continuum.[52]

The contribution of the status-generating equality of military performance to social integration in Israel is thus twofold: on the one hand, it makes participation in the national security effort more rewarding and, on the other, it facilitates the convergence of the military and civilian subsystems.

(3) THE POLITICOLOGICAL PERSPECTIVE

The political role of the military in Israel is characterized by both a high degree of participation in the formation of national security policy and, at the same time, a low degree of involvement in the domestic political game. This pattern of relations between civilian political institutions and the military establishment has evolved through the consolidation process of normative rules of the game in Israeli politics. The maxim of 'depoliticization of the military'[53] is rooted in a broad consensus on the autonomous role accorded the military in its professional capacity. This prevailing consensus on the autonomy of the military sphere is a result of the political pursuit of maximum national consensus regarding national security. Consequentially, military institutions have acquired the status of a 'reserved' sphere of nonpolitical professionalism, similar to the case of Israel's legal institutions, both spheres being regarded as immune to the influence of Israel's intense party politics. The measure of credibility rendered the military institutions as a result of this perceived immunity has been conducive to the rallying of a broad national consensus on security matters, including foreign-policy issues involving security calculations. Israel's involvement in a conflict perceived as a struggle for survival has blurred the distinction between the spheres of foreign policy and defense and has served to subjugate the former to the latter in the decision-making process.[54]

The perceived military threat posed by the Arab–Israeli conflict has reinforced the pervasive attitude toward conformity for the sake of national unity. Thus potentially controversial political issues tend to be presented as military-strategic and technical issues. Consequentially, the broad scope of the military sphere is lent legitimacy – a tendency which is also reinforced by the perception of rules governing the conduct of nation-actors in the international political arena as power politics oriented and dominated by strategic considerations.[55]

The perception of security in terms of a threat associated with affiliation to the Jewish collectivity is responsible for the Israeli tendency to regard the threat to survival of the state as a political entity as a threat to the physical survival of Israel's entire Jewish population.[56] This tendency is rooted not only in the Jewish historical experience in the diaspora, particularly the Holocaust, but also in the history of the Jewish–Arab conflict in the pre-state period. In the first violent expressions of Arab resistance to the Zionist enterprise, the boundary line between the threat to the collectivity and the threat to the individual identified with the collectivity, was blurred. The terrorist character of actions taken against the State of Israel, which are defined in the Israeli security terminology as 'current' (as opposed to 'basic') security problems, also contributed to the perception of the threat to national security as a threat to the physical survival of the Jews of Israel as individuals.[57]

Hence, Zionism as the guiding ideology for Jewish national revival was based on the premise of promoting security interests for the purpose of survival. It is against this background that Israeli threat perceptions vis-à-vis the conflict with our Arab neighbors are best understood.

Moreover, the status of the Arab–Israeli conflict itself has been perceived as a state of 'dormant war'.[58] The blurred distinction between times of war and times of peace has been a consequence of the failure to reach a more binding peace agreement than an armistice since 1949. The emphasis that the armistice did not imply the termination of belligerency is a reflection of the prevailing 'Israeli theory of Arab encirclement'[59] which underlies the consensus which regards the Arab–Israeli conflict as a parametric 'given'.[60] This perception of the conflict is the point of departure for the assignment of highest national priority to security and to the legitimation rendered to the use of military forces in neither war nor peace conditions. Such factors as Israel's lack of geographic depth and quantitative inferiority in both population and resources have also served to reinforce the siege mentality and provide a rationale for the tendency to worst-case analysis in evaluating the severity of external threats and in responding to them by taking certain military precautions. Moreover, a tendency developed to perceive the entire international arena as essentially conflictual in nature and hence potentially hostile.[61] In this context the pessimistic anticipation of the behavior of world powers and the skeptical attitude toward the norms underlying efforts to institutionalize international politics are reinforced in Israel by a prevailing national image of the predicament of the Jewish people. This climate of opinion and the obsession with military security consequential upon it has been conducive to the development of an institutionalized pattern of civil–military relations which reflect the preponderance of the strategic outlook in the design of Israel's foreign relations.

The focal point for civil–military relations on the institutional political plane is the nature of the relationship between the Minister of Defense and the Chief of Staff of the IDF.[62] Israel's constitutional framework does not provide for a supreme commander of the armed forces. The political leadership of the IDF is, therefore, not vested in a single person but in the Israeli Cabinet as a body. Ministerial responsibility of the Minister of Defense for the political direction of the armed forces is constitutionally derived from the 'collective responsibility' of the Cabinet. In practice, however, civilian control of the armed forces is embodied in the authority assigned to the minister over the leader of the military hierarchy – the General Chief of Staff.[63] The exercise of this control is therefore dependent on both official and nonofficial definitions and perceptions of the respective roles played by the Minister of Defense and the IDF Chief of Staff.

The division of responsibility between these two offices was recently examined by the October 1973 War Commission of Inquiry headed by Judge Agranat, which concluded that the Minister of Defense should not be expected to assume the responsibility of a 'super chief of staff'.[64]

This affirmation of military autonomy in its professional capacity did not solve the problem of the permeable boundary which separates the political and military-professional aspects of national security. The institutional implications of this permeability – loose procedures, ambiguous 'rules of the game', obscure organizational modes of oper-ation, ad hoc divisions of responsibility, and ad persona role definitions – have led to conflicts of authority between civilian and military decision-makers, at times involving farreaching consequences. The issue over discerning the responsibilities of the Minister of Defense from those of the Chief of Staff, for example, has been at the root of some of Israel's most acute domestic political crises: the Lavon Affair whose first stage in 1955 led to Ben-Gurion's return to an active role in politics upon the resignation of Defense Minister Lavon, and whose second stage in 1961 brought about the fall of the government and early elections; the 'waiting period' crisis of May 1967 which resulted in the formation of a new 'national emergency' government with Moshe Dayan as Minister of Defense – a portfolio previously held by Prime Minister Eshkol himself; the 1974 public debate over the responsibility of Defense Minister Dayan for the October 1973 intelligence failure and poor performance of the IDF in the early stages of the war – a debate which eventually led to the fall of the Golda Meir government and its replacement by the Rabin government. These political controversies notwithstanding, the prevailing tendency has been to involve the military in the process of foreign-policy formation by relying on the IDF General Staff's professional advice and the utilization of the IDF's planning and intelligence apparatus. IDF chiefs of staff and frequently the heads of General Staff's intelligence branch as well, were often invited to attend both Cabinet meetings and meetings of the ministerial committee on security affairs.[65]

Furthermore, the IDF intelligence apparatus has been institutionalized as officially responsible for providing the government with what is known as the 'national assessment' on all matters concerning war-waging and preparedness for war.[66] Nevertheless, the political echelons have retained ultimate responsibility for decision-making, even in security matters. Thus, for example, Prime Minister Levi Eshkol did not respond to the pressure from the military echelon during the period preceding the Six Day War to open hostilities at the end of May 1967.[67] Thus the outbreak of war was postponed for over a week despite the professional opinion of the military that every day of waiting placed new difficulties before the IDF and was likely to add to the number of its casualties. On the morning of Yom Kippur 1973, too, it was Prime Minister Golda Meir who took the fateful decisions to mobilize the reserves and to refrain from a pre-emptive strike, giving her support to Chief of Staff, General David Elazar on the first issue and to the Minister of Defense, Moshe Dayan, on the second.[68]

It is also noteworthy that since Israel still relies on a conventional defense posture, the professional role of the IDF General Staff is perceived as confined to the planning and conduct of conventional warfare. Decisions concerning the development of Israel's nuclear option has remained within the realm of civilian responsibility or the Ministry of Defense.

The IDF General Staff has been prevented from maintaining monopolistic control over national security interests mainly owing to the institutional functions and political status of the civilian component of the defense establishment, particularly the Ministry of Defense. In this manner, the influential position of the Minister of Defense has facilitated a reconciliation of democratic principles with the extended role of the military in a society where national security is central in importance. While this discretion of the civilian component of the defense establishment has reduced the potentiality of conflict between the civilian and military spheres, it has sometimes contributed to conflict within the civilian sphere itself, that is, the Israeli political system.

In 1955 Ben Gurion expressed the opinion that the function of the Ministry of Defense should be to dissect foreign-policy formulation, while the function of the Foreign Ministry should be to explain this policy.[69] A year later conclusions drawn from this attitude forced the resignation of Foreign Minister Sharett who refused to adapt himself to this conception of his ministry's role.[70] A controversy of a similar institutional nature, though focusing on different substantive issues, occurred in the late 1950s and early 1960s. During this period, arms procurement connections played such a crucial role in Israel's relations with France (and later for a short period with Germany as well) that Deputy Minister of Defense Shimon Peres established a direct political connection with the French and German defense ministries, alongside the diplomatic and political connections maintained by Foreign Minister Golda Meir.[71]

The unique status of the Minister of Defense had also been demonstrated in the merging of the offices of the Prime Minister and the Defense Minister both during Ben-Gurion's period of premiership and at the beginning of Levi Eshkol's term of office, up until the outbreak of the Six Day War. In 1955, Ben-Gurion also served as Defense Minister in Moshe Sharett's government until he became Prime Minister again at the end of the same year.

The Knesset has adopted another institutional measure for maintaining a balance between the military and diplomatic dimensions of foreign policy. Unlike the practice in most other Western parliaments, a joint committee for foreign and defense affairs was appointed instead of two separate committees corresponding to each ministry.

The centrality and salience of military security under conditions where an obscure boundary exists between military and civilian political roles, constitutes a potential threat to the supremacy of the civilian political authority. In Israel, however, this supremacy has never been seriously challenged. The military establishment has complied with the fundamental rules of the game of democratic politics by normative consent. Furthermore, any potential points of tension have been eased by the tendency toward positive response to military demands in matters of national security on the part of civilian decision-makers. In this way, not only has consensus or 'rules of the game' been maintained, but specific modes of existing military influence over political decision-making have evolved which did not undermine the ultimate supremacy of civilian political authority. The accepted channels for direct and indirect military participation in the government may be outlined as follows:

(a) Professional military advice

The high priority assigned military-strategic considerations in foreign-policy decisions and the prevailing broad definition of the sphere of military professionalism in Israel has led to an extended role played by senior military officers as consultants and advisers to political decision-makers. This is reflected in such institutionalized procedures as the invitation of chiefs of staff to Cabinet meetings[72] and the GHQ planning branch preparation of position papers for political decision-makers.[73] Politically minded chiefs of staff such as Moshe Dayan in the 1950s and Yitzhak Rabin in the 1960s have utilized this advisory capacity not only to promote their own political ideas but, in some cases, to initiate certain policy decisions as well. It was General Dayan who initiated the transformation of the Israeli policy of reprisals into a systematic strategy of controlled retaliation based on the utilization of the concept 'military operations in peace time' as a political instrument.[74] Dayan's successor, General Laskov and Laskov's successor, General Zur, on the other hand, refrained from active participation in policy formation. General Rabin served under Prime Minister and Minister of Defense Levi Eshkol whose dependence on Rabin's professional advice once again resulted in a considerable extension of the chief of staff's political role. Consequently, General Rabin played a central role in the formulation of Israel's policy toward Syria – first during the incident when Syria attempted to divert the sources of the Jordan river, and later on, in the context of Israel's response to Syrian support of Palestinian guerrilla operations against Israel.[75]

(b)　Intelligence inputs control

The role of the IDF's GHQ intelligence branch as the government's main source of current intelligence data, together with its almost monopolistic position as the provider of both military and political intelligence assessments, has enabled the General Staff to influence decision-makers' cognizance of the strategic and political situation. The most salient example of the impact of military selectivity in providing intelligence information to the government is demonstrated by the case of the 'low-probability-of-war' assessment in October 1973 which led to Israel's being politically and militarily surprised by the outbreak of war.[76] In this case, the Agranat Commission concluded that the cognitive error was made within the military intelligence system, yet it is conceivable that the control of military intelligence inputs into the political decision-making apparatus may in different circumstances be exploited in order to promote policies advocated by the military command.

(c)　Diplomacy in uniform

In the 'neither-war-nor-peace' framework of Arab–Israeli relations, the almost exclusive form of diplomatic exchange has been that of military diplomacy. Military men in uniform represented the parties in the 1949 armistice negotiations in Rhodes and in the mixed armistice commissions.[77] The negotiations which led to the signing of the first disengagement of forces agreement with Egypt after the October 1973 War were conducted by military men at kilometer 101 on the road to Cairo.[78] Following the Sadat visit to Jerusalem, Israel was represented diplomatically in Egypt by a military mission for the first half of 1978.[79] The role of diplomats in uniform in Israeli diplomacy, however, has not been confined to the context of Arab–Israeli relations. During the French–British–Israeli negotiations which led to the coordinated Sinai Campaign and Suez operation it was the Israeli Chief of Staff, Dayan, who contrived the scheme for what came later to be known as the British–French–Israeli 'collusion'.[80]

(d)　The military as a political pressure group

The exertion of pressure by the military sphere on security policy formation is facilitated by: the military's institutional role in the formation of national security policy, the high accessibility of politicians to senior military officers due to the social linkage of these elites, and the military's capacity to influence public opinion via channels of communication at their disposal – the IDF Spokesman's office, a radio station, a news weekly, and control of press censorship.[81] In the history of civil–

military relations in Israel, there is at least one example of systematic use of these facilities for the purpose of manipulating the civilian decision-making bodies to adopt a military strategy advocated by the chief of staff. During the period 1954–5 Chief of Staff Moshe Dayan effectively utilized all the political resources available to the General Staff in order to induce Prime Minister Sharett to adopt a tough policy of retaliation in response to terrorist infiltrations along Israel's borders with Jordan and Egypt.[82] In several instances, Sharett conceded under the weight of public opinion, party considerations and consistent military lobbying, and reluctantly approved reprisal raids which he considered useless or even damaging. In this manner, the pressure-group practices of the military establishment, led by Dayan, contributed to the escalation which eventually brought about the outbreak of the 1956 Israeli–Egyptian War. Another example of pressure-group-like behavior of men in uniform was the lobbying by members of the General Staff for an immediate pre-emptive strike in May 1967.[83]

(e) Military doctrines and tacit doctrines

Though the IDF has never adopted a coherent body of operative pre-scriptions which can be labeled a military doctrine, its organizational structure, order of battle and modes of operation reflect the impact of a cluster of prevailing concepts which actually prescribes the general outline for military planning and military instruction. In spite of its flexibility and nonbinding nature this cluster of concepts is sufficiently integral and effective to constitute a tacit military doctrine of the IDF.[84] This tacit doctrine affects Israel's defense posture through its impact on military planning and order of battle. In this respect, it determines to a consider-able extent the degree to which various strategic options are backed by military capabilities. Hence, Israel's tacit military doctrine imposes effective constraints on the discretion of the civilian decision-makers responsible for the forming of national security policies.

The most salient example of the impact of tacit military doctrines on the range of options in political decision-making is that of the IDF's offensive doctrine on the eve of the Six Day War.[85] Since the mid-1950s the IDF command actually made no serious effort to prepare for absorbing an enemy's first strike before 'carrying the war into the enemy's territory.'[86] The underlying assumption of the Israeli military thinking was that Israel would be able to pre-empt an enemy attack and strike first. The first strike assumption was most apparent in the operational planning of the Israeli air force whose command concentrated its efforts on developing a capability for destroying the enemy's air force on the ground in the first hours of the war.[87] Thus, when the Egyptian army concen-trated along the Israeli–Egyptian armistice line in a potentially offensive disposition, the need to pre-empt in order to secure military success became a major consideration in determining the Israeli response to the Egyptian threat. The government was under considerable pressure from the whole defense establishment to end the 'waiting period' and prevent the enemy from taking the military initiative. It is noteworthy, however, that the offensive doctrine was not just a consequence of military operational and tactical preferences of the IDF command. It was rooted in the basic geographic and demographic conditions of Israel which put Israel in an inferior strategic position vis-à-vis its hostile Arab neighbors. The vulnerability of the core area of Israel to an enemy's surprise attack, and the need to offset Arab quantitive superiority by reliance on the reserves, had induced the IDF to prefer the offensive option with its first-strike consequences.[88] The link between the doctrine and the conditions which are its source are also apparent in the 1967 crisis since one of the main factors which led to the decision to implement the doctrine was the burden of full IDF mobilization on Israel's economy and society. The experience of the 'waiting period' thus showed that in the context of the Israeli defense posture of the mid-1960s *casus mobili* is apt to become *casus belli*. This lesson, and that of the limited range of options in the absence of reliable first-strike absorption capability, led to a modification in Israel's strategic doctrine. A new element of 'defensible borders' has been introduced into Israeli strategic thinking in order to provide the IDF with 'strategic depth' considered necessary for the development of 'absorption capability.'[89]

(f) Retired officers in politics and government

The high prestige of the IDF and the centrality of national security issues in Israeli politics has been at the root of the 'demand' for retired high-ranking officers on the part of political parties which aimed at exploiting the generals' appeal to the public. The early-retirement scheme, on the other hand, created a 'supply' of former senior officers, some of whom have had political aspirations. Hence the number of Israeli generals in the Cabinet, in Parliament and in the civil service tended to increase.[90] Students of civil–military relations in Israel who observed this phenomenon referred to it as a potential channel of military influence on politics.[91] This approach has been challenged by studies of political attitudes of retired officers which did not support the hypothesis that their common experience would result in the sharing of political views. Indeed, the diversity of political opinion among them did not differ in essence from the diversity of opinion among other elite groups.[92] Nor did those of them who chose politics as their 'second career' tend to have similar political styles and modes of operation. They were not particularly inclined to adopt either an authoritarian approach to domestic politics or a hawkish outlook on foreign and defense issues. The contribution of retired officers who joined the political elite to the militarization of politics thus remained negligible. However, their participation in political decision-making bodies even reduced the dependence of civilian decision-makers on the expert advice of officers in uniform. The General Staff has thus been actually deprived of its monopolistic position as a provider of military expertise to the civilian decision-making apparatus. Moreover, the need of the military establishment to respond to competent, well-informed and sometimes critical civilian opinion on military affairs implied a higher level of accountability of the military to its civilian political environment. This impact of the political participation of retired officers remained, however, conditional on the diverse political opinion and nonuniform social outlook of the military elite. Recent studies of officers' career patterns and of attitudes of retired officers suggest that the relatively 'civilianized' outlook has become less characteristic of the IDF officer corps compared with the past.[93] Officers recently retired tend to cultivate a more narrow professional image and to be more inclined toward sharing hawkish and right-of-center political views. This tendency is compatible with trends in Israeli society and politics which culminated in the success of the rightwing nationalist Likud block in the 1977 general election. The diminution in the social impact of the previously predominant ethos of a pioneering society, associative with the politics and culture of the Israeli Labor movement, has been supposedly reflected in the military sphere in less civilianized social characteristics and less divergent political opinion among the officer corps.

(g) 'Military industrial complex'

The economic role of the military is one of the less studied aspects of civil–military relations in Israel. Studies of the economics of national security in Israel tend to focus on defense expenditure.[94] The share of the defense expenditure in the government budget (about 50 percent in the peak year of 1973) and its share of the GNP (about 38 percent in 1973, and 27–9 percent in the two following years) are in this context less relevant to the question of whether a 'military industrial complex' evolves in Israel than the share of domestic defense expenditure (that is, excluding expenditure in foreign currency) in the GNP (17 percent in 1973, 15 percent in 1974, 13 percent in 1975). However, defense expenditure in general, or even the share of the labor force employed by the defense sector of the economy (about 25 percent) are indicative of the economic role of the defense establishment as a whole rather than in that of the IDF. It is the civilian Ministry of Defense rather than the armed forces, as such, that is formally responsible for most of the economic activity related to defense. Nevertheless, the military is directly, or indirectly, involved in most of the projects of the defense sector of the economy.[95] In many projects, the role of the civilian ministry is confined to the legal and financial aspects, while the military is responsible for specifying technical prescriptions, supervising works, controlling quality, and so on. Another feature of the defense economy which affects the role of the military in it, is the difference between the primarily government-owned armament industry and the suppliers of other industrial products and contractors of the IDF which are mostly nongovernmental enterprises. The variety of institutional contacts and complicity of relations between the military and nonmilitary components of the defense economy makes it most difficult to examine the impact of the Israeli version of the 'military industrial complex' on both tendencies of the militarization of society and the civilianization of the military.

The abovementioned linkages between military and political institutions – military advice, intelligence estimates, diplomacy in uniform, pressure-group activities, political impact of military doctrines, retired officers in politics and government, and the military-industrial complex – represent channels for military influence on government in a political system which permits a relatively high degree of fusion between military and civilian institutions. The existence of institutional linkages between the military and civilian subsystems of the Israeli polity facilitates these 'fusionist' tendencies.[96] Another facilitating condition has been the tendency toward convergence of the military and civilian systems in terms of: (a) organizational modes of operation (particularistic, nonauthoritarian); (b) elite perceptions of international environment (*realpolitik* and power-politics oriented); (c) dominant political culture (democratic-coalescent).[97] Convergence in the case of Israel thus represented a limited and normatively restricted militarization of the civilian political institutions, on the one hand, and a partial civilianization of the military institutions, on the other. It is, however, noteworthy that exchange processes between the military and civilian subsystems of the Israeli polity are governed by normatively sanctioned rules of the game. Most of the inputs of the military subsystem to the civilian one, and vice versa, take place in a structured environment composed of those institutional linkages which are rendered legitimate for this purpose in the context of the prevailing Israeli political culture. Moreover, not only the channels of such an exchange but also its content are subject to restriction rooted in public consensus. This content is thus expected to be compatible with the maxim of depolitization of the military, which in Israeli usage means neutrality in terms of party politics and avoidance of political commitment in fields unrelated to national security. In this manner, the Israeli political culture provides for democratic ideological and political pluralism while maintaining practices highly conducive to military involvement in political decision-making.

CONCLUSIONS

In spite of the many references to Israel and the IDF in comparative works on civil–military relations, none of the existing conceptual frameworks in the field appear to be fully applicable to the case of Israel. The complexity and unique features of the case of Israel against the background of relative poverty of conceptualization in most comparative works in the field account for the tendency among students of civil–military relations in Israel to focus on the characteristics of the case rather than engage themselves in theorizing.

Works on the case of Israel may, however, bear upon developments in the comparative study of civil–military relations as it demonstrates some of the central issues for which theoretical approaches in the field are expected to account.

Three of these issues seem to be particularly significant in this context. The first issue relates to the multidimensional characteristics of civil–military relations. The available data on the case of Israel is not compatible with the proposition that militarism – that is, military values, power and prestige – necessarily tends to spill over from one dimension to another. In post-Yom Kippur War Israel, a considerable increase in the share of the military in the allocation of national resources coincided with diminution in its political role and social prestige.

The second issue relates to convergence and divergence of the military and civilian subsystems of society. Convergence may be a consequence of either 'militarization of society' or of 'civilianization of the military'. The case of Israel demonstrates that a nation-in-arms level of convergence may be the outcome of both tendencies developing simultaneously. In this context partial 'militarization' of the civilian subsystem and partial 'civilianization' of the military subsystem may be complementary to one another in terms of their contribution to convergence of the two subsystems. For example, the convergence of the two systems in terms of elite value orientations embraces both a quasi-militaristic perception of the role of violence in international politics by the civilian elites and a nonauthoritarian outlook at the military elite. The content of the inputs of the military subsystem to the civilian one, and vice versa, bears upon the capacity of the Israeli polity to function as a multiparty democracy while responding to the national security requirements, deriving from involvement in protracted intense conflict and maintaining a high degree of centrality of the military in society. The normative inputs of the civilian subsystem to the military one are relevant mostly to domestic politics, while the normative inputs of the military to society, at large, focus on values relevant to the maintenance of national security in conditions of acute conflict and sporadic outbreaks of hostilities.

The tendencies to distinguish between national security and other spheres of public policy is evident in Israel in an institutional context as well. In this context, it relates to a third central issue in the comparative study of civil–military relations: the degree of permeability of the boundary of the military subsystem. The boundary of the military subsystem in Israel can be labeled fragmented, as the norms prevailing in Israeli society tend to be permissive in regard to military participation in national security policy-making, and highly restrictive in regard to military involvement in other spheres of public policy-making. The boundary most relevant for the control of military intervention in civilian policy-making in Israel is thus the boundary between national security in the broad sense of the term and other spheres of public policy, rather than the boundary between military and political institutions.

The norms governing the exchange which takes place across this boundary render legitimate only certain kinds of inputs and outputs with different norms applying to inputs and outputs. In other words, the normative rules of the game of civil–military relations in Israel do not stipulate symmetrical exchange between the military and civilian subsystems. This tendency is particularly marked in the context of the social-stratificational dimension of civil–military relations. In this context, the utilization of status attributes rooted in military service in civilian life is fully legitimized but not vice versa.

The permissive approach to the utilization of military status attributes in civilian life constitutes a contribution to the balance of rewards and deprivations of Israeli individuals in the context of the overall national security effort. The deprivations associated with this effort cannot, however, be fully compensated by rewards of social status. The rewards of social status are thus reinforced by rewards derived from participation in a collective endeavor perceived as 'central' in two senses: contribution to the survival of the collectivity and reaffirmation of the legitimate right of access to the shared symbols of collective identity. In the case of Israel, these symbols are linked with the ethos of Jewish National emancipation. The Israeli national security effort is thus 'national' in the sense of nationalism rather than in the sense of nationality.

The community-based nationalistic tradition that underlies the Israeli national security effort, renders legitimate the exceptional status of national security among the various spheres of organized social action. The formal-universalistic rules of the game which characterize the civic tradition of statehood are not fully applied to the sphere of national security. The exceptional permeability of the boundary between military and civilian institutions in matters related to national security can in this context be attributed to the permissiveness of the political rules of the game associated with the nationalist community-based tradition.

The three aspects of civil–military relations discussed above – the degree of spillover of militaristic values from one dimension of civil–military relations to another; the degree of convergence between the military and civilian subsystems; the degree of permeability of the military subsystem boundary – relate, in the case of Israel, to a normatively sanctioned capacity of the Israeli elites to differentiate between dimensions of relations, between value contents, and between spheres of organized social action.

The pattern of civil–military relations in Israel is structured, and yet flexible to a degree, due to its tolerance of inconsistencies legitimized by public consensus. In such a framework, inclinations toward militarization of society are controllable even under conditions of centrality of national security as the fusion of the military and civilian subsystems is restricted to one sphere. In this context, it is possible to suggest a tentative answer to the central question referred to in the introduction to this chapter: the survival of multiparty democratic polities under conditions of centrality of military institutions, values and elites. The answer is threefold: (1) the differentiation between dimensions of civil–military relations facilitated the simultaneous occurrence of processes of militarization and civilianization balancing one another; (2) the differentiation between value contents in terms of their relevance to either national security or domestic politics facilitated convergence between the military and civilian subsystems based on a consensus between military and civilian elites; (3) the differentiation between national security and other spheres of public policy facilitated the control of civil–military fusionist tendencies on the basis of a fragmented rather than 'permeable' or 'integral' boundary.

In a broader perspective, the question of preservation of democratic institutions under conditions of centrality of the military can be perceived as a facet of the more general question of preservation of civic values in conditions of an acute international conflict. The inconsistencies inherent in the Israeli response to this challenge led a former commander of the Israeli air force to label Israeli society 'schizophrenic'. Our analysis shows, however, that at least as far as civil–military relations are concerned, this 'schizophrenia' has been instrumental to the ordinary functioning of Israeli society as a stable multiparty democracy.

NOTES

1   B. Halpern, 'The role of the military in Israel,' in P. Johnson (ed.), *The Role of the Military in Underdeveloped Countries* (Princeton, NJ: Princeton University Press, 1962).

2   For a similar approach see Gabriel Ben Dor in 'Politics and the military in Israel in the seventies,' in M. Lissak and E. Guttman (eds), *Ha'Ma'arechet Ha'Politit Be'Yisrael* (The Political System of Israel) (Tel Aviv: Am Oved, 1977) (Hebrew).

3   The potentialities of the study of deviant cases in comparative politics are discussed in A. Lijphart's 'Comparative politics and the comparative method,' *American Political Science Review*, vol. 65, no. 3 (September 1971), p. 691. For reference to the features of Israeli society as constituting a deviant case, see D. Horowitz and I. Lissak, *Origins of the Israeli Polity* (Chicago: University of Chicago Press, 1978).

4   The functioning of Israel's multiparty democracy in conditions of conflict conducive to military intervention in politics, has been referred to in most studies of civil–military relations in Israel, for example, Halpern, in Johnson (ed.) op. cit.; J. C. Hurewitz, 'The role of the military in society and government of Israel,' in S. N. Fisher (ed.), *The Military in the Middle East* (Columbus, Ohio: Ohio University Press, 1963), pp. 87–104; A. Perlmutter, *Military and Politics in Israel* (London: Cass, 1968), pp. 82–126; Ben Dor, in Lissak and Guttmann (eds), op. cit.; D. Horowitz, 'Is Israel a garrison state?', *Jerusalem Quarterly*, no. 4 (Summer 1977), pp. 58–75 (Hebrew); A. Perlmutter, *Politics and the Military in Israel* (London: Cass, 1978).

5   The concept of the 'garrison state' was suggested by Harold Lasswell in 'The garrison state,' *American Journal of Sociology*, vol. 46 (1941), pp. 455–68; the term 'the nation-in-arms' (*Das Volk in Waffen*) is associated with the name of the German military theoretician C. Von Der Goltz. See C. Von Der Goltz, *The Nation in Arms* (London: Macmillan, 1906). The two models are referred to in this chapter in order to demonstrate issues in civil–military relations. They are not considered representative of recent studies in civil–military relations. More influential in this respect were the works of Huntington, Finer, Janowitz, Andreski, Rapoport, and others published in the 1950s and 1960s, for example S. E. Huntington, *The Soldier and the State* (Cambridge, Mass.: Belknof, 1957); S. E. Finer, *The Man on Horseback* (London: Pall Mall, 1962); M. Janowitz, *The Professional Soldier* (Glencoe, Ill.: The Free Press, 1960); S. Andreski, *Military Organization and Society*, 2nd edn, (Berkeley, Calif.: University of California Press, 1968) (first published 1954); D. Rapoport, 'A comparative theory of military and political types,' in S. E. Huntington (ed.), *Changing Patterns of Military Politics*, (Glencoe, Ill.: The Free Press, 1962).

6   A. Qazzaz, 'Army and society in Israel,' *Pacific Sociological Review*, vol. 16, no. 2 (April 1973), pp. 143–65.

7   The tendency of Israeli officers to associate democracy with the fusion of army and society was most clearly expressed by the first commander of Israel's staff and command college in an address to the college graduates, later published in the IDF's official military journal: Colonel, later General, A. Rabinowitz (Yariv), 'the IDF as an army of a democratic state is an inseparable part of the nation and the state,' *Ma'arachot*, no. 96 (November 1955) (Hebrew); see also an interview with Israeli former chiefs of staff in *Maariv* (news daily) (6 February 1973) (Hebrew).

8   See A. R. Luckham, 'A comparative typology of civil–military relations,' *Government and Opposition*, vol. 6 (Winter 1971), pp. 5–35.

9   While Luckham refers to both Israel and Switzerland as 'nations-in-arms,' other more detailed comparisons of the role of the military in the two countries have placed more emphasis on the differences between them. See D. Horowitz and B. Kimmerling,

'Some implications of the military service and the reserve system in Israel,' *Archives Européennes de Sociologie*, vol. 15 (1974), pp. 262–76.

10 Harold D. Lasswell, 'The garrison state hypothesis today,' in S. P. Huntington (ed.), *Changing Patterns of Military Politics*, p. 65.

11 According to Lasswell himself, 'There will be an energetic struggle to incorporate young and old into the destiny and mission of the state' and that 'compulsion . . . is to be expected as a patent instrument for internal control of the garrison state . . .' (Lasswell, 'The garrison state').

12 The particular status of national security in the prevailing Israeli 'concept of national security' is examined in D. Horowitz, 'The Israeli concept of national security and the prospects for peace in the Middle East,' in G. Sheffer (ed.), *Dynamics of a Conflict* (Atlantic Highlands, NJ: Humanities Press, 1975), pp. 235–75. For a different view, see Perlmutter, *Military and Politics in Israel*, pp. 127–36, who perceives the IDF as an agent of 'nation-building' in the broader sense of the term. The different evaluations of the Israeli normative approach to civil–military relations can be attributed in part to actual changes in Israeli attitudes since the publication of Perlmutter's book.

13 In certain cases, the IDF general staff was not even ready to back the government in its use of security arguments for political purposes. See A. Rubinstein, 'The army in a role not its own,' *Ha'aretz* (news daily) (14 June 1973) (Hebrew).

14 The political issue of the boundaries of the sphere of national security in the context of press censorship is examined in Dina Goren, *Itonut De'Medinat Matzor* (The Press in a Besieged State) (Jerusalem: Magnes Press, 1975) (Hebrew). See also R. Kahana and S. Knaan, *Hitnahagut Ha'Itonait Be'Matzavey metach Bithoni Ve'Hashpaata Al Tmichat Ha'tzibur Ba'Memshala* (The Behavior of the Press under Conditions of Security Tension and Its Impact on the Public Support of the Government) (Jerusalem: The Hebrew University, Eshkol Institute Publication, 1973) (Hebrew).

15 The issue was raised in 1977 when air controllers of the IDF took over the controls of the Ben Gurion Airport, Israel's main civilian airport, which serves the armed forces as well.

16 The post-Yom Kippur War mood was expressed in an unprecedented open criticism of the IDF in the Hebrew press, for example, E. Hover, 'Credibility gap – why?,' *Yediot Ahronot* (news daily) (26 October 1973) (Hebrew); S. Teveth, 'The rotten fruit of lack of discipline,' *Ha'aretz* (news daily) (13 November 1973) (Hebrew); General (Res.) H. Herzog, 'The Minister of Defense should not be a military man,' *Ha'aretz* (news daily) (2 January 1974) (Hebrew); Z. Schiff, 'The IDF needs a shake,' *Ha'aretz* (8 January 1974) (Hebrew); the weekly *Ha'olam Ha'Ze*, nos 1,915–20 (Hebrew) even published a series of articles on internal rivalries and intrigues in the IDF under the title, 'The family of fighters who fight each other.' This wave of criticism constitutes a departure from earlier practices described by Kahana and Knaan in *Hitnahagut Ha'Itonait . . .* See above, note 14. It is also significant that the official commission of inquiry on the Yom Kippur War (The Agranat Commission), explicitly rejected the view that the main problem of the IDF is to recover 'the trust of the people in the army' and maintained that the public is aware of what happens in the army and its trust depends on a climate of 'proper discipline,' 'mutual trust' and 'initiative and dedication in the IDF itself.' *The Commission of Inquiry – The Yom Kippur War*, Press Communique, (30 January 1975, p. 37) (Hebrew).

17 E. Luttwak and D. Horowitz, *The Israeli Army* (New York: Harper & Row, 1975), p. xiii.

18 Permanent residents of Israel subject to military jurisdiction include: those who serve in regular or reserve service; those who volunteer for reserve service while in service; those who committed an offense when in service and have since ceased to be soldiers; those who were given weapons by the army; those who are legally under guard of the military or work in the service of the military or enterprise which serves the army and is declared as such by the Minister of Defense; or are on a mission for the army. See 'Military justice law,' *State of Israel – Sefer Ha'Chukim* (1955), no. 18, p. 17 (Hebrew). An amendment to this law, *State of Israel – Sefer Ha'Chukim* (1964), no. 432, p. 148 (Hebrew), adds to it all those who belong to the reserve forces and have committed one of the offenses listed in the amendment.

19 The military age was originally defined as '18 to 49.' See *State of Israel – Sefer Ha'Chukim*, no. 296 (24 September 1959) (Hebrew). But on 13 November 1969 an

emergency regulation was issued according to which the age of reserve service was extended to 54, see *State of Israel – Kovetz Ha'Takanot*, no. 2,480 (13 November 1969), p. 444 (Hebrew).

20 Reservists served a few months after each of the three wars of Israel: the Sinai Campaign of 1956, the Six Day War of 1967, and the Yom Kippur War of 1973. After the Yom Kippur War, many reservists continued to serve 2–3 months a year until the signing of the disengagement of forces agreements in 1975.

21 On the meaning of military service in terms of the individual's balance of deprivations and rewards, see Horowitz and Kimmerling, op. cit.

22 See Horowitz, 'Is Israel a garrison state?'

23 See, for example, E. Salpeter, 'Orientals move up in the army command scale,' *Ha'aretz* (14 June 1971) (Hebrew). Noteworthy in this context is Ben Gurion's publicly expressed wish to see in his lifetime a Yemenite chief of staff. On Ben Gurion's sensitivity to participation of new immigrants and oriental Jews in particular in the IDF, see extracts from Dayan's diary in M. Dayan, *Avnei Derech* (Tel Aviv: Idanim), pp. 159–60 (Hebrew).

24 See Dinur Benzion's introduction to *Sefer Toldot Ha'Haganah* (the History of the Haganah), vol. I, (Tel Aviv: Hasifria Hzionit and Maarachot, 1956) (Hebrew).

25 See, for example, David Ben Gurion's statement on self-reliance as a 'basic principle of Zionism,' *Davar* (news daily) (16 October 1947) (Hebrew). This pre-independence statement reflected Ben Gurion's perception which led him later to maintain that what counts is 'not what the gentiles say but what the Jews do.' On the ideological roots of this approach see D. Horowitz and M. Lissak, op. cit., pp. 122–35.

26 The phrase 'Judaism with muscles' was coined by Max Nordau, Theodore Herzl's closest associate. Later it was popular among the followers of the rightwing Revisionist Movement, led by Vladimir Jabotinsky and in the ranks of the underground military organization, associated with this movement, the IZL (Irgun Zvai Leumi), headed by Menachem Begin.

27 Former Prime Minister Rabin expressed this tendency when he said in a meeting with students, 'once the Jewish people did not believe *Mein Kampf*. I do not suggest that it not believe the Palestinian Covenant,' *Maariv*, (28 December 1975) (Hebrew). This kind of association was even more characteristic of Prime Ministers Ben Gurion and Golda Meir and presently, Menachem Begin. For criticism of this approach, see A. Rubinstein, 'Schizophrenia is not a foreign policy,' *Ha'aretz* (news daily) (18 April 1971); an interview with the author Amoz Oz in *Davar* (news daily) (19 September 1971).

28 On the issue of Israeli identity in this context see Horowitz and Kimmerling, op. cit., pp. 265–8.

29 While in the elections to the first and second Knesset (Israeli Parliament), all permanent residents of Israel were eligible to vote, since the 1965 election, only citizens of Israel are eligible to vote. This stipulation of the law excluded from the electorate those Jews who immigrated to Israel but did not accept Israeli citizenship. See 'The Knesset – basic law,' *State of Israel – Sefer Ha'Chukim*, no. 244 (20 February 1958), p. 69 (Hebrew).

30 'The Law of Return – 1950,' *State of Israel – Sefer Ha'Chukim*, no. 51 (6 July 1950), p. 174 (Hebrew), recognizes the right of every Jew to immigrate to Israel. Immigrants coming to Israel under this provision of the law are entitled to Israeli citizenship according to the 'Law of Citizenship.'

31 'Citizenship Law,' *State of Israel – Sefer Ha'Chukim*, no. 95 (8 April 1952), p. 146 (Hebrew).

32 See Defense Service Law 1959 (consolidated version), *State of Israel – Sefer Ha'Chukim* (1959), p. 286 (Hebrew).

33 An exceptional case of conscript service of non-Jews is that of the Druze community. This exception has been considered a reward rather than a duty since it implies a degree of participation which qualifies the Druze minority as a group which is considered to be 'in', even with respect to the informal criteria of Israeli identity. The particular conditions which led to the granting of this exceptional status to the Druze community are examined in G. Ben Dor, 'The military and politics of integration and innovation: the case of the Druze minority in Israel,' *Asian and African Studies*, vol. 9 (1973), pp. 339–70.

34 According to the Defense Service Law 1959 (consolidated version), *State of Israel – Sefer Ha'Chukim*, no. 296 (1959), p. 286 (Hebrew): 'A female person of military age who has proved in such a manner and to such an authority as shall be prescribed in regulations that reasons of conscience or religious conviction prevent her from serving in defense service shall be exempt from the duty of that service.' A loosening of the procedure for getting such an exemption following a coalition-forming agreement with the orthodox religious party, Agudat Israel, has become a major issue in Israeli politics in 1978.

35 While religious girls are exempted, according to the law, the de facto exemption of rabbinical students from regular service is based on an administrative arrangement which is, therefore, formally defined as 'postponement' of service rather than exemption.

36 On the sociological implications of this differential burden see Horowitz and Kimmerling, op. cit., pp. 268–72.

37 On the unequal burden of reservists in emergency service in the post-Yom Kippur War period, see Z. Schiff, 'An expedition force or a people's army,' *Ha'aretz* (15 January 1974) (Hebrew).

38 See Y. Peri, 'Ideological portrait of the Israeli military elite,' *Jerusalem Quarterly*, no. 3 (Spring 1977), pp. 28–41.

39 See Colonel A. Rabinowitz (Yariv), in an address to graduates of the staff and command college, (see n. 7); Lt Col. Baruch Levi on education for civilian values, in *Ma'arachot*, no. 96, pp. 48–50 (Hebrew).

40 For a more detailed presentation of this approach see Horowitz, 'Is Israel a garrison state?'

41 The Israeli army's official position, which deplores such abuses of authority, is expressed in an article by General (Res.) H. Laskov (a former chief of staff of the IDF) in the official Israeli military journal, 'The human doctrine,' *Ma'arachot*, no. 255 (April 1977), pp. 34–7 (Hebrew). See also Colonel (Res.) M. Pe'il, 'The meaning of discipline,' *Ma'arachot*, no. 188 (1968) (Hebrew).

42 Such a change in style of leadership on assuming the Chief of Staff position is described by Dayan in *Avnei Derech*, pp. 116–20 (Hebrew). The different Israeli position on external discipline is reflected also in the debate between two senior officers in the Israeli army's official military journal, *Ma'arachot*. The leadership-by-personal-example view is expressed by Colonel (Res.) M. Pe'il in 'How the officer should educate,' *Ma'arachot*, no. 180, (December 1966), pp. 14–16 (Hebrew). The 'external discipline' school view is expressed by Brigadier M. Zipori in a reply to the above article, *Ma'arachot*, no. 181 (1967) (Hebrew).

43 The term was coined by the commentator 'Palles' (S. Gross) in *Ha'aretz* (10 July 1975). For evaluations of the impact of the Palmach and Haganah on the IDF see Luttwak and Horowitz, op. cit., pp. 1–27, 43–5, 51–70; Perlmutter, *Military and Politics in Israel*, pp. 32–53.

44 The views of the Agranat Commission on discipline were expressed in an appendix to its report (Appendix B). See *Commission of Inquiry – The Yom Kippur War, Press Communique* (30 January 1975), pp. 33–6 (Hebrew).

45 It was claimed that the high proportion of kibbutz and moshav members in elite units and in the command echelon of the IDF is a consequence of the reinforcing effect of their civilian peer-group association on their motivation and performance during their military service. See Amir Yehuda, 'Kibbutz children in the IDF,' *Megamoth*, vol. 15, no. 2–3 (August 1967), pp. 250–8 (Hebrew).

46 For example, A. Qazzaz, op. cit.

47 See Y. Peri and M. Lissak, 'Retired officers in Israel and the emergence of a new elite,' in G. Harries-Jenkins and J. van Dorn (eds), *The Military and the Problem of Legitimacy* (Beverly Hills, Calif.: Sage, 1976), pp. 175–82; E. Salpeter, 'Retired senior officers,' *Ha'aretz* (15 June 1973) (Hebrew); D. Friedman, 'Connections as qualifications,' *Ha'aretz* (14 June 1973) (Hebrew).

48 See Luttwak and Horowitz, op. cit., pp. 117–18, 181–4; see also Y. Erez, 'The momentum of rotation in the IDF: new intake of colonels,' *Maariv* (23 September 1973) (Hebrew).

49 The sociological implications of this type of mixed reserve and professional officer corps are discussed in M. Lissak's paper presented at the 1978 Conference of the Inter-

national Sociological Association at Upsala, Sweden. A Hebrew version of this paper appeared in *Medina, Mimshal Ve'Yachasim Ben-Leumiim*, no. 12 (Summer 1978), pp. 27–45.

50 The close contacts among the various Israeli elites, including the military elite, are examined in A. Weingrod and M. Gurevitch, 'Contact networks in the Israeli national elite,' *Megamoth*, vol. 22, no. 4 (September 1976), pp. 358–78 (Hebrew).

51 See M. Lissak, 'The IDF as an agent of socialization and education – a study of role expansion in a democratic society,' in M. R. Van Gills (ed.), *The Perceived Role of the Military* (Rotterdam: Rotterdam University Press, 1971), pp. 325–40.

52 Hence, the de facto exemption of the extreme non-Zionist ultra-orthodox community from military service as opposed to the overrepresentation of kibbutz and moshav members in elite units and the officer corps, as well as the difference in treatment of the Druze, as compared with that accorded the Arab Muslims (see above, notes 33, 34, 35, 45).

53 The term 'politicization' in reference to the IDF is often used as derogatory word: for example, Mr Sharrett, *Yoman Ishi* (Personal Diary) (Tel Aviv: Sifriat Maariv, 1978), Vol. 1, p. 29 (Hebrew); M. Bar Zohar, *Ben Gurion* (Tel Aviv: Am Oved, 1977), pp. 831–47 (Hebrew); G. Karoz, 'The IDF and the parties,' *Yediot Ahronot* (7 April 1972) (Hebrew); S. Teveth, 'The rotten fruit of lack of discipline,' *Haaretz* (13 November 1973) (Hebrew). The concept of 'depoliticization' was one of Ben Gurion's contributions to the Israeli attitudes toward national security, see Ben Gurion's speech on 27 October 1949 in *Ihud and Yehud Dvorim Af Bitahon Yisrael* (Tel Aviv: Ma'arachot Publishing House, 1971) (Hebrew). Ben Gurion himself, however, was accused of political considerations in promotions by Generals (Res.) H. Bar Lev, *Maariv* (31 December 1971) (Hebrew); Y. Yadin, *Maariv* (6 May 1973) (Hebrew), and M. Peled, *Maariv* (10 March 1972) (Hebrew).

54 See D. Horowitz, 'The Israeli concept of national security and the prospects of peace in the Middle East.'

55 See M. Brecher, *The Foreign Policy System of Israel*, (London: Oxford University Press, 1972), pp. 261–7, 269–79, 335–49.

56 This perception is a source of deep anxiety which finds expression in literature that reflects the 'sense of living on the edge of an encroaching wilderness . . .,' E. Ben Ezer, 'War and siege in Israeli literature, 1948–1962,' *Jerusalem Quarterly*, no. 2 (Winter 1977), pp. 94–112.

57 The term 'current security' in Israeli terminology refers to the threat of terrorist and guerrilla warfare, while 'basic' security applies to the threat to Israeli existence from a major war. On 'current' and 'basic' security, see Y. Allon, in *Divrei Haknesset* (Parliamentary Proceedings, Verbatim Report) (3 February 1956) (Hebrew); D. Ben Gurion, ibid. (2 January 1950) (Hebrew); M. Dayan, 'Pe'ilut Tzvai'i Biyemai Shalom', *Ma'arachot*, vols 118–19 (April 1967), pp. 54–60 (Hebrew); and S. Peres in *Niv Hakvutza* (June 1954) (Hebrew).

58 The term 'dormant war' was coined by General Y. Rabin (later Prime Minister of Israel) in an address delivered at the memorial for Yitzhak Sadeh (Tel Aviv, 21 September 1967). As to its meaning in the context of the Israeli concept of national security, see D. Horowitz, *The Israeli Concept of Defensible Borders* (Jerusalem: The Leonard Davis Institute, Jerusalem Papers on Peace Problems, 1975), pp. 8–9.

59 Perlmutter, *The Military and Politics in Israel*, p. 81.

60 On the implications of the treatment of the conflict as given for Israeli strategic thinking, see D. Horowitz, 'Belligerency without war,' in *Molad* (1972), pp. 36–55 (Hebrew); A. Hareven, 'Peace as an anxiety,' *Maariv* (10 May 1978) (Hebrew).

61 See above, note 55.

62 For examples of controversies related to this issue see Luttwak and Horowitz, op. cit., pp. 133–7; U. Milstein, 'Struggles of succession,' *Maariv* (20 September 1974) (Hebrew). The legal background to the problem was referred to in the Agranat Commission interim reports, see *Commission of Inquiry – Yom Kippur War – Interim Report* (1 April 1974) (Hebrew). See also B. Nahis, 'Who appoints the Chief of Staff?' *Ha'aretz* (12 February 1974) (Hebrew); A. Rubinstein, 'The Agranat Report – legal remarks,' *Ha'aretz* (9 April 1974) (Hebrew); M. Golan, 'The Chief of Staff authority catch,' *Ha'aretz* (22 August 1974) (Hebrew).

63 'The Army (Basic Law),' *State of Israel – Sefer Ha'chukim*, no. 806 (9 April 1976)

(Hebrew), stipulates that 'a) the highest command echelon of the Army is the Chief of Staff; b) the Chief of Staff is under the authority of the Cabinet and subject to the Minister of Defense; c) The Chief of Staff is appointed by the Cabinet according to the recommendation of the Minister of Defense.' Until 1976, the authority of the Minister of Defense was based on the 'Israel Defense Forces Order – 1948,' *State of Israel – Iton Rishmi* (31 May 1948, p. 9) (Hebrew), which stipulated that the ministry responsible for the implementation of the order is the Ministry of Defense.

64 *Commission of Inquiry – Yom Kippur War – Interim Report* (1 April 1974), para. 17 (Hebrew).

65 Ben Gurion as Prime Minister and Minister of Defense did not find it necessary to invite the Chief of Staff to Cabinet meetings on national defense issues. L. Eshkol introduced this practice as part of the division of work between himself as Prime Minister and Minister of Defense and Chief of Staff Rabin. During Golda Meir's term of office, the Chief of Staff had become an almost integral part of the Cabinet, see M. Golan, 'The chief of staff authority catch,' *Ha'aretz* (22 August 1974) (Hebrew).

66 On the consequences of the military intelligence status see *Commission of Inquiry – Yom Kippur War – Interim Report 11* (10 July 1974) (Hebrew). For views of former intelligence officers on the institutional division of responsibility between the various Israeli services see 'The credibility of the military intelligence branch' (an interview with three former heads of military intelligence, General (Res.) Y. Harkabi, M. Amir, and Herzog), *Yediot Ahronot* (21 July 1974) (Hebrew); Y. Karoz, 'The intelligence services: a year after the earthquake,' *Yediot Ahronot* (26 July 1974) (Hebrew). For a criticism of the system by a senior commentator see Z. Schiff, 'The empire of the military intelligence branch,' *Ha'aretz* (22 August 1974) (Hebrew).

67 The attempts in May 1967 to persuade Prime Minister Eshkol to pre-empt were described in public by several members of the 1967 IDF General Staff, for example, H. Bar Lev in an interview with S. Nakdimon, *Yediot Ahronot* (5 June 1973) (Hebrew); E. Weizman in an interview with D. Goldstein, *Maariv* (5 June 1973) (Hebrew), and M. Peled, in an article in *Maariv*, (16 May 1969) (Hebrew). Eshkol, nevertheless, refrained from authorizing the opening of hostilities until the first week of June 1967.

68 See *Commission of Inquiry – Yom Kippur War – Interim Report* (1 April 1974) (Hebrew).

69 See M. Sharrett, *Yoman Ishi*, Vol. 4, p. 117.

70 See M. Sharrett, *Yoman Ishi*, Vol. 4, pp. 1,128, 1,130, 1,131, 1,146.

71 Peres himself described his diplomatic initiatives in S. Peres, *David's Sling* (London: Weidenfeld & Nicolson, 1970), ch. 7. His account confirms the description of his role in M. Bar Zohar, *Gesher Al Ha'Yam Ha'Tichon* (Bridge Over the Mediterranean) (Tel Aviv: Am Hasefer, 1964) (Hebrew). The criticism of this role of expansion of the Ministry of Defense was expressed in the Knesset in a speech by S. Hogan who maintained that 'the Ministry of Defense became the Foreign Ministry while the Foreign Ministry became the servant of the Ministry of Defense,' *Divrei Haknesset* (15 July 1964) (Hebrew).

72 See note 65.

73 The planning branch of the IDF – GHA – has become a separate branch only after the Yom Kippur War. Earlier it was a department of the General Staff Branch (it provided services to both the IDF and the Ministry of Defense and was subject to both the Chief of Staff and the Minister of Defense). The branch head, General A. Tamir, and some of his aides have played an important role in both the disengagement of forces negotiations of 1975 and peace negotiations of 1978. In the beginning of 1979, the branch was split into a military planning branch of GHQ, and a strategic planning branch in the Ministry of Defense.

74 For Dayan's own presentation of the strategic rationale of the reprisals see M. Dayan, 'Military operations in peace time,' *Ma'arachot*, no. 118–19 (1969) (Hebrew). On Dayan's role in initiating reprisals sometimes without the authorization of Prime Minister M. Sharrett, see Sharrett's diary, *Yoman Ishi*, Vol. 2, pp. 431, 447, 476, 514, 526, 596, 606–7, 673 (Hebrew). See also S. Aronson and D. Horowitz, 'The strategy of controlled retaliation,' *Medina U'Mimshal*, vol. 1, no. 1 (Summer 1971) (Hebrew).

75 See M. A. Gilboa, *Shanim Shisha Yamin* (Tel Aviv: Am Oved, 1968) pp. 45–9, 55–60, 72–4 (Hebrew).

76 See A. Shloim, 'Failures in national intelligence estimates: the case of the Yom Kippur

War,' *World Politics* (April 1976), pp. 348–80; M. Handel, 'The Yom Kippur war: the inevitability of surprise,' *International Studies Quarterly* (September 1977). See also Z. Schiff's series of articles on the Israeli intelligence in *Ha'aretz* (21 June, 27 June and 25 June 1974) (Hebrew).

77 For an example of the role of 'diplomats in uniform' in the context of the signing of armistice agreements, see Moshe Dayan's memoirs, *Avnei Derech*, pp. 79–92 (Hebrew).

78 Generals A. Yariv (Res.), M. Gur (later Chief of Staff), H. Shapir, A. Tamir, and S. Gazit were all involved in the various stages of the negotiations on the post-Yom Kippur War disengagement agreements with the Egyptians.

79 The Israeli military delegation which stayed in Egypt in 1978, maintained direct contacts with the Egyptian military authorities even in periods of deadlock in the peace negotiations. The head of the delegation was General A. Tamir who was later replaced by one of his aides in the planning branch of the IDF.

80 For Dayan's own account of his role in contriving the scheme for the French–British–Israeli 'collusion', see Dayan, *Avnei Derech*, pp. 218–71 (Hebrew). See also Bar Zohar, *Ben Gurion*, Vol. 3, pp. 1,232–961.

81 The IDF media is one of the products of the role expansion tendencies of the IDF's second Chief of Staff, General Y. Yadin. See Luttwak and Horowitz, op. cit., pp. 80–8. It was, however, the fourth Chief of Staff, Dayan, who utilized both the IDF and the civilian media as political instruments in his attempts to influence the foreign and defense policies of the Sharrett Government. See Sharrett, *Yoman Ishi*, Vol. 2, pp. 514, 550, 556–7, 581; Vol. 3, pp. 642, 649, 669, 689, 816, 829–30 (Hebrew).

82 The most extreme example of politicization of the Chief of Staff position by Dayan was his attempt to form a new political alliance of politicians and young activists from the settlement movements (*moshavim* and *kibbutzim*) for the replacement of leadership of the government and Mapai Party by representatives of the new generation. On one occasion, Dayan even took off his insignia of rank and delivered a speech before a civilian audience against the defeatism of the older generation, calling for a change of leadership. See Sharrett, *Yoman Ishi*, Vol. 3, pp. 324–5, 332; Vol. 4, p. 1,084 (Hebrew). For Dayan's activities of a political nature, see also the account of Dayan's resignation threat in August 1955, in Dayan, *Avnei Derech*, pp. 150–2, and notes 74, 80, 87 (Hebrew).

83 See note 67.

84 See M. Handel, *Israel's Political–Military Doctrine* (Cambridge, Mass.: Harvard University Center for International Affairs Occasional Papers, no. 31, 1973); D. Horowitz, *The Israeli Concept of Defensible Borders* (Jerusalem: Leonard Davis Institute, 1975) (Hebrew); General (Res.) I. Tal, 'Israel's doctrine of national security: background and dynamics,' *Jerusalem Quarterly*, no. 4 (Summer 1977), pp. 44–57.

85 For comprehensive presentations of the offensive doctrine see Y. Allon, *Massach Shel Chol* (Tel Aviv: Ha'Kibbutz Hameuchad, 1958); Tal, 'Israel's doctrine of military security,' pp. 44–57. For references to the role of the offensive approach in the context of the 1967 'Waiting Period' and Six Day War see Generals (Res.) Y. Gavish in *Yediot Ahronot* (3 April 1970); Y. Rabin (3 June 1971); H. Bar Lev (31 May 1973); E. Weizman, *Maariv* (5 June 1973) (Hebrew).

86 Colonel (Res.) and Professor of Military History S. Wallach examines this concept in an article in *Yediot Ahronot* (25 October 1968). For a broader analysis of Israel's military geography in this context, see S. J. Rosen, *Military Geography and the Military Balance in the Arab–Israeli Conflict* (Jerusalem: Leonard Davis Institute, 1977). See also Y. Levson, *The Demilitarization of Sinai* (Jerusalem: Leonard Davis Institute, 1974).

87 See General (Res.) E. Weizman, *Lecha Shamayim, Lecha Aretz* (Tel Aviv: Sifriat Maariv, 1975) (Hebrew). General Weizman commanded the Israeli Air Force when this concept was adopted and was head of the general staff branch of the IDF in 1967 when it was implemented.

88 For a description of the background for this preference of the IDF see Luttwak and Horowitz, op. cit., pp. 165–201.

89 For a detailed description of the circumstances in which the concept of defensible borders had been adopted see D. Horowitz, *The Israeli Concept of Defensible Borders*, pp. 1–15.

90   The number of retired generals in the Cabinet reached its peak at the end of 1977 when no less than five generals served in the Begin government. The number was later reduced to four with the resignation of one of them. In the Rabin government there were four retired generals, one of which later resigned.

91   See Peri and Lissak, in Harries-Jenkins and van Dorn (eds), op. cit.

92   See Peri, 'Ideological portrait of the Israeli military elite.'

93   On the conclusions of these studies see S. Weis, 'Army and politics in Israel – 1978,' *Davar Hashavua* (weekly) (11 August 1978) (Hebrew).

94   For example, D. Kochav, 'Kalkalat Yisrael Nochach Tzorchei Ha-Bitachon,' (The economy of Israel and the needs of security), in A. Hareven and Y. Podan (eds), *Ben Milchama Le'Hesderim* (Between War and Settlement) (Tel Aviv: Zeman Biton Modin, 1978), pp. 151–61 (Hebrew).

95   The largest industrial enterprise in Israel is the Ministry of Defense-controlled Israel Aviation Industry. The most significant contribution of this enterprise to Israel's military arsenal is the 'Kfir' fighter aircraft built according to the specifications of the Israeli Air Force. On the other hand, another significant Israeli military product, the 'Merkava' tank, is directly produced by the IDF Armament Corps.

96   For an approach to civil–military relations which emphasizes the institutional linkages between the subsystems, see M. Lissak, 'Some Reflections on Convergence and Structural Linkages: The All-Volunteer and Conscription Armies,' a paper presented to the Armed Forces and Society Section in the 9th World Congress at the International Sociological Association at Upsala, August 1978.

97   On the conceptions of convergence and divergence see C. Moskos, 'Armed forces and American Society: convergence and divergence,' in Moskos (ed.), *Public Opinion and the Military Establishment* (Beverly Hills, Calif.: Sage, 1971); A. D. Biderman and L. M. Shark, 'The convergence of military and civilian occupational structures,' *American Journal of Sociology*, vol. 3, no. 4 (January 1968); D. R. Segal *et al.*, 'Convergence isomorphism and independence at the civil–military interface,' *Journal of Political and Military Sociology*, vol. 2, no. 2 (Fall 1974).

Part Two

Civil–Military Relations in Socialist Societies

5 Military Intervention in the Soviet Union: Scenario for Post-Hegemonial Synthesis

ROMAN KOLKOWICZ

(1) INTRODUCTION

'Military and political institutions are inseparable: in a certain sense they are mutually dependent variables. A change in the character of one produces a corresponding change in the other.'[1] David Rapoport's perceptive observation of the ways civil and military authorities interact is particularly applicable to the Soviet case, where the party and the military have been inextricably intermeshed since the Revolution. As the character of the dominant Communist Party evolved, and as the society and state changed, so did the party.[2] Our concern here is with consequences of ongoing and future systemic changes in the Soviet Union and their effects on the party's hegemonial authority and, more specifically, on the roles of the military.

Most Western studies of Soviet party–military relations focused on the past; that is, they tended to examine that relationship within a political system firmly dominated by the ruling Communist Party. That dominant position of the ruling party was never in question, and even those Western analysts who postulated the existence of disagreement and conflict between the military and party never really departed from that common assumption. Indeed, there was good reason for such orthodoxy, since the party has retained control and full authority within the state throughout the six decades of Soviet history.

It is, however, necessary to go beyond such assumptions of the past to consider what sorts of developments might bring about changes in the party's hegemonial position in the state, and how these might affect the role of the military and its relationship to the party. This is not a purely abstract, hypothetical problem since certain internal and contextual changes and some recent developments in Soviet institutional politics suggest that the Communist Party's traditional hegemonial position may be eroding. The party has lost much of its revolutionary elan, it has become a bloated bureaucracy, content to manage a vast bureaucratic state, in partnership with several powerful institutions in a coalition of bureaucracies. The party leadership is in the hands of an ideologically bankrupt gerontocracy that presides over a government and state comprised of several bureaucratic institutions whose particular interests

and priorities do not always coincide. The tight centralism of the earlier
Soviet period is being progressively challenged by restless nationalities,
dissident groupings, emboldened allies, alienated former allies and
demanding clients. The older self-denying, rallying and mobilizing values
and norms of the revolutionary and post-revolutionary periods are being
replaced in society by the trends of embourgeoisment consonant with
the détentist preachments of the regime, despite the engineered efforts to
create a 'nation-in-arms' mood in society.[3] The growing commitments and
involvements of the state in foreign, military, and quasi-revolutionary
adventures add more complications and strains to the party leadership's
burdens of decision-making, as well as the adjudication of priorities and
claims among the contending bureaucracies at home and the grasping
clients abroad.

Indeed, as Soviet state and society are becoming more settled,
economically more viable, and militarily more powerful, they are also
engendering corollary developments which are logically inevitable: the
decline and decay of totalitarian strictures and revolutionary dynamism
encourage institutional and social differentiation and particularism, and a
persistent rise of expectations with a corresponding decline in adherence
to the center. The party's policy of providing more bread, more circuses
and more legions does create responsiveness and short-run support for
the party's policies from the major institutions and strata in society;
however, this expanding Soviet imperium harbors certain profound
dangers: expectations raised are very difficult to deny and curb; détentism
and embourgeoisment cannot readily be transformed into mobilizational
demands for sacrifice, revolutionary asceticism and totalitarian discipline,
particularly when called to do so by a 'leadership of clerks,' bureaucratic
satraps whose legitimacy is becoming questionable. Crises of internal
disarray, of political decline and ideological decay, or of severe external
challenge and threat, cannot very well be managed in the long run by
such leadership. A different form of leadership, or a different mix of
bureaucratic hierarchs, would be needed to protect the party, the state,
and society. New mobilizational demands would require different bases
and claims to legitimacy.

It is the premise of this chapter that such critical future developments
are not unlikely given some present patterns of Soviet events, and that
one highly probable form of post-hegemonial leadership would be
centered on the military.

It is against this background of perceived and potential changes in the
Soviet Union that we consider future party–military relations. Several
plausible scenarios of the relationship can be projected depending on the
mix of the systemic, institutional and political variables, including:

Retrogressive Patterns: a reversal to a subordinate role of the military
   vis-à-vis the party, analogous to the Stalinist period, could occur in the
   event of emergence of a powerful general secretary of the party; or a
   less radical retrogression to the Khruschevite pattern of selective co-
   optation of the military into political and bureaucratic policy bodies of
   the state.

Continuation of status quo: an extended period of party–military interdependence and institutional accommodation.

Radical Discontinuities: military coups, anti-party insurrection, military
government. While any one of these scenarios is, in principle, plausible
(particularly since we postulate a weakening party leadership, an
erosion of its claim to legitimacy, and a failure to properly satisfy
demands and perform adequate 'systemic maintenance') we shall dis-
count these as unlikely scenarios for the foreseeable future.

These scenarios possess various degrees of plausibility, depending upon
one's assumptions about the direction of internal changes in the Soviet
Union and the scope and success of foreign commitments of the party and
the government. The most interesting, and also the most probable,
scenario envisaged by this author is one that may be described as:

Incremental Patterns: the militarization of the party and the post-
hegemonial synthesis of communism, nationalism and militarism. The
relations between the party and the military would undergo subtle, yet
fundamental, changes. The military, in this scenario, would assume a
much more active role in decision-making in the party and government,
becoming a senior partner of the civilian apparat of the CPSU. This
occurrence is postulated on severe disintegrative internal developments
in the Soviet Union and in its sphere of influence, brought about or
exacerbated by severe external stress; in other words, during or after a
prolonged crisis period that would tax the reactive, mobilizing,
coercive, inspirational capabilities of the party leadership and of the
apparat.

It is postulated here that if such patterns and conditions of Soviet
politics persist, the party leadership will find itself progressively more
dependent upon the military for the efficient maintenance of internal
stability, political and economic programs, retention of the party's central
role within the alliance systems, and efficient conduct of foreign and
defense policies. It is further assumed that the party and military leadership would probably arrive at a *modus vivendi* for their adjusted and
changed institutional and political relationship. In sum, it is postulated
here that as the hegemonial power and position of the party declines and
erodes, the military will assume a leading transition role within the state,
without necessarily formally challenging the party's hegemonial position.
In such an event, the military would seek to vitalize society and state by
seeking to rally the people and institutions around a popular and mobiliz-
ationally attractive synthesis of nationalism, communism, and militarism –
the three fundamental and traditional rallying points of Soviet Russia.

(2) THE MILITARY IN STATE AND SOCIETY

The founding fathers of Marxism–Leninism and of the Soviet Union had
only a vague notion about the role of the military in a post-revolutionary

society. Although Marx, Engels and Lenin contemplated differing roles for revolutionary armed forces, they were in agreement on one fundamental axiom: 'In a communist society no one will even think about a standing army. Why would one need it?'[4] After all, to Lenin 'a standing army is an army that is divorced from the people.'[5] The idea of a massive professional standing army in a post-revolutionary society was considered an anathema, a heretical concept that violated fundamental aspects of revolutionary ideology.

This erstwhile revolutionary 'heresy' has become the orthodoxy of politics. Indeed, the Soviet military today is a vast and complex institution whose interests strongly influence the country's social, economic, and even political life. The military has become a state within a state: it is a primary consumer of scarce resources, of skilled manpower and scientific-technological talent; the military runs a vast educational network that parallels and often excels that of the civilian sector; the military has become a visible and pervasive presence in society through its control of a network of mass-voluntary, para-military youth organizations, and military preparedness and civil-defense training activities. The military is also strongly represented in the highest decision-making bodies of the party, the government, and economic planning functions.

What are the implications of this steady growth of the military's role and influence in the Soviet Union? Does it perhaps suggest an eventual militarization of the Communist Party and government? Is this evidence of a concerted program for war-preparedness and offensive intentions? Are we witnessing the emergence of a garrison state, a nation in arms, a modern Sparta in Marxist tunics? It is important to consider these questions because Western perceptions of Soviet politics rarely touch upon the military's internal roles and influence. These perceptions of the internal Soviet political process were first shaped by Stalinoid, Cold War antagonisms, and more recently, by the more benign perceptions and fantasies of détentism. In either case, Western scholars and analysts rarely concerned themselves with the military's internal role and influence. They saw the Red Army essentially as metal eaters, weapon carriers, and trigger pullers for the party.

The Soviet Union is, in many ways, an ideal country for the military to play important internal roles. The history of imperial Russia and of the Soviet Union is a tale of conquest, invasion, war, and violence. It is therefore understandable that Russian leaders placed a great trust in their military and relied on it to defend the country from foreign aggression. However, while the military's role as the defender of the country has been generally understood, there is much less understanding in the West of the important internal roles of the military. The vast size and geographic/linguistic/ethnic/racial diversity of Russia has perennially presented administrative and political problems for Moscow, and led to a strong reliance on the military for the maintenance of internal stability, law and order, national coherence, and the legitimacy of Moscow's authority. The military was considered to be loyal to the center and able to provide the necessary instrument for bureaucratic and political control. The replacement of the imperial autocracy with Bolshevik authoritarianism or totalitarianism did not significantly affect the military's role, although it did change the dynamics of their relations and the rules of the game. The military's roles, internal and external, continued to develop and grow in the tacit, subterranean manner suitable to the Stalinist regime. Post-Stalin, the military has continued to assume public, social, and political roles commensurate with its position in the state.

The military was seen early on by Communist Party leaders as an excellent instrument for the systematic and rapid execution of the party's primary objectives. Stalin and his successors considered the military an institution that could help eradicate some of the pernicious, entrenched remnants of the bourgeois/imperial past, inculcate desirable habits and patterns in generations of young people, and assist in a swift integration of the diverse Russian society. Thus, to the evils of ethnicity, regionalism/ parochialism, separatism, and traditionalism, the military could counterpose, by means of training, education and discipline, the values and policies of Russification, national patriotism, communization, centralization, integration and modernization. In other words, the army with its national network of installations, schools, and bases would serve as a school for communism, and would thus in a short time create the New Soviet Man. And it would do this as a by-product of its primary mission, the defense of the country, and do it economically and systematically.

The Soviet military did indeed perform many of these vital integrative and modernizing functions in the early decades of Soviet history. In recent years, the military has expanded both the scope and direction of this eductional function by taking a leading role in the development and inculcation of patriotic and military values in the Russian masses.

(a) 'Militarization' of Society[6]

There are several ways in which the Soviet population becomes exposed to military discipline and war-preparedness.

(i) *Pre-induction military training*
The Soviet army combines the advantages of a volunteer army with compulsory military service. The Soviet military establishment encompasses over 3·5 million men in direct active duty, to which we may add other military and para-military components (such as command staff, training cadres, KGB/MVD militarized units, DOSAAF cadres, and so on) that would bring the total to above 5 million. About one-third of the manpower in the armed forces consists of career officers and NCOs, and the other two-thirds is made up of conscripts under the universal military service law of 1967. Since only about one-half of the 18-year-olds in the manpower pool are inducted into the army, the military seeks to prepare the noninductees for military/war contingencies through various programs.

Actually, the military preparation of the young begins at the age 10–15 (via the Young Pioneers programs, embracing about 16 million). Members of the next older group, the *Komsomol,* are organized into permanent military detachments of Eaglets *(Orlenok)* constituting a quasi-militia of 16–18-year-olds. They receive compulsory military

training at their secondary schools and through mass-volunteer organizations of DOSAAF. The latter comprises about 40 million people, distributed in primary organizations of about 300,000. The vast majority of
instructors in these para-military training programs consist of reserve
officers who teach on a full- or half-time basis. Some of the training is
quite advanced, including piloting jet planes, operating radars, para-
chuting, sentry duty, and so on. The performance standards are rather
uneven and vary from organization to organization.

(ii)   *Civil Defense*

This program embraces the whole Soviet population. It is directed by a
senior general in the Defense Ministry, and has been expanding in scope
and intensity in recent years. Through the civil defense programs, the
military fosters and maintains a war-preparedness attitude, certain kinds
of discipline, and para-military habits in the populace. The programs have
received more serious attention from the party and the military lately and
have subsequently been expanded and intensified: in 1971, civil defense
training was introduced into the second grade of primary schools
(formerly it began in fifth grade); it became mandatory in technical and
higher institutes of learning. The population has been increasingly
incorporated into civil defense formations with specialized functions.
These formations increasingly cooperate with regular army units, and
thus serve as quasi-military units, providing intensive training and
exercises for the most efficient evacuation of populace and placing
increasingly more intensive psychological/indroctrinational pressures on
the populace to adapt to a war-preparedness milieu.

(b)   'Militarization' of the Economy, Science, Technology

The defense establishment has enjoyed a preferential position in the
planning of economic and scientific goals and priorities in the Soviet
Union. This special treatment of the military goes back to the early years
of the Soviet state, when the expectations of a world revolution failed to
materialize and the Soviet Union found itself to be the only socialist
country, encircled and isolated within a hostile capitalist and fascist
environment. Stalin had, at the time, radically transformed Soviet
economy, agriculture, and industry in order to rapidly develop a modern
defense industry that was to serve as the basis for a large and powerful
military establishment. Economic planning under the Stalinist Five Year
Plans was built around the needs and demands of defense, and was
described by Western economic experts as follows:[7]

> First allocate to the military establishments the resources (labor,
> materials, capital) needed to fulfill strategic requirements . . . Second,
> maximize the flow of resources into the heavy industrial sector. Third,
> distribute residuals of unrequired and unsuitable resources among
> other sectors, such as agriculture and light industry.

The current economic planning in Russia is not quite as rigidly pro-defense; nor does it follow the stilted and arbitrary Stalinist models. However, the defense establishment remains the favorite institution, whose interests and demands are usually defined by the Politburo as the highest priorities within the state. Among recent Western estimates of the defense sector's share of the Soviet GNP and budgetary slice, there appears to be a general agreement that the defense sector continues to absorb a large share of the GNP (11–13 percent *v.* US 6 percent). Some analysts maintain that the Soviet defense expenditures grew at an annual rate of 10 percent in the period 1958–70, 8–10 percent in the period 1971–5, and that the trend in the share of the Soviet GNP allocated to defense was 10–12 percent in 1955, 8 percent in 1958, 12 percent in 1970, and 14–15 percent in 1975; further projections see 18 percent in 1980. Recent estimates of the defense budget of the Soviet Union show a constant upward movement from 110 billion in 1974 to about 127 billion in 1976 with projections of 140+ billion in 1979–80.[8]

The defense establishment has clearly established its primacy in the economy, as well as in the research and development and scientific and educational sectors of the state. The Soviet defense industry forms a separate sector of the economy. It enjoys 'first priority in the allocation of materials and engineering-technical personnel, who along with the workers are better paid than those in the civilian economy.'[9] The Ministry of Defense enjoys a special position in the economic-technological sectors of the state. It has what David Holloway has called 'consumer sovereignty'[10] – the ability to impose its wishes and preferences on the whole production process – an economic privilege no other group has. The military also dominates the planning and priorities of the scientific and research and development sectors of the state.

The military educational system contains 125 military higher schools (13 percent of all higher schools in the country), leading to an observation by Colonel William Odom[11] that one in every seven college-level institutions in the USSR is an officer-commissioning school roughly analogous to West Point, Annapolis, and Colorado Springs. This has created a large military intelligentsia in the most extensive and intensive officer educational system in the world.

The military has jealously guarded this preferential position in the society and economy, and military spokesmen have, at times, publicly defended this position by attacking even leading party members. This was reflected, for example, in military figures' vitriolic attacks on Khrushchev shortly after his ouster, because Khrushchev had tried to curb the escalating defense budgets and reduce the wasteful practices of defense industry establishments that were hiding under the veil of secrecy. The military accused him of dangerous and harebrained advocacy of the 'primacy of the stomach' and 'goulash communism' because in 1964 Krushchev maintained that 'the tasks of defense industry could be solved more successfully with less expenditures,' and that 'we are now considering the possibility of a further reduction in the size of our armed forces . . . to reduce military expenditures next year' because 'the defense of the country is at suitable levels.'[12] Khrushchev's successors were eager to go on record as rejecting these anti-defense ideas, and asserted that 'the

Communist Party continues to believe that it is its sacred duty to strengthen the defense of the USSR.'[13] And when Brezhnev gingerly sought to remind the military after Khrushchev's ouster that 'the national economy must develop harmoniously, it must serve to achieve . . . constant rise in the people's living standards,' and therefore 'further development of heavy industry must be subordinated to the requirements . . . of the whole economy,'[14] the party leader received a public reminder from the Chief of the General Staff, Marshal Zakharov who, in attacking Khrushchev, served notice to other political leaders. Zakharov asserted that 'subjectivism (arbitrary interference by political amateurs in matters of defense) is particularly dangerous in military affairs . . . and it is the sacred duty of the military cadres to protect these military sciences from everything that detracts from their authority.' And to drive his point home with particular authority, he cited Lenin in support of the primacy of defense interests in economic planning for the country: 'The Soviet people have in the past not for a moment failed to carry out V. I. Lenin's legacy: always be on the alert, protect the defense capabilities of the country and our Red Army like the apple of our eye.'[15]

(c)   Political–Bureaucratic Interpenetration of Party and Government

The military and defense-industrial sector are represented directly in a number of important party and governmental policy-making bodies, where they can substantially influence choices and priorities, advocate special interests, and participate in some of the vital decisions affecting the whole system. In the post-Stalinist, collective leadership, bureaucratic-coalition form of governing, access to, and presence in, the collective, consensus-based, policy-making bodies convey power.

— The defense establishment has about 45 representatives on the Central Committee of the party (12 percent).
— It is represented in the highly important Defense Council (formerly Higher Military Council) where party, government and military leaders deal with the most vital matters of defense policy.
— The defense sector is heavily represented in the Council of Ministers, where it sprawls over eight separate ministries, ranging from the Ministry of Defense to the Ministry of Medium Machines (euphemism for nuclear programs building.)

And of course, until Marshal Grechko's death, the military had a professional officer representing it in the Politburo. Since then, it is represented by a civilian – Ustinov – but one with a lifetime involvement with defense matters, who speaks for the military in the top party body.[16]

Even this brief account of the internal role of the military conveys a picture of its pervasive presence, institutional interpenetration, and expanding social, economic, and political weight within the state. This steady incremental growth of the military's role can be accounted for by reference to such contributing factors as: the expanding scope of Soviet foreign and defense policies that depend primarily on military capabilities; the ossification of the party apparat and its leadership, and the waning of revolutionary elan within society; the problems of transition of power and succession modes that have endowed the military with an increasingly important arbitrating and tacit veto power in the face of competing intra-party factions, and the military's increasing internal role as the 'integrator' and educator of the diverse Soviet national, linguistic, religious, ethnic and class-based groupings and sectors of the vast state.

We shall examine these developments within the framework of contributing factors to systemic change in the Soviet Union, seeing them as some of the 'auspicious conditions' for the postulated scenario of post-hegemonial synthesis and military ascendance within the state.

(3) SYSTEMIC CHANGE IN THE SOVIET UNION: PARTY'S PROBLEMS, MILITARY ADVANTAGE

Western social scientists, in general, and analysts of Soviet politics, in particular, have been challenged and stymied by the post-totalitarian dilemma. The stark, black-and-white outlines of the totalitarian model of the Soviet system, which was perceived as a passive society dominated by an elite that was determined to maximize its own power and to transform society on the basis of its own ideological perceptions, is now perceived as defunct, having been undermined by sweeping changes in the state and society. The unanimity that the totalitarian model enjoyed among Western scholars gave way to a veritable cacophony of inventive, imaginative or simply outrageous alternate constructs, models, and typologies, all trying to describe and label what this post-totalitarian Russia was about.

The search for alternate models ranged wide indeed, as reflected in some of the better-known efforts, from Allen Kassof's 'The administered society: totalitarianism without terror;'[17] T. H. Rigby's 'organizational society'[18] ('a command dominated society'); Zbigniew Brzezinski and Samuel Huntington's 'ideological system,'[19] including Gordon Skilling's 'pluralism of elites,'[20] and J. Hough's 'institutional pluralism,'[21] as well as conundrums on the way to becoming models, such as Brzezinski's 'transformation or disintegration;'[22] J. Hough's 'petrification of pluralism,'[23] and on to 'oligarchic petrification,' and so on.

We shall not add to the growing treasury of post-totalitarian, all-encompassing explanatory theories or models of the Soviet Union. We shall, however, seek to identify a number of significant developments in that system that are: changing the older patterns of institutional interaction; shifting the power alignments among the bureaucracies and the party; and challenging the party's claims to a monopoly of power and as sole source of systemic legitimacy. Underlying our analysis of these phenomena is a basic assumption that the rigidities and strictures of the totalitarian past have given way to a dynamic and rather inchoate process of adjustment and adaptation to the new conditions by the several major bureaucratic institutions and other aggregates within the state.

We postulate here the possibility of 'systemic change' in the Soviet Union that would result in the decline of the party's temporal and secular power and the military's assumption of a greater political authority within the party and state. We shall first identify erosive developments that are assumed to lead to the systemic change: problems of legitimacy, authority, performance and maintenance.

(a) Problems of Legitimacy and Authority: The Ossification of the Party and the Waning of Revolutionary Elan

In explaining the 'routinization of charisma' Max Weber asserted that:

> It is the universal fate of all parties, which almost without exception originated as charismatic followings, either of legitimate rulers or of Caesarist pretenders, or of demagogues in the style of Pericles, or Cleon or LaSalle, when once they slip into everyday routine of a permanent organization, to remodel themselves into a body led by notables.[24]

The 'notables' we are presently concerned with are the leaders of the Communist Party of the Soviet Union, who have indeed routinized the revolutionary charisma of their predecessors and have maintained a progressively more tenuous hold on society and state in Soviet Russia. If the earlier, totalitarian, Stalinist period may be described as one of 'charismatic leadership,' the present situation in the Soviet state is more closely reflected in the 'post-charismatic' (post-totalitarian) reflections of Weber:

> The swing of the pendulum between charismatic obedience and submission to 'notables' has now been replaced by the struggle between the bureaucratic party organization and the party leadership. The Party organization has fallen more and more securely into the hands of the professional party officials and the further the process of bureaucration has gone.[25]

Indeed, as he suggests, 'it is as a rule easy for the party organization to achieve this castration of charisma.'[26] This evocative phrase does reflect the Soviet situation, the decay of revolutionary dynamism, the erosion of the party's claims to legitimacy, and the spectacular growth of bureaucratic institutions within the state.

In his analysis of the post-totalitarian trends in Soviet politcs, Jerry Hough maintains that the post-Krushchev leadership of the Communist Party has modified its role in society and state from a dominant to an adjudicating, arbitrating type:

> Whereas Stalin in his last years ignored the policy suggestions of the institutional centers of power, and whereas Khrushchev challenged the basic interests of almost every one of these centers, the present leadership has not done major battle with any important segment of the establishment and seems, on the contrary, to have acceded to the most central desires of each.[27]

The party leadership seems to desire an untroubled status quo, to avoid hard and risk-prone choices and decisions that might threaten the delicate balance of the bureaucratic coalition within the party and the Politburo: 'The unwillingness or inability of the present leadership to remove members of the administrative elite has been matched by its abstention from imposing any major policy change that would seriously diminish the status of any important institutional group.'[38] The leadership is seen to 'assume the role not of the major policy initiator but of a broker mediating competing claims of powerful interests.'[29] And the party over which this gerontocracy presides has changed drastically in its makeup, membership, role, and vitality. In its drive to broaden the base of the party, to make it a party of all the people, the leadership risks the danger 'that the legitimacy of the party as instrument of the proletariat will be undermined' since it is 'totally impossible for such a party to be some kind of priesthood that stands outside of society' but rather one where 'virtually all societal interests have penetrated into the party,' and where approximately '30% of all citizens with completed higher education in 1973 were Party members, and over 50% of the men with such an education'[30] belonged to it.

The problems of mass party are compounded due to the 'logic of rule' which affects the party apparatus and the controllers in the center as well as those in the provinces, because they very often come from the agencies being controlled. And finally, the drive to mass party membership creates 'a foremost danger that many persons will proclaim total loyalty to the Party's cause and will pretend ideological orthodoxy simply to obtain the jobs and material advantages associated with membership.'[31] This trend has, as its consequence, an influx into the party of people with little talent, prescribed administrative positions, and thus a most ineffective administrative system. In general, one may perceive a pattern of erosion of party authority and legitimacy that undermines the authoritarian features of the system. There are several such erosive trends: (1) the rising educational level of the Soviet elite, (2) the gradual disappearance of the economic-social force that generates a propensity toward authoritarianism, (3) the erosion of ideological certainty under the impact of events in the outside world, and (4) the tendency for dissenters to come from the upper stratum of society, a situation which makes it difficult for an elite to suppress its own.

Although one need not accept all of these developments as contributing factors to the decline of the party's authority and legitimacy, nevertheless, in aggregate, they convey the inexorable momentum of decline of hegemonial power of the party.

Milovan Djilas whose insights about the ideological decay of communist parties are both perceptive and authoritative thus describes the 'castration of charisma' and the dominant new class of the *apparatchiki:*

> The heroic era of communism is past. The epoch of its great leaders has ended. The epoch of practical men has set in. The new class has been created. It is at the height of its power and wealth, but it is without new ideas. It has nothing more to tell the people. The only thing that remains is for it to justify itself.[32]

(b) Problems of Performance: Expanding Foreign Commitments, Greater Reliance on the Military

The Soviet Union has grown over the years from a rather small, regional, and defensive military power into the present superpower configuration. The sheer size, scope, and reach of the military establishment is over-whelming. The internal resources that are made available to the defense establishment are not only very large (the defense budget comprises about 13–15 percent of the GNP), they also enjoy the highest priority in terms of scarce resources, skilled manpower, and the most advanced scientific-technological capabilities.[33]

Starting from a rather vulnerable, defensive and contained continental position, the Soviet Union has in the past two decades expanded into the global arena on land, sea, and in space, sharply increasing its commitments abroad. The primary motor and vehicle for this expansion has been the military establishment: Soviet arms, technology, military expertise, and advisory missions have become the most effective exports and influence-building commodities of the Kremlin in the Third World, and the Soviet military is its prime beneficiary.

Current Soviet global role and power are the result of steady vision and planning aimed at making the Soviet Union invulnerable and subsequently enabling its expansion abroad. From Lenin onward, party leaders tried to make the best of their temporary weakness and vulnerabilities while planning for the day of great military power. Lenin harangued his disciples:

> As long as, from the economic and military standpoint, we are weaker than the capitalist world, we must adhere to the rule that we must know how to take advantage of the antagonisms and contradictions existing among the imperialists . . . however, as soon as we are strong enough to defeat capitalism as a whole, we shall immediately take it by the scruff of the neck.[34]

In the 1970s, Soviet leadership does not talk about weakness or vulnerability: they assert that 'the historical initiative is now firmly in the hands of the socialist community,'[35] and though peaceful coexistence with the West is highly desirable, that must not interfere with the historical-revolutionary mission of the Communist Party: to combat capitalism and imperialism by aiding and supporting national revolutionary and liberation movements in the Third World.

> Peaceful coexistence has nothing in common with class peace and does not cast even the slightest doubt upon the oppressed peoples' sacred rights to use all means, including armed struggle, in the cause of their liberation.
>
> Ideologists hostile to socialism are attempting to inculcate in gullible people the idea that in pursuing a policy of peaceful coexistence between states in practice, the Soviet Union is allegedly straying from revolutionary and internationalist principles . . . even go so far as to

claim that the Soviet Union is 'losing interest' in the peoples' liberation movement and reducing its aid to the movement.[36]

Party leaders and the military vigorously reject the above implication asserting that 'limitation of strategic weapons does not eliminate the danger of war' and that 'it would be utopian to assume that peaceful coexistence between countries with different social systems could at once rule out armed clashes . . . that is why all this talk about an end of the "era of wars" and the arrival of an "era of universal peace" is premature and dangerous.'[37]

In rejecting the universal, peaceful and stabilizing 'linkage' implications of détente and 'peaceful coexistence', the military emphasizes the expansionistic thrust of Soviet foreign and military policies: 'There has been and is no revolutionary movement or action by the peoples' masses for national or social liberation that has not received effective aid from the Party of Lenin and the country of October.'[38] In the present era, which is characterized by a strengthening of the positions of socialism and by sharp antagonism between the two social systems, a deepening of the external functions of the Soviet Armed Forces has logically taken place.'[39] The military is seen also as 'a powerful force inhibiting imperialist expansion and export of counterrevolution' and therefore this 'intensification of the international task of the Soviet Armed Forces also objectively conditions the need for their further strengthening. This situation requires unceasing attention to the problem of Soviet military development.'[40]

The evidence, even in the stilted party jargon of the *agitprop*, is persuasive enough: the vital political, ideological, and defense interests of the party and the Soviet government depend on the might of the armed forces. Despite détente, despite arms control, the struggle against imperialism will go on and the Soviets are in the vanguard of that struggle. Translated into everyday language, that means searching for targets of opportunity in the Third World, offering military assistance, seeking some kind of foothold in the process, and then trying to expand Soviet presence and influence in these vital regions. Since the strategic deterrence relationship effectively stabilized East–West relationships, and since the Soviets seek to retain good relations with other industrialized countries for the time being, the old East–West confrontation is being transferred into the Third World, crossing and merging with the newer North–South conflicts.

The Soviet military has in recent years become involved in various countries in the strategically important regions of the Middle East and Africa, from Angola to Mozambique, from Ethiopia to Yemen, from Afghanistan to Iraq. Soviet naval ships roam the oceans of the globe, while their submarines perform deterrence functions and other missions beneath. Soviet generals train the armies and the military technicians of these countries and Soviet marshals negotiate with the political leaders in the name of the Politburo.

Soviet party leaders appear to be firmly committed to a policy of military and political penetration and expansion into the Third World. The most effective instrument for such a new imperial policy is the military. The current party leadership and the marshals and generals are in this together.

The military expansionist policy harbors certain profound risks and dangers; the possibility of superpower confrontation is not remote; getting bogged down in some remote military quagmire is plausible; becoming dragged into undesirable and unprofitable conflict by some client or proxy is not unlikely; risking costly failure is possible. And, in the meantime, all this revolutionary warring costs large amounts of money and material with the risk of high future losses of many Soviet lives. As long as the party retains a solid political base at home and maintains control, there seems to be little to worry about. However, should the domestic political base erode, or should protracted external involvement reduce domestic and alliance performance capabilities, the party leaders would face tough choices and the possibility of trouble. The fundamental problem of leadership in a hegemonial system is that charismatic 'feats' must be performed (or engineered by controlled media), or the institutions and the people must be terrorized into submission. The post-Stalinist party leadership has abjured the massive use of terror, they need, therefore, to 'perform', to deliver to appease the demands of the bureaucracies and the people, or face the consequences.[41] The current party line of 'more bread, more circuses and more legions' cannot last forever. Sooner or later the leaders will have to make some hard choices.

(c)   Problems of Hegemonial Maintenance: Succession and the Military

In his study of civil–military relations in several political systems, Michael Howard observed that 'in States where no orderly transition of power and obedience had yet been established . . . military force is the final and sometimes only arbiter in government.'[42] In the Soviet case, problems of transition of power in the party and the state represent a key source of instability and institutional tensions that contributes to the erosion of the party's legitimacy and authority within the state.

A change of leadership in the Soviet Union is not a process governed either by tradition or established rules. No Soviet party leader has ever voluntarily relinquished his powers, and no provisions exist for the transfer of authority should the incumbent die or be removed as a result of disability or political coercion. This serves to explain why Lenin's infirmity and death, Trotsky's forced removal, and Stalin's death proved to be such critical events. A grave leadership crisis can also be expected to arise from an intra-party coup resulting from realignments of political relationships and loyalties among representatives of those institutions that carry the main political weight in the state. The former leader then finds himself with a *fait accompli* engineered by his opponents, to which he has no choice but to submit. This was the case, though to varying degrees, in the ousters of both Malenkov and Khrushchev.

There is, however, a basic difference in the leadership changes since the death of Stalin: several party leaders competed for the top position thus enabling an institution outside the party-apparat to serve as an arbiter and adjudicator of the leadership competition. That institution is the military, or more specifically, the top leadership of the armed forces. This involvement of the military in the heretofore sacrosanct internal affairs of the party has fundamentally affected the relations between the party and the military. The mystique and engineered charisma of the party leader was destroyed and rather shabby personalized politicking replaced it. The scramble for the military's support and the subsequent need to reward the military for that support, has undoubtedly impressed the marshals and generals in the post-Stalinist state. Although the consequences of that politicized role of the military have not been fully understood, there is little doubt that party leaders will continue to pay careful attention to the military's basic interests and preferences lest they ignore them at their own peril. The Malenkov and Khrushchev episodes are instructive cases in point.[43]

After the death of Stalin, the complex political power system, formerly held together by the dictator as if by a linchpin, became factionalized. Several men with diverse sources of political power entered into a tense, unstable coalition which from the start promised to be short-lived. The spokesmen of three politically powerful institutions – the party apparat, the governmental bureaucracies, and the security organs – maneuvred for position in the ensuing power struggles in the party. Since there was no precedent or procedural mechanism for an intra-party resolution of this political crisis, the military assumed, or was invited to assume, the role of arbiter in the resolution of the grave crisis. Since the security organs under Beria represented a threat to all three institutions (party, government, military) the military arranged to have him arrested, tried in a military tribunal, and executed.

In the subsequent power struggle between the two remaining claimants to Stalin's power mantle, the military again played a vital role. Having little experience with party politics (since Stalin kept them tightly controlled and subordinated), and since neither Malenkov nor Khrushchev had any special connections with the military, it was at first difficult for the marshals and generals to decide which was worthy of their support. However, that ambivalence was quickly resolved once the military made known their institutional preferences and interests, whereupon one of the contenders, Khrushchev, quickly adjusted his public 'platform' and avowed political programs to coincide with those of the military. After that, Malenkov's fate was sealed. Ironically, a decade later, Khrushchev was to suffer the same fate that he had inflicted on Malenkov: having alienated the military and other powerful institutions, Khrushchev was easily ousted from power in 1964 without any fuss or resistance.[44]

It is instructive to briefly review the political maturation of the Soviet military, their initially tentative and timid steps into the political arena, and the subsequent growth of their institutional strength and mounting demands upon the party.

(i) *Military Demands*

In offering their support to a challenger or victor in the two recent power struggles in the party, the military followed a readily perceivable pattern: a direct and indirect declaration of its interests and of demands from the party, followed by vigorous support of the victorious faction. The military's interests and demands are threefold:

(1) *Resource Primacy.* The military seeks assurance that their needs of technology, weapons and associated capabilities will receive a highest priority in the nationally planned economy, assuring a steady flow of such resources into the military establishment. This demand is usually contained in the code words 'heavy industry' which was once spelled out by Marshal Zhukov: 'Above all, the major achievements of heavy industry have permitted us to rearm our army, air forces and navy with first class military material.'[45] Thus, both in the post-Stalinist succession crisis and in the post-Khrushchevite succession period the military loudly proclaimed its 'heavy industry' priorities: Malenkov rejected it in 1953–4, while Khrushchev loudly proclaimed it.

Malenkov stated his views in August 1953, when he stressed the need to assign higher priority to consumer needs and a lower priority to the heavy industrial/defense-oriented sectors of the economy:

> Our main task . . . ensuring the further improvement of the material well-being of the workers, collective farmers, intelligentsia, all the Soviet people . . . to increase significantly the investment of resources in the program for the production of consumer goods.
>
> On the basis of the progress we have already made in the development of heavy industry, we have all the necessary conditions to bring about a sharp rise in the production of consumer goods.[46]

Clearly this was not what the military wanted to hear. And indeed their response came quickly and from various sources, including the authoritative and classified organ of the General Staff: 'Heavy industry is the foundation of foundations of our socialist economy' and 'without heavy industry it is not possible to . . . further the defense capabilities of the Soviet state'[47] as well as the other sectors of the economy.

Several weeks later Khrushchev jumped on the military's bandwagon and thundered that 'the main thing is the further development of heavy industry'[48] thus ensuring the marshals' support in the coming confrontation with Malenkov.

(2) *Mission Rationale.* The military clearly prefers a set of foreign and defense policies which assign a high role to the defense sector by conveying a sense of threat-expectation from outside. This need for 'international tension' is again reflected in the post-Stalinist power struggles, with predictable results. Malenkov pushed for a relaxation of tensions, for a détente with the West, arguing that nuclear war would be suicidal, since there would be no victors or survivors. Khrushchev sharply rejected this at the time, pushing hard for a tough, blustering, and uncompromising strategic and political doctrine which rejected détente and peaceful coexistence proposals and spoke instead of final victory and destruction of the bloodied capitalists.[49]

(3) *Payoffs and Concessions.* Once Khrushchev got rid of Malenkov in February 1955, the military was accorded a number of highly desired and awaited concessions: long postponed promotions to the highest ranks, rehabilitation of purged military heroes, rewriting of history so as to assign the military a heroic and vital role as defender of the country; a number of military officers were promoted to the Central Committee and other bodies of the party; the political organs in the military were curtailed and their representation in the party bodies was reduced; and Marshal Zhukov, the most popular military leader and war hero, was freed from his Stalin-consigned obscurity and steadily promoted until he was Minister of Defense and full member of the sacrosanct Politburo.

The military was asked by Khrushchev to bail him out on several other occasions: during the anti-party plot episode in 1957, Khrushchev's position was, in effect, saved by the military's swift actions and full support. The military also gave Khrushchev strong support in the developing Sino-Soviet crisis and in the Berlin crisis.

However, once Khrushchev was securely in power, having removed or outlived his main challengers in the party, he turned against the military in his efforts to curb their excessive demands for resources and for corporate autonomy. Having frustrated, alienated and disappointed his erstwhile supporters in his struggles against Malenkov, Khrushchev effectively became politically isolated, enabling his enemies and rivals in the party to arrange for his ouster in 1964.

Between 1959 and the time of his ouster Khrushchev challenged the three main military demands. First, he proposed to reduce the military manpower by about one-third; secondly, he actively pursued ways to stabilize relations with the West on the basis of peaceful coexistence and détente, particularly after the Cuban missile crisis fiasco; thirdly, he constantly harangued the military about their wasteful and excessive uses of resources.[50]

In the Khrushchev succession episode, the military still played their supportive arbiter role: but in a much more muted and less public fashion. Predictably, the military leaders were expected to denigrate, and thus effectively destroy, the predecessor's political and party record, his prestige and achievements, thus both justifying his ouster and freeing the new leadership from any associations, commitments or obligations of the ousted Khrushchev. The military was rewarded with a reversal of Khrushchev's reductions in the defense sector and with the launching of a massive arms program that was to eventually match, and in part eclipse, that of the USA. Military leaders were also rewarded with important political roles as heads of important foreign missions, as spokesmen for the party leader in client states, and as dominant members on international negotiating missions that involved arms control and related issues.[51]

The major difference in the two succession episodes, as far as the military's role is concerned, is the fact that after Stalin's death there were no precedents, no rules of the game, for the establishment of a viable coalition of bureaucratic hierarchs in a collective leadership mode. Thus, each contender had to press hard against his opponents and seek allies, while doing much of this political linen-washing in public. The decade of post-Stalinism, the diminution of the security organs as a potential threat to all, and the semi-institutionalization of collective leadership have negated the need for public histrionics. The deal to oust Khrushchev was made *in camera;* the new coalition was agreed upon and the only thing left was to let the incumbent know that he was through.

What does the party leader obtain as his quid pro quo from his military supporters? Military support in the power struggle during the succession episode; a loyal military elite that he can rely on in the future; the acceptance of institutional 'fealty', that is, the party leader's retention of authority to appoint, promote and remove military personnel; the right to define the general and military-specific goals, priorities, and directions for state policy; and acceptance within the military establishment of the party's controlling, educational, and propaganda instruments.

(ii)   *Consequences of Military 'Succession Management'*
The near three-decades-long period of post-Stalinist party–military politics in the Soviet Union suggests that the two institutions have become thoroughly interdependent and that they interpenetrate each other to a remarkable extent. The military has come to the party leader's support on a number of occasions, aiding him in intra-party struggles and in conflicts with other Communist challengers from abroad. The military has also assumed a number of key roles and positions within the system, including those of:

> The main vehicle and supporter of the ever-expanding Soviet external military and political commitments to clients and proxies in Africa, the Middle East and Asia.
> The key stabilizing factor in the restless alliance system in East Europe, where in the final analysis only the military restores order, punishes opponents and serves as the policeman on the beat.
> The main bulwark against the pressures and demands from the former Chinese ally.
> The educator, national integrator and disciplined Spartan model for the restless and diverse young and old from the various geographic, linguistic, national, religious and class-based sectors of society.

The logic of the post-totalitarian rule, and the imperial expansion of the Soviet state, have endowed the military with vital, indispensable tasks and roles. As the party leadership becomes more dependent upon the military for internal, alliance, and external policy purposes, and as the military shows itself to be a loyal, conservative, and stable force within the state, the party becomes, in a sense, the captive of the military: the party leadership's insistence on a protracted internal status quo and avoidance of hard choices and risky decisions, forces them to support, mollify, and rely on the military. There is no alternative institution to perform these varied tasks in a responsible and loyal way. The party and the military have become mutual captives: they need one another and they cannot let go for there are no viable alternatives. Only a systemic change, or a radical regime change, might break that interdependence.

(4) SCENARIO FOR MILITARY INTERVENTION

The Russian Marxist philosopher Berdyaev maintained that 'Bolshevism entered into Russian life as a power which was militarized to the highest degree, but the old Russian state also had always been militarized.'[52] There is nothing startling about the military antecedents and militarized mobilizational methods of the Communist Party of the Soviet Union. The concept of a hegemonial political system hinges on this military content of modern communism, and people as diverse as Max Weber,[53] Werner Sombart,[54] and Frederich Engels have commented on it and found it persuasive.

The ruling Communist parties, however, invariably reject this proposition and assert that the socialist military was born in the womb of revolution. But we do not need to be distracted by these shrill proclamations: the communist states and their ruling parties ride on the backs of their soldiers, not on the revolutionary proletarian masses. The soldiers obtain revolutionary victory and they later protect it; they subsequently assist in the integration of society and in the consolidation of the party's hegemony; they protect the party and state from external aggression and they also serve as the vanguard and vehicle for the export of quasi-revolutions into the Third World. The question here, however, is under what sorts of circumstances might the military perceive the party leadership as becoming an impediment to the proper pursuit of the ideological, political, and institutional objectives of the system? How might the military go about 'intervening' in the internal hierarchy of authority and in the delicate balance of institutional coalitions that govern the state? Although very little has been written on this subject, we ought to try 'thinking about the unthinkable,' the party's potential loss of hegemony and the military's assumption of a leading role in the state.

There seems to be an agreement among the few Western writers on the subject regarding the necessary conditions for military intervention: some sort of internal or external crisis of duration. One analyst suggests that:

> The range of military participation could be expected to expand more rapidly . . . under two sets of particularly propitious circumstances . . . entanglement in war, especially a prolonged conflict . . . the second and more probable scenario would involve a leadership succession crisis or factional struggle in which one or more parties would appeal to the military leaders for support.[55]

Another necessary condition would be some sort of drastic internal disintegration of the political system.

A stalemated party leadership and the decaying of ideology and legitimacy are seen by another analyst as a precondition for change, and in his scenario of four alternative outcomes, two involve some kind of military coup or involvement:

> First, a strong leader might emerge – either through a military coup, or more likely, through consolidation of power by the General Secretary –

and initiate drastic political action. Second, one might see the emergence of a strong leader who would base his policy almost entirely on the narrow interests of the military/heavy industrial elite.[56]

Another student of military affairs considers the case of a state in which the traditional patterns of social cohesion have broken down and have not been replaced by new patterns. He maintains that only a group separated from society can destroy such a syndrome of social and economic disintegration, and 'If the ruling civilians lack political experience and symbols of authority, military personnel may be able to manipulate the symbols of their institutions to rule and introduce some social cohesiveness.'[57]

The central premise of this chapter has been that patterns of political, institutional and social interaction in the Soviet Union since the death of Stalin (that is, post-totalitarian) tend toward a progressive loss of revolutionary elan and political dynamism of the party, an erosion of the sources and claims to legitimacy by the party hierarchs, a progressive weakening of the party's political and institutional maintenance and performance capabilities, coupled with rising demands from various sectors in society. We also indicated that the party's difficulties in retaining its hegemonial powers are becoming complicated by the expanding external commitments of the state, and the restiveness of allies and clients. The Soviet leaders' response to these mounting challenges and complications has been to avoid hard and risky decisions, to avoid confrontations with challengers, and to seek a status quo.

It is postulated here that this state of affairs cannot endure for very long, since the 'logic of rule' provides 'the seeds of its own destruction.' In the event of a grave, protracted crisis that would necessitate a massive and radical internal mobilization of resources and hard decisions entailing great risks, this party leadership which operates by means of an unstable coalition of bureaucracies, would not be able to cope, and the only reliable, loyal and effective institution that would seem able and willing to take over would be the military.

Since the Soviet military has had an unblemished record of non-intervention in the politics of the state – even when frontally challenged and brutally assaulted, and when the very same political authorities were vulnerable and pathetically dependent upon the military – can one assume that the military would cross that threshold and assume power alongside or above the party? This is a hard question which most Soviet analysts tend to avoid. And when confronted with the problem, they tend to be very tentative and ambiguous. Timothy Colton states that while 'there is no doubt that the military possesses in the long run the capacity for disrupting stability and for taking advantage of unstable conditions,' he sees that the 'most probable course is for military influence to increase incrementally at civilian initiative, widening their current beachheads in issue areas such as secondary education, construction, and civil defense.'[58] This does not help much since the military has already gone beyond such modest 'incrementalisms' and even beyond succession crisis involvements at the invitation of party leaders.

(a)   Soviet Military in Politics

The hegemonial political system has been described elsewhere[59] as a quasi-military and militant political system whose internal bureaucratic structures, hierarchical authority, centralized mobilizational style, controlled-violence mode, high threat expectation, and demands for unquestioned obedience all suggest similarities with military organizations. It was also suggested that although the ethos of the system tends to be nonmilitary or even anti-military, nevertheless, the prevailing operative values and norms tend to derive from the military. In other words, though the party borrows from the military its ethos, styles, rituals and methods, it also seeks to suppress the military's quest for institutional and corporate identity, and seeks instead to subordinate and dominate it, a brutal form of institutional *Gleichschaltung*.

Yet that privileged but abused and patronized institution, the military, remains year after year a most loyal, reliable, supportive entity, faithfully doing the party's bidding and demanding merely the tools and professional freedom to perform at highest efficiency. This ambivalent relationship between the hegemonial party and its military remains opaque to most Western analysts. One thing, however, is clear: the ability both to develop and strengthen the military, and to control it, depends upon a firm, efficient, and dynamic leadership in the party. Once that leadership shows signs of weakness, indecisiveness, and loss of will and elan, the military's subordinate role changes. The Soviet officer corps' peculiar love–hate attitude toward Stalin reflects these ambivalences of the military in its relations with the party leaders.

The party and the military in the Soviet Union have grown ever more interdependent over the years, with the party using the military and its style, and the military taking advantage of the party's growing reliance upon them. This once dominant/subordinate relationship has gradually changed into one of near equals. As the party's leadership and authority erodes, the military proportionately gains. However, their relationship is not of the zero-sum game, pure conflict variety; indeed, the military does need the party to provide the steady flow of technology, weaponry, manpower, ideological rationale and legitimacy of its external and internal missions. Thus, in the event of a systemic shift, resulting in the party's loss of hegemonial authority, it is assumed here that the military would seek to fuse with the party to an even greater degree by assuming authoritative power positions without abolishing the facade of party hegemonial primacy.

The Soviet military has much at stake in the perpetuation of the Communist Party's authority within the state, since under the conditions of progressive interdependence and interpenetration of the two institutions, the military finds most, or all, of its interests satisfied. The bureaucratic coalition form of party leadership serves the military's interests admirably. Moreover, the military, as history has shown, has evolved from the earlier Trotsky and Tukhachevsky revolutionary periods, into an internally conservative, patriotic, loyal and nationalistic institution. Thus, unless the party leadership became incapacitated, collapsed, or failed through internal or external crisis or intra-party power struggles, the military would tend to stay out of politics. However, in the event of such a crisis situation, the military would be likely to assume power in order to protect the state and society and its own interests, to mobilize support and to maintain order and stability.

The officer corps is quite capable of assuming such roles. It is highly educated, with a specific emphasis on engineering, technological, and managerial training: 45 percent of the officers are engineers and technicians with higher degrees, with the proportion rising to 75 percent in the rocket forces. All commanders at brigade level and above, and 80 percent of those at regimental and lower levels, have higher degrees, that is, a BS equivalent or better. The Head of the MPA, General Epishev, boasts that the Soviet officer corps 'is made up of highly intellectual and militarily cultured people.'[60]

The officer corps, and the military in general, are a truly national institution, operating at various levels and in all parts of the country. Unlike the single-characteristic description of other armies, the Soviet military combines, in various degrees, all three roles and functions of the 'nation in arms', the 'military-and-civilian', and even to some degree those of the 'praetorian' armies. That is, the military serves the state as an instrument of foreign policy, it is at times employed in domestic politics, and it also performs general administrative functions.[61]

The military is also the carrier of historical and nationalistic traditions and memories, particularly memories of wars against dangerous foreign aggressors. The military evokes positive and supportive responses from among the populace in times of crisis.

The military is a nationwide institution that can be mobilized quickly by means of its excellent communications and transportation network and its strength can be focused and deployed in a rational and planned manner. The military also has a monopoly of violence and thus is capable of imposing order and stability and restraining factional and dissident groups that might wish to take advantage of the crisis at the center.

It is clear that the military has the capability to intervene in the politics of the party and government. If the military is clearly persuaded that a collapse of regime, a protracted crisis, or serious disintegration of government or society is in the offing, it would be able, and probably willing, to assume power in a transition mode. It is assumed here that the Soviet military would not wish to remain in the political arena in the long run, nor would it wish to formally abrogate the party's claims to hegemonial legitimacy and authority. Nevertheless, the hegemonial power of the party would become irrevocably changed, and we shall, therefore, consider the post-hegemonial role of the military.

(b) Post-Hegemonial Synthesis: Nationalism, Communism, Militarism

In his analysis of the nature of charismatic domination, Max Weber observed that 'all charisma, in every hour of its existence, finds itself on this road from a passionate life . . . to slow suffocation under the weight of material interests.'[62] In the subsequent 'routinization' of charisma, Weber maintains that:

> As soon as charismatic domination loses its passionate belief, which distinguishes it from the traditionalism of everyday life, and its purely personal basis, then a link with tradition becomes, not perhaps the only possibility, but certainly by far the most appropriate.[63]

And since 'pure' charismatic domination is highly unstable, it is at the crucial point of transition, when the question arises of succession to charismatic leadership or to one possessing claims to it, that 'charisma invariably turns on to the path of statute and tradition.'[64]

We postulate here that in a post-hegemonial Soviet system, the forces of tradition would primarily identify with the military, and those of institutionalized and routinized 'charisma' embodied in the Communist Party apparat would tend toward a closer interrelationship, in which the older *forms* of party legitimacy and hegemony would be retained, while the inner *content* would be filled by the military.

Weber was aware that although there is a consistent interrelationship between the forces of charisma and tradition they remain nevertheless 'at base hostile and alien to each other.' However, he also assumed that they were bound toward one another. If we accept the proposition here that the military is representative of the forces of tradition, then its inherently nationalistic and patriotic leanings on the one hand, and its strong antipathy to the spent, routinized, institutionalized 'charisma' of the apparat *clerici* make sense. Despite their mutual antipathies they both share a predisposition toward nationalistic leanings in disregard of the party's ideological strictures against it. Alfred Vagts and John Stuart Mill understood the logic of the adherence to national awareness and traditions as being 'deepest and strongest' among the military.[65]

Hans Kohn has observed that paradoxically 'nowhere is the emphasis on national sovereignty and its sanctity as strong as in Communist societies.'[66] This is paradoxical because Marxists–Leninists have consistently maintained that nationalism is a by-product of the modern capitalist bourgeois state, and they insist that class rather than nation is the proper basis for social differentiation.[67] Yet, Soviet party leaders from Lenin and Stalin to Brezhnev have found the appeals of nationalism to be a very powerful force and thus useful when manipulated by the party. During World War II, Stalin indulged in a veritable orgy of patriotic, historical and nationalistic imageries, which he manipulated by means of propaganda, because he clearly understood that soldiers were more likely to fight and risk their life for something they instinctively understood and could identify with rather than with some abstractions and stilted sociological formulae and ideological slogans of the Communist Party.

It is postulated here that in the event of a post-hegemonial military assumption of power in the Soviet Union, the officers would very likely seek wide comprehensive support and a legitimacy base within the country, and that they would therefore appeal to the sentiments and values of nationalism and patriotism, as well as to those of communism, and finally to the values and virtues of their own military institution. This synthesis of the three most powerful ideologies in the country would enable the military to more effectively mobilize all strata in society, appeal to the sentiments of sacrifice and bravery in times of great stress, and cross-cut through the divisions and boundaries of localism, regionalism, national separatism of the smaller republics, and of class and institutional diversities.

The appeals to communism would also make good sense since the Marxist–Leninist teachings provide the fundamental and sole formal body of ideas and norms for the system, and generations of citizens have lived with and internalized them. Moreover, without the retention of the communist ideology, the *raison* for the party's existence would be gone. And the hordes of party *apparatchiki* and governmental bureaucrats have no other frame of reference for their planning and rationalizing processes for the society.

The appeals to militarism, or more properly to military values and traditions, would tend to serve as a mobilizational instrument closely related to that of patriotism and nationalism, and would also help create a basis for legitimacy for the military's assumption of authority in the state. This close relationship between the military and the nation and the party was described by General Epishev: 'The Soviet Armed Forces are the favorite creation of the Soviet people and the Communist Party. The people and the Armed Forces of the Soviet Union are a single whole. Soviet soldiers are flesh and blood of their people.'[68]

The synthesis of nationalism, communism, and militarism would provide the necessary national base for a new form of government with a mixed legitimacy. The synthesis and its appeals would be likely to revitalize the stagnant Soviet system and provide the necessary momentum and sense of participation and involvement in an exciting experiment that would appeal to various sectors of the vast country and thus provide a better integrative mechanism than the past sterile formulations of the CPSU *apparatchiki*. In the longer run, such a post-hegemonial regime may engender forms of 'Jacobin nationalism' which in the past developed in times of war and rebellion and internal crisis and was marked by its reliance on 'force and militarism . . . characterized by missionary zeal and intolerance toward internal dissent.'[69] It may also tend toward 'integral nationalism' which tends to be militaristic and imperialistic.[70] Nationalism remains a potent force in Russia and 'in a world of rapid change and alienation, and nightmare not far beyond the horizon, nationalism can be a comforting thing.'[71]

A revitalized, mobilized, and integrated society under the joint leadership of the military and the party would create a formidable and purposeful juggernaut. Although a synthesis of nationalistic, Communist, and militaristic values and forces may seem in the long run to be a combustible and unstable mixture, nevertheless, they could be welded by a strong and popular leadership into a formidable political and military force: a far cry from the current leadership of old, tired, and routinized men who manage the vast Soviet system by committee and coalition methods.

Freed from the earlier strictures, domestic concerns, and constraints of the cautious, prudent and vulnerable party *clerici*, the now vitalized, internally cohesive, and domestically supported party–military fusion – these two groups of 'specialists in violence' – would be free to project their enormous power into the external environment of the Soviet state. It is probably difficult for us to recall that Stalin was a rather timid military planner, in the sense that he remained throughout most of his life in a defensive, protective and regionally delimited military strategic position, fearing, above all, the spectre of confrontation with the West; that Malenkov during his brief interregnum, abjured war, spoke of nuclear suicidal madness, and preached the doctrine of détente; that Khrushchev, despite his braggadocio, remained a peace-seeking and détente-seeking leader, hoping to curtail the terrible burden of the military establishment on the Soviet economy; and that Brezhnev and Kosygin have staked their political careers on détente, arms control, and stable deterrence, while at the same time building an enormous military juggernaut, seeking nuclear parity.

It is the military, sitting on top of a vast nuclear and conventional armory, restrained until recently by the party to occasional police actions in the fraternal states of its alliance, who are eager to burst out of these confines and try itself in the spurious glory of the battlefield. The abstract metaphors and paradigms of deterrence strategy are quite familiar to the generals and marshals of the Soviet military; however, the long-denied freedom to unfurl the banners and roll the tanks, fly the fighters and bombers, and sail the navies under flag into enemy waters and terri- tories, makes the peacetime officer corps restive. The grand, global vision of the military was expressed by Marshal Grechko, their Minister of Defense, who asserted that:

> At the present stage, the historic mission of the Soviet Armed Forces is not restricted to their function in defending our Motherland . . . but to support the national liberation struggle and resolutely resist imperialist aggression in whatever distant region of our planet it may appear.[72]

(5) SUMMARY AND CONCLUSIONS

This scenario of military 'intervention' in Soviet politics is premised in several developments having to do with the loss of the party's revolution- ary and organizational elan, and with its growing dependence upon the military for the execution of a variety of internal and external tasks. Our projections are rooted in the presently ongoing developments and in pos- tulated developments that are logically persuasive and empirically possible.

The Soviet military's intervention capability and probability have been generally disregarded and negated by Western analysts of the Soviet Union. To be sure, as long as Stalin dominated the system, there was little that any institution could do, except submit to the dictator's will. After his death, Soviet politics became a new game. Most Western analysts, however, remained mesmerized by the totalitarian paradigm and the party's propaganda, which simply denied the existence of the military as a separate institution with interest, capabilities, ideas and preferences. A kind of *Kadavergehorchsamkeit* projection was imposed on the Soviet military by Western analysts, depriving it of any life, ideas, or identity of its own. The party's frequent raging against transgressions in the military were disregarded in the West; the Zhukov affair was dismissed as a storm in the samovar; the thrust of military leaders into prominent positions of institutional and political authority was explained away. The fact that military organizations in other authoritarian or totalitarian systems had at various times troubled mightily their own leaders was also rationalized: the troubles of Mao with the Lin Piaos and with other marshals; the problems of Hitler with his generals and marshals; the problems of Mussolini with his generals and marshals.

Western scholarly research of complex foreign political systems has often suffered from what might be called paradigm-hubris, or in the vernacular, from ethnocentricity and cultural parochialism. The imposition of Western developmental models on a multiplicity of widely divergent nations and states in the Third World, and the ensuing failures and irrelevancies of such culture-biased constructs, are too well known to need retelling. The imposition of Western strategic deterrence paradigms upon non-Western governments and states is also sufficiently known not to need elaboration; however, the imposition of Western notions, models, and deductive theories of civil–military relations on to the communist states needs further telling. However, this is not the proper place for it.

The Soviet military is clearly capable of intervening in the affairs of the party and the government. The military refrained from intervention in the past, despite provocation and opportunity. We postulated here certain conditions that would motivate the military to intervene and then seek to broaden the political and participatory base of such a crisis-born regime. It is assumed here that such a military-dominated coalition in the Soviet Union would seek to combine the three central national and systemic values in a post-hegemonial synthesis, thus obtaining legitimacy and mobilizational responsiveness from the diverse sectors of society.

It was postulated in this chapter that if the patterns of ideological stagnation, bureaucratic immobilism, and institutional petrification continue, and the expanding costly and risky external military and political commitments of the government are maintained and increased, and the erosive internal corollaries intensified – that under such circumstances the party leadership will find itself progressively more dependent upon the military. That dependence would entail reliance on their efficient maintenance of the party's hegemonial position at home, and of Soviet influence within their alliances, and on their efficient conduct of foreign, economic, and military policies. It is also assumed that the military would, under propitious circumstances, assume the leading political role in the party and state. Such circumstances are assumed to involve a systemic crisis of legitimacy, succession, internal disruptions, or external threat. Once the party leadership would show itself to be incapable of coping with the critical situation, the military would then step in and assume roles as: the protector of the CPSU's waning legitimacy; the integrator of the disparate and diversified socio-political structures, forces, and movements at home and in the bloc; the quasi-revolutionary agent of the party's interests in the Third World; and the traditional defender of the homeland.

Schematically, such a postulated change in party–military institutional relations may be depicted as a fourth phase of a historical evolutionary pattern (see Table 5.1).[73]

Table 5.1

Soviet Political System	Party–Military Institutional Relations	Military's Political Role vis-à-vis CPSU	Systemic Priorities	Soviet Military Power vis-à-vis USA
Stalinist (Totalitarian)	Military Dependence	Subordination	Integration	Vulnerable
Khrushchev (Post-Totalitarian)	Institutional Interdependence	Cooptation	Transformation	Inferior
Brezhnev (Collective Leadership Institutionalized)	Political and Institutional Interdependence	Accommodation	Expansion	Equal
Post-Hegemonial	Political Interdependence/ Institutional Independence	Participation/ Domination	Expansion/ Contraction	Equal/ Superior

NOTES

1 In Samuel Huntington (ed.), *Changing Patterns of Military Politics* (Glencoe, Ill.: The Free Press, 1962).
2 See fn. 1, in my chapter on 'Toward a theory of civil–military relations in Communist (hegemonial) systems', (Chapter 10, below).
3 See Herbert Goldhammer, *Soviet Military Management at Troop Level,* ch. 3: 'A nation in arms,' R-1513-PR, May 1974, (Santa Monica, Calif.: RAND Corporation).
4 Cited in *The Soviet Military and the Communist Party* (Princeton, NJ: Princeton University Press, 1967), p. xviii.
5 ibid.
6 William E. Odom, 'The "militarization" of Soviet society,' *Problems of Communism* (September–October, 1976).
7 US Congress, Joint Economic Committee, *Allocation of Resources in the Soviet Union and China – 1979, Hearings before the Subcommittee on Priorities and Economy in Government,* 96th Congress, 1st Session (1979).
8 ibid.
9 David Holloway, 'Soviet Military R&D: Managing the Research-Production Cycle,' in John R. Thomas and Ursula M. Kruse-Vaucienne (eds) *Soviet Science and Technology* (Washington, DC: National Science Foundation, 1977).
10 ibid, p. 204.
11 Odom, op. cit.
12 In *Pravda* (15 December 1963).
13 *Pravda* (12 July 1965).

14   In *Pravda* (7 November 1964).
15   In *Krasnaia Zvezda* (4 February 1965).
16   See Harriet Fast Scott and William F. Scott, *The Armed Forces of the USSR*, ch. 4: 'The Soviet High Command,' (Boulder, Colo.: Westview Press, 1979).
17   Allen Kassof, 'The administered society: totalitarianism without terror,' *World Politics*, (July 1964), pp. 558–75.
18   T. H. Rigby 'Traditional, market, and organizational societies and the USSR,' ibid., pp. 539–57.
19   Zbigniew Brzezinski and Samuel P. Huntington, *Political Power USA/USSR* (New York: Viking Press, 1964).
20   Gordon Skilling and Franklyn Griffiths, (eds) *Interest Groups in Soviet Politics* (Princeton, NJ: Princeton University Press, 1971).
21   Jerry F. Hough, *The Soviet Union and Social Science Theory* (Cambridge, Mass.: Harvard University Press, 1977), 'Introduction' and ch. 1.
22   Z. Brzezinski, 'The Soviet political system: transformation or degeneration,' *Problems of Communism* (January–February, 1966).
23   Jerry F. Hough, 'The Soviet system: petrification or pluralism?', *Problems of Communism* (March–April, 1972).
24   Max Weber, *Selections in Translation*, ed. W. G. Runciman (Cambridge, Mass.: Cambridge University Press, 1978), p. 245.
25   ibid., p. 246.
26   ibid., p. 247.
27   Hough, *The Soviet Union and Social Science Theory*, p. 28.
28   ibid., p. 29.
29   ibid.
30   ibid., p. 7. See also chapter on 'Party saturation' detailing the statistics of growth of party membership by age, education, sex, etc.
31   ibid., p. 6. See also chapter on 'The bureaucratic model and the nature of the Soviet system' for a perceptive analysis of the bureaucratization of the Soviet system, on the evolvement of a 'government by clerks' (Brzezinski) and on the intractable innovation-resistant system of management of the government and economy.
32   Scott and Scott, op. cit., ch. 9: 'the Soviet military–industrial complex and defense costs,' contains a thorough discussion of the subject.
33   V.I. Lenin, 'Speech delivered at a meeting on activists of the Moscow Party organization of the RCI (b), December 6, 1920', cited in Foy D. Kohler *et al.*, (eds), *From Cold War to Peaceful Coexistence*, (Miami: Center for Advanced International Studies, 1973).
34   *Kommunist*, no. 9 (June 1972), 'Editorial.'
35   Milovan Djilas, 'The new class,' in A. P. Mendel (ed.), *Essential Works of Marxism* (New York: Bantam Books, Matrix edn, 1965), p. 332.
36   CPSU Central Committee, Theses of December 1969, cited in Kohler *et al.* (eds), op. cit., p. 72; also V. Korionov, 'The socialist policy of peace,' *Pravda* (13 July 1972).
37   ibid.
38   CPSU Central Committee, Theses for Lenin's Birth Centennary, *Pravda* (23 December 1969).
39   General A. A. Epishev, 'The historical mission of the socialist state army,' *Kommunist*, no. 7 (May 1972).
40   *Kommunist Vooruzhennykh Sil*, no. 16 (August 1972), cited in Kohler *et al.* (eds), op. cit. p. 234.
41   The victors' swift retribution and condemnation of the loser is reflected in this scathing authoritative editorial in *Pravda*, only a few days after Khrushchev's ouster: 'The Party of Lenin is an enemy of subjectivism and inertia in communist construction. Wild planning, premature and hasty conclusions, hasty and realistic decisions and actions, boasting and blather . . . are alien to it.' *Pravda* (17 October 1964).
42   Michael Howard, *Soldiers and Governments: Nine Studies in Civil–Military Relations* (London: Eyre & Spottiswoode, 1957), 'Introduction.'
43   For descriptions of the politics of the Stalinist successions, see Robert Conquest, *Power and Policy in the USSR* (New York: St Martins Press, 1961); Lazar Pistrak, *The Grand Tactician; Khrushchev's Rise to Power* (New York: Praeger, 1961); Myron Rush, *The Rise of Khrushchev* (Washington: Public Affairs Press, 1958). The ouster of

Khrushchev has been examined by many Western analysts including: P. B. Reddaway, 'The fall of Khrushchev,' *Survey*, no. 56 (July 1965); the November 1964 (11) issue of *Osteuropa*, containing articles on the theme 'Nach Chruschtschow,' by Richard Lowenthal, David Burg, and Herman Achminow; also a series of contributions on the theme of 'The coup and after' by Merle Fainsod, Robert Conquest, and Adam Ulam in the January–February and May–June issues of *Problems of Communism* (1965).

44 The reasons for his 'resignation' were given as 'advanced age and deterioration in the state of his health,' *Pravda* (16 October 1964).

45 *Pravda* (9 August 1953).

46 Marshal Zhukov, 'Order of the Day,' (23 February 1955); see also speeches by top military leaders forcefully reiterating the 'heavy industry primacy' theme: Marshal I. S. Konev ('. . . the general line of the party in economic sphere that foresees the development of heavy industry by every conceivable means, will be firmly continued,' in *Pravda* 23 February 1955, about a week before the decisive meeting of the Central Committee and its announcement of the Malenkov 'resignation' asserted that 'Heavy industry – the foundation of the might of the Soviet state.'

47 *Voennaia Mysl'*, no. 10 (October 1953), p. 8.

48 In *Pravda* (28 December 1954).

49 Malenkov maintained in 1954 that 'a thermonuclear war would result in a new world slaughter' and 'would mean the destruction of world civilization,' in *Pravda* (13 March 1954); also, that 'the danger of war was to a great extent lessened' due to the sufficiency of various weapons capable of 'checking the aggressors,' in *Izvestiia*, (12 March 1954). Soon after Malenkov's ouster, the party's main theoretical journal formally asserted: 'No matter how severe the consequences of atomic war, they cannot be identified with the fall of world civilizations,' *Kommunist*, no. 4 (April 1955), pp. 16–17.

50 In *Pravda* (26 April 1963).

51 See Scott and Scott, op. cit., ch. 4: 'The Soviet High Command' for some descriptions of prominent military leaders in the post-Khrushchev period. Some, like Marshals Ogarkov, Zakharov, had been entrusted by the party with vital, and politically sensitive missions on SALT delegations and Soviet–Egyptian joint military and political missions.

52 In *The Origins of Russian Communism* (Ann Arbor, Mich.: University of Michigan Press, 1960), p. 120, cited in Odom, op. cit., p. 35.

53 Weber, op. cit., pp. 234–5; in chapters on 'Origins of industrial capitalism,' 'The development of bureaucracy,' *passim*.

54 Werner Sombart, *Krieg und Kapitalismus* (1913); see also Martin Berger, *Engels, Armies, and Revolution* (Hamden, Conn.: Archon Books, 1977).

55 Timothy J. Colton, *Commissars, Commanders and Civil Authority* (Cambridge, Mass.: Harvard University Press, 1979), p. 287.

56 Hough, *The Soviet Union and Social Science Theory*, p. 43. The other two alternatives (leadership stalemate and classical pluralism) appear to be not very promising or significant.

57 Amos Perlmutter, *The Military and Politics in Modern Times* (New Haven, Conn.: Yale University Press, 1977), p. 96.

58 Colton, op. cit., pp. 285, 286.

59 See Chapter 10, below, on 'Theory of civil–military relations in Communist (hegemonial) systems.'

60 General of the Army A. A. Epishev, *Some Aspects of Party–Political Work in the Soviet Armed Forces*, (Moscow: Progress Publishers, 1975), p. 87.

61 David Rapoport, 'A comparative theory of military and political types,' in Samuel P. Huntington (ed.), *Changing Patterns of Military Politics*, (Glencoe, Ill.: The Free Press, 1962).

62 Weber, op. cit., p. 235.

63 ibid., p. 237.

64 ibid., p. 238.

65 Alfred Vagts, *A History of Militarism* (London: Allen & Unwin, 1938), p. 31; also Colton, op. cit., p. 258.

66 Hans Kohn, 'A new look at nationalism,' in Louis L. Snyder (ed.), *The Dynamics of Nationalism* (New York: Van Nostrand, 1964), p. 365.

67 Oscar Janowsky, 'Bolshevism and nationalism,' in ibid., pp. 222–3.

68 Epishev, op. cit.

69   Carlton J. H. Hayes, 'The major types of nationalism,' in Snyder (ed.), op. cit., pp. 51–2.
70   ibid.
71   ibid.
72   cited in Scott and Scott, op. cit., p. 57.
73   See chapter 10, below, on 'Theory of civil–military relations in Communist (hegemonial) systems.'

6 The Military as a Political Actor in China

ELLIS JOFFE

Any attempt to discuss the Chinese military as a political actor has to begin with the premise that the actor has changed his role several times. Throughout the history of the People's Republic of China, the People's Liberation Army (PLA) has occupied a pivotal position in the Chinese political system. In the decade that preceded Mao's death in 1976, and in the period of transition to the post-Mao era, the role of the PLA was central and crucial, at times towering in importance over all other political institutions. This role, however, has not been uniform but has undergone sweeping shifts.

After a decade of limited involvement in politics during the 1950s, the army started to intrude, in a restricted and gradual fashion, into the political process in the early 1960s. This intrusion was followed by deepening political involvement which culminated in large-scale inter-vention and a takeover of civil functions by the military in the closing stages of the Cultural Revolution at the end of the decade. The political domination of the army then triggered a reaction which resulted in a gradual disengagement of the military from politics. But the process of disengagement was partial, and the military continued to be involved in the political conflicts that dominated the Chinese scene in the twilight years of the Maoist era. When a succession struggle broke out shortly after Mao's death, the army intervened again, and although its inter-vention was limited by the circumstances of the struggle, it was decisive in determining the outcome, and gave the army new power in the post-Mao political system. However, neither this system nor the army's place in it can be said to have solidified into an enduring mold.

In view of this, the political role of the Chinese military cannot be examined from the vantage point of a fixed model, for such a model has simply not emerged until now. An assessment of this role, therefore, has to look at the whole process of military involvement in political affairs. A brief overview of this process is the purpose of the present chapter.

THE ARMY IN THE FIRST DECADE

For more than a decade after the establishment of the People's Republic of China in 1949, the involvement of the military in politics was limited – limited to the role prescribed for it by the party. To be sure, this role went far beyond the performance of purely military functions.[1] During this period the army carried out a wide variety of nonmilitary tasks, which derived from its revolutionary legacy and from current needs, and which added a unique dimension to the role of the military. Its nonmilitary activities expanded or contracted in line with the direction of the party leadership and at no time did the military make a move to extend these activities on its own nor did it display any sign of resorting to force for the advancement of its institutional interests. The role of the PLA during this decade was thus qualitatively different from the role it came to play increasingly from the mid-1960s, and an appreciation of this difference is essential to an understanding of the army's changing political involvement. The difference stemmed from both the reasons for, and the nature of, the army's nonmilitary activities.

When the Chinese Communist forces swept over the mainland in the final phases of the civil war, the political organs of the new regime were initially established and consolidated in the conquered areas by the PLA units which had moved into those areas. This process began as soon as a town or county were taken over. One of the first tasks of the military commander was to set up a Military Control Committee as the supreme administrative organ. The chairman of the Military Control Committee, who usually also held the post of mayor in the cities and towns, was almost always the senior officer of the military unit. The Military Control Committee set up the local 'people's government' and organized 'takeover committees' which assumed control of government offices, major utilities, communications, schools, and military installations. At the end of 1949, the country was divided into six Great Administrative Areas, each with its own regional government organization modeled on the pattern of the central government. This setup was dictated by the unevenness of takeover, the diversity of the country, and the inability of the central government to exercise direct control effectively immediately after its establishment. The four regions which were the last to come under Communist control were each garrisoned by the Field Army that had moved into the area. The highest organ of government in these regions was the Military–Administrative Committee, which was dominated by military personnel. Until 1954, when the abolition of these committees completed the transfer of power to civilian institutions, local government in large parts of China was controlled by the military.[2]

In addition to its involvement in local administration, the army also took part in other nonmilitary activities. During the early 1950s, its contribution to production was largely limited to helping civilians in times of emergency, such as during floods or periods of drought, although in Sinkiang the military spearheaded the development of industry, agriculture, and mining. The army also took an active part in carrying out land reform. In the second part of the decade, the PLA's nonmilitary activities increased considerably, reaching a high point during the Great Leap Forward, when in 1958 the troops reportedly contributed some 59 million manpower days to industrial and agricultural production.[3]

The involvement of the military in political and civil affairs during the early years differed in several key respects from the role which it assumed increasingly from the mid-1960s. First, the military in the early period performed nonmilitary tasks as an arm of a unified leadership in Peking, whereas in the later period the army entered the political arena as a partisan participant in a power struggle that split the leadership. Secondly, because the leadership was unified during the early period, the involvement of the military in political tasks did not create rifts within the army, as it did in later years. Thirdly, the army in the initial years assumed political and administrative functions under the direction of the party because the party had not yet developed the necessary mechanisms for carrying out these functions, whereas at the end of the second decade the military took over such tasks not to supplement the party organs but as a substitute for these organs, which were dismantled during the Cultural Revolution. Fourthly, in the early period there was little role-differentiation between the top civilian and military leaders, whereas by the mid-1960s functional specialization and professionalism had developed to a point where civilian and military leaders were members of distinct and frequently competing bureaucratic hierarchies. To sum up, in contrast to the situation that developed from the mid-1960s, in the first decade the party delegated important nonmilitary functions to the army, but a united party leadership retained firm control over the military. And, for its part, the army accepted this control without question and aided the party as its agent but did not compete with it or pose a challenge to its position of primacy.

The subordination of the military to the party was convincingly demonstrated by the smooth transfer of power from military to civilian organs. Although many observers predicted at the time that the military would not relinquish their grip on the regional levers of power and that China would revert to a system of regional satrapies similar to the situation in the period of 'warlordism', nothing of the sort occurred. And this did not occur because of several overriding factors – factors which have remained operative throughout the history of the People's Republic of China, and which have prevented its breakup into regional components even during times of acute stress at the center. One factor was the great integrative power of modern Chinese nationalism, which has animated all the Chinese Communist leaders. Another was the commitment of China's military leaders to the principle of central control, a commitment born out of their nationalism and buttressed by their indoctrination, training, and experience. A third was the organizational capacity of the party to enforce its control over the army through an elaborate hierarchy of political organs – party committees, political commissars and political departments – which runs parallel to the military chain of command.

Once the civil organs were ready to assume the tasks of administration, the military withdrew swiftly and quietly from political affairs. The field armies were broken up and their component armies were placed directly under central control. The senior military leaders who had headed both the regional administrations and the field armies were transferred to Peking.[4] The PLA, as noted, continued to perform a wide variety of non-military tasks – from actively participating in mass campaigns to helping peasants – but it did so under party direction and control.

The subordination of the PLA to the party does not mean, of course, that the military did not chafe under party control or that the party–PLA relationship was free of stresses and strains. Quite the opposite was true. The modernization of the Chinese army, which was greatly accelerated by the Korean War and by Soviet military aid and advice, brought into being a professional officer corps, composed partly of young graduates of the newly founded military academies and partly of veteran commanders who reoriented their thinking along more professional lines. This officer corps developed professional perspectives on military strategy, organization, and the role of the army in society that differed in several fundamental respects from the more politically oriented approach of the party leadership and some senior military figures. In the policymaking councils, the military tended to act as a pressure group advocating its own views on subjects affecting the armed forces. As a result, the party–PLA relationship was increasingly strained by controversy and conflict during the second part of the decade. The festering tensions reached a high point during the Great Leap Forward of the late 1950s, when the party leadership tried to reassert political control over the armed forces, and to reestablish mass-oriented practices in the army and in its relations with society.[5]

The source of these tensions was not the opposition of army officers to controls and revolutionary practices per se, but to the extreme fashion in which the party tried to apply these controls and practices in the ideologically charged atmosphere of the Great Leap Forward. The officers were clearly prepared to work out and maintain a balance between political and professional requirements – between the two poles of the 'red and expert' equation. The center of gravity in this equation had moved decisively to the side of the 'experts' during the period of military modernization, but instead of redressing it cautiously and with moderation, the party in the late 1950s moved to the other extreme and tried to establish the supremacy of political considerations in all facets of the army's activities. This was done, moreover, in a high-handed manner which evidently offended the officers and posed what they perceived to be a threat to China's military capabilities. The upshot was that the officer corps did not passively go along with the party's efforts, but resisted these efforts verbally and actively – by putting forth arguments in support of their views, and by refraining from implementing the party's policies. The climax of these tensions, which became intertwined with the opposition of some senior military leaders to the party's economic policies and to the growing rift with the Soviet Union, was the dismissal in 1959 of the then Minister of Defense, Marshal P'eng Teh-huai, and several of his associates.

These conflicts, however, did not extend to the basic question of military subservience to the party, and they were played out within the implicitly accepted parameters of dissent and debate. P'eng Teh-huai overstepped these bounds – by pushing his views too strongly and in a manner which Mao chose to interpret as a personal challenge to the Chairman's policies. For his efforts, P'eng was sacked, but his removal did not elicit an overt reaction in the officer corps. This decision, like other decisions reached by the party leadership, was accepted by the army in disciplined fashion. In short, the army vigorously advocated its views, but did not move out of its barracks to force acceptance of those views.

Thus, during the 1950s the military participated in political affairs on two levels: as a force aiding the party in the execution of policies in the localities, and as an interest group in national decision-making forums (it is plain that in the Politburo, and probably in the Central Committee as well, military men also expressed views on nonmilitary matters). On both levels, military participation was characterized by the army's subordination to party control and by its noninterference in the resolution of political conflicts. Against this background, the gradually deepening involvement of the military in politics during the 1960s represented a clear break with the pattern of the preceding decade, and it is misleading to view it, as some observers have, as a linear development and merely an extension of the military's previous role.

THE ORIGINS OF MILITARY INTERVENTION

The transformation of the pattern of military participation began gradually and almost imperceptibly in the early 1960s in response to a changing political situation.[6] Dominating this situation was the incipient intra-party conflict over power and policy that was to explode with untrammeled fury several years later in the Cultural Revolution. Fueled by the failure of the Great Leap Forward and centering on the fundamental issue of China's development strategy, the conflict entered a critical phase after 1962 as those party leaders opposed to Mao's insistence upon steering China along a more revolutionary course sought to evade his directives by blocking them on the level of policy implementation. As the gap between declaratory policy and actual implementation widened, Mao and his supporters became increasingly disenchanted with the party bureaucracy and its top leaders. This disenchantment led Mao to the conclusion that it was necessary to shake up the party and to re-infuse it with revolutionary values in order to overcome its bureaucratic ossification.

To this end, Mao turned to the army. Under the leadership of Lin Piao, who had replaced P'eng Teh-huai as Defense Minister in 1959, the problems caused by the growth of professionalism in the officer corps had been overcome, and the army's revolutionary qualities had been revived. While Lin's program within the army prudently maintained a balance between political and professional requirements, there is no doubt that the revolutionary vigor of the PLA in the early 1960s contrasted sharply with the increasing bureaucratism and unresponsiveness of the party apparatus. Consequently, Mao began to use the PLA in order to prod the party, with the result that the army was drawn into the political arena – not, as previously, to carry out the policies of a united leadership, but rather to support the Maoists against other groups in an increasingly divided leadership.[7]

The initial impetus for this new type of military involvement in politics thus came from outside the army rather than from within it. Although it is clear that the military leadership, or at least the dominant group within it, willingly responded to Mao's initiative, it seems equally clear that the military leaders could hardly have foreseen that this new involvement in politics would eventually lead to the army's elevation to the top of the power pyramid – a dramatic development that occurred in the turmoil of the Cultural Revolution and could not have been predicted, or even desired, by most of the leaders, both political and military. There is, therefore, no basis for maintaining, as many analysts have, that the army's entry into politics in the early 1960s was the first step in a grand design conceived by the military under Lin Piao to capture political power in China. As far as can be determined, the political ascent of the army was neither planned nor predetermined, but was rather the product of unforeseen and, at least to some military leaders, unwelcome circumstances. The Chinese military, in short, did not grab political power; instead, political power gravitated to the military through a complex process extending over several years.

This process began to unfold in 1963 with a series of countrywide campaigns highlighting the revolutionary qualities of the army and holding it up as a model for the nation to follow. The purpose of the campaigns was a limited one: to reinvigorate the party by infusing it with a revolutionary spirit and style of work, but not to replace it in its leading role by the army. Starting with drives publicizing individual army heroes and model units, the campaigns reached a highpoint in 1964 with a major national movement to 'learn from the army.' As part of this movement, a new apparatus modeled on the army's political organization and staffed by military officers was established in governmental and economic organs to ensure that the army's political techniques would be copied and carried out.[8] The party, however, stiffened its resistence and intensified its tactics of subtly sabotaging Maoist directives. As the contrast between the party and the army from the Maoist perspective sharpened, the stage was set for the epic struggle between the Maoists, supported by the military, and the party. This was the origin of the Cultural Revolution.[9]

However, before the Maoists could use the army as a base for an assault on the centers of resistance in the party, they had to eliminate opposition within the military High Command itself to the growing politicization of the PLA. This opposition surfaced primarily in response to the escalation of the war in Vietnam, and its chief spokesman was the Chief of Staff Lo Jui-ch'ing. Deeply concerned about the possibility that the USA would initiate hostilities against China as an outgrowth of the war, Lo took issue with the Maoist position that a 'people's war' strategy was adequate to meet such a threat and argued for a more conventional strategy and more emphasis on military preparations. He opposed the increasing preoccupation of the army with political affairs and in 1964 initiated a campaign to increase and improve military training at the expense of political activities. Some time after November 1965 Lo was dismissed and the way was cleared for the Maoists to launch the Cultural Revolution with the support of the PLA leadership.[10]

But while Mao, in unleashing the Cultural Revolution, relied on the army as his power base, the role of the military in the early phases of the upheaval continued to be limited. For the period until the end of 1966, a distinction must be drawn between the parts played by the military leadership itself and by the army as a nationwide organization. The central army command did, indeed, play a pivotal role from the beginning of the Cultural Revolution struggle, rendering crucial support to the Maoists, but the army as a whole remained for the time being on the sidelines, although it did provide logistical and, probably, organizational support to the Red Guards.[11]

THE ARMY INTERVENES

The character and extent of the army's involvement in the Cultural Revolution changed sharply after January 1967. In what was probably the single most important decision affecting the role of the military, the army was ordered to intervene in the struggles that were then raging in many parts of China. This dramatic transformation of the army's role stemmed from the inability of the Maoists to purge the party bureaucracy by using the Red Guards. Thwarted in their efforts by the unexpectedly forceful resistance of the party organizations, and faced with mounting chaos as a result of these efforts, the Maoists decided that the only alternative to calling off the Cultural Revolution was to call in the army on the side of the 'revolutionary' forces. For, by the end of 1966, only the PLA had the power, the discipline, and the nationwide organization needed to determine the outcome of the struggle. Involving the PLA in a political struggle, however, was a momentous move that was opposed by some of the top-ranking army leaders who predicted – correctly, as it turned out – that it would subject the PLA to dangerous strains. But their opposition was overridden, and in January 1967 the PLA was ordered to intervene in order to aid the 'revolutionary' forces to 'seize power.'[12]

The intervention immediately cast the army as the main actor in the unfolding drama.[13] From this juncture onward, the entire direction of the Cultural Revolution was determined decisively by the role of the PLA and its interaction with the principal political forces operating in the turbulent arena of power politics. In Peking, these forces consisted of a handful of Maoist leaders, now polarized into radical and moderate wings. In the provinces, they consisted of millions of Red Guards, by now split into a bewildering multitude of massive and frequently rival organizations.

Contrary to the directives of the Maoist radicals in Peking, and to the expectations of the Red Guards in the provinces, the army, in coordination with the moderate leaders in Peking, intervened in the nationwide struggle not as a radical revolutionary force, but rather as a moderating and stabilizing element. Instead of supporting the Red Guards in their attempts to establish a new mass-based order to replace the shattered party organizations, the army engineered a compromise arrangement: Revolutionary Committees, based on the so-called 'triple alliance' of Red Guards, veteran officials, and army representatives. In practice, the army commanders generally tended, in the interests of order as well as for personal reasons, to ally with the veteran officials against the Red Guards in the formation of Revolutionary Committees. The formation of the provincial committees, however, turned out to be a long and strife-ridden process due to factional infighting. Therefore, pending their establishment, the army moved in to fill the power vacuum created by the paralysis of party and administrative organs by establishing Military Control Committees which assumed major political and civil functions in the localities, in effect replacing the party as the paramount political force throughout China.[14]

Saddled with the impossible task of pursuing the contradictory objectives of restoring order and aiding the Red Guards, army commanders by and large opted for order rather than revolution. This aroused the opposition of radical revolutionary activists to which the army responded with varying degrees of toughness. The forcefulness of the army's response was conditioned, to a very large extent, by the shifts in the balance of power between the radical and moderate leaders who constituted the ruling group in Peking. By the time the curtain was rung down on the Cultural Revolution at the 9th Party Congress in April 1969, the Red Guard organizations had been largely broken up, and the power of the radical group in Peking had been considerably diminished. In what was probably the most important short-term result of the Cultural Revolution – a result that was plainly unforeseen by any of the principal participants – the army emerged from the upheaval not only as the dominant political and administrative authority in the provinces but also – consequently – as a powerful force in the central policymaking councils.

The termination of the Cultural Revolution occurred against the background of serious clashes between Chinese and Soviet troops on the Ussuri River which had erupted about a month before the 9th Party Congress. The connection, if any, between these clashes and the internal activities of the PLA is not clear but it seems that Lin Piao used the mounting tension on the border to rally support behind the PLA and, temporarily at least, the position of the PLA appears to have been strengthened.

The army's greatly increased political power at the end of the Cultural Revolution was strikingly apparent in the composition of the most important organs of regional authority. Of the chairmen of the 29 province-level Revolutionary Committees, 21 were military men, while 235 of the 479 standing committee members, or almost 50 percent, came from the army.[15] Moreover, the army's share of representation increased shortly after the Cultural Revolution as regional leadership organs were reorganized. Local-level administrations were also dominated by the military.

The enhanced power position of the military at the provincial and local levels was reflected in the top-level national policymaking organs. Of the 170 full members of the Central Committee, about 45 percent were military men, while about half the members of the Politburo could be classed as having a primary identification with the military. The influence of the army was also reflected in military procurement which began to rise sharply in 1968 and reached a peak in 1971 – when output was estimated at double that of 1967 – before falling off again.[16] The close connection between the growth of the military's regional power and its strengthened position at the national level was evidenced by the fact that about 65 percent of the military representatives in the Central Committee (about

28 percent of the total committee membership) came from the provinces.

These developments had farreaching political implications. The regional predominance of the military, with its strong reflection at the center, meant not only that regional interests would have increased weight in the formulation of national policy, but – more importantly – that the regional military commanders, holding the levers of political power in the provinces, would in effect be able to control how national policy would be carried out in their respective areas. In sum, if the army's intervention in the Cultural Revolution resulted in a pronounced shift of political power to the military, it was the regional commanders within the army who were the main beneficiaries of the shift.

The political ascendancy of the army in the localities raised critical questions with respect to the future role of the regional military in Chinese politics. As a consequence of their actions during the Cultural Revolution, the regional military authorities came to enjoy a large degree of de facto autonomy vis-à-vis the center, and in many instances they used their autonomy to circumvent or reinterpret central directives that they considered inimical to their interests and needs.[17] This autonomy was the product of the peculiar conditions that had prevailed during the Cultural Revolution and, to a lesser degree, in its immediate aftermath: the weakness of the center, which was divided among conflicting groups and consequently issued vague and sometimes contradictory directives; the entanglement of the military commanders on the spot in local factional conflicts which often forced them to make political decisions on the basis of their own judgement; and the virtual elimination of the party apparatus as an effective mechanism for exercising control over military commanders in the localities. But power, once acquired, under whatever circumstances, is not easily relinquished, and the question was whether the military would continue to hold on to political power in China's localities. This question was particularly pertinent in the light of China's past period of regionalism, born out of the country's size, diversity, and regional economic self-sufficiency.

Against the background of past precedents and current conditions some observers predicted that China would disintegrate, in fact if not in name, into a system of regional military governorships reminiscent of the 'warlord' period. Such predictions, however, failed to take into account the basic fact that the autonomist tendencies of the regional military commanders remained subject to important limitations. For one thing, nationalism continued to be a paramount integrative force and the center, whatever its weaknesses caused by internal dissension, remained the repository of national authority and, as such, commanded the basic allegiance of the military. For another, the regional commanders themselves, because of their strong sense of professional discipline and their basic commitment to national unity, restrained themselves from taking any action, even when they had the opportunity to do so, that would endanger national unity or cast doubt on their loyalty to the center.[18] At no time was this attitude of the regional commanders more strikingly demonstrated than during the Wuhan Incident of July 1967, when regional commanders refrained from supporting the open insubordination of the Wuhan commander, Ch'en Tsai-tao, despite the fact that most of them acted just like Ch'en in their own localities in suppressing the radical Red Guard organizations. These commanders, however, had stopped short of outright defiance of the center, whereas Ch'en crossed this sensitive line. By this action, Ch'en isolated himself. While other commanders probably sympathized with his predicament, they nonetheless evidently sanctioned his dismissal in the overriding interest of safeguarding national unity.[19] Also militating against the military becoming permanent political rulers in the provinces was the fact that many military commanders obviously got deeply involved in political affairs against their wishes and better judgement, and they viewed this involvement as incompatible with their professional military requirements. And, indeed, later developments demonstrated that they were prepared to disengage from this involvement once the political circumstances were appropriate.

The intervention of the army in the political conflict had farreaching effects not only on its position in the political system but also on intra-military politics. It is axiomatic that when an army enters politics, politics enter the army – and the PLA has been no exception. Although internal cleavages and conflicts had characterized the Chinese Communist military to some degree throughout its history, such divisions were revived and sharply intensified within the PLA in the heat of the Cultural Revolution struggle, and new ones crystallized. The post-Cultural Revolution cleavages ran along a variety of lines: center–regional, bureaucratic-*v.*-field army, interservice, and political-*v.*-professional.[20] The most serious appeared to be the cleavage between the central military leadership and the regional army commanders. This cleavage was cogently manifested at critical junctures in the Cultural Revolution when the High Command dispatched main force units, which were directly subordinate to it, to strife-torn areas where regional military authorities had sided with local party organizations against the Red Guards.

What significance do such cleavages have in the context of the army's role in politics? For one thing, they indicate that it is somewhat misleading to speak of 'the army' as a unitary actor, since different groups are likely to have competing interests and perspectives and to act accordingly. Such groups, moreover, are apt to form coalitions – sometimes tacit rather than explicit – with groups in the civilian hierarchies that have similar views and interests. One example may be found in the tacit cooperation that developed between regional army commanders and moderate elements in the Maoist leadership during the Cultural Revolution. A later example is the support which appears to have been given by some regional army commanders and professional military officers to the Mao–Chou group in its conflict with Defense Minister Lin Piao and the central military leadership in 1971 – about which more later. As the PLA becomes less involved in political affairs and concentrates increasingly on its professional tasks – as has been the case in the post-Mao era – intra-army tensions, which had been aggravated by pressures from the outside, can be expected to subside. Factions, of course, will continue to exist like in any army, but to the extent that these factions are anchored in differences over issues, the issues will probably be military rather than political. Given the veil of secrecy enveloping intra-army relations in China, a major problem that faces the analyst in this area is to identify factions within the military and to trace their activities. There is no doubt that factionalism has to be taken into account in assessing the army's role in politics. Its impact should not be overrated, however, as internal army rivalries seem, generally speaking, to have been kept within bounds by recognition of a broader 'military' interest as well as by the restraints of military discipline.

AFTERMATH OF THE CULTURAL REVOLUTION

Although the army's involvement in politics was an outgrowth of the Cultural Revolution, the end of that upheaval did not lead immediately to a military withdrawal from the political arena. On the contrary, for some two years after the Cultural Revolution, the army consolidated its political position and strengthened its domination of the regional power structures. These processes took place primarily in the course of the reconstruction of the party organization, which began after the end of the turmoil.[21]

The reconstruction of the party was marked by constant conflict between regional army leaders and remnant radical elements over the allocation of power in the reconstituted party organs, especially in the Party Committees at the provincial level. Since the reconstituted Party Committees were supposed to have higher authority than the army-dominated Revolutionary Committees, the radicals viewed the rebuilding of the party as an opportunity to gain the power that they had been prevented by the army from gaining in the Revolutionary Committees. The army commanders, however, showed no disposition to accommodate the radicals. Although many of them had been reluctant to become involved in the political turmoil in the first place, they displayed an even greater reluctance to hand over power to the same radical elements with whom they had clashed violently and whose policies they opposed. In fact, given the bitterness and hostility that had developed between the radicals and most local army commanders, the latter had good reason to fear that a reascendance of the radicals would bring retaliation against the army – a prospect that they were naturally unwilling to help bring about. Whether or not they would, at this stage, have been more ready to step aside in favor of veteran, conservative party officials whose basic views on national policy they shared is not certain. What is certain is that they were not prepared to step aside as long as the danger of a radical come-back persisted.

Consequently, instead of giving up their political posts, the military commanders used these posts to ensure that the reconstruction of the party organs would not result in a reduction of their power. This they did primarily by supervising the process of reorganization, and the results were apparent in the composition of the reconstituted Party Committees, where the military was able to get its representatives appointed to positions paralleling those they had held in the Revolutionary Committees. Thus, twenty-one of the twenty-nine first secretaries of the new Party Committees in the provinces were military officers (commanders or political commissars), while 62 percent of the members of provincial party secretariats also were from the military – representing a 12 percent increase over its share of such positions under the interim Revolutionary Committees. It seems probable, in light of these results at the provincial level, that the military retained its dominant position in the lower-level party bodies and other reconstructed local organizations as well.

However, the struggles that accompanied the reconstruction of the party apparatus apparently fueled a new conflict that now began to build up at the level of the central leadership. Many aspects of this complex conflict still remain obscure, but one element was the political dominance of the PLA and the related personal ambitions of its commander and Mao's designated successor, Lin Piao. It appears that Mao, alarmed at the reluctance of the top military leaders to relinquish the political preeminence that they had acquired at the expense of the party during and after the Cultural Revolution, now swung his weight behind a coalition of moderate and radical elements in the leadership – both of whom found the army's political ascendancy unpalatable – in a power struggle against Defense Minister Lin Piao and several top members of the army General Staff. In this crucial confrontation, the Mao-Chou coalition succeeded in winning the support or acquiescence of those regional army commanders and professional officers who had been antagonized by Lin's excessive politicization of the army and by his alliance with the extreme radicals, especially Ch'en Po-ta, a veteran leftwing ideologue and driving force behind the Cultural Revolution, whom the military professionals had good reason to despise. The struggle reached a spectacular climax in September 1971 with the mysterious death of Lin Piao and several close associates in a plane crash in Mongolia while they were allegedly attempting to flee to the Soviet Union following an abortive attempt to assassinate Mao.[22]

LIMITED MILITARY DISENGAGEMENT FROM POLITICS

Although the 'Lin Piao Affair' was a limited struggle at the center, its outcome marked an important turning point in the political role of the army and its relationship to the party. The elimination of Lin and his supporters removed a major obstacle to redressing the balance between the party and the army, and the central leadership proceeded – despite continued internal divisions on various issues – to mount a determined drive in that direction. As a result, the post-Lin Piao period witnessed a gradual but marked disengagement of the army from the political arena and a reassertion of the party's political primacy. The disengagement process had three main facets: first, a scaling down of the army's excessive involvement in civil affairs; secondly, a reaffirmation of professional military values within the army, at the expense of extreme politicization; and, thirdly, a reduction of the army's position of strength in the national and regional organs of political power.

Indications of the first of these facets took various forms. One was a renewal of exhortations and instructions to the military to subordinate themselves to the leadership of the party;[23] to display modesty and prudence in their relations with civilian cadres and the masses;[24] to observe military discipline and concentrate on army affairs.[25] Another was an increasing flow of publicity about the rebuilding of party organizations and their resumption of 'normal' operations,[26] accompanied by the virtual disappearance of reports – which earlier had flooded the media – describing the involvement of military units in civil functions. Further reinforcing these developments was the gradual reappearance in public life of veteran party cadres who had dropped out of sight under radical assault during the Cultural Revolution.[27] To what extent these manifestations mirrored reality is difficult to judge, but – taken cumulatively – they definitely suggested a significant lowering of the army's profile on the political scene. This is not to say that the army ceased to play any role in civil affairs, but only to indicate that there was a gradual reversion to its former role – that is, noninterference in politics and the performance of limited nonmilitary tasks under the direction of the party rather than in competition with it. These tasks obviously included the maintenance of public order, as was demonstrated by the dispatch of troops to factories in Hangchow in July 1975 to restore production disrupted by factional strife.

The second facet of the disengagement process was a renewed emphasis on professionalism and military proficiency within the armed forces. In a concerted effort to redress the balance between politicization and professionalism in the military establishment, the central leadership subjected the policies of the late Lin Piao to severe attack on the grounds that they had neglected the military functions of the army in favor of excessive politicization, and it called upon army leaders to concentrate their energies on raising professional military standards.[28] It also proceeded to rehabilitate a number of professional officers, who had been purged in the Cultural Revolution, the most notable example being the late Lo Jui-ch'ing, who had been dismissed as PLA Chief of Staff because of his emphasis on a highly professionalized defense establishment and the need to mend relations with the Soviet Union as a source of advanced military technology. This reordering of the army's priorities doubtless coincided with the views of a great many professional officers who had been unhappy about the army's entanglement in politics from the start. Its rationale in the context of the regime's perception of the army's proper role was quite clear: soldiers who concentrated on improving their specialized military skills would be less likely to involve themselves in politics.

In retrospect it appears that the campaign in support of military professionalism did not achieve substantial results. It tapered off in 1973, at the time of, and largely due to, radical counterattacks on the trends of moderation and the rehabilitation of purged leaders that had been set in motion after the Cultural Revolution by moderate elements in the leadership. From then on until after the death of Mao and the purge of the radical leaders little was heard in favor of military professionalism – but much was said against it. According to accusations against the purged radical leaders – now labeled the 'gang of four' – these leaders had been responsible for creating a climate of acute anti-professionalism in the military, as well as other, fields, and they were quick to pounce on the proponents of any view that advanced the special interests of the military.[29] The reported result was a serious deterioration in the armed forces – their weaponry, discipline, training, and organization.[30] Even allowing for the exaggerations characteristic of charges against fallen opponents, the revelations in these charges merely confirmed what Western military experts have been saying for years – that the weapons systems of the Chinese armed forces are ten to twenty years out of date. In part, this was undoubtedly due to the influence of the radical leaders.

There were, however, other reasons which restricted the pursuit of professional interests by the military, and some of these reasons derived directly from the political involvement of the army. For one thing, this involvement absorbed the energies of its officers and men and diverted the focus of its activities away from military matters. For another, the demise of Lin Piao and his associates, which had been caused to a large extent by the political ascendancy of the military, left the PLA without a strong voice within the ruling elite for several years. It also weakened the position of the military at other levels, due to the purge of officers with real or suspected Lin Piao connections, and due to the pall of suspicion which the affair cast over the military. Thus, whatever the political gains that accrued to the army from its involvement in nonmilitary affairs, there is no doubt that this involvement had a deleterious effect on its military posture. These effects could not be rectified as long as the radical leaders held power and as long as the army remained absorbed in political affairs – and these two aspects were interrelated.

This interrelationship was evident in the third facet of the army's disengagement from politics – the reduction of its political power as measured by military representation in national and regional ruling organs. The behavior of military commanders during the Cultural Revolution and thereafter indicated that, whatever the differences between them, they were agreed that one basic condition had to be met before they gave up their political posts. The condition was that the interests of the military would be protected by the civilian leaders who came in their place. And this meant, at the very least, that military commanders had to be assured that order and stability would be maintained throughout China, for it had been the widespread breakdown of order that had impelled them to move into the political arena in the first place. Such an assurance had to be predicated on the assumption that the direction and execution of national policy would be in the hands of moderate cadres, with whom the military commanders shared a basic vision of the desired social order, regardless of the tensions between them. Since the comeback of such cadres was slow, and since even rehabilitated cadres continued to be exposed to attacks by the radicals, the withdrawal of the military from regional power centers was gradual. From the time of Lin Piao's downfall until Mao's death, nine military officers gave up their concurrent positions as provincial first party secretaries, bringing the number down from twenty-one to thirteen. In each case, the post was taken over by a veteran cadre. Similarly, the 10th Party Congress in August 1973 formalized the rehabilitation of many important party cadres and at the same time reduced the representation of the military in the party's policy-making organs. In the Central Committee, military representation dropped by about 14 percent to some 30 percent, while in the Politburo it declined from about one-half to one-third. These trends pointed both to the process of disengagement and to its limits. That the process had been limited was dramatically demonstrated by the role of the military in the transition to the post-Mao era.

THE MILITARY IN THE TRANSITION TO THE POST-MAO ERA

In the brief power struggle that erupted after Mao's death, the role of the army was crucial. This time, again the involvement of the military in a political conflict was the product of pressures generated by circumstances outside the military establishment, but there is no indication of any hesitation or reluctance on the part of the military to intervene. For one thing, the precedent for military intervention in a political struggle had already been set. More importantly, the military had a vital stake in the outcome of the succession struggle between the contending groups – the so-called moderates and radicals. Without the backing of the military, neither camp had sufficient strength to defeat its opponents swiftly and decisively.

This assessment is based on what is known about the strength of each group. The main strength of the moderate leaders lay in their power bases in the party, the government, and the mass organizations. The death of Mao had removed the main source of strength of the radicals but, like the moderate leaders, they also had power bases in these organs. While the bases of the moderates were plainly more extensive and more powerful, the radicals had concentrated force in the form of well-armed militia units in Shanghai, and, probably to some extent, also in Peking. However, the main power of the radicals lay not so much in the ruling organs as in the capacity of their followers to disrupt the orderly functioning of these organs – by means ranging from publishing media articles to instigating mass action. It was this troublemaking capacity that had enabled the radicals, with Mao's blessing, to prevent the moderate leaders from consolidating their position.

With Mao gone, the primary obstacle to mass action was the army, which had convincingly demonstrated its negative attitude toward disruptive activities during the Cultural Revolution. The radical leaders were well aware of this attitude and of the acute hostility of the senior military leaders. For this reason, they allegedly tried to neutralize these leaders by intervening in army affairs and damaging military unity and discipline.[31] In the unlikely event that they had succeeded in seriously splitting the army, China would have probably been plunged into prolonged internecine strife. Even if they had managed only to keep the army out of the succession struggle, the power of the radicals would have been greatly enhanced. As it turned out, the radicals failed to make significant inroads into the PLA. When it came to the crunch, the army intervened forcefully against them, and the outcome of the struggle was decided with lightning speed.

This intervention had several facets. Most directly, the army carried out the coup against the 'gang of four' and arrested its members. The credit for this operation was given, or rather taken, by the elite guards. There is some uncertainty whether this unit is ultimately subordinate to the PLA High Command, but it is hardly conceivable that the guards would – or could – have acted in the face of united opposition by army leaders. Despite its formidable power, the unit was no match for the army if the army had chosen to block its operation, or even to undo whatever action it had taken. Thus, regardless of how this particular line of command is sorted out, there can be little doubt that the army High Command was, in the final analysis, behind the coup carried out by the elite guards.

Once the coup was over, the army set in motion a major effort to strengthen Hua's position. In editorials and reports purportedly written by various units, the army built up his image and underlined the army's support for the new Chairman. It stressed Hua's legitimacy as Mao's successor, highlighted his virtues, blasted his rivals, and pledged the army's loyalty to him.[32] It emphasized Hua's receptivity to the requirements of the army and hinted that Hua had protected the army from radical assaults during the Cultural Revolution[33] – an extremely sensitive issue, which had been one central factor in the chain of events that led to Lin Piao's downfall.

The army's symbolic support of Hua was not paralleled by a large-scale intervention of military units to prop up the new leadership. This was because no need for such intervention arose, and not because of the army's reticence. The precedent for military intervention to settle political struggles had already been set, and it could be safely assumed that the army would not have hesitated to quell any opposition. This, in any case, was plainly assumed by supporters of the 'gang of four', most notably the leaders of the Shanghai militia, who did not rise in revolt once their leaders had been eliminated. Just to make sure, the army reportedly moved troops into Shanghai after the coup.[34] It also reportedly intervened in Fukien and Hopeh to put down serious disorders, and took over the control of key railway centers, such as Chengchow in Honan, whose operations had been disrupted by infighting.[35] But on the whole, the army remained on the sidelines. However, the threat of its intervention was omnipresent, and this threat, together with its declaration of support for Hua, greatly eased the consolidation of power by Hua and his colleagues. The army thus became the central pillar of the Hua leadership in the transition period. Its prestige, especially that of its veteran leaders, rose sharply. More significantly, so did its power.

This does not mean, of course, that there are no important restraints on the army's power. The influence of army leaders as a bloc is diluted by military factionalism, and they have to compete for power with assertive civilian leaders, whose status has risen immensely since the downfall of the 'gang of four', and whose position is not constantly undermined by the radicals. Moreover, the rules of the game in this competition have been reaffirmed, and the cardinal rule is that 'the party commands the gun.' The implication is that the army leadership – like other leaders – can press for the adoption of its views but it will accept the decisions reached by the top decision-makers. This was the pattern in the first decade of Communist rule, before Mao shattered it by increasingly involving the army in politics. The likelihood that the army will abide by this rule rests ultimately on the assumption of its discipline and self-restraint which derive from its professional ethic, and this ethic has been vigorously revived and reinforced in the post-Mao period. Furthermore, the army has been able to devote itself to the promotion of its professional interests in this period because the Hua leadership has been receptive to its requirements, and because stability across the land has been restored by Hua's policies and by the removal of radical cadres at all levels of the ruling hierarchy. The army, in short, can return to the barracks.

This the army has done – but with important limitations. On the one hand, it has retained a strong voice in decision-making, and it has used this voice to make resounding calls for the fulfillment of its demands for modernization. On the other hand, it has not extended its power from policy formulation to policy-implementation by taking over leadership positions throughout the country. On the contrary, in the post-Mao period the trend has been toward a further disengagement of the military from civil affairs. In other words, what the army seems to want is a major influence in the making of decisions without involving itself in the actual political administration of the country. This it is able to do because it does not need to involve itself in such administration to enhance its power at the center. Its role in the succession crisis and the aftermath of this crisis already gave it considerable power.

These two aspects of the army's role were illuminated by the makeup of the central leadership organs, elected by the 11th Party Congress in September 1977, and by the shifts in the composition of the regional leadership organs. In the highest policy-making body, the Politburo, 12 of the 23 full members could be said to represent the military – as compared with 7 out of 21 in the 10th Politburo and 10 out of 21 in the 9th. Since then changes in the Politburo have brought military representation to 13 out of 28 by the end of 1979, but the military, if united, is still a powerful bloc in the Politburo. The strength of the PLA in the Central Committee remained at about 30 percent. Within the military, the division is roughly 48 percent central military men, and 52 percent regional. In the 9th Central Committee, which was elected right after the Cultural Revolution, 65 percent of the military representatives were from the regions. The trend has thus been toward a decline of the political importance of the regional military as compared with the military men at the center. This trend presumably reflects the withdrawal of the military from an involvement in political administration, which is carried on at the local level, rather than from a participation in policy-making at the national level. It is also apparent in the shifts of provincial first party secretaries. At the end of the Cultural Revolution, 21 of the 29 posts were held by military men.

At the time of Mao's death, 13 of the secretaries were military men. By early 1978, the number had declined to 9, and in the Summer of 1979 it stood at 5.

Thus, in the post-Mao period the military have an important voice in the decision-making councils, and they have used their position of power to vigorously press their demands for military modernization and for upgrading the army's professional standards. These demands aroused debates between some elements in the military and the civilian party leaders, presumably supported by other elements in the military, on issues relating primarily to the pace of modernization.[36]

If the officers expected that the leadership would accede to their call for a rapid and large-scale weapons modernization, they were disappointed. The most they gained was a concession that pending the development of China's industrial base the armed forces would modernize in a limited and selective fashion. Although this was far short of their original appeals, the officers made no attempt to force the adoption of their views.

The assertiveness of the military is thus clearly tempered by two fundamental and interrelated restraints: its acceptance of party supremacy and its discipline. Firmly anchored in the sensitivity of the officers to national needs and in their professionalism, these restraints have guided the behavior of the military throughout the history of the People's Republic and did not collapse even during times of great stress.

The assertiveness of the military in articulating their specific interests must also be seen against the background of political controls in the armed forces. These controls have been reaffirmed by an emphasis on the importance of party organs in the PLA, on political work in the armed forces, and on revolutionary practices. The emphasis on the organizational subordination of the PLA to the party seems to have been accepted by the professional officers without dissent. This is because political control in the post-Mao period has been applied in a moderate and flexible manner that obviously has not infringed upon the professional requirements of the military, for the stated objective of political work in the PLA in the post-Mao period has been to raise the combat capability of the PLA.[37] Although the declared desire of the leadership is to restore the balance between political and professional requirements – to make the army both 'red and expert' – it is the 'experts' who have gained the upper hand.

CONCLUDING REMARKS

Three years into the post-Mao era it is still too early to point to a model of the Chinese military as a political actor. The convulsions of the recent past suggest that a long period of stability should elapse before conclusions are drawn about a permanent pattern of the army's role in politics. Nonetheless, the trend is clear. While the military leadership remains a major force in the formulation of national policy, the army has increasingly reverted to its military role. Whether the army stays out of politics depends to a decisive degree, if past experience is any guide, on political developments outside the PLA. For this experience has demonstrated that the involvement of the Chinese military in politics has been primarily the result of pressures generated by the breakdown of leadership consensus and cohesion and the ensuing eruption of nationwide conflicts and collapse of political institutions. The political role of the military is thus contingent above all upon the state of national politics.

NOTES

1 See John Gittings, *The Role of the Chinese Army* (London: Oxford University Press, 1967), esp. ch. 9; and Ying-mao Kau, *The People's Liberation Army and China's Nation-Building* (White Plains, NY: International Arts and Sciences Press, 1973), esp. ch. 3.
2 Gittings, op. cit., pp. 263–71. See also Dorothy J. Solinger, *Regional Government and Political Integration in Southwest China in 1949–1953: A Case Study* (Berkeley, Calif.: University of California Press, 1977), esp. pp. 84–93, 156–63.
3 Ellis Joffe, *Party and Army: Professionalism and Political Control in the Chinese Officer Corps, 1949–1964* (Cambridge, Mass.: Harvard University Press, 1965), p. 85.
4 Gittings, op. cit., pp. 271–4. See also Solinger, op. cit., esp. ch. 8.
5 On these developments, See Joffe, *Party and Army*.
6 On this period, see the author's *Between Two Plenums: China's Intra-leadership Conflict, 1959–1962* (Michigan Papers in Chinese Studies, no. 22, 1975); and Stuart R. Schram, 'The cultural revolution in historical perspective,' in Stuart R. Schram (ed.), *Authority, Participation and Cultural Change in China* (London: Cambridge University Press, 1973), pp. 69–85.
7 See the author's 'The Chinese army under Lin Piao: prelude to political intervention,' in John M. H. Lindbeck (ed.), *China: Management of a Revolutionary Society* (Seattle, Wash.: University of Washington Press, 1971), pp. 343–74.
8 ibid. Also see Gittings, op. cit., pp. 254–8.
9 See the author's 'The Chinese army under Lin Piao,' pp. 365–6, and A. Doak Barnett, *Uncertain Passage: China's Transition to the Post-Mao Era* (Washington, DC: The Brookings Institution, 1974), pp. 76–9.
10 Cf. Harry Harding and Melvin Gurtov, *The Purge of Lo Jiu-ch'ing: The Politics of Chinese Strategic Planning* (Santa Monica, Calif.: RAND Corporation, 1971).
11 ibid., p. 79.
12 For the text of the directive ordering the PLA to intervene, see *Current Background* (US Consulate-General, Hong Kong), no. 852, pp. 49–50.
13 Ellis Joffe, 'The Chinese army in the Cultural Revolution: the politics of intervention,' *Current Scene* (Hong Kong, 7 December 1970), vol. 8, no. 18, pp. 1–25.
14 See Stanley Karnow, *Mao and China: From Revolution to Revolution* (New York: Macmillan, 1972), pp. 292, 297.
15 On the army's representation among the standing members of provincial Revolutionary Committees, see Jürgen Domes, 'Party politics and the Cultural Revolution,' in Frank N. Trager and William Henderson (eds), *Communist China, 1949–1969: A Twenty-Year Assessment* (New York: New York University Press, 1970), p. 90.
16 Sydney H. Jammes, 'The Chinese defense burden, 1965–1974,' *China: A Reassessment of the Economy*. A Compendium of Papers Submitted to the Joint Economic Committee of the Congress of the United States (Washington, DC: Government Printing Office, 1975), pp. 462–3.
17 Karnow, op. cit., ch. 13.
18 Cf. Barnett, op. cit., pp. 95–8, and Parris H. Chang, 'Regional military power: the aftermath of the Cultural Revolution,' *Asian Survey* (December 1972), pp. 1,008–10.
19 Joffe, 'The Chinese army in the Cultural Revolution,' pp. 16–17. See also Thomas W. Robinson, 'The Wuhan Incident: local strife and provincial rebellion during the Cultural Revolution,' *China Quarterly* (July–September 1971), pp. 413–38.

20 For the most thorough exposition of Chinese military factionalism, see William W. Whitson and Huang Chan-hsia, *The Chinese High Command: A History of Communist Military Politics, 1927–71* (New York: Praeger, 1973).

21 See the author's 'The Chinese army after the Cultural Revolution: the effects of intervention,' *China Quarterly* (July–September 1973), pp. 472–3. See also, Barnett, op. cit., pp. 83–4.

22 For accounts and interpretations of the 'Lin Piao Affair,' see Philip Bridgham, 'The fall of Lin Piao,' *China Quarterly* (July–September 1973), pp. 427–9; this author's 'The Chinese army after the Cultural Revolution,' pp. 468–77; Joseph Lelyveld, 'The ghost of Lin Piao,' *New York Times Magazine* (27 January 1974); Ying-mao Kau and Pierre M. Perrolle, 'The Politics of Lin Piao's abortive military coup,' *Asian Survey* (June 1974), pp. 558–77.

23 For example, Szechwan Provincial Radio (Chengru), 26 December 1971; Anhwei Provincial Radio (Hofei), 9 January 1972; Heilungkiang Provincial Radio (Harbin), 16 June 1972; Hunan Provincial Radio (Hunan), 17 February 1973; Kirin Provincial Radio (Changchun), 20 November 1974; and Kiangsu Provincial Radio (Nanking), 22 January 1975. All radio reports cited in this chapter may be found in English translation in Foreign Broadcast Information Service, *Daily Report: People's Republic of China* (Washington, DC).

24 For example, collection of articles in *Union Research Service* (Hong Kong), vol. 66, no. 5 (18 January 1972); also, Szechwan Provincial Radio, 27 April 1972; Heilungkiang Provincial Radio, 21 June 1972; Hainan Island Radio (Haikow), 26 January 1973; Provincial Radio, 25 August 1973.

25 For example, Peking Radio, Lomestic Service, 13 September 1971; Heilungkiang Provincial Radio, 6 November 1971. See also 'Outline of education on situation for companies,' translated in *Issues and Studies* (Taipei), vol. 10, no. 10 (July 1974), p. 97.

26 See Barnett, op. cit., pp. 47–66.

27 See Parris H. Chang, 'Political rehabilitation of cadres in China: a traveller's view,' *China Quarterly* (April–June 1973), pp. 331–40.

28 For example, see the collection of articles in *Union Research Service*, vol. 66, no. 3 (11 January 1972); also, Fukien Provincial Radio (Foochow), 12 April 1972; Lhasa Radio, 27 April 1972; Shanghai Radio, 26 July 1972, and 31 July 1974; Peking Radio, Domestic Service, 29 April 1973; and Yunan Provincial Radio (Kunming), 7 May 1973.

29 For example, Peking Domestic Service, 5 February 1977.

30 For example, Peking Domestic Service, 10 April 1977; NCNA, 23 February 1978; Peking Domestic Service, 25 June, 1977; Peking Domestic Service, 24 February 1978.

31 For example, Peking Domestic Service, 16 April 1978.

32 For example, NCNA, 8 November 1976; NCNA, 23 December 1976; *Jen-min Jih-pao*, 31 October 1976, in *Survey of People's Republic of China Press*, no. 46 (US Consulate-General, Hong Kong, 1976), pp. 7–9.

33 Peking Domestic Service, 25 April 1977.

34 Chi Hsin, *The Case of the Gang of Four* (Hong Kong: Cosmos Books, 1977), pp. 38–42.

35 *China Trade Report* (September 1977).

36 See Ellis Joffe and Gerald Segal 'The Chinese army and professionalism,' *Problems of Communism* (November–December 1978), pp. 9–19.

37 For example, Peking Domestic Service, 12 April 1978; NCNA Domestic Service, 25 May 1978 and 10 June 1978. See also speeches by Wei Kuo-ch'ing, director of the PLA's General Political Department, and Teng Hsiap-p'ing, vice-chairman of the Chinese Communist Party and Chief of Staff of the PLA, at the all-army political conference held in late May and early June 1978. NCA Domestic Service, 5 June and 7 June 1978.

7 The Military as a Political Actor in Poland

ANDRZEJ KORBONSKI AND SARAH M. TERRY

Anyone attempting to examine the role of the military in Poland's domestic politics since World War II is faced with both an easy and a difficult task. On the one hand, for reasons discussed below, relatively little has been written and published on the military in Communist Poland so that the entire topic has been for many years a *tabula rasa*. This, in turn, has meant that any new piece of concrete information was, almost inevitably, bound to make a major contribution to our knowledge of the subject and that it should be relatively easy to enlarge that knowledge at an exponential rate.[1]

Scholarly neglect of the role of the military in Communist Poland, as well as in the rest of Eastern Europe, can be explained in a variety of ways. For a long time, research on Communist systems was pre-empted by the so-called 'totalitarian' model and its variants which usually implied that while other political systems could 'change,' 'develop,' 'modernize,' or 'stagnate,' Communist polities had to remain static, being sui generis and firmly anchored in the 'totalitarian,' 'mobilization,' or 'command' modes. It is by now clear, however, that the premise of the totalitarian model, as literally interpreted, has been proven false and that, indeed, Communist societies (Poland included) like all others have been undergoing significant change, at least in the past two decades.

Absence of scholarly research on the role of the military in the Polish political system can also be explained, in part, by a paucity of data. It is indisputable that data constraints are of an order of magnitude more severe than those encountered by students of Western or even Third World countries. Yet it can be argued that the information problem with regard to the role of the military in Poland and other Communist systems, albeit difficult, is no more intractable than that concerning other key aspects or components of these systems. The pioneering studies of the military in the Soviet Union have amply demonstrated the richness of some categories of data.[2] Sinologists have been demonstrating to us, that within societies until recently much more 'closed' than the East European systems, studies of the military are feasible.[3] All these studies utilized three basic analytical models – the conflict, the congruence, and the participation paradigms.[4] In Poland, military publications of various kinds contain information that can be tapped for this research purpose.[5]

We decided, then, to investigate the role of the armed forces in Poland in the belief that the military has had a considerable and frequently unappreciated impact on political and social processes in that country, and with the conviction that the data problems are not insurmountable. It is our working hypothesis that in Poland, the East European country with the largest military establishment, the army has been involved sporadically in the political processes since the mid-1950s, and that on several occasions, it has played the pivotal role of political arbiter, especially during succession crises or challenges to the leadership in 1968, 1970, and 1976. To put it somewhat differently, we believe that the armed forces in Poland have gradually been assuming an important, and occasionally even an autonomous, role in the political process, and we intend to test that proposition in a preliminary fashion.

In examining the role of the military in Polish politics, we essentially continued the pioneering research of Jerzy Wiatr and Dale Herspring, both of whom have made our task incomparably easier.[6] There are, as always, several ways in which to approach the subject. One would be to apply the Almondian developmental framework and to analyze the role of the military in the processes of state- and nation-building, partici-pation, and last but certainly not least in this particular case, subsystem autonomy.[7] There is little doubt that the Polish military played an important role in all these stages, at times even acting as a catalyst or instrument of change. Another method would be to treat the military as a special-interest group and to insert it into the five-part Huntingtonian systemic model.[8] We would then trace the interaction of the military with the remaining four variables of the system – culture, leadership, struc-tures, and policies. Finally, as suggested earlier, we could analyze the political involvement of the Polish military with the aid of one of the three approaches focused, respectively, on conflict, congruence, and participation.

The analytical framework that we have chosen will combine several of the above approaches by focusing on the interplay of several factors which in the past thirty years or so have resulted in a cumulative growth of the Polish military's role – changing from the initial role of selective *co-optation* into the Communist Party structures, and leading through periods of political *subordination* to the ruling party's decision-making bodies, to subsequent *accommodation* with the party, and to the present stage of *participation* in managing the country's affairs.[9]

It may be argued that in Poland each of these significant role changes not only paralleled major phases in the more general process of political development, but that the process has also exhibited a circular pattern. Thus the initial stage of intense national integration or nation-building coincided with a limited degree of the military's co-optation into the party. The phase of totalitarian political penetration, which might be viewed also as a process of state-building, overlapped with the subordination of the military. This was followed by the next stage of political and economic reformism away from Stalinism, coinciding with growing demands for expanded participation and greater welfare that, in turn, paralleled the process of accommodation between the party and the military. Finally, the present situation is characterized by growing politico-military participation in decision-making which illustrates the increase in subsystem autonomy.

We shall concentrate largely on the last two stages in the process of the military's evolving political involvement – the *accommodation* and the *participation* stages.[10] This is due partly to space limitations, but mostly to the well-recognized fact that it was only in 1956 that the Polish military succeeded in resurrecting its corporate identity and in reasserting its role as an important *independent national* actor on the domestic political arena. It was also 1956, the *annus mirabilis* in recent East European history, that marked the beginning of the process of accommodation between the military and the party, replacing the previous subordinate relationship which deprived the military of any freedom of action and which, therefore, from the analytical point of view is not intellectually interesting. By way of introduction, we shall begin with a brief summary of the process of Sovietization and subjugation of the Polish military during the Stalinist period, if only to underscore the rather dramatic changes that occurred in 1956 and after.

Viewed from another angle, the various stages in the evolution in the military's role in Polish politics paralleled the evolution of Polish–Soviet relations. One of the key issues in that changing relationship was that for a number of years prior to 1956, the Polish armed forces were perceived by public opinion in the country as having been denied their traditional military function as defender of Poland's independence and national interests, and as being themselves subordinated to Soviet control and interests.[11] There is little doubt that the latter fact was also at least partly responsible for the decline in the prestige of the military as reflected in various public-opinion polls conducted in the 1950s and 1960s.

In analyzing each of the above two stages, we intend to focus on the following four major systemic structural and ideological parameters that have shaped the civil–military relations in Communist Poland for more than three decades:

(1) *Political culture.* We shall consider here primarily the possible impact of the anti-militaristic traditions of Marxism–Leninism that form part of the official ideology, and, on the other hand, changes in popular attitudes toward the military establishment, traditionally regarded as a repository and carrier of national values and as a symbol of national pride, virtue, and identity.

(2) *Elite analysis.* Here we shall explore the relationship between the party and military elites with reference to their structure, composition, and recruitment patterns. While it would be unrealistic to assume the presence of a direct linkage between general background characteristics of elite members and attitudes and policy positions, we shall try to identify, whenever possible, the existing 'affinity groups' or factions within the military, and on that basis to make some inferences about the respective attitudes and policy decisions.

(3) *Group conflict analysis.* The concept of interest groups in Communist political systems continues to be controversial, in that the assumption of the presence of distinct sets of interests and values

shared and articulated by groups and other institutional member-
ships is said to be only relevant for pluralistic societies. Nonetheless,
we believe the concept of interest groups to be a useful analytical
tool for the study of the Polish military, and we shall endeavor to
test some of the underlying theoretical assumptions.[12]

(4)   *Developmental analysis.* Finally, we shall examine the role of the
military as a potential agent of modernization and an instrument of
political, economic, and social change in Poland. As suggested
earlier, the military participated actively in the processes of state- and
nation-building and today it may still be viewed as performing the
crucial function of national, if not always political, integration.

As mentioned earlier, Poland represents today an interesting case of a
country with strong militaristic values and traditions which have been
significantly transformed in the course of the past thirty-odd years.
Following the Communist seizure of power in which the military played a
rather ambiguous role, the armed forces command was first subjugated
and purged, then partially rehabilitated and only relatively recently
accorded once again an important place in the Polish polity. What follows
is an attempt to examine and analyze the role of the military in the
various stages of its evolution since 1956 which, as suggested earlier,
coincided with the military's return to the domestic political arena.

SOVIETIZATION AND SUBJUGATION

The Sovietization and subjugation of the Polish military, which began in
the late 1940s, followed roughly the conventional Stalinist pattern that
was also imposed on the other East European countries. It was part and
parcel of an effort to create a monolithic bloc, a Soviet colonial empire to
be ruled by Moscow. In a nutshell, the process of Stalinization of the
indigenous armed forces had three major consequences: subordination to
the Soviet Union and 'denial of nation-state function,' diminution in the
political role of the military, and growing conflict between national and
ideological and universalistic interests.[13] The most important steps in the
process of Sovietization were as follows:

(1)   Appointment of the Polish-born Soviet Marshal Rokossovsky as Minister of Defense and Commander-in-Chief of the Polish armed forces

The nomination, announced in November 1949, made Poland a unique
example of total domination by the Soviet Union. The Soviet move, which
was not paralleled elsewhere in Eastern Europe, may be explained with
reference to the fact that given Poland's history, the traditional Polish
attitude toward Russia, Poland's critical geographical position, plus Stalin's
paranoia, it was not unreasonable that the Soviet leader should have
wanted to neutralize, if not emasculate, the Polish military. This was done
by the Kremlin, even though there was no evidence that either the Polish
party or the military appeared disloyal toward Moscow, or that they har-
bored stronger Titoist sympathies than their counterparts in the other

satellites. To be sure, the party's Secretary, General Gomulka, was purged together with a handful of the senior party leaders, but the purge was less extensive in Poland than in the rest of the region. As will be seen, the same was true for the purges in the military. Another possible explanation might have been Stalin's desire to humiliate the country as a proof of its total subjugation to Soviet control. Although not entirely credible, the idea cannot be dismissed as totally irrational; after all, only a decade earlier Stalin had forcibly dissolved the Communist Party of Poland for reasons that remain as largely obscure today as they were in 1938.

(2) Mass Purges in the Military

Together with the party, the military became a major target for a massive purge. The purge in the party was focused mostly on such disparate elements as the members of the former Polish Socialist Party which only recently had merged with the Communists, the members of the prewar Communist Party of Poland, Spanish Civil War veterans, Polish Communists who for a variety of reasons had spent the war years in the West, and, last but not least, the members of the wartime Communist resistance movement. Similarly, the purge in the army was selectively directed against the potentially less reliable elements of the officer corps which was composed of several parts. Among the victims of the purge were not only many of the former officers of the Polish army in the West, the members of the non-Communist underground, former German prisoners of war, and officers of the Communist military resistance, but also members of the Polish army organized in the USSR. Most of them were arrested, tried, and given long prison terms. Only relatively few were executed, especially when compared with similar executions in Czechoslovakia and Hungary.[14]

(3) Ascendance of the Secret Police and Internal Security Forces

As elsewhere in the region, the purge of the military in Poland went hand in hand with the military's penetration by the secret police. Moreover, the creation of a separate, fully equipped internal security command represented further weakening of the military's monopoly of armed power and provided additional proof of the party's lack of confidence in the army's reliability as loyal supporter of the regime, as reflected earlier by the appointment of Rokossovsky as Minister of Defense.

(4) Institutional Sovietization of the Military as the Logical Consequence of the above Changes

It brought to completion the process initiated already during the takeover period, and was closely linked with the expansion and militarization of the Polish industry in 1950, after the outbreak of the Korean War.

Thus the military, together with the other elements of the Polish polity and society, were brought under the control of the Stalinist faction in the party in the true totalitarian fashion. Among the consequences of this particular process was the further alienation of the armed forces from the rest of Polish society which viewed the military establishment, headed by Rokossovsky and other Soviet generals, as one of the major instruments of Moscow's control over its satrapy. The estrangement continued the process of a significant change in Poland's traditional political culture which began in the aftermath of World War II.

Insofar as the other analytical parameters were concerned, the policy of Sovietization obviously precluded the emergence of the Polish military as an interest group. Whatever limited autonomy the military enjoyed at the end of the takeover period appeared to be totally eliminated. There was some degree of congruence between the military and the political elites, although the former still consisted of many former Soviet officers who represented a source of potential future friction if not outright conflict. Viewed from the developmental angle the subjugation and Sovietization of the military was part and parcel of the process of Soviet-dominated state-building, the first stage of which coincided with the Communist seizure of power. Although ordinarily the military tends to be seen as an important component of the state, in this particular case the military together with such social or systemic components as the labor unions, youth organizations, or peasant associations, could be considered if not as a necessarily useful transmission belt then, at least as a potential instrument of socialization at the disposal of the state.[15]

THE PARTIAL RECOVERY OF THE MILITARY

The partial recovery of the military's standing and prestige which reached its peak in October 1956 was an integral part of the process of de-Stalinization that started later in Poland than in the rest of the Soviet bloc. However, once under way, the disintegration of the Stalinist system went deeper and further than elsewhere in the region except for Hungary. To put it in a nutshell, the decline in the rule of terror and the power of the secret police, the growing popular dissatisfaction with the regime, economic stagnation, and the deepening conflict within the oligarchy combined finally to overturn the existing political leadership and to return Gomulka to power. This was greatly facilitated by the attitude of an important part of the military establishment which actively pressed for greater liberalization and which in a moment of crisis showed its willingness to defend the new leadership against imminent Soviet attack.

In contrast to other periods of postwar Polish history, the process of de-Stalinization, leading up to and including the traumatic events in October 1956, has been fairly well described and analyzed in the literature.[16] Insofar as the role of the military is concerned, the salient stages in the process included the following:

-   the downgrading of the secret police apparatus which in the Polish context resulted not only from Beria's demise but also from the highly publicized defection and revelations of a high-ranking secret police official;[17]

- the gradual release of political prisoners, including a number of generals and other high-ranking officers, most of whom were subsequently rehabilitated and readmitted into the army;
- the growing schism within the ruling oligarchy, accentuated after the sudden death of the party's Secretary-General Bierut and his replacement by Ochab in March 1956;[18]
- escalating criticism of Stalinist practices in all walks of public life, especially after the 20th Congress of the Soviet Communist Party.

The watershed event was clearly the workers' demonstration in the city of Poznan in June 1956 which necessitated the use of troops. There was conflicting evidence as to whether the soldiers had actually fired at the demonstrators; even if they had, it became fairly obvious to the regime that the military could not be fully trusted in the event of a similar demonstration in the future.[19] There is little doubt that this awareness contributed to the escalation of the split within the party hierarchy and to the increasing demands for a drastic change in the top leadership.

The events of October 1956 are well known and will not be discussed here.[20] The crucial factors were, of course, the overwhelming support of the military for Gomulka and the new leadership, and the determination of the Polish armed forces to resist Soviet intervention aimed at stopping or slowing down the process of liberalization. The immediate result of the changeover was the departure of Marshal Rokossovsky and his replacement in the Ministry of Defense by General Spychalski, a veteran of the Communist underground and a close confidant of Gomulka, with whom he was accused of 'rightist–nationalist deviation' in 1949; he was subsequently arrested, jailed and apparently even tortured, before his release in 1956.

The direct involvement of the military in the process of de-Stalinization and liberalization, and especially the army's willingness to fight if necessary in order to defend the new regime, appeared to stop, at least for a while, the growing alienation of the society from the military. The degree of alienation and indifference vis-à-vis the army was too high, however, to reverse the trend, but for a few months in late 1956 and early 1957 one could witness almost a return to the traditional 'organic unity' between the Polish people and their army. Once the threat of the Soviet intervention began to wane, however, the old distrust of the military reappeared, although clearly not as sharply as in the preceding period. Hence it may be speculated that the popular attitude of indifference toward, or even contempt for, the military had become one of the more interesting permanent features of the Polish political culture.[21]

Obviously, one of the more important reasons for the rapprochement between the military, on the one hand, and both the regime and the rest of society on the other, was the re-emergence of powerful nationalist sentiments within both the military and society at large. In the military this was primarily reflected in the early return to the USSR of those Soviet officers who had occupied leading positions in the Polish army, often for more than a decade.[22] Their places were filled by their Polish counterparts chosen by the new regime which, in this way, laid the foundations for a party–military coalition which survived more or less intact for the next fifteen years or so.

Finally, the October changeover meant a farreaching rehabilitation of various groups and individuals who had been branded as people's enemies and persecuted throughout most of the Stalinist period. Among them were members of the Communist and non-Communist resistance, veterans of the Spanish Civil War and former German prisoners of war. Many of them participated actively in the takeover only to be dismissed at its end and often imprisoned after 1949. Upon rehabilitation, some returned to active duty while others joined the revived veterans' organization known as ZBoWiD which quickly became one of the most powerful interest groups in the country and, in time, came to be used as an important political base for potential aspirants for top leadership.[23]

THE UNEASY ALLIANCE

As suggested earlier, the ouster of Marshal Rokossovsky and the Soviet military advisers was followed by the creation of what initially appeared to be a strong alliance between the party and the military. In fact, the relationship was anything but close and smooth as indicated by the events of 1967–8, which demonstrated that continuing attempts at closing the gap between the military and the rest of Polish society have largely failed. Eventually, the military, increasingly dissatisfied with Gomulka's faltering leadership, became involved in the intense factional conflict that weakened the party in the late 1960s and led to Gomulka's ouster in December 1970.

In its early stage, however, the party–military alliance seemed close. The new Minister of Defense, General Spychalski, was made a member of the Central Committee and together with a few other veterans of the wartime Communist underground formed the core of the Gomulka regime. Other key positions in the military were also occupied by members of the wartime Communist resistance and Polish army in the Soviet Union who filled the slots left vacant by the departing Soviet officers.[24] The closer relationship between the party and the military after 1956 was also reflected in the growth of party membership within the officer corps which increased from 40 percent in 1949 to about 67 percent in 1958.[25] At the same time, however, class origin, which in the early postwar period served as the main criterion for officer recruitment, gave way to the level of educational achievement which, beginning in the mid-1950s, became the main criterion for entry into the Polish army officer corps.[26]

The 're-Polonisation' of the officer corps was closely linked with the growing prestige of the military which seemed slowly to regain its traditional role as the sole bearer of arms. The drastic reduction in the power of the secret police and the downgrading of the internal security troops removed to some extent potential competition and challenge to the military's monopoly of organized armed power. For a while, at least, the armed forces basked in the limelight of euphoric nationalistic feeling directed against the Soviet Union and some of its clients. Although its prestige continued to lag, by its readiness to confront the Red Army, the Polish military, most likely, recovered some measure of popularity among the masses.[27]

However, the wild exuberance that characterized the first year or so of Gomulka's rule soon gave way to a feeling of *déjà vu* and resignation. Clearly, some of it was due to Gomulka's return to the Soviet fold consummated at the famous meeting of the eleven ruling parties in Moscow, in November 1957, to honor the 40th anniversary of the Bolshevik Revolution. Deprived of hoped-for Chinese support, the Polish leader was forced to accept and to acknowledge once again the Soviet hegemony in the region.[28]

Little is known about the military's role in the process of fencemending with the USSR and the rest of the Warsaw alliance. It may be speculated that the military raised no objection to closer relations with Moscow, as long as the latter were placed on a more equal basis than in the past, as reflected in the new 'status of forces' agreement signed in November 1956. This agreement, together with a number of other Polish–Soviet treaties signed at the same time, removed several of the most vexing anomalies and irritants that had characterized the Polish–Soviet relations since the end of the war, especially in the economic arena. As such, it did go a long way in satisfying the military's demand for a greater equality between Warsaw and Moscow.

The process of apparent accommodation between the party and the military did not get very far. Despite the mutual support and cooperation between the political and military leadership at a critical juncture in October 1956, the appointment of Spychalski as Minister of Defense symbolized the continued subjugation of the professional officer corps, now to Gomulka rather than to Rokossovsky. Thus, despite the removal of the latter and of the other Soviet officers, the new situation led to a continuation of frustrations, to cleavages within the officer corps, and to a growing resentment of Spychalski. The cleavages within the military elites paralleled to some extent the growing rifts within the party. Moreover, the past relationship of party versus the military, which characterized the earlier stages in the civil–military relations in Poland, was now replaced by a more complex matrix that involved the military, the apparat, the secret police and the bureaucracy, each of which has continued to articulate its own particular interests.

The next decade witnessed a gradual erosion of the party–military alliance, culminating in the major purge of the officer corps in 1967–8 that was closely linked with the anti-Semitic campaign of the same period. On the other hand, the failure to solve the country's basic economic problems resulted in a rapid decline in popular support for Gomulka, who by 1967 found himself under a severe attack from various directions within and outside the party. Among the former, the most significant was the so-called 'Partisan' faction which soon made a fairly obvious bid for power. The strength of the 'Partisans,' led by the former Communist resistance leader Moczar, lay in their unabashedly nationalistic, if not outright chauvinistic, stance, their relatively close personal ties with segments of the military and the party intelligentsia, and in their control of the veterans' association, ZboWiD.[29]

Although the 'Partisans' appeared as the most visible faction within the military High Command, there were at least two other groupings that continued to exert some influence within the military establishment: the 'Russians' who included mostly Soviet army officers who for a variety of reasons did not take part in the exodus of the Soviet military advisers after October 1956, and the 'Liberals' who consisted primarily of the veterans of the wartime Communist resistance and who tended to be closely identified with the brief liberalization period in the late 1950s. In the early 1960s, they were on the way out as victims of the growing conservatism of the Gomulka regime.[30]

The opportunity for the 'Partisans' to expand their influence in the Polish military establishment arose in 1967, in connection with the Six Day War in the Middle East. Without going into the details, the overwhelming Israeli victory was openly applauded by a number of high-ranking Polish officers. They were soon given discharges as the first victims in the ensuing vicious struggle for power between the Gomulka faction and the 'Partisans.'[31] As is well known, Gomulka was saved at the last minute by Brezhnev who had his hands full with the Czechoslovak crisis of 1968 and who was clearly reluctant to face another emergency in Poland. The Polish leader managed to survive for more than two years before he was forced out and replaced by Gierek in the wake of the Baltic Coast riots in December 1970.

The part played by the military in the factional struggle is not easily reconstructed. It may be assumed that although the nominal head of the Polish armed forces, Marshal Spychalski, was a loyal supporter of Gomulka, some segments of the military hierarchy sympathized with the 'Partisans' with whom they felt a closer affinity reinforced by the shared traditions of nationalism and anti-Semitism. Hence, there is no evidence of any mass resentment of, or resistance to, the purging of officers of Jewish background in 1967 and after, which illustrated rather well the weakness of professional pride and military esprit de corps when faced with an attack from the outside.[32] On the contrary, one might speculate that the purge was widely applauded as creating some room at the top for followers of the 'Partisans', just as the departure of the Soviet military advisers a decade earlier opened many avenues for advancement. However, the 'Partisans' suffered a blow in 1965, when the control over the so-called 'Internal Security Corps' was transferred from the Ministry of the Interior, headed by Moczar, to the Ministry of Defense which remained loyal to Gomulka.

Furthermore, the 'Partisans' hopes of capturing the High Command of the armed forces were dashed in April 1968 by the appointment of General Jaruzelski as Minister of Defense, replacing Spychalski who was elevated to the largely ceremonial chairmanship of the State Council, the collective presidency of the country. In the context of civil–military relations in Poland, Jaruzelski's nomination was an important turning point in that it symbolized the emergence in its own right of the professional officer corps. Thus, it may be argued that it was only in 1968 that *accommodation* became a truly relevant and accurate description of the political–military relationship in Poland.

In light of this, it is really not surprising that the Polish military did not support Gomulka in his hour of need in December 1970. On the contrary, there is some circumstantial evidence suggesting that the military High Command favored Gomulka's ouster and Gierek's succession, and the fact that the Minister of Defense, General Jaruzelski, not only retained his post in the Cabinet but also his seat in the new Politburo, speaks for itself. It was clearly a reward for the military's refusal to prevent the changeover.[33]

The seeming rapprochement between the party and military in the late 1950s had not resulted in any major change in the popular attitude toward the military which continued to be held in low esteem by the population.[34] Nonetheless, the decade of the 1960s witnessed the emergence of the military as a pressure group, emphasizing its own distinct, professional identity and purpose, and articulating its own particular interests. This strong insistence on a separate identity became especially visible during the riots of December 1970 which, as the military was only too eager to stress, were suppressed by the police and internal security detachments with regular army units remaining largely neutral on the sidelines. The military High Command took every opportunity to present the army to the public at large as a purely professional force which, when called upon, apparently refused to perform police duties for the Gomulka regime fighting desperately for its political survival.[35]

A closer look at the transfer of power from Gomulka to Gierek in December 1970, makes it clear that by refusing to move against the striking shipyard workers or to defend Gomulka against attacks from within the party, the military leadership, probably for the first time in Polish postwar history, exercised its veto power, thus becoming a key arbiter on the domestic political scene. To put it differently, although it was the Polish working class that succeeded in overthrowing the unpopular party leadership, it was only able to do so with the tacit approval of the military leadership which most likely could have prevented Gomulka's ouster. Whether December 1970 witnessed the birth of a workers–army alliance that replaced the party–military coalition, was too early to tell, yet the possibility of such an alliance could not have been lost on the incoming Gierek leadership. One might also view the Polish military as trying to assume the mantle of a 'Guardian of the Nation' by remaining above factional politics.[36]

The question may be raised as to why the military apparently preferred Gierek to Moczar, the leader of the 'Partisans' who, as suggested earlier, enjoyed considerable support within the officer corps. It may be hypothesized here that the top military command was somewhat distrustful of Moczar as a potential candidate for the highest post in the nation. While he may have been preferable to Gomulka, his colorful past and a rather obvious appetite for power, made Moczar suspect as an ideal partner in the party–military coalition.

One may assume that even though Moczar's positions on various issues, including his implicit appeal to anti-Soviet sentiments, had attraction for some in the armed forces, there must have been some apprehension that once in power he might rely most heavily on his already formidable base of support in the security forces. In other words, by supporting Moczar against Gierek, the military would be running the risk of contributing to the rise of a potential, strong institutional competitor. With his impressive record as the party leader in Silesia, Gierek appeared as a much more stable and reliable ally who could be counted upon to maintain stability both at home and in Poland's foreign relations.

There is little doubt that the 1960s represented a period of rapid political and socio-economic change in Eastern Europe which, for various reasons, seemed to affect Poland less than such countries as Czechoslovakia, Hungary, and even Romania. Whereas Czechoslovakia had its 'Prague Spring,' Hungary its New Economic Mechanism, and Romania its challenge to the Warsaw Pact and the Soviet domination of the alliance, the attention of the Polish leaders appeared focused on feuding with the Church, fighting the students, and fomenting anti-Semitism, while the country was stagnating on all fronts. It was the awareness of the lack of progress, especially on the economic front, that most likely persuaded the military to cast its lot with the Gierek group which was perceived as being more dynamic and pragmatic, and eager to get the country moving again.

CIVIL–MILITARY RELATIONS IN POLAND IN THE 1970s: PARTICIPATION OR PARTNERSHIP?

At this stage it is necessary to define more clearly the nature of the military's role in political decision-making and the types of decisions in which the Polish military participated in the 1970s. With respect to the latter, Polish military elites could not participate in the sense that their Soviet counterparts – or the Chinese, Romanian, and Yugoslav military did – that is, they did not play a significant role in the formulation of such major policies as defense strategy, internal political stabilization and/or foreign policy.[37] Rather, its participation was limited to less important domestic questions such as economic policy and performance inasmuch as they affected the country's military strength and potential and, willy nilly, to the question of maintaining law and order within the country in the event of a major domestic unrest. The infrequent official statements concerning military strategy and doctrine mirrored closely the standard Soviet pronouncements, reflecting little original Polish thinking on the subject.[38]

Thus, prevented from participating in most issue-areas which are traditionally the focus of the military's interests, the Polish military's concern for domestic stability may have distorted what would otherwise be the expected pattern of economic priorities. In other words, since internal stability in Poland in the 1970s depended not simply on modernization and economic efficiency but on an immediate improvement in consumer satisfaction, the military may have found itself in the anomalous position of favoring consumer-oriented policies at the expense of investments in heavy industry.

Together with the rest of the Polish society, the military could not help being impressed with the initial record and performance of the Gierek team. It is also possible that the military was consulted by Gierek regarding his new economic strategy which emphasized large-scale modernization of the Polish industrial base with the help of mass infusion of Western technology financed by Western government and bank credits. The relations between the new regime and the military seemed relatively close, at least on the surface, and Gierek's ouster of his two initial supporters and latter competitors – Moczar and Szlachcic, both identified as leaders of the 'Partisan' faction – was apparently not opposed by the military.[39]

There has been no evidence of any deterioration in the party–military relationship in the mid-1970s, when the Polish economy began to slow down following the spectacular growth period earlier in the decade, and when the announcement of the constitutional revisions resulted in the emergence of a first serious dissident movement in late 1975. The concessions granted the opposition by the Gierek regime must have had the approval of the military who, one may guess, was probably less than happy with the original revisions emphasizing the leading role of the Soviet Union in the region, and stressing the special exalted position of the Communist Party at home.

The first apparent confrontation between the party and the military took place in the course of 1976. By that time, it was common knowledge that the Polish economy had been in serious difficulties which, among other things, were reflected in growing shortages of certain foodstuffs and consumer goods which, in turn, resulted in growing popular dissatisfaction. As is generally known, one of the suggested remedies was to be a comprehensive reform of retail prices which was intended to raise the general price level of goods to bring demand closer to supply and make the whole price structure at the retail level more rational. In anticipation of the increase in prices, it became generally known some time in late spring that the military and the security organs received wage adjustments which were to compensate them for the rise in the cost of living. It was obvious that by engaging in this rather crude technique of social engineering the party was not going to take any chances, and it wanted to be able to count on the undivided support of the army and the police in the event of a violent reaction à la December 1970. It was equally clear, however, that no one in the party or in the government seriously anticipated the repetition of the scenario of six years earlier.[40]

The rest is history. The sharp and largely uncompensated increase in the retail prices of meat and other foodstuffs resulted in violent strikes in several key industrial cities, forcing the regime in less than twenty-four hours to call off the price reform and postpone it indefinitely. Little is known of what transpired in those twenty-four hours, but it may be assumed that the top party leadership found itself under powerful pressure to surrender to the workers' demands and acknowledge defeat. The latter, needless to say, represented a tremendous loss of face for the Gierek regime, not only at home but also abroad, and it may be speculated that the major, if not the sole, reason for the government giving way on this particular issue was the fact that it was not able to enforce its initial decision to raise the prices. It appears that at the crucial meeting of the Politburo called in the wake of the strikes, the Minister of Defense moved to call off the rise declaring that 'the soldiers would not shoot at the workers.'[41]

Thus in June 1976, the Polish military once again reasserted its position as the key actor on the domestic political arena whose veto or approval has ultimately proved decisive in time of emergency. At least twice in barely six years, the military forced the civilian leadership to grant significant concessions to the population, and twice the armed forces and the working class found themselves on the same side of the barricade in the conflict with the ruling oligarchy, thus duplicating the situation of October 1956 when the Warsaw workers and soldiers were ready to resist Soviet forces advancing toward the Polish capital.

The internal political situation in Poland since 1976 has been characterized by considerable instability, with the Gierek regime a target of attacks and criticism from within and outside the party. The party itself has become again sharply divided, with Gierek occupying the middle and, most likely, the weakest position between the conservative central apparat and the more pragmatic younger regional party secretaries. The bone of contention among these three groups has been mostly economic policy and, presumably, the attitude toward the political opposition which acquired considerable momentum in the early fall of 1974, with the formation of the so-called Workers' Defense Committee (KOR). Neither of the factions has been strong enough to push through its favored program in the face of the opposition by the others.

The military's stand vis-a-vis the economic crisis and the dissidents is not easily discerned. One possible intepretation is that the High Command has favored the maintenance of the status quo, at least in the short run, and therefore it has not opposed Gierek and the centrist faction. It might have adopted this stance in the expectation of an early improvement in the economic situation, or in order to maintain at least some semblance of stability and agreement among the factions. In political terms, the emphasis on the status quo meant continued absence of extreme solutions and radical reforms and the presence of incremental improvements in domestic economic policy, gradual expansion of commercial, cultural, and even political contacts with the West, and the policy of benign neglect toward the opposition.

It may be argued that any other policy, such as the emergence of an alliance between the military and the *apparatchiki* was bound to contribute to further economic and political instability, possibly involving additional worker riots, a potential general strike, a confrontation between the military and the party rank and file, a direct violent clash between the army, the police and the population, and, ultimately, a possible Soviet intervention to restore order. While it may be assumed that, in contrast to the Czechs, the Polish military would offer armed resistance to the Soviets, it may also be taken for granted that the High Command would just as soon try to avoid a direct confrontation with the Red Army.

Conversely, a coalition between the military and the 'reformers' would also create serious problems, since the bureaucrats in both the party and the government would be likely to resist, if not sabotage, the economic and other reforms which, in turn, could lead to an escalation of the party–military conflict and eventually to systemic instability. Thus the apparent strong preference of the military for the middle-of-the-road approach to the solution of the many difficulties faced by the Polish polity today.

Generally speaking, a good case can be made that the Polish military, having been drawn into domestic politics because of the highly unstable situation, has viewed its support of any particular faction as conditional, contingent upon that faction's ability to maintain stability, the latter in Poland today being defined in terms of economic performance. Thus one could expect the military to shift its support from the center to the 'reformers' or the conservatives if it perceives that either of these groupings is better able to get at the real source of current instability.[42]

CONCLUSION

There were several reasons for investigating the role of the military as a political actor in Poland. One was simply the relative dearth of scholarly research on this particular subject. Another reason was to use Poland in order to test a generalized analytical framework developed for the study of civil–military relations in Communist systems. Finally, we were interested in examining the part played by the military in Polish politics with the aid of four different parameters.

One of the conclusions that emerges from our study is that the party–military relations in Poland since the end of World War II, and especially since 1956, have, in fact, conformed to the pattern suggested at the outset; that is, they moved from a stage of *co-optation* to *subordination, accommodation,* and eventually *participation.* To a large extent, that congruence should not surprise us since the above pattern was originally derived from the study of party–military relations in the USSR. Although Soviet–East European relations have changed over time, and Moscow's junior partners no longer have to imitate and emulate Soviet experience to the smallest detail, this change may have been less true for the relationship between the ruling party and the military where the Soviet model was still used as an example. This was most likely due to the continuing impact of the traditional Marxist–Leninist thinking which tended to influence the behavior and attitude of the party toward the military.

All Communist regimes, at least in their early stages, took the Soviet model of civil–military relations as their reference point. However, in no case were civil–military relations identical to the Soviet practice. On the one hand, the dependent Communist countries have adopted an institutional pattern relatively similar to the Soviet one – at least in theory – although the military has been denied many of its normal functions. Elsewhere, however, the mode of civil–military relations has become domesticated to varying degrees – individualized according to the characteristics of the individual regimes as they have become independent of

Moscow (for example, Yugoslavia, China, Romania, North Korea). What has remained constant throughout the Communist camp has been the traditional insistence on the primacy of politics.

Although Poland in the late 1970s probably no longer viewed itself as Moscow's satellite, the Soviet connection was clearly an important variable in the development of political–military relations in that country. For, as long as the Polish armed forces considered themselves as a faithful member of the Warsaw Pact – an alliance strongly dominated by the Soviet Union – their freedom of maneuver had been severely circumscribed. Here, the comparison with Romania is quite useful. Ceausescu's frequent avowals of Romanian sovereignty, including exclusive command and control of the country's army, clearly have increased the importance of the Romanian military as a domestic and international actor. Until now, the Polish party leadership has not found sufficient courage to come up with a similar declaration of independence, even though it might have tacitly shared the views of its Romanian counterpart. It follows that, at least for the time being, the Polish military has not become fully emancipated as a professional national fighting force, and its ability to articulate its own interests and demands has remained restricted.

Have the 1970s witnessed any serious changes in the parameters that we have used to analyze the role of the military in the Polish socio-political systems? Our preliminary view is that whatever transformation has taken place, it represented essentially a direct continuation of changes initiated in an earlier period. Thus, insofar as the popular attitude toward the military was concerned, the latter has not greatly improved its image which continued to be rather low in comparison with other professional groups and occupations.[43] This rather drastic postwar decline in popular support of, and respect for, the military as the carrier of national values and patriotic pride contrasted sharply with the highly positive attitude that dominated the interwar political scene. It is our belief that the major causes of the lack of respect for the military were mostly the trauma of the wartime occupation, including the heavy human casualties, which raised serious questions in people's minds regarding the exalted role of the military as leaders of the Polish nation, combined with the persisting image of the impotent military as a handmaiden of the increasingly unpopular regime and an obedient tool of the Soviet Union. The low opinion of the armed forces was further augmented by the widely shared perception of the low social status of the military elites in society at large.

Lack of data precludes drawing definite conclusions regarding the differences and similarities between the civil and military elites. We have been able to define some major subcategories and factions within each of the two groupings; we have tried to identify some 'affinity groups' and make inferences about their impact on attitudes and specific policy decisions, but, as always, we have been hampered by our ignorance of the input side of decision-making processes in Communist countries, Poland not excluded.

Has the Polish military in the 1970s behaved or acted more forcefully or decisively like a pressure group, articulating and protecting its own particularistic interests? Here again the answer is not clear, mostly because of lack of evidence. A good case can be made for asserting that, beginning in the second half of the 1950s, the military acquired its own professional identity, separate from that of the party, and police and internal security forces. However, this did not necessarily mean that the armed forces have had to reassert that identity and defend its interests against the other two institutions more intensely and frequently in the decade of the seventies than in the previous ten or fifteen years.[44] There is no evidence of either the party or the police after 1956 trying to reduce the authority of the military. In other words, there has been no real need for the latter to behave as a typical interest group competing with others for power, influence, and human and material resources.

However, on the basis of what is known about the crisis situations in December 1970 and June 1976, it may be concluded that while one might hesitate to view the Polish military as a typical interest group, one could certainly describe it as a 'veto group' without whose approval no major decision was likely to be made in the country. It does not follow that the military is, or has been, consulted at every step of every major decision: it simply means that in the stalemate situation which has characterized the Polish domestic politics for some time now, the military could be called upon to act as the ultimate arbiter whose judgement would be acceptable to the various factions within the party and the government.

It is occasionally suggested that interest group theory, as applied to Communist systems, focuses almost entirely on conflict to the exclusion of shared values and common interests of the main protagonists. We submit that this is a gross misrepresentation of interest group theory, even as applied to Western pluralistic societies where the assumption is that of a fundamental consensus on the nature of the system and of an acceptance by competing groups of established political processes. Thus group conflict on specific issues takes place within that broader consensus, and this is true for the party and the military in Poland which seem to recognize the legitimacy of competing interests in a socialist polity. In fact, it may be argued that in the 1970s the process of accommodation between the party and the military was well on the way to becoming a process of participation.

The same conclusion can be reached when the process is viewed from the developmental perspective. After December 1970, the Polish armed forces seemingly supported the party's decision favoring rapid economic modernization which was also bound to have serious impact on the political system. While itself not an agent of modernization or political change, there is some evidence suggesting that the military has been involved in the major political decisions that affected the course of events and the process of development in Poland in the 1970s.

One point that we would like to put across is that in Poland, in contrast to most, if not all, of the East European countries, there has been little evidence of the 'traditional incompatibility between the value-systems of the military establishment and the Leninist hegemonial party' and of the 'conflict stemming from Party efforts to enforce political control, ideological conformity, and to use the military for socialization in Party beliefs.'[45]

Throughout most of the past three decades, the Polish party could hardly be called 'hegemonial.' On the contrary, in terms of the internal power configuration in Poland, the party has traditionally been one of the weaker political actors, if only because of its proclivity toward factionalism and lack of agreement on fundamentals. Because of it also, the party after the mid-1950s has not been in the position always to challenge and fully control the military.

In the same vein, we would like to take issue with the view that 'the [Polish] Party's willingness to introduce new technology . . . is indicative of its rising confidence in the political reliability of the armed forces. The Polish Party leadership . . . has shown its confidence in its military by permitting extensive modifications in the traditional control mechanisms.'[46] It may be argued, first, that the December 1970 and June 1976 events mentioned earlier, exploded the myth of the political reliability of the Polish military, and, second, that the Polish party, being politically weak, had little or no choice but to modify the existing control arrangements, most likely at the request of the military. The fact that, by the end of 1975, 85 percent of the officer corps belonged to the party, apparently made little or no difference.[47]

Does it all mean that, on the one hand, as suggested by Herspring, 'the Polish armed forces has basically accepted its national leadership and its value system as legitimate'[48] or, on the other, that 'past experience indicates that the military is generally unreliable against internal threats?'[49] We do not think that either proposition is correct. Apart from the fact that the concept of legitimacy is a difficult one to define and operationalize, especially in the Communist context, there is really no sufficient evidence showing full congruence between the party and military value systems. All that can be said is that for the past three decades or so, the Polish military has tolerated the Communist regime and that, presumably, it would be willing to defend the country – and perhaps even the government – against some foreign invaders. Whether this automatically implies legitimization of the Communist rule is too early to say.

One potentially significant process that took place in the 1970s could have had a major impact on the relationship between the political leadership and the military. This was the rapprochement between Poland and West Germany, initiated by the Brandt–Gomulka Treaty of December 1970, and culminating in the establishment of relatively close bilateral diplomatic, cultural, and, above all, economic relations in the mid-1970s. This could have been interpreted by the Polish elites and masses alike as eliminating the German Federal Republic as the major enemy of People's Poland, at least in the foreseeable future. Almost from the moment of the creation of West Germany, the latter was often viewed as the chief raison d'être of the Polish People's Army whose main task was the protection of Poland's western borders against West German revanchism, and hence the Polish–West German treaty might well have given rise to questioning the need for maintaining a large standing army, especially in light of Poland's recent economic difficulties.[50]

Is the Polish military entirely unreliable as the protectors of the established regime against domestic enemies? Here again, the answer is far from clear. To be sure, the regular troops did not shoot at the workers in Poznan in June 1956, at the Baltic Coast in December 1970, or in Radom and Ursus in June 1976. At the same time, however, the High Command did not openly prevent security organs from restoring order, not only in the above places but also on the other occasions such as in Warsaw in March 1968, using often brutal and violent methods. In the final analysis, the military's behavior vis-à-vis internal insurgencies is likely to be guided by its perception of its own interests rather than the existence of a political crisis. Thus, at certain times, the army may well open fire at the demonstrators whereas, at others, it may refuse to do so, if in its judgement, this would benefit it.

Finally, could the Polish military be viewed as an agent of modernization and political change? Our view here is that this particular role has not been very important, especially when compared with the interwar period when the Polish armed forces performed a series of functions associated with state- and nation-building, socialization, and even political participation. After World War II, this role has been drastically diminished as the military's involvement in the processes of the seizure of power and Stalinist consolidation has been marginal. Only in the most recent period could one possibly talk about the military's role in the process of modernization, but even here that role tended to be passive rather than active, and it would not be correct to view the military as an agent of change. More likely, the military has not opposed change, perhaps at times it has even encouraged it, especially in the economic sphere, but this was still a far cry from being in the forefront of the modernization process.

Throughout this chapter we have focused almost entirely on the Polish military's role in domestic politics. What needs to be investigated is that role in the international context, including such issues as the relations between the Polish and Soviet military, the comparison between the civil–military relations in Poland and elsewhere in the region, and also the relationship of the Polish military to the Warsaw Pact. All of these problems are important and require a separate treatment which simply could not be attempted here, if only for reasons of space.

NOTES

The authors wish to thank Dale Herspring, Robin Remington, and Jerzy Wiatr who read the first draft of this chapter and whose penetrating criticism helped to clarify many of our thoughts.

1 To the best of our knowledge, until the mid-1960s the only scholarly research in the English language that dealt with the Polish military in the post-World War II period was a chapter in Ithiel de Sola Pool *et al.*, *Satellite Generals* (Stanford, Calif.: Stanford University Press, 1955), pp. 55–81.

2 For example, Roman Kolkowicz, *The Soviet Military and the Communist Party* (Princeton, NJ: Princeton University Press, 1967); Edward L. Warner, III, *The Military in Contemporary Soviet Politics: An Institutional Analysis* (New York: Praeger, 1977); and Timothy J. Colton, *Commissars, Commanders, and Civilian Authority* (Cambridge, Mass.: Harvard University Press, 1979).

3 Ellis Joffe, *Party and Army: Professionalism and Political Control in the Chinese Officer Corps, 1949–1964* (Cambridge, Mass.: Harvard University Press, 1965); C. Cheng (ed.), *The Politics of the Chinese Red Army* (Stanford, Calif.: The Hoover Institution, 1966).

4 For a summary of these three approaches, see Timothy J. Colton, 'The party–military connection: a participatory model,' in Dale R. Herspring and Ivan Volgyes (eds), *Civil–Military Relations in Communist Systems* (Boulder, Colo.: Westview Press, 1978), pp. 53–75. Recently a fourth approach, the 'developmental' one, has been introduced in the literature. Dale R. Herspring and Ivan Volgyes, 'The military as an agent of political socialization in Eastern Europe,' *Armed Forces and Society*, vol. 3, no. 2 (Winter 1977), pp. 249–69.

5 For example, J. Margules (ed.), *Z zagadnien rozwoju Ludowego Wojska Polskiego* (Warsaw: Wydawnictwo MON, 1964); S. Komornicki (ed.), *Regularne jednostki Ludowego Wojska Polskiego* (Warsaw: Wydawnictwo MON, 1965); W. Jurgielewicz *et al.* (eds), *Ludowe Wojsko Polskie 1943–1973* (Warsaw: Wydawnictwo MON, 1973); K. Frontczak (ed.), *Sily zbrojne Polski Ludowej* (Warsaw: Wydawnictwo MON, 1974); M. Plikus (ed.) *Mala kronika Ludowego Wojska Polskiego 1943–1973* (Warsaw: Wydawnictwo MON, 1975); and M. Anusiewicz and I. Ruszkiewicz, *Tarcza socjalistycznej ojczyzny* (Warsaw: Wydawnictwo MON, 1979). Two journals have also been very useful: *Wojsko Ludowe* (a monthly appearing since 1950), and *Wojskowy Przeglad Historyczny* (a quarterly since 1956).

6 Jerzy J. Waitr, 'Social prestige of the military,' in Jacques van Doorn (ed.), *Military Profession and Military Regimes* (The Hague and Paris: Mouton, 1969), pp. 82–93, and 'The public image of the Polish military: past and present,' in Catherine M. Kelleher (ed.), *Political–Military Systems* (Beverly Hills, Calif.: Sage, 1974), pp. 199–205. Dale R. Herspring, 'Technology and the changing political officer in the armed forces: the Polish and East German cases,' *Studies in Comparative Communism*, vol. 10, no. 4 (Winter 1977), pp. 370–93; and 'Poland and East Germany: the external factor,' ibid., vol. 11, no. 3 (Autumn 1978), pp. 225–36.

7 Gabriel A. Almond and G. Bingham Powell, Jr, *Comparative Politics* (Boston, Mass.: Little, Brown, 1966), pp. 35–7 and 306–10.

8 S. P. Huntington, 'The change to change: modernization, development and politics,' *Comparative Politics*, vol. 3, no. 3 (April 1971), p. 316.

9 This typology is a modification of that developed by Roman Kolkowicz in his 'Civil-Military Relations in Communist Systems: The Case of the Soviet Union' (Paper presented at the Conference of the Inter-University Seminar on Armed Forces and Society, SUNY Buffalo, October 1974).

10 For an analysis of the first two stages – *co-optation* and *subordination* – see Andrzej Korbonski, 'The Polish army: 1945–1980,' in Kenneth R. Adelman (ed.), *Communist Armies in Politics* (Boulder, Colo.: Westview Press, 1981).

11 This point is well made in Alex Alexiev, 'Party–military relations in Eastern Europe: the case of Romania,' *ACIS Working Paper*, no. 15, (January 1979), pp. 5–6.

12 Sarah M. Terry, 'The Case for a "Group" Approach to Polish Politics' (paper presented at the 9th National Convention of the American Association for the Advancement of Slavic Studies, Washington, DC, October 1977).

13 Alexiev, op. cit., pp. 5–6.

14 In 1956, nineteen high-ranking officers were posthumously rehabilitated in Poland. They were shot in 1952 on trumped-up charges. Zbigniew Brzezinski, *The Soviet Bloc*, rev. and enlarged edn (Cambridge, Mass.: Harvard University Press, 1967), p. 526.

15 Herspring and Volgyes, 'The military as an agent of political socialization in Eastern Europe,' pp. 249–69.

16 For example, in Brzezinski, op. cit., pp. 230–68.

17 The Ministry of Public Security was abolished in 1954 and its functions were taken over partly by the Ministry of the Interior and partly by a newly formed Committee on Public Security. For details of the defection, see Jozef Swiatlo, *Za kulisami bezpieki i partii* (no publisher and no date). For an English version of the latter, see *News from Behind the Iron Curtain*, vol. 4, no. 3 (March 1955), pp. 3–86.

18 For details, see Peter Raina, *Political Opposition in Poland 1954–1977* (London: Poets and Printers Press, 1978), pp. 37–8.

19 Apparently, 'the soldiers of the Poznan garrison remained passive and in some cases willingly handed over their weapons to the crowd.' M. K. Dziewanowski, *The*

Communist Party of Poland, 2nd edn (Cambridge, Mass.: Harvard University Press, 1976), p. 265.

20 For an interesting recent summary, see George Sakwa, 'The Polish 'October:' a reappraisal through historiography,' *Polish Review,* vol. 23, no. 3 (1978), pp. 62–78.

21 According to a comprehensive analysis of occupational prestige in Poland in 1958, the inhabitants of Warsaw ranked army officers 20th out of 27 occupations, while inhabitants of rural areas gave them a higher ranking, 9th out of 21 occupations. Michal Pohoski, Kazimierz M. Slomczynski, and Wlodzimierz Wesolowski, 'Occupational prestige in Poland,' *Polish Sociological Bulletin,* no. 4 (1976), pp. 70–1.

22 According to a Polish source, the percentage of Soviet officers in the Polish army declined from 3·6 percent in 1950 to 0·4 percent in 1955. Tadeusz Konecki, 'Zawodowe szkolnictwo Ludowego Wojska Polskiego w pierwszym powojennym dziesiecioleciu,' *Wojskowy Przeglad Historyczny,* vol. 19, no. 2 (April–June 1974), p. 358.

23 *ZBoWiD* is the acronym for *Zwiazek Bojownikow o Wolnosc i Demokracje* (Association of Fighters for Freedom and Democracy).

24 For details, see Michal Checinski, ''Ludowe Wojsko Polskie'' przed i po Marcu 1968,' *Zeszyty Historyczne,* no. 44 (1978), pp. 16–19.

25 Dale R. Herspring, 'The Changing Role of the Party–Political Apparatus in the Polish and East German Armed Forces' (Paper presented at the 8th National Convention of the American Association for the Advancement of Slavic Studies, St Louis, Missouri, October 1976).

26 For a discussion of this problem, see J. Graczyk, 'Problems of recruitment and selection in the Polish People's Armed Forces,' in Morris Janowitz and Jacques van Doorn (eds), *On Military Ideology* (Rotterdam: Rotterdam University Press, 1971), pp. 199–208, and 'Social promotion in the Polish People's Army,' in van Doorn (ed.), *Military Profession and Military Regimes,* pp. 73–81. See also, Laszlo Revesz, 'Die Polnische Volksarmee,' in Peter Gosztony (ed.), *Zur Geschichte der europaischen Volksarmeen* (Bonn–Bad Godesberg: Hohwacht, 1976), p. 34.

27 An interesting effort aimed indirectly at raising or resurrecting the prestige of the military, focused on a farreaching debate about traditions of heroism and military glory, and the value of political idealism versus political realism or pragmatism. Adam Bromke, *Poland's Politics* (Cambridge, Mass.: Harvard University Press, 1967), pp. 189–206. See also, George Kolankiewicz and Ray Taras, 'Poland: socialism for everyman,' in Archie Brown and Jack Gray (eds), *Political Culture and Political Change in Communist States* (London: Macmillan, 1977), p. 116; Jerzy J. Wiatr, 'The public image of the Polish military' in Kelleher (ed.), op. cit; and Mieczyslaw Michalik, 'Normative linkages between civilian and military sectors of Polish society,' in Gwyn Harries-Jenkins and Jacques van Doorn (eds), *The Military and the Problem of Legitimacy* (Beverly Hills, Calif.: Sage, 1976), pp. 159–74.

28 Brzezinski, op. cit., pp. 279–308.

29 Dziewanowski, op. cit., pp. 291–2.

30 Checinski, op. cit., pp. 14–18. See also, Joachim Georg Gorlich, 'Tendenzen und Strömungen innerhalb der polnischen militarischen Führung,' *Wehrwissenschaftliche Rundschau,* vol. 18, no. 7 (1968), pp. 377–8.

31 Dziewanowski, op. cit., pp. 296–301, and Gorlich, op. cit., pp. 379–80.

32 Checinski, op. cit., pp. 24–30. See also, Anonymous, 'USSR and the politics of Polish antisemitism 1956–68,' *Soviet Jewish Affairs,* no. 1 (June 1971), pp. 33–8, and H. Laeuen, 'Die Märzunruhen in Polen und ihre Folgen: (II) Partisanen gegen Zionisten,' *Osteuropa,* vol. 19, no. 2 (February 1969), pp. 110–24.

33 Jaruzelski discussed the behavior of the Polish military during the December 1970 crisis at the 8th Plenary Meeting of the Central Committee of the Polish Communist Party on 6–7 February 1971. Radio Free Europe Research, *Polish Press Survey,* no. 2,317 (10 August 1971).

34 For an interesting comparative analysis of the prestige of the military, including Poland, Denmark, West Germany, Indonesia, Pakistan, and the USA, see Wiatr, 'Social prestige of the military,' in van Doorn (ed.), op. cit., pp. 73–81. According to Wiatr, 'One country in the group of seven has consistently much lower prestige of the military profession than the remaining six. This one is Poland,' (p. 77).

35 For an extensive discussion of the military's behavior in December 1970, see Michael Costello, 'The party and military in Poland,' Radio Free Europe Research, *Poland,* no.

12 (26 April 1971).

36 We owe this suggestion to Robin Remington.

37 For an interesting discussion of this question, see Colton, in Herspring and Volgyes (eds), op. cit., pp. 62–73.

38 Henryk Michalski, 'Refleksje o podstawach, charakterze i tresci doktryny wojennej PRL,' *Wojsko Ludowe,* vol. 23, no. 7 (July 1972), pp. 8–16, and 'Niektore teoretyczne problemy strategii wojennej w warunkach PRL,' ibid., vol. 22, no. 8 (August 1972), pp. 9–16.

39 Apparently one of the chief leaders of the 'Partisans', General Korczynski, who was also Commander-in-Chief of the Territorial Defense Forces, was accused of ordering his troops to fire at the Baltic coast strikers. H. Laeuen, 'Moczar's Entmachtung,' *Osteuropa,* vol. 27, no. 1 (January 1972), pp. 37–8. See also, Michael Costello, 'The political fortunes of Mieczyslaw Moczar,' Radio Free Europe Research, *Poland,* no. 15 (2 June 1971).

40 At the same time, however, several hundred potential troublemakers – worker-activists, student leaders, and others – were suddenly called up into the army shortly before the announcement of price increases, ostensibly to participate in summer training exercises. There is some evidence that the initiative for this precautionary action originated with the Ministry of the Interior rather than that of National Defense. Andrzej Solecki, 'Dlaczego nie zostalem czerwcowym warcholem?' *Kultura* (Paris), no. 11/350 (November 1976), pp. 11–34.

41 Personal interviews, Warsaw, June 1976.

42 In the summer of 1979, Jaruzelski was widely mentioned in Warsaw as the most likely successor to the ailing Premier Jaroszewicz. It was said that he was well regarded as an organizer and as one of the very few people capable of getting the country out of the economic morass.

43 In 1975, the inhabitants of Warsaw ranked army officers 13th out of 27 occupations, while the inhabitants of rural areas ranked them 10th out of 21 occupations. Pohoski, Slomczynski and Wesolowski, op. cit., pp. 70–1. In comparison with 1958 the officers' prestige improved in the eyes of Warsaw citizens but remained essentially unchanged in the rural areas. The aggregate ranking put officers as 11th out of 30 occupations (p. 75).

44 This was true even though the relative representation of the military on the Central Committee in the 1970s was below that in the 1950s and 1960s. Dale R. Herspring, 'The Polish military and the policy process' (unpublished paper), p. 20.

45 Alexiev, op. cit., p. 36.

46 Herspring, 'Technology and the changing political officer in the armed forces,' p. 392.

47 Herspring, 'The changing role of the party–political apparatus,' p. 29. The corresponding ratio for 1968 was 80 percent. Also 53 percent of warrant officers, 48 percent of noncommissioned officers and 10 percent of enlisted men belonged to the party. P. I. Efimov (ed.), *Boevoy Soyuz Bratskikh Armii* (Moscow: Voenizdat, 1974), p. 151.

48 Herspring, 'The changing role of the party–political apparatus,' p. 32.

49 Dale R. Herspring and Ivan Volgyes, 'Toward a conceptualization of political reliability in the East European Warsaw Pact armies,' *Armed Forces and Society,* vol. 6, no. 2 (Winter 1980), p. 291.

50 It appears, however, that the German threat can be resurrected at a moment's notice. Thus, in late 1978, a senior party official stated that Poland needed a strong army, among other things, because of the modernization of the Bundeswehr and Germany's continuing desire for border adjustments. Stanislaw Wronski, 'W 35-lecie Ludowego Wojska Polskiego,' *Nowe Drogi,* no. 10 (October 1978), p. 12.

8 The Role of the Military in Yugoslavia: An Historical Sketch

A. ROSS JOHNSON

Studies of Yugoslavia have neglected the military. This research lacuna is both puzzling and troublesome. The Yugoslav People's Army (YPA) in its Partisan incarnation was the founding instrument of Communist Yugoslavia. The army began to play a more active role in the Yugoslav political arena in the 1970s. It will continue to play an important role in the post-Tito political constellation. This chapter, derived from research in progress on the postwar development of the YPA, provides an historical context for analyses of the present and likely future role of the Yugoslav military.[1] The chapter will first sketch the evolving military mission of the Yugoslav armed forces and then treat the YPA's socio-political role.[2]

THE PARTISAN ARMY: 1941-5[3]

The YPA was the founding instrument of Communist Yugoslavia. Originally known as the People's Liberation Army (PLA), it was created by the Communist Party of Yugoslavia (CPY) after 1941 to fight what Tito and his subordinates in the CPY leadership conceived as a dual war for both national liberation from Axis occupation and for social revolution. Tito fully recognized the overwhelming attractiveness to Yugoslavs of the cause of liberation (as opposed to revolution), and skillfully exploited that appeal in developing the Partisan movement; the party downplayed both its control of the Partisans and its revolutionary social objectives.[4] The PLA developed initially from 'proletarian brigades' organized after December 1941 and staffed largely by Yugoslavs who had fled the cities in the face of German occupation. While the proletarian brigades had relatively high interregional mobility, they were not the model for the PLA: in 1942 Tito decided against attempting to establish such units on a wide scale and subsequently emphasized regionally based units. By 1945, the PLA had grown into a force of some 800,000 soldiers organized in forty-eight divisions and four armies.

Rapid growth and internal stratification of the PLA conditioned the evolution of its officer corps. The military organizers of the Partisan movement with the 'Spaniards' – prewar Communists who had served in the International Brigades of the Spanish Civil War – who dominated the major PLA commands, including all four army commands in 1945.[5] Twenty-nine 'Spaniards' became Partisan generals. Prewar military officers played a significant role only in the Partisan navy (245 former naval officers occupied all leading naval posts in October 1944) and the Partisan air force (Stanišić, 1973, p. 387). Most wartime officers lacked previous military experience and were elevated from the ranks of the Partisans. Like other revolutionary armies, the PLA initially lacked hierarchical differentiation; formal ranks were introduced only in 1943.

National equality was emphasized in the development of the Partisan army; the party's slogan of 'brotherhood and unity,' signifying opposition both to the Serb hegemony of interwar Yugoslavia and the national fratricide of World War II, was another key to the Partisans' success.[6] Apart from the proletarian brigades, whose special status has been noted, the PLA was, until late 1944, comprised of regional units commanded principally by officers of the respective region and national group, subordinated to regional commands, and utilizing the respective regional language or dialect for command. The only demographic anomaly occurred in Croatia; there the Partisans' major initial support came from the Serb minority concentrated in Lika, Kordun, and Slavonia that was the object of a policy of physical extermination by the Axis satellite 'Independent State of Croatia.'[7]

The CPY organized the PLA; it maintained its influence over a rapidly expanding PLA through multiple channels. The PLA's Supreme Command, organized by Tito in 1941, was coterminous in membership with the party Politburo. Regional commands were organized on a similar basis. Party activists were appointed to the posts of political commissars at all levels of the PLA, and shared responsibility with unit commanders – the familiar 'dual command' principle characteristic of (and modeled after) the Soviet army in the prewar period. Utilizing political commissars to maintain political control over the expanding PLA, the party feared 'militarization' of the party itself – a fear understandable in view of the fact that the CPY grew in size from 12,000 members in 1941 to 140,000 members in 1945 (with only 3,000 of the 1941 contingent surviving the war). To protect the autonomy of party cells in military units, party secretaries were secretly appointed; nominally they occupied the function of deputy commissar. The commissar and the party secretary were in turn subordinated to yet another channel of party control. Party Central Committee emissaries were dispatched first to brigades (usually 3 emissaries), and in mid-1943 to divisions (4 to 5 emissaries) to organize 'Political Sections' that were considered integral parts of the Central Committee. It was this Political Section, working with the commissar, the party secretary, and the youth organization secretary, that served as the linkage for transmittal of political directives to military units. The Political Sections were maintained until the end of 1944 (Stanišić, 1973, ch. 6). These instruments, secretly employed, indeed allowed the CPY leadership to totally dominate the PLA, while maintaining the integrity of the party itself.

POSTWAR CONSOLIDATION AND SOVIET THREAT: 1946–55

After 1945 and the consolidation of the Communist system in Yugoslavia, the PLA (now called, first, the 'Yugoslav Army' and then the 'Yugoslav People's Army') was transformed from a revolutionary Partisan army into a standing army, and a more conventional professional military institution. Strict party control of the army was maintained through political channels: unified party–political organs in the YPA were subordinated to its Political Administration that was (as in other Communist countries today) a section of the party Central Committee. The Main Political Administration was initially headed by Party Secretary Vukmanović-Tempo (who was also military prosecutor and head of KOS, the military counterintelligence service). Commissars continued to function in all military units; the commissar was generally more powerful than the commander. The command hierarchy itself was dominated by Tito, who was both Supreme Commander and, until 1953, Secretary of Defense.

Once the YPA had suppressed the remaining domestic opposition to Communist rule, it became preoccupied with external security. Concern with a Western threat was soon matched by apprehension about Soviet intentions. Tito had successfully insisted to Stalin in 1944 that none of the Soviet forces that had helped to liberate parts of eastern Yugoslavia remain after the war. But Yugoslavia quickly became dependent on the USSR for military training and equipment. Soviet military advisers were posted to Yugoslavia in large numbers. Most Yugoslav senior officers went to the USSR for training, and Tito looked to Moscow for assistance in modernizing the YPA. Friction developed between Soviet and Yugoslav military personnel, however, and by 1947 Tito had come to view these incidents as part of a general Soviet effort to gain control of the YPA. In December 1947, Tito adopted a defiant stand on the issue of the independence of the YPA – the first issue so confronted in the developing general conflict with Stalin (Johnson, 1972, pp. 34–5).

Following the outbreak of open conflict with the USSR in 1948, Yugoslavia faced a threat of external intervention. With Soviet renunciation in 1949 of the Soviet–Yugoslav friendship treaty, the staging of troop maneuvers in neighboring satellite countries, and a series of border incidents, Yugoslavia lived in the shadow of Soviet military invasion. The YPA was redeployed and enlarged to meet the Soviet threat. A domestic arms industry was established in the interior of the country. By 1952, Yugoslavia was devoting nearly a quarter of national income to defense, and the YPA had been expanded to a half-million men. A US military assistance program was formally begun in 1953 and provided grant aid worth three-fourths of a billion dollars by 1958. These defense preparations were primarily in the hands of the YPA. Doctrinally and organizationally, it emphasized conventional defense more than the Partisan operations of World War II (Johnson, 1974, p. 43).

As the YPA expanded in the early 1950s, the prerogatives and authority of its professional commanders were strengthened. Surfacing of the Stalin–Tito conflict led to several high-level, pro-Soviet defections within the military[8], and these touched off an extensive political search for possible 'Cominformists' (that is, pro-Soviet elements) within the YPA that initially strengthened the hand of political officers. But as early as February 1949, the formal authority of the commander vis-à-vis the commissar was elevated. A qualitative strengthening of the position of the professional command echelon occurred in early 1953 as a direct consequence of the 6th Party Congress directives to remove the party from a direct command role in Yugoslav society. This general political imperative to redefine the party's role in the military was doubtless reinforced by the military requirement of more authority for the command hierarchy, given the extent and nature of the YPA buildup that was then under way. In February 1953, the Soviet-inspired system of unified party–political control organs was dismantled. The Main Political Administration (as a party Central Committee section) was abolished, as was the position of commissar at all levels. The political organs of the YPA were now subordinated to commanders up and down the military hierarchy; the military party organization, too, was strongly influenced by the commanders, for their deputies for political affairs also assumed the post of party secretary (Kovačević, 1968, pp. 16–19). As a consequence, then, of the intersection of political and military developments – the 6th Party Congress that redefined the role of the party in Yugoslavia and the massive conventional military buildup in the face of the Soviet threat – professionalism and institutional autonomy were emphasized in the YPA, more so than in many other Yugoslav institutions.

DEMOBILIZATION AND MODERNIZATION: 1956–67

Following Stalin's death in 1953 and Khrushchev's conciliatory visit to Belgrade in 1955, Soviet–Yugoslav relations improved and in the mid-1960s again became warm. In Yugoslav eyes, the Soviet threat receded; defense spending was reduced and the YPA greatly limited in size, so that by 1968 Yugoslavia devoted less than 6 percent of national income to defense, and the YPA had been reduced to nearly 200,000 men (Johnson, 1974, p. 43). Early retirement of YPA officers was encouraged after 1956; by 1968 26,000 officers had retired, including 2,500 officers (and 38 generals) in 1967–8 alone (*Prva konferencija,* 1969, p. 17). Social tensions inevitably resulted and some of the retired officers, lamenting the loss of their positions, actively opposed party policies of the day that emphasized economic modernization and social differentiation. In the 1960s, Yugoslavia again became dependent on the USSR for advanced weaponry (although it accepted these armaments on terms compatible with its independence) and resumed exchange of official military delegations with the Soviet bloc. During this period, military ties with Western countries lapsed. At times, particularly in connection with the 1967 Middle East war, the Yugoslav military seemed to be more concerned with a potential military threat from the West than from the East.

The Soviet-led invasion of Czechoslovakia in August 1968 reawakened Yugoslavia to the reality of the Soviet threat, perhaps the most significant long-term consequence of that invasion outside the Soviet bloc. While the resulting crisis atmosphere (that included widespread mobilization) relaxed within a few weeks (*New York Times*, 1969), the shock of Czechoslovakia caused Yugoslavia to take its defense more seriously. A renewed massive conventional military buildup was out of the question for several reasons: pressing economic difficulties; the more decentralized political system of the late 1960s; and the military inadequacy of whatever conventional force Yugoslavia might organize to meet the threat presented by the massive and highly mobile Soviet military establishment. Re-embracing the concept of a 'nation in arms' and re-emphasizing the Partisan heritage, Yugoslavia developed its present system of *opštenarodna odbrana* or 'total national defense.'

DEVELOPMENT OF TOTAL NATIONAL DEFENSE: 1969–80

The primary organizational consequence of the adoption of 'total national defense' was the establishment on republican lines of territorial defense forces (TDF) as units of citizen-soldiers. The TDF developed into a force of perhaps one million men (with auxiliaries) that is financed on a sub-federal, that is, republican and local basis.[10] The TDF is comprised of small factory-defense units, company-size local units, and larger, well-equipped mobile units intended for use throughout a republic. TDF units are subordinated to local and republican defense commands; at each level TDF commanders are responsible both to local political authorities and to the superior TDF command. TDF units fall under YPA command only when engaged in joint tactical operations. On the other hand, should an entire republic be overrun by the enemy, the republican defense command would assume control of all military units on its territory. Complementing the TDF is a network of civil defense organs. All in all, 9 percent of the Yugoslav population – nearly 2 million people – are claimed to be included in organized defense efforts (Ljubičić, 1977).

Implementation of total national defense thus entailed a profound change in the role of the YPA, which lost its monopoly of responsibility for defense and became nominally (although not de facto) one of two co-equal components of the newly named Armed Forces of Yugoslavia. The YPA is no longer *the* Yugoslav military institution, but is now complemented by the larger TDF. On the other hand, Yugoslavia has not accepted for the YPA the Swiss model of a professional training corps for a single militia of citizen-soldiers; the active YPA must be able, on its own, both to resist limited incursion and to delay massive attack long enough for the country to carry out total mobilization; in the latter case, it would still play a key role. Specific changes in YPA organization have resulted, including further manpower reductions, a sharp lowering of YPA reserve levels (and virtual abolishment of the YPA's inactive reserve), and transfer of many support and logistic functions to the TDF or civilian sector.

The relationship of the YPA to the TDF has been a dynamic one. Established at the height of republican self-assertiveness in Yugoslavia at the turn of the 1970s, the regional character of the TDF was originally emphasized at the expense of YPA influence, even though TDF commands were from the outset staffed exclusively by YPA reserve or, in some cases, active officers. Most importantly, the TDF chain of command originally extended directly from the Supreme Commander to the republican commands, bypassing the Federal Defense Secretariat and the YPA General Staff. After 1972, as some republican rights were curtailed at the expense of greater federal authority in the political system generally, more emphasis was placed on the role of the TDF as part of a 'unified defense system;' now the General Staff was inserted into the TDF chain of command, and this was symptomatic of greater influence of the YPA over the development of the TDF at all levels. This influence notwithstanding, the TDF remains politically responsive to local and republican political authorities, who continue to nominate candidates for TDF command posts and whose right to organize and direct national defense in their respective territories was legitimized in the 1974 Yugoslav constitution. Their involvement in defense matters represents a significant return to the Partisan heritage and dilution of the exclusive responsibility for defense that the YPA bore between 1945 and 1968.

Total national defense is officially described in Yugoslavia as a system of defense against any, and all, enemies. In fact, since 1968 the principal threat preoccupation of the YPA and TDF has been the Soviet Union – notwithstanding the continuation of military relations with the USSR and its allies, and concern with other, particularly subversive and terrorist, threats from the West. After 1968, Yugoslavia resumed exchange of military delegations with Western countries. It continued to depend on the Soviet Union for certain advanced heavy weaponry, since its interest in diversifying its arms purchases was only slowly reciprocated by Western governments (*The Economist,* 1970, 1976; *Washington Post,* 1978). Yugoslav–US military relations developed further under the Carter Administration; in October 1977, Secretary of Defense Harold Brown visited Yugoslavia, and in September 1978 Yugoslav Defense Secretary Ljubičić visited Washington. The following month, Yugoslav Chief of Staff Potočar visited Peking, initiating a parallel program of Sino-Yugoslav military cooperation.

Yugoslav military doctrine postulates the threat of a sudden massive armored and airborne invasion that corresponds only to Soviet doctrine and capabilities. More fundamentally, the entire system of total national defense was developed in its present form in response to Soviet military action – the invasion of Czechoslovakia – just as the only previous post-war expansion of Yugoslav military capabilities was undertaken in response to Stalin's threats. Yugoslav apprehensions about Soviet intentions were exacerbated greatly by the Soviet invasion of Afghanistan in late 1979.

THE YPA'S INTERNAL ROLE: 1945–80

The YPA's preoccupation with external security over the past thirty years conditioned its role in the Yugoslav political system. Following the

Communist consolidation of power after 1945, the YPA became a more conventional military establishment. The revolutionary multinational army was transformed into an exclusivist, professional, supranational 'Yugoslav' institution that was almost hermetically sealed off from the rest of Yugoslav society. To be sure, the YPA remained a key instrument by which conscript youths were socialized into the values of the Yugoslav Communist system. The YPA continued to cultivate its heritage as the founding instrument of that system. It remained its fundamental buttress. Yet for two decades, the YPA remained outside the mainstream of Yugoslav party–political life. Defense Secretary Ivan Gošnjak and his military subordinates were responsible only to Tito for military affairs, but they played little role in party debates on socio-economic policy in the 1950s and early 1960s.

In the mid-1960s, party reformers feared that this isolation of the military could mean a future 'militaristic' threat to the wideranging economic and political reforms introduced in Yugoslavia at that time. They sought, with considerable success, to dilute the exclusiveness of the military establishment. The reformers forced on the YPA an 'opening to society' (as the process was termed in Yugoslavia) after 1966. Military matters, once a public taboo, began to be discussed in the media. The Federal Assembly began to debate, not just rubber stamp, the defense budget. The party organization in the YPA was reorganized in an effort to limit the authority over it of the command echelon that had dominated the party bodies in the military since the abolishment of commissars in 1953; to encourage horizontal contacts with nonmilitary, territorial party organizations; and to permit greater participation by the military rank-and-file. The purpose of these measures was, in the words of a political officer, to effect 'the real and not formal acceptance in the army [of the] democratic and self-management achievements of our society' (Kovačević, 1968, p. 33).

The lowering of barriers between the military and other elements of Yugoslav society was reinforced by the upsurge of forces of national and regional self-affirmation that led to increased decentralization and pluralism in Yugoslavia in the second half of the 1960s. Under pressure from republican party organizations, the YPA adopted the goal of proportional national representation in its officer corps (in which, for historical reasons, Serbs and Montenegrins had played a disproportionately large role [see Table 8.3]). Republican political authorities outside Serbia and Montenegro sought to enroll more of their youth in military academies (and encouraged the establishment of new officers' training schools in their respective republics for this purpose). The YPA accepted the principle of stationing a percentage of conscripts on the territory of their native republic; formerly it had followed a policy of almost exclusively cross-regional postings. Earlier, Serbian (more precisely, the Belgrade version of Serbian written in the Latin, that is, Croatian alphabet) had been used almost exclusively in the YPA, as in other federal institutions; now opportunities for linguistic and cultural national expression within the YPA were enhanced. The necessity of a unitary language for command and training (that is, Belgrade Serbian) was

brought into question.[12] Most significant of all, the YPA was complemented after 1968 by the republican-based territorial defense forces; the
latter greatly increased contact between YPA officers and other
Yugoslavs and contributed to the breakdown of the isolation of the YPA.

As the military institution was reintegrated into public life in the late
1960s, the military leadership accepted the program of socio-economic
and political reforms, including greater affirmation of national rights,
adopted by the party leadership in the latter half of the 1960s. The
reforms were supported by top generals in public statements and by the
party organization in the army in a series of conferences. That this public
support was not pro forma, but reflected broad acceptance of the reforms
among the military (qualified by reservations about increased
nationalism) was indicated by the reported results of an internal opinion
poll of May 1971. This poll (conducted at the height of the movement for
greater national affirmation in Croatia) indicated less than 5 percent of
the sample clearly opposed to the main lines of the reform (and its
components of political decentralization to the republic and greater
national affirmation in particular), but a majority concerned with the
degree of prominence the 'national question' was then receiving. Seventy-
two percent of the 'higher officers' thought the national question had
been overemphasized in the public discussion of the Constitutional
Amendments of 1971; 54 percent considered 'nationalism and
chauvinism' the greatest single present danger to Yugoslavia.[13] The 1971
poll thus indicated a qualifiedly 'loyalist' majority within the military
(whose apprehensions about the rise of nationalism were a harbinger of
the shift in party policy in late 1971), and a minority undercurrent of
opinion at odds with party policy, then and subsequently, on the basic
direction of reforms. The existence of an undercurrent of dissent advocating 'hard-line' and neo-centrist policies is further corroborated by
critiques of such unorthodox views leveled at the time by top military
leaders.[14] Yet there is no indication that this latter current was significantly stronger in the military than in other Yugoslav groups.[15]

Subsequent developments and retrospective comments by Yugoslav
military leaders critical of nationalism in the YPA, indicated the existence
of an opposite, and even weaker, undercurrent of dissident 'nationalist'
viewpoints.

The significant dilution of the YPA's exclusivist and supranational
character in the late 1960s notwithstanding, the military establishment
remained the strongest and most reliable all-Yugoslav political institution.
In the protracted confrontation with Croatian nationalism (and the
republican party leadership in Zagreb that sought to harness it) in mid-
1971, Tito turned to the military for support. He organized an unusual
series of consultations with senior military figures to buttress his anti-
nationalist remarks of the time. And in December 1971, Tito restated
what was never in question, but which had not been made explicit for
years – that the YPA played an internal political, as well as external
security role in Yugoslavia and would be utilized, if events so dictated, to
suppress a nationalist or other domestic challenge to the integrity of the
Yugoslav state and the maintenance of party rule (Tito, 1971).

In the atmosphere of domestic semi-crisis generated by the party center's confrontation with Croatian nationalists in 1971, and the crackdown on the Serbian party leadership (accused of being too 'liberal') the following year, the civil–military relationship postulated as desirable by the party was modified and, in a sense, reversed. In the late 1960s, party reformers hoped the 'opening to society' would reintegrate an isolated and more conservative military establishment into the mainstream of a 'liberalizing' Yugoslav political system. Military involvement in politics, indeed, further increased. But in the early 1970s, the party leadership re-emphasized the internal political, as well as external security role of the YPA as a loyalist, orthodox institution providing an antidote to permissive nationalism and 'liberalism', and, at a more fundamental level, as the custodian and ultimate guarantor of the Yugoslav state and Communist system. In Tito's words of late 1971, 'our army is also called upon to defend the achievements of our revolution within the country, should that become necessary.' Six years later, Tito re-emphasized this custodial function.

> Brotherhood and unity are inseparably linked with our army . . . I believe that our army is still playing such a role today . . . Our army must not merely watch vigilantly over our borders but also be present inside the country . . . there are also those who write that one day [Yugoslavia] will disintegrate. Nothing like that will happen because our army insures that we will continue to move in the direction we have chosen for the socialist construction of our country. (Tito, 1977)

On another occasion, he implored: 'It is no longer sufficient for our army to be familiar with military affairs. It must also be familiar with political affairs and developments. It must participate in [them]' (Tito, 1974). Many other high-level calls for military participation in politics ensued. For example, addressing an army party conference, Party Executive Bureau Secretary Mirko Popović (1975) called on YPA officers to be politically active in the communities in which they were stationed. As such appeals indicate, Tito and the party called on the military to play a more active political role; the military did not inject itself into the political process.

Re-emphasis on the custodial role of the military in the domestic semi-crisis of 1971–2 encouraged the expression of the concern felt earlier within the military about the negative security implications of the rise of nationalism and, more broadly, the lack of discipline in Yugoslav society at the turn of the 1970s. Apprehension about the negative impact of these developments was indicated in numerous statements by military leaders to the effect that lack of discipline in Yugoslav society was sapping the country's defense strength (Šarac, 1972). Concern of the military elite on this score was reinforced by a threat to the institutional integrity of the YPA itself from extreme nationalist elements in the party. The military leaders' concerns on these matters were expressed frankly in the fall of 1972 by Defense Secretary Ljubičić, who emphasized the need for 'more order, personal and social responsibility, and equity' in Yugoslavia, and reiterated the fact of the YPA's domestic, as well as external security role (Ljubičić, 1972). But it is important to note that in this atmosphere of domestic semi-crisis, no military figure claimed a domestic role for the military independent of the party. In his frank statement just cited, Ljubičić placed unusual emphasis on the role of the party, affirming that the army 'was a part of the self-management system *and the Party*' (emphasis added). Undersecretary of Defense Jovanić (1976) made a similar retrospective claim about his own efforts in the Croatian crisis of 1971, which, he said, were directed toward strengthening the role of the Croatian party organization.

Military involvement in political affairs, in fact, increased in the 1970s (albeit not to the extent some observers suggested). A small group of 'political generals' emerged for the first time since the late 1940s, although they occupied almost exclusively security-related posts: Colonel General Ivan Kukoč was appointed one of the Party Executive Committee secretaries; Colonel General Franjo Herljević assumed the post of Federal Secretary of Internal Affairs; Major General Vuko Gozze-Gučetić became the Public Prosecutor; and Lieutenant Colonel General Ljubiša Čurgus became the head of the Directorate of Civilian Aviation. The appointment of generals to such posts reflected the Tito leadership's heightened concern with terrorist and subversive threats to Yugoslavia in the early 1970s. A few military figures were called upon for other services, both technical and political. Major General Dragislav Radisavljević was put in charge of the civilian airline to improve its efficiency. Army General Kosta Nadj, then semi-retired, was installed as head of the veterans' union in 1974, as part of an effort by the party to dampen the pressure that had emanated from parts of the veterans' organization in 1971–2 for 'stronger measures' against nationalists and 'liberals,' and for more centralist policies.

General Nadj's appointment was accompanied by a major reshuffle of the leadership of the veterans' organization. In isolated cases, recently retired senior officers joined forces with the veterans in urging more conservative policies on the party. But such cases did not demonstrate, as some observers suggested, that the veterans' organization was a hand-maiden of the military establishment. The veterans' organization consti-tutes a significant political force within the Yugoslav system in its own right; local and even republican-level veterans' organizations have at times advocated quite unorthodox (usually 'conservative', but sometimes 'liberal' and 'nationalist') policies. The political weight of the veterans' organization is to be explained by its core membership of prominent 'first fighters' who constituted the cream of the postwar political elite, but who were subsequently shunted off onto the political sidelines. Thus it is not ties with the current military establishment that account for the influence of the veterans' organization. That organization cannot be viewed as a political surrogate for the YPA (Johnson, 1974, pp. 28–9).

A general increase in the political weight of the military was effected at the 10th Party Congress in 1974, when the Central Committee (abolished as such at the 9th Congress of 1969) was reconstituted, and the military party organization formally allocated fifteen seats on it (equivalent to those of a provincial party organization, although less than the twenty allocated to the republican party organizations). This change granted to the army party organization the same status of constituent suborganization granted in 1969 to the republican party organizations. Since two other active military men were included in Central Committee representations from individual republics and provinces, total military representation on the 1974 Central Committee was seventeen or 10 percent of the Central Committee membership. As indicated by Table 8.1, this represented a larger proportion of military members than at any time in the postwar period. The proportion of military representation increased slightly at the 11th Party Congress in June 1978.

But this greater military weight in central party councils did not translate itself into a military presence in nonmilitary bodies at the republican and local levels; claims to such a role were voiced by some military party officials in 1972, but soon dropped. At the republican level, military representation on party Central Committees reached its peak in 1969, and has subsequently declined. Table 8.2 displays the proportion of military representatives on postwar republican and provincial Central Committees. These data indicate that the policies of the mid-1960s aimed at reducing the barriers between the army and the rest of Yugoslav society did lead to greater lateral ties between the army and the republican party organizations. On the other hand, the further increase in a role for military men in the federal party Central Committee after the political turbulence of 1971–2 was accompanied by a constriction of military representation on the republican Central Committees. After 1978, all the military representatives on the republican Central Committees were, with one exception, key officers in the republican territorial defense apparatus, not the YPA.

Nor has the more prominent role of the military in Yugoslavia in the 1970s meant a consolidation of the positions of individual 'political generals'. After the 11th Congress, the only general who was simultaneously a major Yugoslav political figure was Defense Secretary Ljubičić. Some of the other generals who assumed civilian posts at the turn of the 1970s – including Kukoč, Čurgus, and Radisavljević – were replaced at, or soon after, the 11th Congress. Kukoč was replaced by Lieutenant Colonel General Milan Daljević, a more junior officer; Čurgus and Radisavljević, by civilians. Colonel General Ivan Dolničar was appointed Secretary-General of the state presidency in mid-1969, placing a military incumbent in an important administrative, but not policymaking, position.[16] On balance, the greater influence attained by the military in Yugoslavia in the first half of the 1970s was consolidated, but not significantly expanded, in the second half of the decade.

Since 1971, the YPA has reacted to the challenge of the forces of national affirmation in the same way as have other Yugoslav institutions: extreme nationalist demands have been decisively rejected, but opportunities for national self-expression within a context of respect for the integrity of Yugoslav institutions have been expanded. The calls of extreme nationalists in 1970–1 for radical reorganization of the YPA into single-nation units, each with the respective national language of command, have been silenced. But efforts have continued to correct the disproportionate national representation in the officer corps.

Table 8.3 displays the available fragmentary data on the national composition of the officer corps, as a whole, and the general officer corps. These data refute the frequently asserted proposition that Serbs and Montenegrins dominate the military leadership; on the other hand, they point to continued Serb–Montenegrin overrepresentation among field-grade officers. The percentage share of Croats and Slovenes, in particular, among the officer corps as a whole declined between 1946 and 1970, and was therefore all the more a matter of concern to the respective republican party leaderships.

At the insistence of the republican party organizations, the principle of proportional national representation in the officer corps was codified in the 1974 Constitution. Republican party bodies have continued to insist on its implementation[17], and it has been formally accepted by top military organs (*Narodna armija*, 1979). New officer schools have, as noted, been opened in the underrepresented republics. Officer candidates are assured of greater opportunities to be posted to their native regions (*Vjesnik*, 1973). Opportunities for linguistic self-expression in the military have expanded; in 1977, for example, the armed forces service code was, for the first time, published in all the Yugoslav languages. The principle of a unitary language of command and training has been successfully defended, but more scope has been granted, at least in theory, for the use of Croatian along with Serbian military terminology.[18]

The apex of the military leadership may still think of itself as an all-Yugoslav grouping that can function without regard to its national composition (Denitch, 1976, p. 116). But even if supranational impulses survive, the Yugoslav military is clearly aware of the sensitivity of the national issue. It is constrained on many military matters by the multi-national federalized political system of which it is a part. Today it acts as if greater scope for national affirmation within the YPA were essential to the functioning of the military institution. Moreover, it recognizes the crucial symbolic importance for the functioning of the Yugoslav political system of respect for national affirmation within the YPA. The YPA is, in brief, an all-Yugoslav federal, or at least 'federalizing' institution. This development stands to strengthen, not weaken, the military institution in the particular multinational circumstances of Yugoslavia.

The more prominent role of the YPA in the early 1970s has allowed the military establishment, as noted earlier, to defeat the challenges to the YPA's institutional autonomy and primary role in the Yugoslav defense system raised by some of the stronger advocates of territorial defense forces after 1968. Calls from the republican level in 1970–1 claiming a veto right over YPA regional postings, and counterposing the TDF to the YPA have been decisively rejected. The YPA has assumed a more active role in pre-induction military training, further solidifying its monopoly over all military education.

Re-emphasis of the YPA's role evidently undercut the 'hardline' dissident political undercurrent that existed within the YPA at the turn of the 1970s. These dissident views were related to, and in many cases doubtless derived from, reservations held by minority elements of the officer corps about the post-1968 system of total national defense, with its major emphasis on the role of territorial defense forces. What evidence there is, including the reported results of internal YPA opinion polls, indicates overwhelming acceptance of the system of 'total national defense'; the polls and the critical comments of senior military figures suggest again the existence of 'technocratic' (that is, status quo 1965), and 'nationalist' (that is, favoring – at the extreme – republican armies) undercurrents within the officer corps (Lončarević, 1972; *Narodna armija*, 1972, 1976). But the available evidence indicates full backing for the system of total national defense by the military, once a top-level intra-military dispute over the desirability and efficacy of relying heavily on territorial defense forces had been resolved in 1967–8. It is testimony to the continued influence of the Partisan past, the flexibility of outlook of the YPA senior officer corps, and the YPA's responsiveness to party policy and Tito personally that the Yugoslav military evidently adapted without much friction to the system of total national defense that called into question some traditional professional military prerogatives.

In the early 1970s, the military establishment also blunted an incipient challenge from within. In the wake of the political campaign of 1971–2 against 'nationalism' and 'liberalism,' some military party organizations, as mentioned previously, made short-lived claims to influence outside the armed forces. Simultaneously, the military party organization took a more active stance within the YPA, in some cases opposing political to professional military concerns in a manner challenging commanders' prerogatives. By 1975, this tendency had been reversed; the proceedings of the February 1975 military party organization conference indicated a preoccupation with military–technical tasks (*Narodna armija*, 1975). The chief party official in the army subsequently stressed repeatedly that the military party organization's involvement in operational concerns was limited and supportive of the command echelon (Šarac, 1975, 1976). That command echelon is still dominated by the Partisan generation – more precisely, 'Partisan commanders' – individuals who joined the party via the Partisans, typically rose to the position of division commander at the end of the war; and subsequently advanced along a command career path while assimilating the political values of the Titoist system. These 'Partisan commanders' still constitute the core of the Yugoslav military elite; they dominate the party organization in the armed forces as well.

CONCLUSIONS

After World War II, the YPA quickly evolved from a revolutionary Partisan army into a professional military establishment. Created by the Communist Party, the YPA has remained effectively subordinated to overall party control. But the nature of that control has changed; since 1953 it has been exercised 'from above,' through the command echelon, rather than through commissars posted to each level of the hierarchy. Assimilating the changing values of the party, the military leadership has developed a strong loyalty to the Yugoslav state and the Yugoslav Communist political system. The Yugoslav military elite is thoroughly Titoist.[19] Throughout the postwar period, the YPA has been preoccupied with external security, primarily the real or potential Soviet threat; the intensity of Yugoslav defense preparations has varied in the postwar period proportionately to the Soviet threat. Following the Soviet invasion of Afghanistan, the military elite became more concerned with the Soviet threat.

After the mid-1960s, the YPA again became involved in domestic party–political life, not on its own initiative but at the insistence of party leaders and Tito himself. Following the domestic political turmoil of 1971–2, the military re-emphasized its mission to protect, as servant of the party, the integrity of the Yugoslav Communist system and the Yugoslav state against domestic, as well as external, challenges. It evidently sees one of its functions as the promoting of social stability (Kukoč, 1977). The military recognizes the crucial importance of respecting national rights within the YPA for the functioning of both the military institution and the political system of which it is a part. It is committed to a broadly based system of 'total national defense' that has created a symbiotic relationship between the military institution and Yugoslav society as a whole. The military institution cannot be juxtaposed to the party, for it is one of the party's integral parts: the army party organization, dominated by the command echelon, is the ninth component of the federal party, along with the six republican and two provincial party organizations. The military has become a political actor, but not a political arbiter. It is in these terms that the Yugoslav military entered the post-Tito period.

NOTES

1 Existing studies (including works cited in this chapter) are listed in the Bibliography.
2 The final revision of this chapter was made in March 1980, just prior to Tito's death.
3 This section is based primarily on Stanišić (1973). Stanišić, a retired general, was a divisional commissar during World War II; his book, *The CPY and the Development of the Armed Forces of the Revolution, 1941–1945*, is based on archival research and is the authoritative Yugoslav account of the party–army nexus during World War II.
4 At the end of 1941, Tito briefly embraced (but then abandoned) the notion of emphasizing revolutionary 'class' aims and party control of the Partisan movement (Stanišić, 1973, pp. 92–4.
5 Aleš Bebler (1975) described how he implemented in Slovenia guerrilla warfare experience gained in Spain.
6 Serb domination of interwar Yugoslavia was particularly evident in the armed forces. Of the 165 active generals on the eve of World War II, 161 were Serbs, 2 were Croats, and 2 were Slovenes. Thirteen hundred of the 1,500 military cadets were Serbs (Rothschild, 1974, p. 278).
7 Of roughly 5,000 Partisan organizers – the 'First Fighters' who received the 'Partisan Medallion of 1941' and constituted the postwar Yugoslav elite – still alive in Croatia in 1971, 25 percent were Croats, and 49 percent were Serbs (with 3 percent miscellaneous other nationalities, and 18 percent refusing to declare a national affiliation). The respective proportions of these nationalities in the postwar population of Croatia were 78 percent and 15 percent respectively (*NIN*, 1971b).
8 Most prominently, Tito's wartime Chief of Staff, General Arso Jovanović and the

deputy head of the Political Administration in 1948, General Branko Petrićević.
9   For detailed analysis, see Johnson (1971, 1974); Dean (1976).
10   Data on the size of the TDF are not available.
11   The National Defense Law (1974, Article 20) stipulates that the Commander-in-Chief appoints republican defense commanders upon nomination by the republics.
12   These national issues were prominently discussed in the military party organization in early 1969 (*Prva konferencija*, 1969). They were systematically analyzed in a 1970 document of the military party organization, published as a supplement to *Narodna armija* (1970).
13   The poll results grouped Slovene officers with Montenegrin and Serbian officers as most concerned with nationalism (but showed Slovene officers most concerned with economic issues); Croatian and Macedonian officers were least concerned (*NIN*, 1971a).
14   A document of the military party organization (*Narodna armija*, 1970) referred to 'individual' misunderstandings of the reform measures and took issue with the following unorthodox views within the military: that 'state capital' should not be returned to the economy (that is, economic liberalization should not proceed further); that devolution of greater powers to the republics weakened the Yugoslav federation; that no language reform (that is, more use of languages other than Serbian) in the army was needed; that 'we are all Yugoslavs' (that is, that national self-affirmation of individual ethnic groups was not needed); that republican territorial defense headquarters were unnecessary.
15   For example, an opinion poll of the Croation population at large in 1969 indicated 5 percent believed that 'socialism was possible without self-management' (an unorthodox view implying acceptance of a centralized Communist system) (Denitch, 1976, p. 88).
16   For a different view, stressing greater military influence, see Stankovic (1979).
17   See *NIN* (1976). Illustrative of the republican party stands on the issue are statements of Mehmet Bakali (1975), the head of the Kosovo provincial party organization, and the Croatian Party Executive Committee (1976).
18   The 1974 National Defense Law formally defines the language of command and training as 'Serbocroatian or Croatoserbian'; formerly, only the first term was used.
19   Observers have periodically labeled the Yugoslav military as 'pro-Soviet'. An example is Andelman (1978, 1980), who claims it is the judgement of 'most observers' that the military 'is a reservoir of pro-Soviet sympathy within the Yugoslav establishment' and alludes to 'evidence of Soviet penetration of the Yugoslav military.' No evidence has been adduced to support that contention, and I know of no specialist on Yugoslav affairs who shares that judgement. It is the military that has been most directly concerned with the Soviet threat, particularly after 1968. It is the institution that Tito must have watched most carefully (along with the internal security apparatus) for any sign of even incipient pro-Soviet feelings.

BIBLIOGRAPHY

Andelman, David (1978), 'Yugoslavia's army, even divided, is the power,' *New York Times* (5 March).
Andelman, David (1980), 'Yugoslavia: into the post-Tito era,' *Atlantic* (March).
Antic, Zdenko (1967), 'The chief of staff of the Yugoslav army,' *Radio Free Europe Research* (1 August).
Antic, Zdenko (1972), 'National structure of the Yugoslav army leadership,' *Radio Free Europe Research* (12 April).
Bakali, Mahmut (1975), speech, Tanjug, 29 March.
Barton, Allen H., Denitch, Bogdan, and Kadushin, Charles (eds) (1973), *Opinion-Making Elites in Yugoslavia* (New York: Praeger).
Bebler, Aleš (1975), article, *Vjesnik* (5–6 October).
Bebler, Anton (1976), 'Development of sociology of militaria in Yugoslavia,' *Armed Forces and Society*, vol. 3, no. 1
Croatian Party Executive Committee (1976), statement, Tanjug, 17 February.
Dean, Robert W. (1976), 'Civil–military relations in Yugoslavia, 1971–1975,' *Armed Forces and Society*, vol. 3, no. 1.

Denitch, Bogdan D. (1976), *The Legitimation of a Revolution: The Yugoslav Case* (New Haven, Con.: Yale University Press).
Economist, The (1970), article (30 May).
Economist, The (1976), article (20 November).
Gozze-Gućetić, Vuko, Vučinić, Milan, and Petković, Aleksandar (1972), *Komentar saveznog zakona o narodnoj odbrani sa pratećim propisima i zakona o opštenorodnoj odbrani sr Srbije sa pratećim propisima (Commentary on the Federal Law on National Defence with Accompanying Regulations and the Law on Total National Defence of the Federal Republic of Serbia with Accompanying Regulations)* (Belgrade).
Ibrahimpašić, Mensur (1977), *Društvena priroda opštenarodnog odbrambenog rata (The Social Essense of Total National Defensive War)* (Belgrade).
Janković, Blažo (1975), *Četvrta proletarska Crnogorska brigada (The Fourth Proletarian Montenegran Brigade)* (Belgrade: Vojnoizdavački zavod).
Johnson, A. Ross (1971), *The Yugoslav Doctrine of Total National Defense* (Santa Monica, Calif.: Rand Corporation).
Johnson, A. Ross (1972), *The Transformation of Communist Ideology: The Yugoslav Case, 1945–1953* (Cambridge, Mass.: MIT).
Johnson A. Ross (1974), *Yugoslavia: In the Twilight of Tito,* Washington Papers, no. 16 (Beverly Hills, Calif.: Sage).
Jovanić, Djoko (1976), article, *Narodna armija* (1 July).
Kačavenda, Petar Dr (1975), *Skoj i omladina u narodno-oslobodilačkoj vojsci i partizanskim odredima Jugoslavije 1941–1945 (Skoj and the Youth in the People's Liberation Army and Partisan Detachments in Yugoslavia 1941–1945)* (Belgrade).
Kelleher, Catherine McArdle (ed.) (1974), *Political–Military Systems: Comparative Perspectives* (Beverly Hills, Calif.: Sage).
Kovaćević, Sveto (1968), 'Koncipiranje uloge komunista u posleratnom razvitku Jugoslovenske Narodne Armije' ('Conceptualization of the role of communists in the post-war development of the Yugoslav People's Army') in *Zbornik radova,* Politićka Skola JNA, I (Belgrade).
Kukoć, Ivan (1977), interview, *NIN* (20 March).
Lendvai, Paul (1972), *National Tensions in Yugoslavia,* Conflict Studies no. 25 (London, Institute for the Study of Conflict).
Ljubićić, Nikola (1972), speech to the military party organization on 15 November, published in *Vojno Delo,* no. 1 (1973) (key points omitted in mass-media coverage).
Ljubićić, Nikola (1977), speech to the Federal Assembly, Tanjug, 28 December.
Lonćarević, Djuro (1972), speech to the Serbian Party Central Committee, Tanjug, 30 June.
Narodna armija (1970), document on national issues issued by the military party organization, supplement to issue of 15 May.
Narodna armija (1972), article (7 December).
Narodna armija (1975), proceedings of the military party organization conference (27 February).
Narodna armija (1976), article (20 May).
Narodna armija (1979), 'Action program' of the military party organization (11 January).
National Defence Act (1974), published in *Službeni list SFRJ,* vol. 22.
New York Times (1969), article (15 April).
NIN (1970), article (20 September).
NIN (1971a), article (20 June).
NIN (1971b), article (19 September).
NIN (1976), article (14 March).
Osnovi opštenarodne odbrane SFRJ (Foundations of Total National Defense in the SFRY) (1975), Vols I and 2 (Belgrade).
Popović, Mirko (1975), speech, Tanjug, 20 February.
Prva konferencija SKJ u JNA (First Conference of the LCY in the YPA) (1969), Belgrade.
Remington, Robin A. (1974), 'Armed forces and society in Yugoslavia,' in Kelleher (ed.) (1974).
Roberts, Adam (1976), *Nations in Arms: The Theory and Practice of Territorial Defense* (New York: Praeger).
Rothschild, Joseph (1974), *East Central Europe between the Two World Wars* (Seattle, Wash.: University of Washington Press).
Rusinow, Dennison I., (1972), *Crisis in Croatia,* American Universities Fieldstaff Reports

(4 pts) (Hanover, NH: American Unversities Fieldstaff).
Šarac, Džemail (1972), speech, *Borba* (22 January).
Šarac, Džemail (1975), chapter, in *Total National Defense in Theory and Practice* (1975).
Šarac, Džemail (1976), speech to the military party organization, *Narodna armija* (20 May).
Stanišić, Milija (1973), *KPJ u izgradnji oružanih snaga revolucije 1941–1945 (The CPY and the Development of the Armed Forces of the Revolution 1941–1945)* (Belgrade: Vojnoizdavački zavod).
Stankovic, Slobodan (1979), More power for army generals in Yugoslavia,' *Radio Free Europe Research*, no. 145/79 (29 June).
Tanasković, Rajko (1970), *Faktori izgradnje i organizacije oružanih snaga (Factors in the Development and Organization of the Armed Forces)*, (Belgrade: Vojnoizdavački zavod).
Tito (1971), speech, *Borba* (24 December).
Tito (1974), speech, Radio Belgrade (8 January).
Tito (1977), speech to the military leadership, Tanjug, 22 December.
Total National Defence in Theory and Practice (1975) (Belgrade: *Narodna armija*).
Vjesnik (1973) ('Croatia in the YPA') (5 May).
Vojna enciklopedija (Military Encyclopedia) (1958–1968), 1st edn, 8 vols (Belgrade).
Vojna enciklopedija (Military Encyclopedia) (1970–5), 2nd edn, 11 vols (Belgrade).
Washington Post (1978), article (29 September).

Table 8.1 *Military Representation in Postwar LCY Central Committees*

Date		Number	Percentage of Total CC Membership
1978	(11th Congress)	18	11
1974	(10th Congress)	17	10
1969	(9th Congress Presidium)	3	6
1964	(8th Congress)	9	6
1958	(7th Congress)	4	3
1952	(6th Congress)	6	6
1948	(5th Congress)	2	3

Source: Official proceedings of each party congress.

Table 8.2 *Military Representation in Postwar Republican Party Central Committees*

Republic/Province	Percentage of Total CC Membership						
	1949	1954	1959–60	1965–6	1968[a]	1974	1978
Bosnia-Hercegovina	4	c	0	0	4	1	0
Croatia	5	0	1	2	4[b]	1	2
Kosovo	(First separate congress held in 1968) 0					2	2
Macedonia	2	0	0	0	6	1	1
Montenegro	5	0	c	0	3	0	1
Serbia	3	1	0	0	2	2	1
Slovenia	0	6	c	0	4	1	1
Vojvodina	(First separate congress held in 1968) 0					1	2

Notes:
[a] As of early 1970.
[b] Reduced to 0 in 1972, when all three military representatives were expelled from the Croatian CC.
[c] Data not available

Source: Official accounts of the respective congresses, published as books or in the regional press. I am indebted to Zdenko Antic for assistance in locating this documentation.

Table 8.3   *Nationality of Officer Corps (percentages, rounded)*

Nationality	General Officers 1970[1]	Delegates to 1969 Army Party Conference[4]	Officer Corps 1970[1]	Officer Corps 1946[2]	Total Population 1971[3]	Total Population 1948[3]
Serb	46·7	40	57·4[b]	51·0	39·7	41·5
Croat	19·3	21	14·7	22·7	22·1	24·0
Slav Muslim	3·2	1	4·0[a]	1·9	8·4	5·1[d]
Slovene	6·3	9	5·2	9·7	8·2	8·9
Albanian	0	2	1·2	c	6·4	4·8
Macedonian	3·9	12	5·6	3·6	5·8	5·2
Montenegrin	19·3	13	10·3[b]	9·2	2·5	2·7
Hungarian	0·4	1	0·6	c	2·3	3·2
Other	0·9	1	1·0[a]	1·9[c]	4·6	4·6

Notes:
a   Approximation.
b   Serbs and Montenegrins together constitute 67·7 percent of the officer corps; breakdown is estimated. Discrepancies in addition due to rounding.
c   Includes Hungarians and Albanians.
d   'Muslim' was not a recognized national group in 1948; this was the percentage of the 'undeclared' group, mainly Slav Muslims.

Sources:
1   Derived from data in *NIN* (1970). This source gives the following rank order (only) of the nationality of generals occupying 'leading positions' in the Defense Secretariat: Serb, Croat, Montenegrin, Muslim, Slovene, Macedonian. These calculations differ slightly from those made by Antic (1972).
2   Stanišić (1973), p. 409, citing data in the FSND Personnel Administration. Similar figures are given in Kaćavenda (1975), p. 389.
3   Official census data.
4   *Prva konferencija*, (1969), p. 389.

9 Party–Military Relations in Eastern Europe: The Case of Romania*

ALEX ALEXIEV

CIVIL–MILITARY RELATIONS IN EASTERN EUROPE: AN INTRODUCTION

Western studies of civil–military relations in Communist societies have until now focused primarily on the two dominant and politically independent Communist countries: the Soviet Union and China.[1] Very little attention to date has been paid to dependent European Communist countries, despite their obvious political significance in the context of the gradual disintegration of the monolithic Communist system and the evolution of autochthonous models of socialist development. The few studies that have attempted to deal with the issue in Warsaw Pact states have focused, for the most part, on individual aspects of civil–military relations. Notable among those have been attempts to examine party efforts to use the military as an agent for socialization in party-held values;[2] the impact of technology on party–military relations;[3] the importance of the military establishment as a springboard for a political career, and so on.[4] Most of these studies have used analytical concepts borrowed from studies of civil–military relations in the dominant Communist countries. Party–military interaction is presented more often than not simply as an expression of the party desire to ensure an officer corps that is both 'red' and 'expert,' that is, ideologically reliable and professionally competent. Similarly, the military is seen as primarily interested in high levels of resource allocations and technology acquisition. Although this approach does illuminate some important aspects of party–military relations that seem common to all Communist polities, it also obscures what may be very important differences in the nature of civil–military relations in the dependent countries, as opposed to the

* An earlier verson of this paper appeared as ACIS Working Paper no. 15 (University of California, Los Angeles Center for International and Strategic Affairs, January 1979). I am deeply indebted to Professor Roman Kolkowicz of UCLA for his perceptive criticism and suggestions offered generously throughout the writing of this chapter. I have also benefited from the comments and criticism on an earlier draft by Ross Johnson of the RAND Corporation, and Dale Herspring of the State Department. I would also like to thank Heidi Aspaturian at CISA for her many useful editorial suggestions.

dominant ones. As a result, no conscious effort has so far been made to distinguish specific East European conditions that affect the military from those common to all states with a Communist social system. Nor have there been any attempts to examine the impact that some of the recent wideranging changes in the political environments of the East European countries have had on party–military relations. This chapter proposes to identify some of the most salient of these specific East European conditions, and to analyze their relevance by focusing on the evolution of party–military relations in Romania.

Before proceeding to discuss the differences in the environments of the dominant and the dependent Communist military establishments, it will be useful to briefly review the three main analytical models that Western scholars have developed in their attempts to explain the nature of civil–military relations in Communist societies, particularly the Soviet Union.[5] The earliest, most comprehensive, and most well-known model was developed by Roman Kolkowicz in his pioneering study, *The Soviet Military and the Communist Party*. This approach, known as the Institutional Conflict Model, describes the two major protagonists in civil–military relations – the party and the officer corps – as cohesive institutions with distinct identities, value systems, and institutional desiderata. According to Kolkowicz, the Soviet military espouses a belief system which stresses the military virtues of duty, honor, obedience, and heroism, as well as esprit de corps, elitism, and societal exclusivity. The party, on the other hand, preaches an egalitarian, materialistic, and universalist ideology that is basically anti-militaristic. The incompatible value systems of the party and military and the everpresent party desire for total control over the military (which clashes with the natural military striving for professional autonomy) keeps relations between the two in a state of constant tension and conflict.

Kolkowicz's thesis has been challenged by William Odom, who has asserted that party–military relations in the Soviet Union are character-ized by consensus rather than conflict.[6] Odom's model, which has been called the Institutional Congruence Model,[7] assumes that the two insti-tutions share similar value systems and rejects the relevance of one of Kolkowicz's key variables – military professionalism. Odom thus sees the military's primary role as one of faithfully executing party policies with which it agrees. According to this model conflict, to the extent that it is present, is not inter-institutional but intra-institutional, that is, present within both institutions on any given military issue.

Recently, another approach has been offered by Timothy Colton. His model, which falls somewhere between the two discussed above and could be called the Participation Model, sees military participation in politics (as opposed to Kolkowicz's concept of party control) as the main feature of party–military relations. In Colton's view, the interaction between the two institutions is characterized not by conflict, but by 'structural interpenetration, broadly compatible goals and the operation of informal cross-institutional linkages.'[8]

Application of the above analytical constructs to the study of party–military relations in Eastern Europe soon reveals that none of them alone is capable of explaining the party–military situation in the region. At the same time, all three are extremely useful in increasing our understanding of specific periods in the evolution of party–military relations. I propose to present here a model which conceives of party–military interaction in Eastern Europe as proceeding through the stages of conflict, accommodation, and participation, leading ultimately to a symbiotic relationship.

THE EAST EUROPEAN ENVIRONMENT AND THE MILITARY

In Eastern Europe, the potential for conflict between the party and the military, at a given stage of their interaction, has perhaps been more pronounced than in the Soviet Union due to the specific local political conditions. There are two important periods in the post-World War II history of party–military relations in the region. The first, generally lasting into the mid-1950s, was a period of brutal suppression and subordination of the military to the party, followed by sweeping Stalinization and Russification of the national armies. Characteristic of this period were wideranging purges of the officer corps, the introduction of pervasive political controls, the unquestioned primacy of the political officer over the military professional, and the total suppression of the military's national character. During the second phase, whose beginning roughly coincided with the start of the de-Stalinization campaign in the mid-1950s, the East European armies underwent a process of professionalization, modernization, and renationalization, and emerged as modern, national military establishments. Here it is of critical importance to note that all Communist armies have remained nation-state dependent. As such, they continue to hold the view that their identity and fundamental purpose depend on the existence of a well-defined, national-political entity and a set of quintessential national (often of a geopolitical nature) interests. Indeed, there has been very little genuine supranational integration of the socialist countries in the military field, and there is, as yet, no convincing evidence that any of the East European Communist armies has become more loyal to a supranational or an ideological factor than it is to perceived national interests. It is quite significant, for example, that the Soviet Union has never been able to use the East European military establishments to resolve conflicts, crises, or anti-Soviet upheavals in their respective countries. This has been the case even when these nations have taken an openly anti-Soviet position, as Yugoslavia and Albania did in 1948 and 1960, or directly challenged the Communist regime itself, as was the case with Hungary in 1956. The traditional organic relationship between the army and the nation-state, succinctly summed up in Von Moltke's aphorism 'keine Grenzen, keine Militär' (no borders, no military), persists in Communist states. It remains vitally relevant for understanding the nature of political–military interaction in Eastern Europe.

In short, there is good reason to believe that the East European military establishments have preserved their national orientation. The East European Communist parties, on the other hand, have remained throughout most of this period subordinated to an external force, that is, the Soviet Union. As a result, they have espoused sweeping universalist-chiliastic objectives that are inherently anti-national and could, at least theoretically, be expected to come into conflict with the national loyalties of the military.

Most of the other specifically East European conditions affecting the military establishment, and therefore party–military interaction, also derive from the political relationship between the East European states and the Soviet Union. The complete political subordination of the East European regimes to Moscow after World War II has had the following important consequences for the military:

(1) *Subordination to the Soviet military and denial of nation-state function.* Under Soviet auspices the East European military establishments have been formally integrated into a quasi-alliance (the Warsaw Pact) of questionable military value, where their only clearly defined function seems to be political and organizational subordination to the Soviet military. By entrusting this quasi-alliance with the collective defense of the socialist commonwealth, the Soviets have, in effect, denied the East European militaries their essential nation-state function, that is, the defense of their countries, as well as all prerogatives proceeding from that function, such as the formulation of a national defense doctrine, and so on. This situation could be expected to arouse negative feelings among the East European military establishments, who continue to see themselves as the major protectors of the national interests. It is no coincidence, in this respect, that one of the first demands made during the Prague Spring of 1968 and the Romanian drive for independence was for reassertion of national control over the military, and the formulation of a *national* defense doctrine.

(2) *Diminished political role and clout.* Under the conditions of Soviet military and political domination, the East European militaries have never had political influence with the party comparable to that of the Soviet military, or other independent Communist countries. This is because the Red Army has always been the ultimate and reliable guarantor of the local parties' continuous hegemony of power. This has, of course, obviated to a considerable extent party need for support from its own military, and thus correspondingly decreased the military's political role.

(3) *Divergent perceptions of national versus ideological desiderata.* Military establishments in both the dominant and dependent countries are likely to stress national over ideological desiderata. However, in the dominant countries, the two may be difficult to separate, while in the dependent states they will be impossible to confuse. To give one example of this dichotomy, it may be very easy for a Soviet officer to rationalize that the Soviet invasion of Czechoslovakia, or involvement in Angola, serves the national interests of the Soviet state, quite apart from any ideological motivation; but it would be exceedingly difficult for a Polish officer to see his participation in a Soviet–Chinese war, or in a Soviet-organized invasion of Yugoslavia as even remotely relevant to Polish national interests. Thus, Marxist–Leninist ideology of the Soviet type, and military nationalism could, under certain conditions, be fairly com-

patible in a dominant state, yet remain basically antagonistic in dependent East European polities.

The specific characteristics, enumerated above, of the East European political environment have a critical impact on the mode of party–military relations in the area.* In particular, they provide for a model of conflict, or accommodation, between the party and the military that is quite distinct from the Soviet one. The divergent institutional desiderata of an East European military establishment and an orthodox Leninist party, aside from those issues of conflict that are common to all Communist states, could be contrasted as follows:

Military Desiderata	Party Desiderata
Nationalist values	Universalist values
Loyalty to national political factor	Loyalty to external political factor
National military prerogative	Supranational military prerogative
National military autonomy	Supranational military integration
High domestic political input	Low domestic political input

This is obviously an ideal typology which is unlikely to occur in a real-life situation. Indeed, the East European parties probably conformed totally to the above 'party desiderata' formula only during the relatively brief Stalinist period. Nonetheless, it provides some important clues, not only to the sources of conflict, but also to the direction in which party–military relations in Eastern Europe are likely to evolve. It implies, above all, that any party attempt to move away from external political dependence and inter-nationalist ideology and toward a more nationally oriented posture, would result in a proportionate alleviation of party–military tensions, as well as in a corresponding enhancement of the army's political role. A significant modification of party ideology, including foreign–political emancipation, could conceivably lead to a party–military accommodation, and even alliance, based on a new consensus regarding national objectives.

The remainder of this chapter will examine the hypothesis that such a process of accommodation has been taking place in Romania since it began its quest for independence in the early 1960s. A brief discussion of the Romanian drive for independence will provide a background to the analysis to follow. An attempt will then be made to construct a framework for the analysis of Romanian nationalism as a major factor affecting party–military interaction. Finally, three distinct aspects of the evolution of Romanian party–military relations will be examined in detail.

---

* It is recognized here that the attempt to group together and treat as an entity all East European Warsaw Pact countries on anything but the most general level, could present serious problems due to widely diverse individual features such as military–political traditions, geopolitical circumstances, external threat perception, etc. Nonetheless, all of them, with the exception of East Germany, exhibit generally similar characteristics with respect to military–political interaction, which at the same time are quite distinct from those prevailing in the Soviet Union.

ROMANIA'S QUEST FOR INDEPENDENCE

Although it originally began as a revolt against Soviet policies of economic integration and division of labor, which were reportedly designed to relegate Romania to a predominantly agricultural, 'vegetable garden of COMECON' role, the Romanian pursuit of independence has quickly taken the form of a marked deviation from accepted norms of foreign–political, economic, and military–political behavior in the Soviet bloc. An early turning point was reached in August of 1968, when party leader Ceausescu boldly denounced the Soviet invasion of Czechoslovakia and declared Romania's resolve to resist militarily a Soviet incursion into Romania.[9] Since then the common denominator of all Romanian policies has been a dogged determination to place perceived national interests above those of international communism and the Soviet Union, whenever they have conflicted. In the realm of foreign policy, besides the above-mentioned stand on Czechoslovakia, Romania has openly clashed with the Soviet Union on a number of issues in various international forums; improved relations with the West despite Soviet misgivings; refused to sever relations with Israel in 1967; established close relations with fellow maverick Yugoslavia; and maintained extensive and cordial ties with China. Lately, Romania has also declared itself a developing country and has made numerous overtures to the nonaligned movement. On the economic front, Bucharest has strongly restated its disapproval of economic integration within the Soviet orbit, and considerably expanded cooperation with the Western countries. Further, the Romanians have begun to call for a 'new international economic order,' a demand which is implicitly as critical of Soviet international economic behavior, as it is of capitalism. With respect to military policy, Romania, though nominally still a member of the Warsaw Pact, has refused to participate in, or allow, military maneuvers on its soil, and has become a vocal advocate of the abolition of military blocs, the liquidation of foreign bases, and withdrawal of foreign troops. Domestically, the country has marshalled all its energies and resources for a determined drive toward economic–industrial development. The wideranging foreign–political emancipation, however, has not been accompanied by internal political liberalization, and Romania remains one of the most repressive East European states.

PARTY–MILITARY RELATIONS IN ROMANIA: A FRAMEWORK OF ANALYSIS

The impact of the Romanian pursuit of independence, it is suggested here, has dramatically changed the political environments of the party and military institutions. These new environments reflect the changing political realities, institutional objectives, and options available. Their basic parameters are as follows:

(1) *Party Environmental Parameters*

(a) Determination to continue course of Romanian independence.

(b) Acute external threat.

(c) Determination to pursue unabated industrialization and economic modernization drive.

(d) Need to secure domestic support in order to offset loss of traditional external support.

(e) Reliance on the military for protection of the regime from external threat.

(2) *Military Environmental Parameters*

(a) Military recast into traditional role of guardian of the nation.

(b) Military emancipation from subservient position within both the multilateral (Warsaw Pact) and bilateral (Soviet–Romanian) context.

(c) Termination of total military subordination to the party, characteristic of Stalinist period.

(d) Military identification with, and support for, party policies of independence and economic development.

The radical change in the political circumstances of the party and the military has forced a revision of the traditional modes of party–military interaction. The two most salient and novel elements that have contributed to the crystalization of a qualitatively new relationship are party dependence on the military, and party need for modicum of public support. Realizing that failure to win the support of the military and gain some public acceptance for its policies would spell political doom for the party leadership, and inevitable *Gleichschaltung* into Soviet bloc orthodoxy, the party has made this objective a major determinant of its strategy and attitudes. Accordingly, the party has introduced nationalism as the surrogate ideology of Romanian autonomy, and this, in turn, has had a profound impact on political–military relations. By implicitly revising its doctrinal–philosophical values to accommodate nationalism, the party has moved away from an internationalist outlook, and embraced values dear to the military. As a result, an important rapprochement between the two institutions' world views has occurred. It is suggested here that this emerging philosophical compatibility, and the party's continued reliance on the military for protection from Soviet threat, are the major forces behind the process of civil–military accommodation in Romania. The pages that follow will examine nationalism as the major catalyst of party–military relations, and the following developments in the accommodation process:

(1) *Rehabilitation of the Military*

(a) Positive re-evaluation of the historical societal role and function of the military.

(b) Rehabilitation of pre-World War II military establishment image and political role.

(2) *Emerging Military Institutional Autonomy*

(a) Reorganization of army political structures.

(b)   Promulgation of a new defense doctrine stressing national defense.
(c)   Military input in increased defense effort, the setting up of an indigenous arms industry, and weapons acquisition from non-Soviet sources.
(d)   Growing military participation in foreign–political matters involving the military.

(3)   *Evolution of Party–Military Relations Into a Symbiotic Relationship*

(a)   Incorporation of quintessential military values into party ideology and new societal value system.
(b)   Intensified military involvement in socio-political and economic management.

NATIONALISM REDIVIVUS

The new party-promoted Romanian nationalism has two distinct dimensions: a theoretical-doctrinal revision of the concepts of nation and nation-state, and a positive reinterpretation of the Romanian past and national traditions in order to show that Communist Romania is the legitimate heir to historic Romania and its traditions.[10] Both of these are highly significant for our study insofar as they show a major modification of the party Marxist–Leninist *Weltanschauung*.

The new Romanian interpretation of the role of the nation and the state in socialist society has become a cornerstone of Romanian ideology. Essentially, Romanian ideologists have tried to present the nation as indispensable to both the Romanian people's historical development and to the construction of advanced socialist and communist society. Romanian nationalism of the past and its present equivalent, socialist patriotism, are simultaneously credited with providing the impetus behind the historical achievements of the Romanian people. The political significance of these developments is twofold: they not only imply a major revision of the sacrosanct Marxist tenets of historical materialism and the class struggle, but also constitute an outright denial that proletarian internationalism is the guiding principle of relations among socialist countries.[11] Having asserted the primacy of the nation, party theoreticians proceed to impute the nation's alleged progressive role to the Romanian nation-state. The nation-state is thus presented as the legitimate expression of the nation.[12] Moreover, it is presented as the only possible way in which society can achieve its fullest development and communism be constructed. The elevation of the nation-state to a primary position as purveyor and defender of Romanian interests has been accompanied by an unequivocal rejection of both suprastate mechanisms in the relations between socialist countries and the doctrine of limited sovereignty. Suprastate arrangements, argue the Romanians, require functional transfer of sovereignty from the nation-state. This, they assert, is not only unnecessary, but inevitably leads to inequality and domination.[13] Attempts to suppress the nation-state in the international system are 'in contradiction with laws of human progress.'[14] This thesis has found practical expression in Romanian recalcitrance over matters of cooperation with such supranational bodies as the Warsaw Pact and COMECON. An integral aspect of the Romanian rehabilitation of nationalism has been the offiicial insistence on the national character of sovereignty. National sovereignty and independence, as well as the obligation to defend them, are seen as residing exclusively in the nation-state, and subject strictly to international law, rather than proletarian internationalism. This aspect of Romanian ideology, which is reflected in the new Romanian defense concept, to be discussed later, directly contradicts the doctrine of limited sovereignty, first formulated by Soviet theoreticians as a justification of the 1968 invasion of Czechoslovakia.[15] The defense of Romanian independence and sovereignty are thus declared a strictly national prerogative, and the failure to safeguard them is equated, in Ceausescu's words, with 'abdicating revolutionary Marxist–Leninist principles and sliding down the slippery road of cosmopolitanism and national nihilism.'[16]

Along with the revision of some basic theoretical tenets of Marxism–Leninism, as practiced in the Soviet bloc, the new Romanian nationalism has resulted in an extensive, and at times spectacular, rewriting of Romanian history.[17] The net result has been an almost total revision of Romanian Communist historiography prior to the deviation, and interpretations of historical material that increasingly resemble prewar bourgeois historiography. Though the scope of this chapter prohibits a detailed discussion of this development, we shall list some of its most interesting aspects. One of these has been the 'rediscovery' of a succession of 'progressive' Romanian feudal princes and military chieftains, now extolled as noble fighters for Romanian unification. In one instance, a sixteenth-century Romanian prince, Michael the Brave, who official historians not too long ago decribed as a 'feudal boyar and a rapacious invader of peasants' lands,'[18] has now been proclaimed by Ceausescu himself as 'a luminous, progressive personality in the golden annals of Romanian history.'[19] The same treatment is accorded to all perceived historical attempts to create a unitary Romanian state. Another significant aspect of historical revisionism is the quiet rehabilitation of the irredentist policies of Romanian bourgeois governments. A case in point is the sympathy and approval which party historians now extend to the ancien régime's policies for recovering national irridenta in Bessarabia and Bukovina at Soviet expense.[20] An important corollary of the party volte-face on Bessarabia has been open official denunciation of the RCP's prewar anti-national, that is, pro-Soviet attitudes.[21]

The new Romanian nationalism, reborn under party auspices, however, is not of the traditional utopian-romantic kind, nor is it simply an expression of external-political aspirations. Rather, it is a calculated policy to elicit support for broader party objectives and is used primarily as a mobilization tool. However, in pursuing a nationalistic course, the party itself has undergone a process of resocialization in nationalistic values. This has, in turn, made it more receptive to intrinsic military values. A logical consequence of this process has been the party decision to restore the formerly downgraded military to its traditional position as repository of national ideals.

THE MILITARY REHABILITATED

In general, the official reinterpretation of the historical role and image of the Romanian military has been characterized by a determined effort to present it as an invariably progressive force in the struggle for achieving Romanian national ideals. In pursuing this objective, the RCP has not only parted company with the traditional Marxist condemnation of bourgeois military establishments as reliable tools for ruling class oppression, but also publicly admitted its own erroneous stands on the question in the past.

The rehabilitation drive has centered on reasserting the 'progressive' character of military traditions, the crucial role of the military in achieving national unification and repelling assorted aggressors, the organic ties between the military and the people, and the allegedly correct political orientation of the military throughout Romanian history. According to the new interpretation, the progressive traditions of the Romanian military stem from the fact that the army has never been used against the masses, but only to protect the people from foreign enemies. According to Ceausescu, 'the Romanian armies have covered themselves with everlasting glory in the fight waged in defense of our national being.'[22] It has further been stated that the military's view that its sole function is 'safeguarding the national existence' is the basis of the 'historic bond between the people and the military.'[23] It is this link with the people that is said to account for the military's progressive character.

As Ceausescu has elaborated: 'As a matter of fact, the old traditions of the Army at various historical stages prove that the Army has always supported the people's interests, that it has always been the basic force in the struggle against foreign domination'.[24] And, of course, the progressive traditions of the old Romanian army are said to be reflected in today's army which is 'the highest and most progressive continuation of the old military traditions of the Romanian people.'[25]

The official campaign to rehabilitate the prewar military focuses on the period after World War I. Particular attention is given to such important events in Romanian history as the reunification of the country in 1918, its subsequent dismemberment in 1940, and Romanian participation in World War II. This period is of special interest also because the new Romanian interpretations stand in direct contradiction to Stalinist Romanian historiography and present Soviet historiography. The army, for example, has been pictured as spearheading the successful drive to incorporate Transylvania, Northern Bukovina and Bessarabia in the mother country,[26] an action which Soviet historians usually describe as an imperialist annexation of sovereign Soviet territories.[27] The positive re-evaluation of the military establishment's role in the interwar years involves presenting it as a strictly defensive, status quo-oriented force. This approach is in line with the generally sympathetic portrayal of Romanian foreign policy and objectives of the time.[28] Far from being 'an aggressive military encampment as stated by some foreign [read Soviet] historians,' Romania and its army are depicted as a dedicated force for peace.[29] Curiously, the prewar regime is subjected to criticism only for weakening the defense potential of the country and neglecting the war industry.[30] The events of the summer of 1940, leading to the surrender of considerable parts of Romanian territory (Northern Bukovina and Bessarabia to the Soviet Union, Northern Transylvania to Hungary), are interpreted in a fashion that exonerates the Romanian military from any responsibility for Romania's ready submission to the threat of force. A treasonous ruling class is blamed for the military's failure to fulfill its sacred duty of defending the territorial integrity of the fatherland.[31]

By far the most striking case of historical revisionism involving the military deals with Romanian participation in World War II. Under the Fascistoid government of Marshal Antonescu, Romania participated actively and enthusiastically in the war against the Soviet Union from the very first day. In the process, Romanian troops occupied considerable Soviet territories, took part in battles as far east as Stalingrad, and suffered tremendous casualties.[32] In August of 1944, after the Soviet army had already crossed the Romanian borders, a palace coup overthrew the Antonescu regime and Romania gingerly switched sides, fighting the last nine months of the war on the side of the Allies. The strategy of the new Romanian historiography in dealing with the war has been to maintain an almost complete silence on the first four years of the war, and emphasize military cooperation with progressive forces in the overthrow of Antonescu. Further, the Romanian army is now credited with single-handedly liberating the country from the Nazis, and providing a sizable military contribution to the Allied war effort. Of great significance here are attempts to present the military as an anti-Fascist force participating in the anti-Fascist struggle alongside the party. While the party has always been hailed as the main organizer and executor of the 23 August coup and subsequent events (in actuality the Romanian Communist Party, with a prewar membership of less than 1,000, was, at best, a marginal political force), official recognition of a military role is a novel and highly significant element. It has prompted a drastic re-evaluation of the political attitudes of the army and, in particular, its leadership. A fascinating example of this approach has been provided by a group of military historians in a study of the political attitudes of Romanian wartime generals.[33] According to the study, during the war only 17 of 387 active Romanian generals supported the regime's policy of alliance with Germany.[34] Moreover, those 17 pro-German generals 'had either been removed early in 1941, or arrested at the outset, or in the course of the insurrection.'[35] In other words, the study implies that the highest officers of an army that fought side by side with the Germans for four years were almost totally united in their anti-German attitudes, and that pro-German sentiments were somehow cause for dismissal from the service. Further discussion of the 'correct' political orientation of the military leadership is available, for instance, in a study of the Romanian General Staff by Colonel General Ion Gheorghe. In addition to extolling the professionalism of the General Staff, Gheorghe praises it for 'significant contributions to the clarification of urgent political and diplomatic problems.'[36] Numerous other studies dealing with party work in the army have come to similar conclusions.[37] These new Romanian interpretations stand in direct contradiction to some recent Soviet writings on the subject.[38]

Several other points concerning the rewritten history of the 23 August coup are also worth noting. Contrary to the RCP's earlier position that the party alone initiated Antonescu's overthrow and that the Red Army liberated Romania,[39] the new version credits an alliance between the party, the military, and other progressive elements, including the king, with these achievements. In particular, its account of the coup suggests that the Communists played at best a secondary role.[40] In short, the success of the uprising is now attributed to a party–military–other progressive forces–anti-fascist alliance, rather than to the party alone. Significantly, special praise is bestowed on the 'farsighted' party policy of seeking the cooperation of the military leadership. In one case, this alleged party attitude is compared implicitly to the 'historical compromise' concept of the Italian Communist Party of today.[41] The army is also now credited with liberating the country on its own and with substantially assisting the Allied cause.[42] This Romanian contention is again rejected outright by the Soviets.[43]

Perhaps the most spectacular case of historical revisionism yet has been the recent partial rehabilitation of Marshal Antonescu, the military dictator, leader of the army and traditional bête noire for the party. This self-styled Romanian Conducator (Fuehrer), who ruled in alliance with the Fascist Iron Guard movement and was eventually hanged by the Communist government as a war criminal, has suddenly reappeared on the Romanian scene in a fairly favorable light. Through the medium of a historical novel, which was published in large quantities and became a national bestseller overnight, Antonescu has now been resurrected as a strong, albeit tragic figure, who had the interests of his country at heart, but was doomed by the tragic circumstances in which Romania found itself in the early 1940s.[44] His alliance with Hitler is explained, in Antonescu's words, as the unpleasant choice of the lesser of two evils, the other one being 'Freemasons, Jews, and Bolsheviks.' The novel also goes a long way toward absolving the army for its attack on the Soviet Union by implying that the military's motivation was simply the recovery of annexed Romanian territories. Antonescu has been further exonerated in two recent articles. In these, the Marshal is depicted as having become disillusioned with Hitler and willing to reach an accommodation with the Allies and withdraw Romania from the war.[45] Moreover, the Conducator is alleged to have strongly disapproved of the activities of his allies, the Iron Guard, most notably their atrocities against the Romanian Jews, and to have shared the army's 'profound hostility' toward them.[46]

Several aspects of the rehabilitation of the prewar Romanian military establishment are of particular relevance to party–military relations of the present time. The emphasis on the progressive historical and societal role of the army in Romania before the war, not only satisfies the military predilection for professional and institutional continuity, but, by implication, enhances its present status as a social force. The significance of the attempts to present the alleged party–military alliance as the decisive factor in the realization of Romanian national objectives during the war is rather obvious as well. Not so clear, are the implications of the political rehabilitation of the prewar top brass. The positive treatment accorded to the army wartime leadership in the rehabilitation campaign appears to open the question of party policies toward the military in the immediate postwar period. As is well known, after the war the Romanian officer corps was subjected to an extensive purge in which most of the command personnel, currently hailed as ardent patriots and political progressives, were ousted, incarcerated and, in some cases, even liquidated.[47] So far, there have been few signs of a party desire to re-examine its attitudes toward the army during the Stalinist period. Nonetheless, there are some signs that this may yet come. One indication was the 1968 rehabilitation of two groups of army officers purged and sentenced to long prison terms in the early 1950s. This case is of particular significance since these officers were tried and sentenced on apparently fabricated charges during Ceausescu's tenure as Chief of the Main Political Administration of the Romanian army.[48] Another example concerns a 1971 decree restoring the right to military pension to officers who have been demoted or whose rank has been revoked.[49] Finally, in 1974, twenty-three purged prewar generals, many of them with extensive combat experience against the Soviet Union, were promoted by Ceausescu to generals of the reserve.[50]

THE MILITARY AUTONOMOUS

Under the conditions of changing party perceptions, the military establishment has gradually assumed an increasingly autonomous professional and institutional function within the Romanian body politic. The emerging military autonomy has both an internal and a foreign-political dimension. Domestically, the military no longer finds itself totally subordinated to the political factor as it was during the Stalinist period. It has also acquired growing responsibility in the areas of traditional military jurisdiction, such as military defense doctrine, military organization, armaments, and so on. On the external plane, the Romanian military has achieved a considerable degree of emancipation from foreign control, both in the context of the Warsaw Pact and Soviet–Romanian bilateral relations. On another level, the military has begun to provide substantial institutional input in state conduct of foreign-policy matters of a military nature.

Reorganization of Army Political Structures

The extent of military emancipation from excessive political control and interference is difficult to ascertain conclusively due to the sensitive nature of the issue and the absence of any open discussion of party–military interaction. Officially, party and military officials alike continue to advocate strict political hegemony in all military matters. Nonetheless, some important structural changes in the mechanisms of party–military interaction suggest a more equitable relationship. These include the reorganization of the Main Political Administration, the Ministry of Defense, and the formation of a National Defense Council. The Main Political Administration, a traditional party watchdog in the military establishment, was abolished by the Romanians in 1964 and replaced by a Higher Political Council. The Higher Political Council is subordinated to the Defense Council, which is not a party body as such, and not to the Central Committee of the party, as is the case with the Main Political Administrations in the other Warsaw Pact countries. Significantly, the membership of the Higher Political Council includes, ex officio, a number of career soldiers, such as the commanders of armed forces branches, the Minister of Defense, and other officials of the Defense Ministry. It would appear that professional military men have thus been given a voice in determining party–political initiatives in the army. Furthermore, the Defense Council, which is directly responsible for Higher Political Council activities as well as all other defense-related policy, is not merely a party but also a constitutional body, subordinated to the party as well as the State Council (or the National Assembly while in session).[51] Another indication of military emancipation from excessive controls is the recent reorganization of the Interior Ministry, and the secret police. Communist regimes, Romania's included, have invariably used these organs for controlling the military, a practice undoubtedly detested by military professionals. The Interior Ministry in Romania has now been placed under the jurisdiction of the Defense Council, with its security activities, that is, the secret police, responsible to the Central Committee of the party and the command of the armed forces.[52] This arrangement is without precedent in the Warsaw Pact states and is highly significant. Additional evidence of the military establishment's enhanced status is provided by the 1972 Decree for Reorganization of the Ministry of National Defense.[53] The decree, which widens the jurisdictional domain of the ministry, specifically charges it with 'organizing, direction, and guiding political education in the army,' as well as the military training of high party and state officials.[54]

An examination of some recent Romanian works suggests further that the Romanian military has attempted to deal with the problem of dual (military and political) authority that traditionally plagues Communist armies. In a recent authoritative book on military organization by a military collective, the authors strongly advocate the concept of 'unity of command' (similar to the Russian notion of *edinnonachalie* – 'one-man command'), and argue that the military commander is both the main promoter and representative of party and state policy and responsible for political education of the troops.[55] The political organs (Councils) are listed only in third place (after military commanders and Military Councils) among those responsible for carrying out the party line.[56] It should be explained that in the Romanian army, the secretaries of the Political Councils (branches of the Higher Political Council at every level), who are appointed rather than elected from the local party cell, are deputy commanders of their particular unit and are nominally in charge of political training. The fact that the military commander, rather than the political officer, is described as the party's main activist in the unit, ostensibly on the basis of the unity-of-command principle, is an interesting development that suggests an increased military assertiveness. In addition to stressing the primacy of the commander in political matters, which logically would make the party officer superfluous, military writers have argued openly for stronger professional input in the decision-making process. They have suggested that 'every act of leadership' should be characterized by a 'bivalent approach' which 'ties together professional competence and political responsibility.'[57] Some indication of party awareness of military sensitivity on this point and its willingness to accommodate it could be glimpsed in a 1969 Army Day speech by Ceausescu, in which he admonished his audience to 'respect the Army's own command principles' while carrying out military and political training.[58]

The New Romanian Defense Doctrine

The increased party reliance on the army for protection from external threat has also enhanced the military establishment's professional autonomy and prestige. The most conspicuous development in this respect has been the re-emergence of the army as the societal institution solely responsible for the country's defense. This radical change in the position of the Romanian military, which formerly occupied an ill-defined secondary role in a superpower-dominated pseudo-alliance, has been legitimated by Romania's new defense doctrine. The new Romanian doctrine of national defense, conceived and promulgated in the wake of the Soviet invasion of Czechoslovakia, exhibits several unique features that have significant bearing on the military institutional posture, apart from their foreign-political implications.[59] The major conceptual premise and innovation of the doctrine, as compared to Warsaw Pact defense concepts, is its emphasis on the national character of Romanian defense, which 'cannot be conceived or exist outside Romanian society.'[60] In the Warsaw Pact countries, the *collective defense* of the socialist commonwealth continues to be the major defense imperative. Another highly significant novelty in the new defense concept is its adoption of the notion of people's war as the basic method of fighting a defensive war. This aspect of the Romanian doctrine, which appears to be closely patterned on the Yugoslav idea of 'all-people's war,' calls for the participation of the entire population in preparation for the defense of the homeland.[61] It envisages territorial defense which is to be accomplished by a wide variety of civil–military organizations such as 'patriotic guards,' local anti-aircraft defense units, youth military training detachments, etc. Though some of these units existed before as voluntary groups, the new law has made them compulsory forms of civilian participation in the country's defense effort.[62] All of the above units are placed directly under the jurisdiction of the Ministry of National Defense in terms of training, control, and guidance.[63] In this way, the professional military establishment has been made responsible for the military training of all Romanian citizens. It is worth noting that military training of nonmembers of the armed forces in other Warsaw Pact members is provided by paramilitary organizations, such as the Soviet DOSAAF, which are independent from the military. Finally, the defense law stipulates the setting up of local defense councils at every administrative level. These are entrusted with a wide variety of functions within the socio-economic sphere pertaining to defense. Again, local military commanders are assured substantial input via ex officio membership.

The Military in Arms Production and Foreign Policy

The strong advocacy of Romanian national sovereignty in all defense matters has had a considerable effect on military involvement in the area of indigenous arms production, which, through a traditional area of military interest, had been virtually nonexistent prior to Romania's independent course. A logical consequence of the independent Romanian defense stance was a concerted drive to develop a domestic military-industrial capacity. This effort gathered momentum after the Soviet invasion of Czechoslovakia in 1968. Designed to free Romania from its almost total dependence on the Soviet Union for military hardware, this novel (for a Warsaw Pact member) Romanian development provides yet another indication of the military's growing professional independence. Judging from the legal provisions governing arms production, as well as the growing body of literature dealing with the subject in the military press and elsewhere, the military has been accorded a dominant position in setting up the priorities and controlling the new military industry. In particular, the defense establishment has been given preponderance over other state institutions in matters concerning the planning, production, and financing of defense-related equipment.[64] In the related area of defense technology transfer, the military has been put in charge of all foreign trade activities related to defense equipment.[65] In the process of developing an indigenous arms industry, the Romanians have already achieved some important successes, given the relatively undeveloped technological-industrial base of the country. Primarily to serve the needs of a people's war and to reduce dependence on the Soviet Union, Romania has engaged in production of various types of ammunition, armored vehicles, artillery, and even laser-guidance technology.[66] More important, and politically sensitive, have been numerous joint projects and licensing agreements with non-Warsaw Pact countries. The most important of these has been the joint Yugoslav–Romanian development of a supersonic twin-jet fighter outfitted with British engines, which is the first non-Soviet military aircraft to be introduced by a Warsaw Pact member.[67] Other significant developments include the production, under license, of French Alouette and Puma helicopters and British Rolls-Royce engines. It has even been speculated that Romania is interested in acquiring American military aircraft.[68] In a move that must be considered a major challenge to the Soviets, the Romanians have also acquired a number of Chinese naval vessels, which are now also produced under license.[69]

The intensity of the defense production effort is shown in the drastic increase of research and development appropriations and the steadily growing (by about 20 percent a year) general defense outlays.[70] With respect to defense expenditures, a number of articles by military writers seem to have been composed specifically to counter criticism of the increased defense burden. These pieces support defense spending by pointing out that technological spillover into the civilian sector, and foreign currency savings, have benefited the economy. They also stress the vital political dimension of the defense effort.[71]

Rather substantial military participation is also observable in the sphere of Romanian foreign policy. Military activities in foreign policy have come to be regarded as an integral part of the Romanian pursuit of independence and, as such, are vigorously promoted and encouraged by the party. Particular attention has been given to developing military ties with countries 'embarked upon the path of independence,' and with the Western countries.[72] While the greatest contribution the Romanian military can make to cooperation with the Warsaw Pact members is said to be the strengthening of Romania's own defense, military relations with independent and/or capitalist countries are described as strengthening the processes of international understanding and détente.[73] Indeed, a look at the foreign activities of Romanian defense officials would clearly show that establishing ties with non-Warsaw Pact countries has the highest priority. Military–political relations are particularly close with neighboring Yugoslavia, as evidenced by joint arms production efforts and regular consultative meetings, and probably influenced by the similar threat perception of the two countries. The most dramatic development, however, has been intensified contacts with NATO countries. After the first visit of a Romanian military official to a NATO country – Chief of General Staff, Colonel General Ion Gheorghe to France in 1971 – exchanges of military delegations between NATO and Romania have become routine.[74] On a number of occasions, high-powered Romanian military delegations have visited Britain, France, Italy, and the USA, while the Romanian military have played host to the British, French, and Italian Defense Ministers and Chiefs of General Staff, and the US Army Chief of Staff.[75] There is also some evidence that the rather frequent diplomatic excursions of Romanian military figures are more than ceremonial courtesy calls. For example, Britain and France – the two Western countries with which exchanges have been most frequent – have become Romania's partners in some sizable projects of a military-technical character. Perhaps the favorite foreign recipient of the Romanian military's attention has been China. In apparent disregard of Soviet sensitivities, Romania has maintained close and productive relations with the People's Republic since 1965.[76] It has also been speculated that Romania is engaged in selling military equipment, which is another area of military responsibility.[77] According to one source, a Romanian military vehicle is being exported to over fifty countries, including NATO member Greece.[78]

THE MILITARY ENGAGÉ

So far we have examined the evolution of party–military relations in Romania by concentrating on the processes of refurbishing the military image, under the impact of the new nationalistic revival, and the reinvestment of the army with institutional autonomy, within its traditional societal dominion. The analytical focus of the study will now shift toward an investigation of party co-optation of the military establishment in the political process and absorption of intrinsic military values in its socio-political *Weltanschauung,* leading to an evolving symbiotic relationship. Decisive for this development, which we believe characterizes the present phase of party–military interaction, has been a changing party perception of its socio-political goals and foreign and domestic political exigencies.[79]

Since the early 1970s, some significant new nuances have appeared in the party's interpretation of the goals and methods that are guiding Romanian socio-political development along the road to socialism. First noticeable at the National Party Conference in July of 1972, they were further developed and reconfirmed at the 11th Congress of the Romanian Communist Party in 1974 and the Congress on Political Education and Socialist Culture in 1976. Essentially, the party has restated and made more specific its developmental blueprint, while reformulating mobilizational methods for achieving it. The new party orientation, involving substantial doctrinal-ideological revision, has basically been a reaction to some disturbing external and domestic stimuli. Externally, an intensified Soviet effort to enforce conformity in the bloc, and its continuing insistence on proletarian internationalism (a traditional euphemism for Soviet hegemony) has increased the Romanian sense of insecurity, which had abated somewhat after the Soviet failure to invade Romania in 1968. Particularly disturbing, have been recent harsh Soviet denunciations of nationalism as intrinsically anti-Communist, and the newly espoused notion that a single integrated socialist nation is evolving in the Soviet bloc.[80] All of this has probably convinced the Romanians that their independence is still not accepted as a fait accompli and should not be taken for granted.

Domestically, the party has been faced with a number of difficult problems. With the novelty and excitement of national reassertion wearing off, the continuing success of party mobilizational policies has been placed in jeopardy. This problem has been compounded by official awareness that public tolerance of both the economic hardships accompanying development, and unmitigated domestic authoritarianism and repression, may have its limits. A different potential challenge is posed by the rising technocratic-managerial stratum. Although this elite possesses vital developmental expertise, its ideological credentials are dubious. Thus, the potential confluence of a number of negative developments – slackening ideological fervor, social unrest, and serious economic difficulties – into a powerful challenge to the party course, coupled with the ever-present external threat, must have convinced the party that urgent pre-emptive measures were called for.

The party has responded with a new mobilizational drive with a slightly different ideological emphasis. The overriding societal goals of foreign-political independence and accelerated economic development have again been forcefully restated. A sense of urgency has been added to the economic aspect by declaring Romania a 'socialist developing country' and by setting specific developmental target deadlines. According to these, Romania has to graduate from its 'developing' stage by 1980 and emerge as a developed industrial country by 1990.[81] The major doctrinal innovations have taken place in the party-controlled mechanics of mobilization. Important among these have been the drive to fuse party and state functions, an intense anti-bureaucratic campaign, stress on national unity and purpose, and last but not least, a call to mold a 'new man' in Romania. The campaign to combine the party and state functions is primarily designed to streamline the process of governing by reducing the dual party and state character of administration.[82] It has been carried out by considerable reorganization and restructuring of the apparatus. In the process the traditional boundaries dividing the party from the rest of society have become somewhat blurred. The fusion of the party and the state has become part of a larger effort to create national unity among all elements of Romanian society – women, the minorities, the peasants, and even the Orthodox Church.[83] The ideological creed behind the efforts to forge national unity rests on concrete Romanian developmental and national imperatives, rather than on traditional Marxist–Leninist doctrinal postulates. The ultimate product of the unified, homogenized, and thoroughly idealogized Romanian society is to be the creation of a 'new man'. This new hypothetical *Homo Romaniens* is quite distinct from the 'new Communist man' of Soviet doctrinal parlance; he exhibits none of the universalist revolutionary propensities of the latter, but is seen as a fervent Romanian patriot and a dedicated builder of the Romanian 'multilaterally developed socialist society.'[84] As such, his 'highest duty' is the 'defense of the Fatherland and the revolutionary achievements of the people.'[85] Ideally, then, the 'new man' would be a militant propagator of Romanian socialism and, at the same time, a socialist citizen-in-arms.

The Military as an Agent for Patriotic Socialization

Aware that external threat and lack of genuine national popularity make its position tenuous, the party has introduced these innovations in an effort to widen its narrow political base, while preserving its leading role. In its quest for national unity the party has found a natural ally in the military. The two institutions' growing affinity has been based on the remarkable compatibility between the party's new value system and traditional military beliefs. Party emphasis on unity of action, discipline, hard work, hierarchical leadership, and national purpose has struck a responsive chord among military men, who have always considered the above values as integral components of the military ethos. On the other hand, the military establishment, which, along with the party, is the best organized and most powerful institution in the country, has emerged as an ideal channel for socialization and mobilization of the masses in the new spirit. This, however, is not the old type of political socialization for which the party used the military during the Stalinist period, but a qualitatively new, military–political socialization, which appears to serve the institutional and philosophical needs of the military as much as it does those of the party.

The actual involvement of the military in socio-political activities has taken two general directions. First, the military has assumed wideranging responsibilities for the patriotic-political training of Romanian youth, as well as the population at large. These new responsibilities have been carried out both inside and, increasingly, outside the army's institutional structures. The primary importance accorded to this aspect of military activity can be inferred from the evermore frequent attempts to picture the military as the 'high school of the nation.'[86] The Romanian concept of the army as the 'school of the nation,' it should be noted, is qualitatively different from the Soviet 'school for communism' notion. Implicit in the Romanian concept is military participation in efforts to instill in the youth patriotic-political values that are, in fact, part of the military value system, rather than indoctrination in strictly ideological, party-held beliefs, as is the case in the Soviet Union and other orthodox Communist polities.[87] It could be argued that the Romanian concept is far more similar to the old Prussian view of the army as a *Schule der Nation* whose primary purpose was nationalistic indoctrination. Along with providing traditional military training, the army is now asked to impart political and cultural knowledge and, most importantly, to thoroughly imbue the nation's youth with the spirit of socialist patriotism, a current euphemism for Romanian nationalism.[88] In pursuing its educational tasks, the military is expected to contribute to the shaping of the 'new man.'[89] It pays special attention to socialization work outside its institutional boundaries. Party support for military involvement in the society at large has become an important aspect of the accommodation process. In a typical comment, Ceausescu has expressed the party belief that military involvement is essential: 'Not one commander and not one army political activist must content himself with his activity in the units but must participate in the social, political, and educational activities being carried out throughout the country.' Ceausescu has gone on to urge 'the wonderful corps of command and political officers to become a strong detachment of the party and state in the entire activity of socialist and Communist construction in Romania.'[90] There is considerable evidence that the army has indeed become widely involved in the cultivation of nationalism in Romanian society. Particularly noteworthy are military efforts to instill patriotic values among Romanian youth. The Young Pioneers (ages 7 through 13), and even pre-school children, recently organized in the patriotic 'Falcons of the Fatherland' organization, are taught in direct cooperation with the military, 'the patriotic attitude of civic duty.'[91] Military participation involves actual paramilitary training, providing military-educational materials, setting up special 'Friends of the Military' circles and awarding military meritorious badges to the 'little defenders of the Fatherland.'[92] Military educational and training activities with high school students are quite extensive. The army apparently runs a comprehensive program complete with 'courses about the glorious fighting past of the Romanian people' and the 'heroism of Romanian soldiers throughout the centuries,' as well as military training sessions and summer military-educational camps for high school students. The magnitude of this program can be estimated from information contained in a 1972 report, which revealed that 650,000 Romanian students were receiving military training in the school system alone.[93] Continuously stressed is the necessity of active army participation in all aspects of ideopolitical and military education of the adult population, under the auspices of the Law on National Defense. The main task here is the cultivation of 'indissoluble ties' between the army and the people, and 'the love and respect for the armed forces' which is said to be the source of army invincibility.[94]

The Military in the Economy

In addition to patriotic indoctrination, the army is playing an increasingly active part on the socio-economic front. A highly instructive case of military involvement in the civilian economic realm is the Defense Ministry's assuming responsibility for civil aviation, which formerly was handled by the Ministry of Transportation.[95] The transfer was said to be warranted because of the need 'not only to improve coordination of civil aviation, but also to make certain that there is, at all times, steadfast discipline in this field.'[96] Under military administration, civil aviation and the airlines would now be run by a commander 'under the principle of unified command,' which apparently required, among other things, 'mandatory uniforms for civilian employees.'[97] In a related development, all professional training of civil aviation personnel has been transferred to military schools and the School for Civil Aeronautics abolished.[98] Again, one of the main reasons given was the need to achieve the 'necessary military discipline and order.'[99] The same thing has happened in the naval area, where the Civil Naval Institute was dissolved and the training of merchant marine cadres transferred to a newly created Military Naval Institute.[100] The Romanian army has been entrusted with direct participation in economic projects where work, according to Ceausescu, should 'proceed at a military pace.'[101] Among the important projects for which the army has assumed responsibility are the construction of a Danube–Black Sea canal and a seaport at Mangalia. On this last point, however, army enthusiasm for direct economic participation may not be unqualified. Traditionally, military establishments have resented attempts to use them as a source of cheap labor, and it remains to be seen whether army dedication to national developmental goals has changed military attitudes in this respect. More significant politically are instances of military officers assuming command positions in the civilian economy. In a 1974 speech to party activists, for example, Ceausescu announced the introduction of a system of 'commands' at important projects, implying that work there was to proceed along military organizational lines, with the possibility of military men assuming central control.[102] In the same speech, Ceausescu further disclosed that an army general had been appointed to head the 'command' in the trouble-ridden port authority of Constanta, and, on a later occasion, praised the results achieved under this arrangement.[103] In a similar development, an admiral was appointed Deputy Minister of the Ministry of Transportation and Communications, as well as head of the Department of Naval Transport, which apparently was experiencing considerable difficulties.[104]

The Military in Politics

Substantial evidence also attests to the intensified recruitment of military professionals for important political positions. A number of political appointments of military officers have been accompanied by extensive reshuffling of the army hierarchy, which has given rise to speculations about problems in the military sphere. However, with one important exception, none of the officers transferred seems to have suffered a loss of stature and political influence. Thus, a more plausible explanation of this development would be that the party is carrying out its expressed intention of strengthening political–military control in sensitive areas by involving the military in a more decisive manner.[105] This hypothesis appears to be corroborated by the significant number of professional soldiers elected to the highest party bodies at the 11th Congress of the Romanian Communist Party in 1974.

Major military figures recently shifted to political positions have included the Defense Minister, Deputy Defense Ministers, Chiefs of Staff, and so on. Former long-term Defense Minister Ion Ionita was relieved of his post in June of 1976 and appointed Deputy Premier. Just a few days later he was elected to the Political Executive Council, the top party body. Western media have speculated that, in his new position, Ionita has been put in charge of the defense-industrial sector of the economy.[106] Another professional soldier, and a former head of the Higher Political Council, Lieutenant General Ion Dinca, was recently appointed to the powerful position of First Secretary of the Bucharest party organization.[107] He has, at the same time, been made President of the Bucharest People's Council, which is the top government job in the city. On top of these appointments, Dinca was elected an alternate member of the Executive Council. Before his latest appointments, Dinca served as the Chairman of the Commission on Defense in the Grand National Assembly. Dinca's deputy in the Bucharest city government is another distinguished career officer, Colonel General Ion Gheorghe. Gheorghe, who was Chief of Staff and Deputy Defense Minister until December of 1974, also has wider responsibilities as the Vice-Chairman of the Commission on People's Councils and State Administration in the National Assembly.[108] At the time, Western sources interpreted Gheorghe's appointment to the Bucharest post as a party move to assure better control and discipline in the city's ailing industry by placing a 'strong man' in charge.[109] The present situation where two generals are in total control of Bucharest's party and government organizations is certainly as significant as it is unprecedented. An example of political upward mobility is also provided in the case of Lieutenant General Ion Hortopan. Over the last two years, Hortopan has been elected to full membership in the party Central Committee at the 11th Congress of the RCP in 1974, Deputy Chairman of the Commission on Defense in the National Assembly in 1975 and, finally, member of the highest government body, the State Council, in July of 1976. It is significant that most of the professional officers appointed to top civilian jobs are usually given dual party and state responsibilities.

SUMMARY AND CONCLUSIONS

This study has attempted to analyze civil–military relations in Romania by first delineating the general East European characteristics of party–military interaction, and then examining the impact of political environmental changes in the Romanian case. Party–military relations in the East European countries, it has been suggested, are influenced by two sets of circumstances: those characteristic of Communist societies in general, and those determined by conditions peculiar to Eastern Europe. Included in the first category are the traditional incompatibility between the value systems of the military establishment and the Leninist hegemonial party, and the conflict stemming from party efforts to enforce effective political control, ideological conformity, and to use the military for socialization in party beliefs. More important, it has been suggested here, are institutional behavior determinants conditioned by the fact that the East European parties have been ideologically and politically subordinated to an outside power, the Soviet Union. Because the East European polities have been subservient to the USSR in virtually all major facets of their ideological, military, economic, and political life, the East European military establishments have been relegated to a secondary, dependent role and denied their national defense prerogative. Thus, the party espousal of an internationalist ideology and acquiescence to Soviet political domination comes into conflict with the military's basically nationalistic orientation. The basic theoretical proposition of this study is that, given party inability to eradicate nationalistic military ideals and instill an internationalist outlook, a farreaching rapprochement between the two institutions could come about only as a result of party modification of its universalist philosophy accompanied by a more independent foreign-political stance. Such a development has been characteristic of the Romanian drive for national and political independence.

The most important consequence of Romania's pursuit of independence from Soviet hegemony has been the end of Soviet patronage and protection of the Romanian Communist Party, and the emergence of external threat. In order to cope with these new political exigencies, the party has been forced to accommodate, and rely on, the military. The party has sought to bring about such an accommodation, and, at the same time solicit public support, by actively cultivating nationalism and granting the military considerable institutional autonomy. With its new nationalistic overtones, the party world view has become compatible with the nationalistic orientation of the army. On the other hand, under the changed Romanian circumstances, the military has come to identify more closely not only with the party's foreign-political initiatives, but with its domestic desiderata as well. This, I would suggest, has been the direct result of party movement away from moot millenarian objectives and toward specific national developmental goals, such as reaching a developed industrial status by 1990. In this respect, party dedication to developmental imperatives, national purpose, and firm political authority undoubtedly appeals to the military's institutional affinity for discipline, mission, and authoritarian leadership. On the basis of this newly evolved congruence in perceptions of national foreign-political and domestic objectives, party–military interaction in Romania may have gone beyond accommodation and toward a genuine symbiotic relationship and interdependence, characterized by substantial military involvement in all spheres of societal activity. This is not to suggest that this relationship is of a permanent or even stable nature. Any number of factors, such as a party tilt back to a pro-Soviet position, serious domestic disorders, or economic failure could easily upset it. Nonetheless, if the party's present commitment to independence, an all-out industrialization effort and a dictatorial political system continues, further militarization of the Romanian mobilization system can be expected.

NOTES

1 See Roman Kolkowicz, *The Soviet Military and the Communist Party* (Princeton, NJ: Princeton University Press, 1967); John Gittings, *The Role of the Chinese Army* (London: Oxford University Press, 1967); Ellis Joffe, *Party and Army: Professionalism and Political Control in the Chinese Officer Corps, 1949–1964* (Cambridge, Mass.: Harvard University Press, 1965); and C. Cheng (ed.), *The Politics of the Chinese Red Army* (Stanford, Calif.: The Hoover Institution, 1966).

2 Dale R. Herspring and Ivan Volgyes, 'The military as an agent of political socialization in Eastern Europe: a comparative framework,' *Armed Forces and Society*, vol. 3, no. 2 (Winter 1977).

3 Dale R. Herspring, *East German Civil–Military Relations: The Impact of Technology* (New York: Praeger, 1973).

4 Carl Beck and Karen Rawling, 'The military as a channel of entry into positions of leadership in Communist Party systems,' *Armed Forces and Society*, vol. 3, no. 2 (Winter 1977).

5 A perceptive analysis of these models can be found in Timothy J. Colton, 'The party–military connection: a participatory model,' in Dale R. Herspring and Ivan Volgyes (eds), *Civil–Military Relations in Communist Systems* (Boulder, Colo.: Westview Press, 1978).

6 William Odom, 'The party–military connection: a critique,' *Problems of Communism*, vol. 22, no. 5 (September–October, 1973).

7 Colton, op. cit.

8 ibid.

9 See Ceausescu's speech at the Bucharest rally on the day of the Soviet invasion of Czechoslovakia, 21 August 1968 (translation in *FBIS Daily Report Eastern Europe*, no. 164, 21 August, 1968).

10 See, for example, Elena Florea, *Natiunea Romana si socialismul* (The Romanian Nation and Socialism) (Bucharest: Publishing House of the Academy of the Socialist Republic of Romania, 1974). For a general discussion of Romanian nationalism, see Viktor Meier, *Neuer Nationalismus in Suedosteuropas* (New Nationalism in Southeastern Europe) (Opladen: C.W. Leske Verlag, 1968); and Stephen Fischer Galati, 'Romanian nationalism,' in P. Sugar and I. Lederer (eds), *Nationalism in Eastern Europe* (Seattle, Wash.: University of Washington Press, 1969).

11 For the Romanian argument that the class struggle has an exclusively national character, see Alexandru Tanase, 'The permanence of the nation and the real significance of internationalism,' *LUMEA*, no. 14 (1 April 1976).

12 For a discussion of this point, see C. Vlad, *Eseuri despre natiune* (Essays on the Nation) (Bucharest: Editura Politica, 1971).

13 Martin Nedelea, 'Independence and interdependence,' Era Socialista, no. 15 (1976) (translated in *Joint Publications Research Service (JPRS)*, no. 1,283 (25 August 1976).

14 Nicolae Dumitru, 'The nation and the nation-state – factors of progress and civilization,' *Era Socialista*, no. 16 (August 1976). Also see the excellent discussion in

Michael Cismarescu, 'Die Nation und die Rumaenische Voelkerrects Doktrin' (The Nation and the Romanian International Law Doctrine), *Osteuropa*, no. 12 (December 1974).

15 The doctrine of limited sovereignty, better known as the Brezhnev Doctrine, espouses the concept of collective socialist sovereignty which is said to transcend the nation-state sovereignty of individual socialist countries and obligates the socialist common-wealth to 'defend' the achievements of socialism in any of its member countries.

16 Cited in Robert King, 'Romania reasserts position on national independence and sovereignty,' *Radio Free Europe Research 94* (28 April 1976).

17 A discussion of historical revisionism will be found in the work of the Romanian emigre scholar Dionisie Ghermani, *Die Kommunistische Umdeutung der Rumaenischen Geschichte* (The Communist Revision of Romanian History) (Munich: Suedost-Institut, 1967).

18 Cited in George Ciuranescu, 'Michael the Brave – evaluations and revaluations of the Wallachian prince,' *Radio Free Europe Research 191* (1 September 1976).

19 ibid.

20 See, for example, M. Musate and Gh. Ionita, 'The fundamental problems of the history of the Romanian people.' *Anale de Istorie*, no. 1 (January–February, 1976); M. Musate, 'The Romanian people's achievements in 1918 and their international confirmation,' *Anale de Istorie*, no. 2 (April–May, 1976); and Ion Popescu-Pituri, 'From the Romanian people's past of fighting to defend the sovereignty and indepen-dence of the homeland,' *Anale de Istorie*, no. 1 (January–February, 1976). This, understandably, has provoked a heated exchange between Soviet and Romanian historians in which the Romanians have invoked no less an authority than Marx him-self to prove the legitimacy of their claim. See Karl Marx, *Insemnari despre Romani (Manuscrise inedite)* (Notes on the Romanians. Unpublished Manuscripts) (Bucharest: Editura Politica, 1964). For the Soviet–Romanian debate over Bessarabia, see Robert King, *Minorities under Communism: Nationalities as a Source of Tension among Balkan Communist States* (Cambridge, Mass.: Harvard University Press, 1973), pp. 220–41. For the Soviet interpretation, see Artem Lazarev, *Moldavskaya Sovetskaya Gosudarstvennost i Bessarabyski Vopros* (The Statehood of Soviet Moldavia and the Bessarabian Question) (Kishinev: Politizdat, 1974); and also the article by A. Yazkova in *Novoye vremya* (29 November 1968).

21 See Ceausescu's speech at the 45th anniversary of the founding of the Romanian Communist Party in 1966, in which he sharply criticized the resolution of the 5th Congress of the RCP in 1932 for advocating the reincorporation of Bessarabia into the Soviet Union (*Scinteia*, 7 May 1966). For a critical discussion of the negative influence of the Comintern on the policies of the RCP, see M. Stanescu and N. Popescu, 'The Romanian Communist Party and the congresses of the Third International,' *Anale de Istorie*, no. 5 (September–October, 1975).

22 Speech by Ceausescu at the 24 October 1974 Army Day meeting, in *Romania, Documents – Events*, no. 49 (October 1974), p. 30.

23 Col. Pavel Ciuhureanu, 'Scientific meeting: the Romanian army traditions and contemporaneity,' *Viitorul Social*, no. 1 (1975), pp. 174–6.

24 Speech by Ceausescu at 30th anniversary of the formation of 'Tudor Vladimirescu' division, Radio Bucharest, 1 October 1973 (translated in FBIS *Daily Report Eastern Europe*, no. 191 (2 October 1973).

25 Ciuhureanu, op. cit., p. 174. In an apparent effort to create a visual impression of military continuity, the Romanians have reintroduced the old prewar uniforms, helmet, and salute. See *Der Spiegel* (19 August 1974).

26 Stefan Pascu, 'Moments in the Romanian people's struggle for the formation of a unified national state,' *Magazin Istoric*, no. 26 (February 1976) (translated in *JPRS*, 2 April 1976, pp. 49–52).

27 ibid., p. 49.

28 See Eliza Campus, *Politika externa a Romaniei in perioada interbelica* (The Foreign Policy of Romania in the Interwar Period) (Bucharest: Editura Politica, 1975).

29 Ciuhureanu, op. cit., p. 175.

30 ibid.

31 See, for example, an article commemorating the *Era Socialista* demonstrations against the Vienna Diktat in August of 1940 in no. 14 (1975).

32 According to Soviet sources, Romania fielded some 30 divisions on the Soviet front and suffered 600,000 casualties of which 400,000 were killed. See Marshal A. Grechko (ed.), *Osvobovitelnaya missiya Sovetskikh vooruzhenikh sil v vtoroi mirovoi voine* (The Liberation Mission of the Soviet Armed Forces in the Second World War) (Moscow: Voenizdat, 1974), p. 133.

33 Cols. I. Ceausescu, M. Ionescu, and I. Talpes, 'Considerations on the attitudes of the Romanian generals toward the national anti-fascist and anti-imperialist armed insurrection of August 1944' *Revue Roumaine d'Etudes Internationales* (25 March 1974), pp. 237–48.

34 ibid., p. 244.

35 ibid., p. 244.

36 Lt Gen. Ion Gheorghe, 'The High National Staff during the national anti-fascist insurrection of August 1944,' cited in Ciuhureanu, op. cit., p. 176.

37 Also see Col. Ilie Ceausescu, 'Aspecte contradictorii in atitudenea unor forte politice burgheze din Romania fata de probleme le militaire si politice ale tarii in perioada Septembrie 1941–August 1944' (Contradictory aspects in the attitudes of some bourgeois political forces toward the military and political problems of the country in the period September 1941–August 1944), in *File din istoria militara a poporolui Roman* (Pages from the Military History of the Romanian People) (Bucharest: Editura Militara, 1973); and Constantin Nicolae, *Din activitatea Partidului Comunist Roman pentru atragerea armatei Romane la lupta de restabilize a independentei si suverenitatei patriei (1940–1944)* (On the Activities of the RCP for Involving the Romanian Army in the Struggle for the Restoration of the Independence and Sovereignty of the Fatherland 1940–1944) (Bucharest: Editura Militara, 1971).

38 The Soviet wartime Chief of Staff, for example, argues that even after the insurrection, the Romanian army continued to be dominated by reactionary officers, refused to surrender and carried on combat operations on the side of the Hitlerites. He also accuses the Romanian General Staff of having attempted to hinder the development of the uprising and pledging free passage to the German troops. See S. M. Shtemenko, 'The liberation of Romania,' in *The General Staff in the War Years*, bk. 2 (translated in *JRPS*, no. 65733, (22 September 1975), p. 105.

39 See G. Gheorghiu-Dej, 'Five years since the liberation of Romania,' in *Articles and Speeches*, 3rd edn (Bucharest, 1952), p. 337.

40 The existence of the anti-Antonescu conspiratorial 'military committee' was acknowledged for the first time in an article published in the August 1964 issue of *Lupta de Clasa*. An admission of party distortion of the historical truth is also provided in a new version of the circumstances surrounding the arrest of Antonescu on the day of the coup. Until recently party historians have maintained that the actual arrest of the pro-Fascist leadership had been carried out by a group of Communists led by the well-known party leader Emil Bodnaras. This view, dominant for some twenty years after the actual events, has now been directly contradicted in an article by an eye-witness, the former king's adjutant, General Emilian Ionescu. The article, published surprisingly in an authoritative party journal, revealed that Marshal Antonescu, as well as Prime Minister Mihai Antonescu, had not been arrested by Bodnaras, but by a group of monarchist officers under the command of a Major Dumitrescu. See *Anale de Istorie ale Partidului*, no. 5 (1965), cited in *Wissentschaftlicher Dienst Suedosteuropa* (11 October 1974), p. 198.

41 See Gh. Ionita and N. Nicolaescu, 'On compromise and conciliation in the history of the Romanian people,' *Revista de Istorie* (September 1976), pp. 1,279–94.

42 See, for example, Col. General Ion Coman, 'Romania with all forces in the services of victory,' *LUMEA* (10 April 1975); also, Gh. Ionita, 'All for the front, All for victory! Romania's substantial contribution to the joint victory over Hitler's Germany,' *Era Socialista*, no. 8 (April 1975).

43 Soviet sources are unanimous in assessing the post-August 1944 Romanian army as demoralized, ill-equipped, and incapable or unwilling to fight independently. This is said to be the major reason why the Romanian army was incorporated in the Soviet Command and given a largely supporting role. More importantly, the Romanian army has been openly accused by Soviet historians of a lack of sincerity in pursuing the military effort, of procrastination, and even collusion with the retreating Germans. Shtemenko, for example, recalls with indignation the Romanian refusal to turn over to

the Soviets captured German generals, while Grechko criticizes the Romanian General Staff for its unwillingness to enhance the combat readiness of the troops. As an illustration, Grechko reveals that the total armor strength of the Romanian front units in February of 1945 consisted of 8 tanks, while, at the same time, 211 tanks were kept in Bucharest. See Grechko, op. cit., pp. 156, 164, 172; Shtemenko, op. cit., p. 172; and A. B. Antosyak, *V. Boyakh za svobodu Romunii* (In the Battles for the Liberation of Romania), (Voenizdat: Moscow, 1974), p. 148.

44   Marin Preda, *Delirul* (The Delirium) (Bucharest, 1975). For an analysis of the novel, see Anneli Maier, 'Marin Preda's *The Delirium:* historical novel or novelistic history?' *Radio Free Europe Research/94* (6 June 1975).

45   See Sergiu Columbeanu, 'Unpublished documentary archives on the international situation of Romania in 1942–1944,' *Revista de Istorie* (May 1975) (translated in *JPRS*, no. 65559, 27 August 1975).

46   Col. Alexandru Savu, 'The Iron Guard rebellion as interpreted by General Hansen,' *Magazin Istoric*, no. 2 (February 1975).

47   For the postwar purges of the Romanian army, see A. B. Antosyak, *et al.*, *Zarozhdenie Narodnikh Armii uchastnits varshavskovo dogovora 1941–1949* (The Formation of the National Armies of the Warsaw Pact Member Countries) (Moscow: Voenizdat, 1975), pp. 204, 209, 218.

48   *Scinteia* (20 September 1968).

49   '*Decree no. 477' Buletinul Oficial*, (31 December 1971).

50   *Muenchener Merkur* (21 September 1974).

51   The Defense Council was set up in 1969 under Law No. 5, published in *Buletinul Oficial*, no. 32 (14 March 1969).

52   See 'Decree no. 121 of the Council of State on the organization and operation of the Ministry of Interior,' *Buletinul Oficial* (8 April 1978), pp. 1–6.

53   'Decree on organization and operation of the Ministry of National Defense,' *Buletinul Oficial*, pt 1, no. 30 (21 November 1972), pp. 1,048–51 (translated in *JPRS*, no. 57812, 19 December 1972).

54   ibid., pp. 40, 41.

55   Lt Gen. C. Zamfirescu *et al.*, *Sistemul militar: organizarea, recrutarea si mobilizarea armatei* (The Military System: Organization, Recruitment and Mobilization of the Armed Forces) (Bucharest: Editura Militara, 1973), p. 68.

56   ibid., p. 66.

57   Col. Iulian Cernat, 'An impressive show of Romanian military thought,' *Viata Militara* (November 1973), pp. 46–52 (translated in *JPRS*, no. 61572, p. 48).

58   *Scinteia* (25 October 1969).

59   The Law of National Defense of the Socialist Republic of Romania was adopted by the National Assembly in late 1972. The text was published in *Scinteia* (29 December 1972), pp. 4–7 (a translation is to be found in *JPRS*, no. 58017, 18 January 1973).

60   The most detailed analysis of the various aspects of national defense is provided in *Apararea Nationala a Romaniei Socialiste* (National Defense in Socialist Romania) (Bucharest: Editura Militara, 1973).

61   For a discussion of the Yugoslav defense doctrine, see A. Ross Johnson, 'Yugoslav total national defense,' *Survival*, vol. 15, no. 2 (March/April, 1973), pp. 54–8. Also see Aurel Braun, 'The Yugoslav–Romanian concept of people's war,' *Canadian Defense Quarterly*, vol. 7 (Summer 1977), pp. 37–43.

62   See Law of National Defense, op. cit., Article 22. For the role and nature of the most important of these units – the 'patriotic guards,' see Cols L. Loghin and Alexandru Petricean, *Garzile patriotice din Romania* (Patriotic Guards in Romania) (Bucharest: Editura Militara, 1974).

63   Law of National Defense, op. cit., Article 24.

64   See the *Decree on Organization and Operation of the Ministry of National Defense*, Section 2: Functions.

65   ibid.

66   See, for example, *US Army Europe and Seventh Army, Identification Guide, Weapons and Equipment, East European Communist Countries (1972–1975)*, and *Viata Militara* (November 1973).

67   The first test flight of the plane called 'IAR 93' in the Romanian version and 'Orao' (Eagle) in the Yugoslav, was reported by the Romanian Agerpress news agency and

the Yugoslav TANJUG on 15 April 1975.

68 See *The Military Balance 1976–1977* (London: Institute for Strategic Studies, 1977), and Agence France Press (10 August 1975).

69 *The Military Balance* reports the deployment of ten Shanghai-class gunboats and one Hu Chwan-class torpedo boat.

70 According to one Romanian source, R&D allocations for the period 1966–70 were 5·7 times higher than the previous period, while planned allocations for the 1971–5 period were said to be over twice as large as the 1966–70 period. Cf. 'Report on a scientific conference on the subject of military applications of the scientific-technological revolution,' *Lupta de Clasa* (December 1971) (translated in *JPRS*, no. 55110, 4 February 1972, p. 47). For the Romanian defense expenditures, see *The Military Balance*.

71 Col. D. Buznea and Lt Col. G. Bondei, 'The technical–scientific potential and its role in providing a national defense capacity,' *Lupta de Clasa* (January 1972) and Col. Gen. C. Sandru, 'The implications of the scientific and technical revolution on defense production,' *Lupta de Clasa* (January 1972).

72 See Nicolae Ceausescu, *Romania on the Way of Building the Multilaterally Developed Socialist Society: Reports, Speeches, Articles, January 1973–July 1973*, (Bucharest: Meridiane Publishing House, 1973), p. 492.

73 ibid., pp. 491 and 492.

74 *Le Monde* (7 December 1971); *Washington Post* (11 March 1975).

75 For information on the various visits, see Agerpress (29 September 1973 and 10 December 1975); *Radio Bucharest* (5 September 1975); *Scinteia* (8 and 14 April, 17 May, 2 October 1975).

76 See 'Romanian–Chinese military relations,' *Radio Free Europe Research/34* (1 October 1976).

77 See *MENA* (Cairo: 13 April 1976).

78 See *Radio Free Europe Research/46* (28 November 1975).

79 In the examination of the changing party attitudes in the early 1970s, I have relied heavily on Kenneth Jowitt's perceptive analysis in 'Political innovation in Rumania,' *Survey*, vol. 20, no. 4 (Fall 1974), pp. 132–51.

80 The Soviet views of these issues can be found in two recent Soviet publications: Veniamin Midtsev, *Revizionism v sluzhbe anti-komunizma* (Revisionism in the Service of Anti-Communism) (Moscow: Politizdat, 1976); and I. N. Fedoseev (ed.), *Nauchnyi komunizm* (Scientific Communism) (Moscow: Politizdat, 1977).

81 For a detailed analysis of the industrialization drive, see Gheorge Oprea, 'The RCP is determinedly promoting a policy of industrialization,' *Viitorul Social*, no. 3 (1976).

82 Robert King 'Reorganisationen in Rumaenien' (Reorganizations in Romania), *Osteuropa*, no. 1 (January 1974).

83 Jowitt, op. cit., p. 137. In its efforts to co-opt the peasants in the drive for unity, the party has of late started to stress the historically progressive role of the peasantry as the traditional reservoir of manpower for the Romanian armies. See, for example, the 'Draft Program for the Eleventh Congress', *Scinteia* (1 October 1974).

84 *Scinteia* (8 October 1976).

85 Wolf Oschlies, 'Ceausescu ruft zum Grossen Sprung' (Ceausescu calls for the Great Leap Forward), *Osteuropa*, no. 5 (May 1975).

86 Speech by Ceausescu at 1 October 1976 meeting with the army 'aktiv', *Scinteia* (3 October 1976) (a translation is available in *FBIS Daily Report Eastern Europe*, 5 October 1976, pp. H2–H10).

87 For a discussion of the Soviet 'school for communism' notion and its impact on party–military relations, see Roman Kolkowicz, 'The impact of modern technology on the Soviet officer corps,' *Orbis* (January 1976).

88 Ciuhureanu, op. cit., p. 22.

89 Ceausescu's speech to army 'aktiv', p. H9.

90 ibid., p. H10.

91 See interview with Professor Florian Moraru, Chief of the Commission for Training for the Defense of the Fatherland of the Pioneer Organization, *Viata Militara* (March 1973), p. 22.

92 ibid., p. 22.

93 *Viata Militara* (July 1972), pp. 23–4.

94　See Ceausescu's speech at Army Day anniversary, and Radio Bucharest (2 February 1972), p. 2.
95　Decree on Organization and Operation of Ministry of National Defense, Section 2, Point Q.
96　Cited in *Radio Free Europe Research/44* (7 December 1972), 'Reorganization and Expansion of the Ministry of National Defense,' p. 5.
97　ibid., p. 6.
98　*Buletinul Oficial* (14 August 1973), pp. 2–3.
99　ibid., p. 2.
100　See 'Decree on the establishment and organization of the Mircea cel Batrin Naval Institute and the Alexanderu Ioan Cuza Naval Military School,' *Buletinul Oficial* (18 September 1973), pp. 2–4.
101　Ceausescu's speech to army 'aktiv', p. H8.
102　*Scinteia* (12 April 1974). The Romanian term used *comandamente,* has the strictly military connotation of 'headquarters'.
103　Jowitt, op. cit., p. 143.
104　The appointment of Vice Admiral Gheorghe Sandu to these positions was reported in *Buletinul Oficial*, pt 1 (17 March 1977).
105　The notable exception referred to involves the so-called Serb case. According to Western sources, in the summer of 1971, General Ion Serb, Commander of the Bucharest garrison, and a number of other unidentified officers, appear to have either plotted to overthrow Ceausescu, or to reveal military secrets to the Soviet Union, or both. Serb is reported to have been executed for his activities. The Romanians have remained silent on the case. For details, see *Die Presse* (Vienna: 17 November 1971) and *Sueddeutsche Zeitung* (Munich: 18 February 1972). For a longer, albeit of necessity speculative, analysis, see Robert R. King, 'Romanian difficulties in military and security affairs,' *Radio Free Europe Research/6* (6 March 1972).
106　*Reuters* (3 July 1976).
107　*Informatia Buchurestului* (19 June 1976).
108　Ion Gheorghe's appointment was reported in *Informatia Buchurestului* (3 December 1975).
109　*Le Monde* (10 December 1975), and *Reuters* (8 December 1975).

Part Three

Systemic Change and the Role of the Military:
Modernization, Development, and
Civil–Military Relations

10 Toward a Theory of Civil–Military Relations in Communist (Hegemonial) Systems

ROMAN KOLKOWICZ

Every Army is established by definite social forces and classes for the defense of their vital interests. The Army is the mirror of society.
General of the Army, A. A. Epishev, Head, Main Political Administration, Soviet Armed Forces

(1) INTRODUCTION

In his *Politics of the Prussian Army*,[1] Gordon Craig observed that, 'we live in an age in which military influence in both foreign and domestic policy is marked and growing, and there is little hope that this tendency will be reversed in the foreseeable future.' He asserted that while the 'ideal aim of the healthy state is that its military establishment shall remain merely the executive will of the sovereign power,' this remains a difficult task, requiring 'delicacy, patience and constant vigilance, for military influence manifests itself . . . in hidden ways, not always easily detected.' It is the concern of this chapter to examine the ways in which the relationship between the military and the sovereign evolves in political systems defined here as hegemonial, and to discern those forces and phenomena that appear to enhance the military's position within one particular hegemonial system, the Soviet Union.

Western research on the military in Communist countries is to a large extent premised in certain cognitive and political distortions. Many researchers in the field began with the premise that the Communist countries are our enemies and threaten our vital interests and even survival; they therefore asked questions concerned primarily with the threat-potential of the Communist military, considering them essentially to be mere extensions of the Communist Party. The military was assumed to be simply an executant of the will of the dictator, the Politburo, or the collective leadership, and thus having no specific, differentiated, institutionalized identity or interests.[2]

Some recent studies of the Soviet military have attempted to modify this stereotype of the Communist military, in general, and of the Soviet military, in particular. These attempts were of several kinds: those that sought to apply certain concepts and analytical methods from Western social sciences to the study of the Communist military in order to test assumptions and hypotheses regarding the nature of party–military relations (that is, the interest group approach, coalition theory, bureaucratic politics theory);[3] others sought to order the evidence into analytic categories (conflict, congruence, participation models);[4] still others essayed to apply some concepts from developmental theory and to look for evidence in support of a modernization role of the military in such systems.[5]

Most of the efforts at 'modernization' of the study of civil–military relations shared a common denominator, an unquestioned set of assumptions about the military's subordination to the party's authority. Civil–military relations in Communist countries were assumed by a number of Western analysts to be frozen in a static, bi-polar (party–military, without intervening institutions), linear (dominant party-subordinate and compliant military), and apolitical condition (the relationship between the two was postulated to be devoid of institutional and political bargaining, pressures, negotiations, or any transactions of a political kind). This model of Soviet party–military relations is particularly bothersome. One is asked to believe that the Communist countries have escaped certain general socio-political forces ('laws') that apply to most other political systems. It is as if some kind of immaculate conception had occurred after the October Revolution, and a wondrous, conflict-free, harmonious system of institutions and bureaucracies had materialized in Russia and the other Communist countries. This notion, a deeply ingrained but unquestioned Western belief, defies understanding, particularly when given the fact that almost everything is political or politicized in the Soviet Union: the boundary between state, society, and the individual is rather ambiguous in a country where the ruling elites of the party subscribe to a modern Hobbesian concept of *kto-kovo*, and suspicion and terror are institutionalized. After all of that, it remains difficult to understand how analysts can still subscribe to the rather simplistic, 'immaculate conception' vision of a society free of institutional/bureaucratic conflict. Even in Nazi Germany, that paradigm of centralized, totalitarian, party-and-Fuehrer-rule, bureaucratic politics and institutional conflicts remained alive, flourishing, and effectively creating semi-autonomous, institutional fiefdoms.[6] These Western analysts apparently seek to out-Marx the Marxists and the Leninists who postulated the end of politics and institutional conflict at the end of history, with the arrival of the millenium; our Western colleagues studying Soviet party–military relations see the end of politics at the beginning of the millenium process. And in any event, the reader need only glance through the history of military institutions and their relations with civil authorities, from the Roman legions and praetorians through the *condottieri* and into the aristocratic–bourgeois stresses of more recent military history, before arriving at the contemporary period of civil–military problems in professional or mass armies.

Concerns with political control of the military are as old as the institution of the military itself. Michael Howard[7] observed in his study on civil–military relations in several countries that 'the problem of civil–military relationships is one which in one form or another all societies have to deal. In States where no orderly transition of power and obedience has yet been established . . . military force is the final, and sometimes only arbiter in government.' Alfred Vagts[8] notes in his impressive study on militarism, 'the natural tendency of armies toward a self-government brooking no outside interference.' The Communist sociologist Wiatr[9] asserts that, 'Every army is not only part of the general social system, but is also a separate, and to some extent autonomous . . . social system.'

The military's search for apartness from society is seen by many scholars as derived from their 'peculiar' profession: 'A class of men set apart from the general mass of the community, trained to particular uses, formed to peculiar notions, governed by peculiar laws, marked by peculiar distinctions.'[10] In Nazi Germany, the closure-prone and politically resistant officer corps was a threat to the party and 'it was therefore natural that Hitler should endeavor to penetrate this phalanx of the officer corps, for every totalitarian state had sooner or later come up against a similar problem.'[11] The Chinese Communists readily understood that 'political power comes out of the barrel of a gun,' and it became a cardinal principle of the Chinese, as articulated by Mao Tse-tung, 'to have the Party control the gun and never allow the gun to control the Party.'

The history of party–military relations in the Soviet Union is a study in distrust and occasional conflict rooted in a certain incompatibility between the hegemonial holder of power in the state and one of its main instruments of power. The distrust and conflict are largely engendered and aggravated by the party's rigid adherence to a monopoly of power and in its expectation of challenge from organized groups in society. The fact that the military has been among the most loyal, supportive, and compliant institutions in the state seems not to have eased perceptibly that fundamental *kto-kovo* paranoia. This wariness is closely tied to the constant unease that afflicts political authorities in hegemonial systems where there is an absence of provision for orderly transfer of power, and the consequent opportunity for rival groups to assert themselves. In this context, the military appears to the party as a potential challenger who must be contained, manipulated, and controlled at all times in order to prevent a serious threat to the party's monopoly of power. Unlike most other institutions, the military represents a special source of concern to the *apparatchik* mind because of the instruments of violence it commands, and because of its organizational and hierarchical structure.

The party's inability or unwillingness to modify its hegemonial position often amplifies the modest efforts of groups or institutions in society toward a modicum of professionalism and institutional privacy to the level of a contest and makes these efforts appear to be a challenge to the party's hegemony. Throughout most of Soviet history, relations between the party and the military have been marked by profound suspicion, frequent tensions, and at times by open conflict. This has been so despite the fact that about 80 percent of all armed forces personnel are Communists or *Komsomols;* that the officer corps is one of the most responsive and responsible groups in the state; that it tends to be closer to the party's values and norms than most others; and that the military has come to the support of party leadership in times of extreme crisis caused by internal, or external threats. The party's extensive efforts to control, manipulate, and indoctrinate the military has not always prevented the crystallization of a 'military' viewpoint; nor has occasional friction between the two institutions been mitigated by an awareness that they are both members of the Establishment. The reason for this must be sought in the unique political context of the Soviet Union, where even the limited, professional, or institutional interests and objectives of the military take on disproportionate importance, largely because of the party's exaggerated distrust of all institutions, and its unconditional insistence on hegemony.

I shall attempt to explain this relationship between the omnipotent party and the military. I had earlier described it as an uneven, asymmetrical kind of interaction, in which one player sees it as a being closer to zero-sum game and the other sees it as a variable sum game, a dynamic process of institutional transactions, marked by mutual dependence and opposition: 'The relations between the Party and the military became a dialogue between two powerful institutional bureaucracies some of whose vital interests have come into conflict.'[12] To use Schelling's terminology,[13] 'pure conflict, in which the interests of two antagonists are completely opposed, is a special case; it would arise in a war of complete extermination, otherwise not even in war.' In the flow of party–military relations, 'winning a conflict does not have a strictly competitive meaning; it is not winning relative to one's adversary. It means gaining relative to one's own value system; and this may be done by bargaining, by mutual accommodation, and by the avoidance of mutually damaging behavior.' In the uneven interaction of the two protagonists, the military appears to subscribe to this variable-sum-game interdependence more carefully than the party. However, in the post-Stalinist period, the party's strategy of interaction with the military is becoming ever closer to that of the military's. Some Western analysts of party–military relations in the Soviet Union have trouble with such an explanation of institutional dialogue.[14] Preferring conventional views of the party's 'totalitarian' domination of the whole cowering system, they are, wittingly or unwittingly, embracing the *agitprop* ideals and formulas regarding total integration of the military with the people and the party. Indeed, the party does deny the military a distinct institutional identity, seeking at all times to reinforce through its control of the media an image of the military as totally submerged within the party and as a fully integrated part of the hegemonial system. Friedrich and Brzezinski have referred to the vast efforts exerted by 'totalitarian' parties 'to prevent the armed forces from developing a distinct identity of their own,' concluding that this creates a situation where the military lives 'in an atmosphere of an armed camp surrounded by enemies.'[15]

I shall propose here that Communist political systems in general, and the Soviet Union in particular, are not, and were not, frozen in a static, 'totalitarian' mold; that political, economic, and social processes within the Soviet Union have effected vital changes in the politics of institutions and bureaucracies within the state; that the changes in the systemic priorities (primary orientation of the state, the political and military policies, and institutional alignments) are in a dynamic process in which the military assumes a progressively influential role. I propose, therefore, a conceptual framework that will help to order the flow and evidence of Soviet political and social history of the past six decades, and that might help to sharpen and systematize the study of party–military relations. I suggest that it may be possible to generalize from this specific Soviet case about political systems that share essential characteristics with the Soviet Union and propose a conceptual framework for the study of civil–military relations in major Communist countries, which are defined here as belonging to hegemonial political systems. I shall examine the relevance and utility of this model within the Soviet context.

It is my hope that this conceptual framework will provide a more useful approach to the study of civil–military relations in Communist systems than some of the other prevailing approaches. This hope is based on the comprehensiveness of the model (it relates the political system, its major institutions, and bureaucracies to the prevailing priorities, values, and the rules of the game) and on the avoidance of certain a priori restrictions and postulates that tend to reduce the utility of other approaches (such as their static-linear-polar totalitarian postulates and their assumptions about the amorphousness and permanent subordination of the undifferentiated military institutions to the party).

It is my intent that this conceptual framework serve as a vital step in the direction of developing a useful theory of civil–military relations in Communist (hegemonial) systems.

(2) A HEGEMONIAL POLITICAL SYSTEM: DEFINITION

A hegemonial political system is characterized by the following:

(a) A single, 'revolutionary,' hierarchically organized party, which claims hegemonial power and authority within the system.

The goals of the hegemonial party are imbedded in the mythos of the system, which also contains the ultimate source of legitimacy for the uses of power and authority within the system. This governing mythos tends to be chiliastic, defining unconditional conflict with intransigent enemies. This mythos is used to mobilize the people and institutions within the system, to extract loyalty, service, and sacrifice.

(b) It is a 'rational' organizational system par excellence, designed for the most efficient mobilization and use of all resources for the most effective maximization of the party's objectives. The central values of the party and the system are modern and efficient methods and means.

The inherent 'logic' and political dynamics of hegemonial systems create overriding demands for 'rationalization' and administrative rationality:

centralization of all political, institutional, bureaucratic, economic, and military authority,

standardization of laws, rules, processes, producer/consumer/distribution patterns,

neutralization of diversities, deviances, and idiosyncracies that might inhibit and constrain centralization and standardization goals, and

integration of the diverse political, economic, institutional, and social entities under the party's hegemonial authority.

(c) The essential hallmark of the hegemonial system is constant activism: it is a dynamic system.

The energies of the system are channelled by the party first *internally* (to establish and maintain hegemonial rule, to eradicate opposition and to create efficient productive and social institutions); *contiguously* (to strengthen the domestic base, to neutralize unfriendly neighbors, to obtain strategic advantage); and, *externally* (to fulfill the chiliastic imperatives of the systemic mythos – this pretending to universal levelling or universal hierarchy-horizontalism or verticalism; communism or fascism and Nazism). The hegemonial party needs to maintain constant activism and mobilism internally and externally; prolonged, sustained periods of nondirected passivity would negatively affect the chiliastic urgencies and imperatives of the mythos; the mobilizational responsiveness of populace and institutions would engender privatism, thus threatening the hegemonial position of the party. The imperatives of the hegemonial system do, therefore, lead to a constant manipulation and channelling of the forces and energies of the system into:

vast mobilizational tasks: Great Leap Forward, Third Revolution, collectivization, industrialization,

internal 'revolutionary' campaigns: purges, terror, cultural revolution, propaganda campaigns,

external 'revolutionary' campaigns: support of wars of national liberation; assistance in revolutionary wars; anti-imperialistic, military assistance, *military aggression.*

(d) The hegemonial system is a quasi-military and militant political system. Its internal bureaucratic structures, hierarchical authority, centralized mobilizational style, controlled violence mode, high threat expectation, and unquestioned obedience all suggest similarities with military organizations. Hegemonial systems also place great emphasis on the primacy of military power for internal and external policy purposes, and therefore subordinate social, governmental, economic, and cultural activities within the system to military priorities. Although the mythos of the hegemonial system tends to be nonmilitary or even anti-military, nevertheless, the prevailing operative values and norms tend to derive from the military. The hegemonial party leadership tends, therefore, to borrow from the military its methods, styles, ethos, and rituals, while at the same time suppressing the military, and seeking to dominate it.

Yet, the party relies on the military in times of crisis caused by external aggression or internal disturbances, for support of its foreign and military policies, and for maintenance of order and compliance among allies of the state.

The military has shown itself, particularly in the Soviet case, to be a very loyal institution, supportive of the party during its periods of great vulnerability, during war, succession crises, and challenges from troublesome allies. It is apparent that the relationship between the Communist Party of the Soviet Union and the military establishment is highly complex, interdependent, and in constant process of change and adaptation.

(e) Hegemonial political systems contain elements of three major 'military types' of organizations: revolutionary, praetorian, and professional corresponding to the 'nation-in-arms', praetorian, and 'civil-and-military' political systems.[16] That is, the military plays a key role as an instrument of foreign policy, it is employed in domestic partisan politics, and performs administrative functions of nonprimary military relevance. While the foreign policy and defense function of the military is clearly perceived, the other two remain as vestigial functions of the developing hegemonial system. The military serves as a national school, as an integrator of diverse sectors of society, and as an institution that is admirably capable of inculcating the values and the norms of the party into young and malleable people; the military and paramilitary organs are also activated at times of internal crisis, leadership struggle, for domestic policing in times of external threat, or for policing contiguous allied states.

The military and the party are parts of a whole, the main organizational structures for the management of a post-revolutionary hegemonial political system, and for its guidance from an embryonic revolutionary utopia into an expanding militant hegemonial system.

(3) PARTY–MILITARY RELATIONS IN THE SOVIET (HEGEMONIAL) SYSTEM: A SYSTEMIC-INSTITUTIONAL-INTERDEPENDENCE MODEL APPROACH

Party–military relations in the Soviet hegemonial political system are essentially determined by three sets of factors: the systemic priorities, the political parameters, and the institutional variables. The interaction of these sets of factors, defined here as the systemic-institutional-interdependence variables, simply stated suggests that the military's role and influence within the system and the degree of its dependence upon the party is a function of certain systemic and institutional priorities and power relationships.

(a) The Systemic Priorities

These define the primary orientation of the state and the party at a given period of historical development, and serve as the central focus for the mobilizational and planning priorities within the system. I have identified three main phases of systemic priorities in the Soviet Union:

(i)   The early postrevolutionary period of *consolidation* of the party's hegemonial authority within the state and the longer corollary phase of *systemic integration* of the complex and heterogenous society into the centralized, hegemonial system. This period coincides with the long Stalinist rule of the Soviet Union; a period of intensive transformation of society and institutions in accordance with the 'totalitarian' model, including the eradication of all dissenting, opposing, or unsympathetic political, social, and ethnic groups. In short, the aim was the creation of a 'new society, new institutions, new socialist man.'

(ii)   The *systemic transition* phase, in the wake of Stalin's death and the de-Stalinization policies, aimed at a loosening of the rigid hold exercised by the terror machine and static bureaucracies on state and society; a search for more rational and effective economic and social policies within the system, as well as the establishment of more realistic and viable relations with other Communist and nonCommunist countries. In short, the process of adaptation of internal and external Soviet policies and institutional processes to the changes inside, in the bloc, and in the international environment of the Soviet state.

(iii)   The contemporary period of *systemic expansion* of Soviet influence, power and presence abroad; this refers to a set of objectives and policies aiming at the creation of vast military capabilities, at least equal to those of the capitalist adversary, and their projection around the globe; the search for 'superpower' status and the corollary prestige and influence; and activist political and economic policies of the government in support of expansion of Soviet power around the globe.

(b)   The Political Parameters

These set out the fundamental rules of the game within the system, define the sources of legitimacy and the proper uses of authority and power, and define the relationship between the hegemonial party and the bureaucratic institutions:

(i)   *party hegemony* within the system, including a monopoly of authority, legitimacy, and power to initiate, prescribe, proscribe, or halt any and all private and public action within the system;

(ii)   *no provision for the transfer of power* within the party and therefore for all practical purposes within the state; there are no traditional, legal, constitutional, or procedural provisions for an orderly and predictable transfer of power within the party, creating thereby a crisis-prone situation during each succession period;

(iii)   the existence of *security and political control organs*, a paramilitary organization parallel to the military and within the military but not directly responsible to it, whose primary responsibility is to oversee, report on, and control the military. The security and paramilitary organs are directed by the top party organs in the Central Committee Secretariat;[17]

(iv) the ideologically and historically sanctioned tradition of the *political supremacy* of military professionalism, and of the residual *anti-militarism* of Marxism–Leninism.[18]

(c) Institutional Variables

This refers to the interaction between the systemic priorities and the political parameters as they affect relationships between the party and the major bureaucratic institutions. The pull here is between the party's compulsion to retain a monopoly of power and the compelling need to share, delegate, or disperse some of it to institutions and functionaries in order to support and advance the systemic priorities:

(i) *Party leadership mode:* leadership within the system implies leadership in the party, varying from Lenin's overwhelming moral authority as the founder of the party, to Stalin's autocratic, centralized, dictatorial *vozhd'* type of leadership, to the improvisational and unstable, evolving, collective leadership in the Khrushchev period, to the current institutionalized form of collective leadership in which the *primus inter pares* serves as power broker within a stable coalition of bureaucratic hierarchs.

(ii) *Role of the security and the paramilitary organs* whose primary function with regard to the military is to serve as the party's 'eyes and ears' within the military, and as an 'equalizer' viz-à-vis the military's inherent institutional power. The more prominent and powerful the position and authority of these organs, the greater the corresponding reduction of the power and influence of the military. There seems to be a built-in hostility and competition between the military and these ancillary party-controlled instruments of control, terror, and coercion.

(iii) *The level of economic and technological development* within the system: although the military was a privileged, primary consumer of goods and services during earlier periods of development of the state, the greater recent abundance of economic and technological resources has enhanced even further the military's position within the system.[19] The modernization of the economy and technology has enabled the military to obtain the most up-to-date weaponry, technology, and equipment, as well as modern managerial and command and control methods. Moreover, the growing complexity of modern management problems of the military has enhanced the military's claims to professional standards and exclusiveness as a means to resist political interference with their institutional and professional autonomy.[20]

(iv) *Level of political development:* this refers to the idiosyncratic mode of political 'development' of the 'totalitarian' system and its institutions in the Soviet Union and its subsequent decline and decay under the pressure of modernization during the systemic transition period. The decline of the developed 'totalitarian' system has enabled a partial emancipation of institutional and personal roles and encouraged incipient, formative forms of interest aggregation and articulation by institutions, including the military.

There are certain problems with this approach to the study of 'political development' in the Soviet Union. The conceptual problematics derive from the persistence of two basic Western concepts of modernization which revolve around the sequential progression of economic and political development. One is a uni-linear concept of an almost sequential process of 'nation-building,' in which political development follows upon economic development, suggesting that only in economically highly developed societies can mature and developed political institutions exist and thrive. In subscribing to such a sequential model of development, analysts perceived the actual or potential roles of the military to be of great importance in 'developing' societies. The military was analyzed in terms of its role as a vehicle or accelerator of economic and political development.[21]

A more recent approach to modernization suggested a reversible model, indicating the possibility of economic development and retardation or retrogression of political development under conditions where modernization proceeds at a very rapid pace. Here the military is seen as an impediment to political development.[22]

In the study of Communist societies – specifically, the Soviet Union – one may want to introduce a third approach. In the USSR (the dominant model for other Communist systems) the Western developmental-modernizing model appears to have been placed on its head. The Soviet state began as a highly complex, political, and organizational system imposed upon a relatively underdeveloped economic substructure. Most of the conditions generally associated in the West with political development were present, such as high political participation, intensive political socialization, effective national integration, 'rational' decision-making, and bureaucratic management. Yet this vastly politically 'developed' apparatus rested on a backward economic substructure, an inheritance of imperial ineptitude and mismanagement, and devastation.

The Soviet leaders reversed the assumed sequential process of economic development preceding political development. A central purpose of these imposed 'developed' political structures and processes was to accelerate economic development, technological innovation, urbanization, and the like. To be sure, it can be argued that much of this so-called 'political development' and these advanced structures and processes remained merely symbolic, empty of content; that the 'totalitarian' ruler and his supportive elites were engaged in meaningless duplications of 'democratic' forms. Yet we cannot dismiss the fact that many of these processes associated with nation-building and modernization were formally present at a very early stage in the history of the Soviet Union.

Thus, in attempting to analyze the role of the military in Communist systems and to relate it to the modernization process within such states, we must employ approaches and methods other than those generally used by Western analysts for the study of the military in 'developed' or 'developing' societies. Moreover, the role of the military, again in an idiosyncratic manner, grew and developed with the progress in economic development and political retrogression from the developed 'totalitarian' model. In this manner, the role of the military in the Soviet Union has followed a somewhat different pattern from that in most 'developed' or 'developing' countries.

(v) *Scope of commitment to foreign and military policies:* The Soviet Union has come a long way from its earlier days of great vulnerability, when a sense of 'capitalist encirclement' and a backward economic and technological structure intensified the inherent Russian and Soviet concerns with isolation and threat. Given the limited industrial/defense capabilities and a sense of beleaguerment, Stalin followed an 'isolationist' defensive, reactive, continentally delimited strategic policy. The overriding systemic priorities of the period prior to World War II were to consolidate the party's (and thus Stalin's) power and authority within the country and to integrate the heterogenous social, economic, geographic, linguistic, and territorial sections of the vast country under the party's leadership. Although the military was to be the prime recipient of the modernizing industry, its internal role remained tightly contained, strictly subordinated, and politically neutralized. It was a time for primacy of the internal security organs and the paramilitary organizations, whose roles and functions were in line with the systemic priorities – inward consolidation and integration.

The Soviet Union has now become a superpower, a military juggernaut, with a vast defense establishment and a global foreign policy: Brezhnev asserted the new position of the Soviet Union claiming that 'no question of any importance in the world can be solved without our participation, without taking into account our economic and military might.'[23] Soviet soldiers, weapons, tanks, and airplanes, and Soviet military techniques, training, and advice are at the forefront of their foreign policy of expansionism and exploration for targets of opportunity in the Third World: 'There has been, and is, no revolutionary movement or action by the people's masses for national or social liberation that has not received effective aid from the party of Lenin and the country of October.'[24] The Head of the Main Political Administration of the Armed Forces, General of the Army, A. Epishev, made the case for the military's extended and crucial role:[25]

> In the present era, which is characterized by a strengthening of the positions of socialism and by sharp antagonism between the two social systems, a deepening of the external function of the Soviet Armed Forces has logically taken place . . . It must be seen that socialism's military might objectively assist the successful development of the revolutionary, liberation movements and that it hinders the exportation of imperialist counterrevolution. In this lies one of the most important manifestations of the external function of the armed forces of a socialist state.

Soviet strategic forces are globally deployed, under the seas, on land, in the air, in space. Soviet conventional forces and weapons are vast, have been modernized and are poised in East Europe, in the Soviet Union, and on its peripheries facing Asia, the Middle East, and Western Europe; they are also becoming more visible, directly or via proxies, in Africa, the Middle East, and Asia. The military component of Soviet foreign policy has become its most effective counter and its cutting edge.

As the scope of Soviet external commitments increases and becomes more complex, so does the party's reliance upon the military. Soviet military leaders serve as the party's quasi-revolutionary agents in the Third World; they head up important diplomatic missions, serve on major international negotiatory teams and, at times, serve as private emissaries of the Politburo.

The military has become a participant and executant in the expanding affairs of the new Soviet imperium, in the foreign and military policies of the party and of the expanding state. The military is the beneficiary of this new demand for its services, and their leaders are responsive to the party's direction and leadership. At the same time, the party's reliance and indebtedness to the military is increasing.

(c) The Systemic-Institutional-Interdependence Variables

The history of party–military relations indicates that the role of the military and its institutional strength vis-à-vis the party have been strongly affected by shifts in the systemic priorities of the state and the party. The systemic priorities reflected the main orientation of the state and party in a given developmental phase of the Soviet Union. These phases were:

(i)   A period of *consolidation* of the party's hegemonial authority and control over the post-revolutionary society and state; and of *integration* of the diverse sectors, people, groups, and the national, racial, linguistic, and geographic entities into a centralized, hegemonial political system.

(ii)   A period of *systemic transition* of the Soviet system from a Stalinist, quasi-revolutionary, terror-ridden, excessively centralized and coerced, integrating system into one that is less coercive, less beleagured, more participatory, mature, and modern post-revolutionary state.

(iii)   The contemporary phase of *expansionism* of the scope, influence, and power outside the system into primarily Third World areas.

In studying these major phases in the development of the Soviet Union, one also perceives roughly corresponding modes of party–military relations:

(i)   An initial phase of the military's near total *dependence* and *subordination* to the party, corresponding roughly with the Stalinist regime.

(ii)   A subsequent phase of growing *interdependence* between the party and the military and of selective *co-optation* of military elites by the party into political affairs, this approximating the Khrushchev regime.

(iii)   The current phase of marked institutional and political *interdependence*, a time of mutual *accommodation* between the party and the military.

Each of these phases in the evolution of party–military relations corresponds to the shifts in the systemic priorities and to the general development of the Soviet Union, from the revolutionary and early post-revolutionary phase to the present superpower status. It thus appears that the systemic priorities and the nature of party–military relations are related and exhibit a congruence:

(i)   An initial phase of military *dependence* and *subordination* to the party coincided with the process of intensive *consolidation* of the party's hegemonial authority and with the *integration* of the country into a hegemonial, centralized system.

(ii) The period of growing institutional *interdependence* between the party and the military and of co-optation of the military elites into bureaucratic and political decision-making bodies coincided with the ongoing *transition* of the Soviet system from the Stalinist to the post-totalitarian model.

(iii) The current period of political and institutional *interdependence* and *accommodation* between the party and the military corresponds to the political and military *expansionism* of the Soviet state.

One may, therefore, be able to present schematically the evolution and process of Soviet party–military relations by relating the given systemic priority with the institutional interdependence variables and indicating the given position of the military vis-à-vis the party:

(i) *Political Consolidation and Systemic Integration Phase (Stalinist):*
Military Subordination to the party
(1) High political (totalitarian) development
(2) Low level of economic development
(3) Dictatorial, *vozhd'* leadership
(4) High role of the terror, security organs
(5) 'Isolationist' foreign policy
(6) Defensive, continental strategic doctrine and policy

(ii) *Systemic Transition Phase (Khrushchev Period):*
Military Co-optation and Growing Interdependence
(1) Decline of totalitarian system
(2) Intensive economic development
(3) Evolving collective leadership
(4) Low role of terror/paramilitary organs
(5) Expanding foreign policy
(6) Expanding regional strategic doctrine and policy

(iii) *Systemic Expansion Phase (Contemporary):*
Party–Military Accommodation, Institutional Interdependence
(1) Decay of totalitarian system
(2) High economic development
(3) Institutionalized collective leadership
(4) Low role of terror/paramilitary organs
(5) Global, superpower foreign policy
(6) Global, activist strategic doctrine and policy

The summary point deriving from the study of the institutional inter-dependence variables is that the stronger the congruence between the given systemic priority and an institution's role and function, the greater that institution's weight and negotiability vis-à-vis the party. The military's particular role and influence in the Soviet Union may also be inferred as being inversely related to the role of the security and paramilitary organs, to the scope of the party's authority and the mode of leadership, as well as to the levels of political 'development' of the system. At the same time, the military's weight and negotiability vis-à-vis the party are directly related to the levels of economic development and the scope and level of commitment to foreign and military policies of the state.

In the following section we shall briefly examine the evolution of party–military relations in the Soviet Union under the three regimes of Stalin, Khrushchev, and Brezhnev in the light of the preceding conceptual framework.

(4) HISTORICAL NARRATIVE: EVOLUTION OF THE MILITARY'S ROLE

(a) Stalinist Subordination

The long tenure of Stalin, as the head of the state and party, is seen here as the hegemonial consolidation and systemic integration phase of the CPSU. Stalin abandoned most of the revolutionary-utopian objectives and values of his predecessors and launched a massive program of collectivization and industrialization. The military establishment was to play a key role in this 'Third Revolution,' both as the beneficiary of the heightened economic productivity and as the protector of the state surrounded by a 'capitalist encirclement.' The military in the Stalinist schema was to remain a giant on a leash: they were to be a privileged elite whose spokesmen were to remain mute, whose authority was to be enjoyed at the pleasure of the party leader, and who had to accept and tolerate in their midst networks of security organs provocateurs, party agitators, and young zealots. The military was conditioned through fear of failure to practice a form of passivism and bureaucratic inertia, thus creating a generation of officers without much independence, esprit de corps, initiative, or innovative nerve. In the purges of 1937–8, Stalin struck a devastating blow at the military, destroying their self-assurance and institutional autonomy, a blow from which they did not recover until the war years. Even then, when the victorious generals and marshals of the Red Army were returning from victories in Germany, Stalin once again shattered the military's self-esteem and institutional strength by lecturing them that 'only childish people think that the laws of the artillery are stronger than the laws of industry,' and by demoting and banishing the most prominent among the military leaders. In the remaining years of Stalinist dictatorship, the military had to endure the megalomania of the leader, and his various forms of chicanery, repression, and humiliation.

(b) Khrushchevite Co-optation

The death of Stalin rapidly changed the rules of the game in the system and introduced new dynamics of interaction between the party and the military. Since several party leaders entered into a struggle for succession, and since the terror machine had been eliminated from the political arena with the arrest of Beria, the military found itself for the first time in a position of potential influence. Their subsequent support of Khrushchev against Malenkov gained additional influence for the military in the affairs of the state and party. With the absence of a powerful, charismatic, and dominant figure at the center, the military made inroads into the important decision-making centers of the party.[26]

However, as long as Marshal Zhukov appeared to be the spokesman for the military, Khrushchev and the party continued to distrust the motives and the objectives of the officer corps. Zhukov's views on the military's role and place in the state were anathema to the party leaders; he was a disciplinarian, a professional, full of contempt for the party amateurs who were meddling in the military's affairs. Moreover, Zhukov enjoyed vast support among the rank and file and among the officers of the Red Army. He was also a popular war hero.

Zhukov's ouster in October 1957 laid the groundwork for a more relaxed and stable form of relationship between the party and the military. A presumably loyal group of military leaders (from the Stalingrad Group) was entrusted with the leading positions in the Ministry of Defense: after the initial purge of the Zhukovites in the military, it appears that an informal sort of co-optation of the military into party affairs and decision-making processes of the state took place. Military leaders who had been destroyed by Stalin in the 1937 purges were rehabilitated; the military was now given preferential treatment in the budgetary allocations and in social planning; and the political control functions in the armed forces were muted.

However, this tranquil period did not last very long. Khrushchev attempted to renege on commitments made to the military and to decrease the size and role of the armed forces, thus threatening institutional empires, careers, and traditions. The relations between Khrushchev and the military continued to deteriorate after the Cuban missile crisis until his ouster in 1964.

(c) Brezhnevite Accommodation

The Soviet military establishment entered the 1980s amidst very auspicious circumstances. Internally, the military is rather quiescent and unified, and generally satisfied with its institutional role, budgetary allocations, modern weapons, and technology, and freedom to manage its internal affairs without excessive interference from the party and political organs. The military also enjoys an unprecedented period of high morale due, in various ways, to the growing strength and modern technology received during the 1970s, which, in effect, made them equal to the military establishment in the USA. Moreover, the military has expanded its reach globally, through its modern and powerful navy, military-space technology, and intensified pressures in the Third World. Having challenged and overcome Khrushchev's policies both of stringent economization and strategic-political adventurism, the military is enjoying a preferential position under the leadership of Brezhnev.

The military's institutional and political influence has been further strengthened by the growing external commitments of the Soviet state, the mounting challenge from China, the complex situation in the Middle East and Central Asia, and the pending negotiations and ratification of SALT. The Sino-Soviet conflict is moving progressively more in the direction of a protracted, low-level military confrontation. The tempting and risky policy opportunities in the Middle East and Central Asia are premised heavily in a military calculus. The Soviet accommodations in the SALT talks were paralleled by concessions to the military by the party leadership.

The present position of the military represents the culmination of a long trend of aggregative growth of the military's institutional strength, corporate autonomy, professional sophistication, and political influence. The question therefore arises, what are the social and political implications of this development?

We may begin by identifying the military's dominant interests and objectives. The military's values and preferences include a set of conservative social and political views. They prefer a society which is stable, fairly conservative, orderly, and committed to the ideas and objectives of the party. They tend to view deviancy, social experimentation, 'liberalism,' and excessive consumerism as antithetic to their own code of values, as well as detrimental to society and state. The military prefers a national planning policy in which the security and strength of the state receive first priority.

The military has progressively indicated an infatuation with technocratic/bureaucratic values and approaches to social and political management. This cult of technology translates itself into the societal setting in terms of the heightened status and prestige of the managerial/bureaucratic types and the minimization of the ideological-theoretical premises of decision- and policy-making. This military preference has also denigrated certain bourgeois influences in the arts, literature, and sciences. This trait of the military parallels the preferences and attitudes of the party leadership which is largely composed of managerial/bureaucratic types, rather than of the ideological revolutionary types. To be sure, the military understands the legitimating functions of ideology and revolutionary rhetoric, as well as necessary mythologies and symbolisms associated with such rhetoric and revolutionary heritage. Public military statements will, therefore, continue to stress the primacy of ideology, the vitality of the revolutionary heritage, and the unchallenged role of the party in affairs of the society and state. Moreover, while the military is progressively more given to technocratic/managerial ways and values, it continues to retain the morale-building and corporative self-identification derived from the more traditional, heroic, and revolutionary values and symbols of the armed forces.

The Soviet military and the party leadership seem to have reached a workable *modus vivendi*, a political and bureaucratic accommodation. This accommodation is likely to be sustained throughout the decade unless certain premises of this accommodation are changed. For example, the re-emergence of the security organs as a potent political actor in

Soviet politics is likely to create friction and tension between them: the re-emergence of a single, Stalinoid type of leader, who would presumably attempt to curb the military's institutional and political influence, would similarly lead to profound resistance and conflicts. The pursuit of foreign or domestic policies by the party leadership which would seriously undermine or threaten the military's basic interests would also create severe internal disturbances.

However, in the absence of such changes, the military is likely to remain a key supportive actor in the present and foreseeable array of Soviet domestic and foreign policies. The military has a vital stake in the support of the present regime, in its policies, and in its relations with the armed forces. The Soviet Union has become a superpower; it now follows, and is likely to continue, an active and dynamic superpower policy, with interests and commitments reaching farther afield in a global scope. The military's role in such a policy will remain vital and prominent. And thus, détente, active international trade, the muting of the excesses of a neo-totalitarian system, the willingness to enter the arms-control negotiations and arms limitations – none of these negate or seriously threaten the military's interests.

The military, despite its occasional internal disagreements and disunity, has become a member of the coalition of bureaucracies which presently rule the Soviet Union. The original props of party hegemony (revolutionary charisma, terror machine, committed party apparat and the sense of an encircled, beleaguered camp) are eroding. The revolutionary dynamism is abating and dwindling, and the Soviet people, their functionaries, professionals, scientists, and workers are increasingly consumer-oriented, tending toward embourgeoisment. They are interested in the good life of the present, and their leaders are fulfilling these needs, while at the same time pursuing superpower, imperial policies abroad. The military is the beneficiary of this balance between domestic stability and external dynamism, since the Brezhnev leadership appears to consider them interdependent. Moreover, despite the massive gains in arms and technology, which brought the Soviet Union into a state of superpower parity, the party leaders continue to view their conflict with China and their explorative policies in the Middle East region as necessitating a powerful and credible military capability.

(5) CONCLUSIONS

Several conclusions emerge from the analysis and empirical evidence of this chapter:

(a) The relations between party and the military in the Soviet (hegemonial) political system are dynamic, changing, and not rigidly frozen in a static, 'totalitarian' atrophy. The military is not, as certain Western analysts insist, an undifferentiated, amorphous, fully integrated, mere 'executant' of the party; indeed, the military does have distinct institutional and professional values, interests, and objectives which it seeks to advance, within the given rules and constraints of the system.

(b) The party and the military in hegemonial systems are highly interdependent institutions: the military provides the party with many of the desirable values, styles, rituals, and methods for the management of the quasi-military and militant hegemonial systems. The military tends to be a most loyal, dependable, and supportive institution vis-à-vis the party, despite the fact that the latter tends to suppress the military's independence and to dominate it by various means. Yet, the party finds itself becoming more dependent on the military as the demands and expectations from the domestic populace and institutions increase, as the party's control of alliance systems declines, and as the very inner dynamism and revolutionary vitality of the party itself erodes.

(c) The relations between the party and the military are shaped by several systemic, political, and institutional factors. Their relations are also affected by the profound suspicion, bordering on paranoia, of the party leaders regarding institutions that have the potential to challenge their hegemonial role, their monopoly of powers. One may describe the party as operating within a very high threat-expectation milieu, where even minor deviations from the rigidly precribed norms of 'proper' institutional behavior are perceived with disproportionate concern and alarm. The relations between the party and the military are marked by uneven and asymmetrical attitudes and responses: the military tends to see the relationship as one of a 'variable-sum-game,' while the party's behavior is closer to a 'zero-sum-game.' To be sure, their interaction is based on mutual dependence and not on pure conflict, where the destruction of the antagonist is the object of the game. Over time, the party's attitude and management of its relations with the military is becoming closer to that of the military, more accommodating than dominating.

(d) What emerges from an analysis of the systemic institutional interdependence variables is that:

(i) The closer the congruence between the given system priority and an institution's role and function, the greater that institution's weight and negotiability vis-à-vis the party.

(ii) The military's role and influence in the Soviet Union may be inferred from the mix of institutional variables: the military's role appears to be inversely related to that of the security and paramilitary organs and to the scope of the party's leadership; and more directly related to the levels of economic development and the level of commitment to foreign and military policies of the state.

The military and the current leadership of the party seem to have established a *modus vivendi* that suits both parties. The military has faithfully supported the party's policies and the party has seen to it that the military's interests are satisfied. There is a complementarity of institutional interests: the Brezhnev regime political line appears to comprise:

(i) controlled expansion of military and political influence abroad, primarily into the Third World in the areas south of Russia,

(ii) normalization, détentification policies vis-à-vis the industrialized world, including arms control,
(iii) controlled consumerism at home in the spirit of détente.

These general policy lines, to the surprise of observers, have gained vigorous military support because the military became their beneficiary:

(i) Expansion abroad legitimizes the steady growth of the defense establishment and the quasi-revolutionary function of the military in Africa and the Middle East.
(ii) Détente does not threaten the military and gives them access to vital Western technologies; arms-control negotiations and agreements do not threaten the military's interests because the military dominates the negotiatory process, serves as the key adviser to the party leaders on these issues, and receives major concessions from the party as a quid pro quo for its acquiescence and support of such agreements.
(iii) The controlled consumerism at home and its attendant threats of embourgeoisment endows the military with crucial roles as Spartan educator, as patriotic revolutionary model, and as purifier of the youth.

NOTES

1 Gordon Craig, *The Politics of the Prussian Army, 1640–1945* (London: Oxford University Press, 1964), pp. xix–xx.
2 See particularly William Odom, 'The party–military connection' in Dale R. Herspring and Ivan Volgyes, (eds), *Civil–Military Relations in Communist Systems* (Boulder, Colo.: Westview Press, 1978), page numbers in citation text refer to this book.

   We ought to welcome Colonel Odom's attempt to expose the rather specialized field of study of Soviet party–military relations to a critical examination. The field has grown over the years in a rather haphazard manner, from the pioneering historical studies of Fedotoff-White, John Erickson, Merle Fainsod, to the professional works of John Mackintosh, Raymond Garthoff and second generation of scholars and analysts that include the books of Timothy Colton, Edward Warner, and Robert Deane. The field, however, is also cluttered with the institutional monographic effluvia from the Cold War period and from more recent times, including some confused popular books on the 'Red Army' and even some misguided and pseudo-authoritative content-analytical blind-men-and-elephant tracts in the social sciences.

   Colonel Odom labors, however, toward that ineluctable goal of area studies and regionalist scholars who are verbally flogged at conferences and in the professional literature because of their narrow parochialism. The assigned professional goal, their duty and aspiration, is to tunnel through the walls of regionalism and connect the byways of the 'area studies' to the 'mainstream'. In the field of civil–military studies, that tends to mean the use of the developmentalists', comparativists' and sociologists' methodological and theoretical machinery by placing it over the 'area study' in a Procrustean coup.

   Although he means to include the whole field of Western studies of the Soviet military, he selected my book (*The Soviet Military and the Communist Party*, Princeton, NJ: Princeton University Press, 1967) as the *Blitzableiter* of his critical wrath. He argues that while 'faulty assumptions have long pervaded most of the literature of Soviet Party–Military Relations' he finds that 'perhaps the most unambiguous statement of them has come from Roman Kolkowicz.' *Das Ding an sich*. Ironically, the Central

Committee theoretical journal *Kommunist* (no. 3, 1968) and the *Soviet Military Review* (January 1969) have found me guilty of the same transgressions, in almost identical terms.

In attempting to clear out the cobwebs of musty Sovietology in the field of party–military relations, Colonel Odom wields a rather hefty critical ax all over the field. He sets out by dismissing Kolkowicz's 'assumptions about the military adversary relation-ships as based on somewhat metaphysical grounds' (p. 29) and as being 'more scholastic than real' (p. 30). Attempts to define military professionalism in the Soviet military by Kolkowicz are seen by Odom as 'analogous to phlogiston', a 'mystical substance that was to explain fire before man understood oxidation' (p. 34). He finds fault with Huntington for 'obscuring the fact that an apolitical military establishment is a mythical convention concocted in the parochial minds of the Europeans' and in general 'offer little analytical assistance and may introduce intellectual confusion' (p. 36). Phillip Selznick is found to suffer from 'category confusion' seemingly not knowing the difference between internal war and external war (p. 49), and Barrington Moore is found wanting since his decision model and treatment of military professionalism remain to Odom 'incomplete' (p. 34). In the specific field of Soviet military studies, Odom finds Timothy Colton guilty of peddling 'vintage Kolkowicz, not a new approach' and for 'perplexing' him because of his 'rubbery terms' forcing the reader to 'proceed in circles'. Even Thomas Wolfe and the late Merle Fainsod are suspect because they believe that the relations between the party and the military in the Soviet Union are not fully harmonious and tranquil. Only Raymond Garthoff, whom Odom finds to be 'a bit more cautious' in his espousals of 'conventional' views of party–military relations in the Soviet Union appears to be almost exempt from the critical jihad of Colonel Odom.

3   Roman Kolkowicz, 'Interest groups in Soviet politics: the case of the military,' in Herspring and Volgyes (eds), op. cit. Also see Dennis Ross, 'Coalition maintenance in the Soviet Union,' *World Politics*, Vol. 32, no. 2 (January 1980).

4   Timothy J. Colton, 'The party–military connection: a participatory model,' in Herspring and Volgyes (eds), op. cit., ch. 4.

5   William Odom, 'Bolshevik ideas on the military's role in modernization,' *Armed Forces and Society*, vol. 3, no. 1 (November 1976), pp. 103–20; see also Ivan Volgyes, 'The military as an agent of political socialization,' in Herspring and Volgyes (eds), op. cit.

6   See Walter Goerlitz, *The German General Staff* (London: Hollis & Carter, 1953), particularly chs 9–14; also, John Wheeler-Bennett, *The Nemesis of Power: The German Army in Politics, 1918–1945* (London: Macmillan, 1953).

7   Michael Howard, *Soldiers and Governments: Nine Studies in Civil–Military Relations* (London: Eyre & Spottiswoode, 1957), 'Introduction'.

8   Alfred Vagts, *A History of Militarism* (New York: Meridian Books, 1959), p. 296.

9   Jerzy Wiatr, *Studia Sociologiczno-Polityczne*, no. 14 (1963), p. 47.

10   Cited in Howard, op. cit., p. 11.

11   Walter Goerlitz, *History of the German General Staff, 1657–1945* (New York: Praeger, 1962), pp. 278–9.

12   See Kolkowicz, 'Interest groups in Soviet politics', p. 15.

13   Thomas C. Schelling, *The Strategy of Conflict* (London: Oxford University Press, 1963), pp. 4–5.

14   See note 1 of this chapter.

15   Carl J. Friedrich and Z. K. Brzezinski, *Totalitarian Dictatorship and Autocracy* (New York: Praeger, 1956), p. 281.

16   See David C. Rapoport, 'A comparative theory of military and political types,' in Samuel P. Huntington (ed.), *Changing Patterns of Military Politics*, (Glencoe, Ill.: The Free Press, 1961), ch. 3; also Amos Perlmutter, *The Military and Politics in Modern Times* (Princeton, NJ: Yale University Press, 1977).

17   The official party's instructions spell out that role very clearly: 'The Communist Party is the organizer and leader of the Soviet Army and Navy. In this lies the main source of the military's strength. The Communist Party exercises its leadership in the Armed Forces through the military councils, commanders, political organs and Party organiz-ations. At the head of the political organs stands the Main Political Administration . . . which operates as a section of the CC CPSU' (*Partiinio-politicheskaia rabota v Sovetskoi Armii i Voenno-Morskom Flote*, Moscow: Voenizdat, 1960, p. 10).

18   The head of the Main Political Administration of the Soviet armed forces, General

Epishev, has described the party's role in the military as follows: 'The Communist Party and its Central Committee control the implementation of the wide range of practical measures in the military field, from the elaboration of theoretical and methodological principles . . . to practical fulfillment of concrete tasks relating to the training and education of the personnel. The collective intellect, will and energy of the Party are alone capable of embracing the entire range of the economic, political and strictly military problems that have to be solved today in enhancing the country's defense capabilities' (A. A. Epishev, *Some Aspects of Party–Political Work in the Soviet Armed Forces,* Moscow: Progress Publishers, 1975, pp. 76–7).

See also *Marxism–Leninism on War and Army* (Moscow: Progress Publishers, 1972), particularly ch. 5: 'The Armed Forces of the Socialist States.' 'The leadership by the Communist Party of the Armed Forces is the fundamental basis underlying Soviet military development' (p. 229).

19 For very candid views of the military on these subjects, and on the need to retain the defense establishment's primacy in economic and budgetary planning, see articles by top Soviet military leaders after the ouster of Khrushchev (who tried to reduce the defense budgets and the military's priority in industrial planning): *Pravda* (2 October 1964). Marshal of the Soviet Union, M. Sakharov, *Krasnaia zvezda* (4 February 1965), and ibid. (23 February 1965); also, *Kommunist,* editorial, no. 7 (May 1965); *Pravda* (17 May 1965); and speech by Brezhnev (3 July 1965).

20 See numerous citations from Soviet sources in 'The dialogue on professional autonomy' and 'The new technology and the rise of the technocrat: effect on party–military relations,' in Roman Kolkowicz, *The Soviet Military and the Communist Party* (Princeton, NJ: Princeton University Press, 1967).

21 A. Perlmutter, 'The praetorian state and the praetorian army,' *Comparative Politics,* vol. 1, no. 3 (April 1969); Lucian Pye, 'Armies in the process of political moderniz-ation,' in J. J. Johnson (ed.), *The Role of the Military in Underdeveloped Countries* (Princeton, NJ: Princeton University Press, 1962); Morroe Berger, *Military Elite and Social Change* (Princeton, NJ: Princeton University Press, 1960); Hans Daalder, *The Role of the Military in the Emerging Countries* (The Hague: Mouton, 1972); Manfred Halpern, *The Politics of Social Change in the Middle East and North Africa* (Princeton, NJ: Princeton University Press, 1963).

22 S. P. Huntington, *Political Order in Changing Societies* (New Haven, Conn.: Yale University Press, 1968).

23 L. I. Brezhnev, speech in Minsk, 14 March 1970, on the Soviet army's 'Dvina' Maneuvres, reported in Foy D. Kohler, *et al., Soviet Strategy for the Seventies* (Center for Advanced International Studies, University of Miami, 1977), p. 228.

24 CPSU Central Committee, 'Theses for Lenin's birth centenary,' *Pravda* (23 December 1969).

25 General of the Army, A. Epishev, 'The historical mission of the Socialist State's army,' *Kommunist,* no. 7 (May 1972).

26 For evidence of this surge of the military from the 'Stalingrad Group' into the Central Committee and commanding military and political positions, see Kolkowicz, *The Soviet Military and the Communist Party.*

11 The Praetorian Army: Insecurity, Venality, and Impotence

DAVID C. RAPOPORT

The great thing about an army officer is that he does what you tell him to do.

Theodore Roosevelt

If we supply an aggregate of human beings, more or less homogeneous in language and religion, with a little assistance and a good deal of advice, if we protect them from external aggression and discourage internal violence, they will speedily and spontaneously organize themselves into a democratic state along modern lines.

Lord Balfour

After World War II, many academics buoyantly pictured the future of the new states created. A decade later, when governments, one by one, began falling to military usurpers, the optimism did not fade – a 'dynamic and self-sacrificing military leadership committed to progress' had seized the helm.[1] So self-evident did the virtues of soldiers seem that two scholars appeared dismayed that armies in black Africa were too small to overturn their governments should the latter fail.[2]

More than a century earlier, a similar faith in the potentialities of armies had been voiced by Marx and Engels who believed that Spanish soldiers would bring their country into the 'modern world'.

What we call the State in a modern sense has from the exclusively provincial life of the people no national embodiment in opposition to the Court, except in the army . . . It was only in the army that everything vital in the Spanish nationality was permitted to concentrate.[3]

The army had 'revolutionary aims' and authentic 'revolutionary elements'. True, its initial political and economic measures failed, but that was because the soldiers' ardor had been *too* great, being foolishly determined to 'prosecute [reforms] at all costs.'[4] Marx and Engels were convinced that the soldiers would learn from their mistakes.

However, as they became more familiar with the Spanish scene, their doubts grew and they began entertaining the notion that Europe was witnessing a phenomenon unknown since the Roman Empire. The soldiers kept *spoiling* the revolution by praetorianism.' In the end, the two writers turned a complete about-face, believing that the army itself had become the greatest obstacle to Spain's development.[5]

Marx and Engels failed to develop a concept of praetorianism which may be the major reason why Marxists subsequently ignored their comments.[6] In the nonMarxist world praetorianism has received some attention. But the concept which I reintroduced two decades ago has been refashioned to mean something else – the antithesis of *civilian* control[7] and a military domination which is 'institutionalized' largely to expand the military's 'corporate interests' at the expense of society as a whole.[8]

By emphasizing the army's strength, contemporary discussions of praetorianism obscure the army's weakness or vulnerabilities. We have no basis, consequently, for discussing the *mutual* interactions of governments and soldiers which, ironically, was the concern of the classical view represented in the experience of Rome and the work of traditional political theorists.[9]

My purpose here is to restate the concept, explore several of its latent meanings, and then examine implications of those meanings for the predicament and agony of the praetorian army. Both ancient and modern examples will be used; my modern illustrations rely on Spanish and Latin American cases more than might seem appropriate here, considering the title of the volume, but the history of modern praetorianism is more extensive there and provides much useful material.[10]

(1) THE CONCEPT

> Augustus . . . [established] a form of government which justified itself on the ground of efficiency and sought to substitute the expert for the amateur.
>
> > G. H. Stevenson, *Roman Provincial Administration*

All reflections on the concept should begin by considering *the* classical experience, or those aspects of it pertinent for our purposes. Praetorianism was the unintended consequence of Augustus's effort to replace the Roman Republic's numerous ad hoc levies by a unified, permanent military order. He rationalized or modernized military administration, and he created *the* Roman army – a voluntary, professional standing force. All soldiers pledged obedience to a commander-in-chief, *imperator* or emperor, who provided a uniform system of pay and promotion based on merit and seniority. Weber characterizes the arrangement as *democratic*, because the emperor was 'a free trustee of the masses . . . unfettered by officers and officials whom he selects freely and personally.'[11]

The Imperial or Praetorian Guard, an elite unit of 9–10,000 tested veterans drawn from social classes most committed to the imperial order, was the capstone of the system. It supplemented Rome's first professional police force organized by Augustus and shielded the emperor from domestic unrest. But, in time, the Guard became a major threat to particular emperors or governments which it normally overthrew by means of a coup d'état. Sometimes, especially in its initial history, the Guard eliminated corrupt or totally incompetent emperors and then chose able replacements. But it violated military discipline in the process, and always received a donative (a grant of money) from the new emperor which, in effect, suggested that he had purchased their loyalty. This image led contemporary and subsequent generations to regard them as incurably venal, and modern dictionaries characterize a praetorian army as a venal or corrupt one.

The concept, then, refers to systems where a bureaucratically administered professional army, paid in coin, intermittently deposes governments by extra-legal acts, the most characteristic being the coup d'état. Military coups presuppose states with sufficient centralization and an army fully identified with the symbols of legitimacy. Because the necessary political and administrative requisites of praetorianism did not exist in the Roman Republic military insurrection could culminate in civil wars, but not in a coup d'état.[12]

A particular praetorian coup may be undertaken for an appropriate and/or popular justification; it may even have beneficial political consequences, but since all praetorian coups *seem* to entail a breach of the military oath and an increase in the army's material amenities, soldiers gain the reputation of callously exploiting the governments' dependence upon them.[13]

The concept has deeper meanings which should compel us to put this moral judgement in a larger perspective, meanings which the Roman experience, or any other for that matter, amply illustrates. The political weakness of governments inescapably involves the army which necessarily is organized to be both a subordinate and dependent part of the system. Hence, if individual governments are blackmailed by their armies, soldiers are weak also and cannot secure themselves from suspicious governments.

The vulnerability of the Guard stems from conditions which are systemic or inherent in every arrangement where governments have the final responsibility for determining the uses of the army, and for recruiting, organizing, equipping, promoting, punishing, and paying individual soldiers. In such circumstances, a government *may* become politically dependent upon its army, but individual soldiers are *always* more directly and obviously permanent dependents (even wards) of the governments they serve. Members of any bureaucratically organized force retain their positions, their income, and even their lives at the lawful discretion of the government. Governments, moreover, have enormous capacities to intrigue or conspire against individual soldiers, and weak and desperate governments will undoubtedly plot, or certainly will be 'seen' as doing so. The first coup in Roman history was not effected *by* the Guard but *against* it, or at least its leadership. This was the conspiracy organized by the Emperor Tiberius who felt too weak to act openly. As often as not the emperors installed by the Guard ruthlessly purged the unit as soon as they had consolidated themselves.[14] The more important an officer was, the more reason he might have to worry about an emperor's anxieties.

Insecurity breeds venality and both contribute ultimately to a deterioration of military potentialities. Four centuries after Augustus established a magnificent army 'there was no people so small that it was unable to do the Romans harm.'[15] The pace of the movement was not uniform. Sometimes, able, dedicated emperors reinvigorated the army, but the overall trend was irresistable.

> The patient's strength dwindled, and his activity was restricted accordingly. As the metabolic efficiency of a diseased man diminishes, more energy is consumed in the simple effort of trying to stay alive; similarly the task of routine administrative maintenance increasingly absorbed Romans. Diocletian had more helpers, but less help, than Marcus Aurelius; the latter in turn envied Augustus, and Augustus understood Livy's astonishment at the endless vitality Rome displayed during the Punic War.[16]

Rome had no binding rule to resolve succession disputes. But the existing notion of legitimacy did limit the political capacities of soldiers. Although they could depose an emperor and virtually choose his successor, they could not abolish the institution of the emperor or rule in their own name.

The significance of this point is driven home in the literature of traditional political theory. Praetorianism there is associated with two different, yet related, conceptions of legitimacy. Prior to the nineteenth century Harrington, Montesquieu, Ferguson, and so on, recognized one basic praetorian type – the despotic – which had particular and unique expressions in Rome, the Ottoman Empire, the Arabic world, and so on. After the French Revolution, Tocqueville and Maine distinguished a second type – the 'democratic' – which was most highly developed in Spain and which, they argued, would become prominent elsewhere as more and more states embraced conceptions of popular legitimacy.[17]

I have discussed aspects of the legitimacy principles in the two praetorian types elsewhere. But several observations are pertinent here. In both cases, as Weber's previously cited observation suggests, a government which has the legal right to organize the army as it sees fit is supposed to originate in a direct affirmation by the public.[18]

The public consists of civil and military elements, the latter being persons subordinated to a code of military discipline, even though they may not be exercising military functions.[19] In a despotism, civil and military 'constituencies' 'nominate' their candidates for the throne separately through designated institutions, though, in fact, the wishes of the soldiers are commonly decisive. Still, the soldiers are limited by 'unalterable' constitutions. The Janissaries could not go outside the House of Ottoman to choose a Sultan; and while the Roman soldiers had a wider range of choice, they could not abolish the Senate, an essential feature of the constitution which existed in part to 'represent' the civil element in confirming a new emperor.

In the democratic state, as opposed to the despotic one, a distinction between the community or the 'people' on the one hand, and their institutions, on the other, is recognized which maximizes potential for instability because the 'people' are entitled to design constitutions as well as choose their governments.[20] Any citizen, including a soldier, may claim to exercise this right which is confirmed by elections, plebiscites, and referenda.

In despotic states, durable constitutions make discussions of praetorian varieties meaningful. A useful typology of democratic forms, on the other hand, may be impossible to devise. So short is the life of many constitutions and so large is the variety which may be produced by a particular state in a brief time.[21] The difficulty suggests that one should pay less attention to typologies and more to the major common feature in the bewildering array of forms, namely the fact that *successive* governments anticipate that they may be deposed by acts of violence, organized usually by members of their standing armies. In a 'fully developed' praetorian state, democratic or despotic, virtually all governments experience military conspiracies, and most will emerge and disappear by means of a military coup d'état.

The term 'praetorian', therefore, pertains to a central feature of a *system* not to that of a government, to a perennial or inherent apprehension. The intensity or significance of that fear may vary considerably. Clearly, every government will attempt to reduce its vulnerability; some will be reasonably successful, but the life of others will be consumed with the single question of physical survival. In any case, the fear persists in latent or manifest form over time, and produces cumulative, as well as immediate, consequences.

The mutual apprehensions of broken pledges and violence should be the initial starting point for all reflections on the dynamics of a praetorian system. These mutual apprehensions prevail in democratic and despotic types, influencing the interactions of governments and soldiers, while shaping every major social institution as well. My concern, here, is with the army itself and my thesis is that the logic of the Roman experience – insecurity breeds venality and impotence – is represented in other praetorian states.

(2) INSECURITY

> When 'group feeling' (the bond between government and public) weakens soldiers become bold . . . their allowances must be increased [and] they become less able to wage wars . . . The dynast cannot get around that.
>
> Ibn Khaldun

> They [Turkish soldiers] are suspicious because they have suffered; they are violent because they are weak.
>
> G. F. Abbot, *Turkey in Transition*

Virtually every discussion of successful military coups since World War II starts precisely at the point where the fourteenth-century theorist Ibn Khaldun began – the precondition of the phenomenon is the weakness of the existing government. But the arguments then move in different directions. For contemporaries the development of cohesion and organiz- ation capacities in armies appears unrelated to, or is independent of, the development of those same qualities in their governments.[22] Ibn Khaldun, on the other hand, visualizes the problem as a systemic one. If govern- ments are weak, their armies are likely to be too, because most measures insecure governments take to defend themselves against their soldiers will weaken their armies; and the attempts of soldiers to protect themselves, or remedy the deficiencies of government, will also have debilitating effects on military organization and cohesion.

It may appear easy for soldiers to rebel successfully. But insurrections have enormous divisive potential for a military body even when they take, as they usually do, the limited form of the coup d'état where soldiers are less likely to be firing on their comrades. The full significance of these divisive acts emerge when they are repeated or become 'normal'. A single lie may be justified and despite certain invidious effects on balance may produce healthy results. But when lies become the 'rule' instead of the exception one must perceive the results differently, and the same thing is true for the coup d'état.[23]

The conspirators strike at the constitutional law, the ultimate authority for discipline; they violate their oaths, and if, as is generally the case, the conspirators are not the highest-ranking officers, they breach the normal structure of command. Every coup d'état *must* create hostilities, anxieties, and suspicions; some soldiers will be opposed simply because they believe in the constitution. Others will be concerned with keeping their oaths, a few will sympathize with the existing government, and most will fear that soldiers might be compelled to fire upon each other. A great majority of the officers will be apprehensive because the coup necessarily originates in a secret plot by a tiny minority, and those not invited to participate must be asking themselves why.

The coup d'état entails surprise always, and those we trust and to whom we expose ourselves are in an excellent position to surprise us. Surprise necessitates secrecy, and to maintain the advantage secrecy confers, conspirators cannot solicit positive support before they strike. Obviously this means that if the first blow miscarries they cannot continue the fight. Nonetheless, success is often possible, because conspirators may be able to count on powerful *negative* sentiments – a distaste for the existing government and a reluctance of most soldiers to fire on their comrades. The personal interests of soldiers must also become immensely significant and exploitable in this context. The bureaucratic nature of the army (that is, the dependency of individuals on the decision of others for their status and livelihood) generates enormous pressures on every officer. To support a failing government can be disastrous, and it may be immensely lucrative to support a likely successor before its position is beyond dispute.

The coup d'état teaches everyone that deceit and cunning, not cohesion and participation, are needed to depose government. The logic of the dynamic is that while the first successful conspiracy is usually organized by the highest-ranking officers, whose position and personal prestige may be needed to secure the entire army's acquiescence, successive ones may be organized by those in the lower ranks whose major advantage is that they are too inconspicuous to draw the government's full attention.[24] The chain of command becomes a perverted arrangement as each fear those below him. It is at least a moot point as to whether those qualities necessary to be a good conspirator (or to wind up on the 'winning side' in a context when conspiracies occur often) are antithetical to the virtues normally associated with being good soldiers.

The aftermath of a coup d'état, even one which successfully avoids violence (and, therefore, the 'necessity' perhaps to kill those who resisted) normally results in a continued erosion of military potential. The reasons are obvious. The pressure to consolidate the conspirators' position immediately will compel the new government to make many changes in the chain of command. Political considerations will be paramount in determining who gets promoted, discharged, rotated, and so on. As one might expect there are numerous instances of frightened and disappointed officers organizing countercoups, before the conspirators can entrench themselves.[25]

Praetorian governments have utilized many mechanisms to reduce their vulnerability. (I can only enumerate a few here, and those external to the regular forces (that is, secret police and paramilitary units) will be ignored.) Sometimes, a measure may increase the reliability of an army initially, and even inadvertently increase its military strength. But the development of maximum military potential can never result as an unintended by-product. In any case, the long-run or cumulative impact of many typical measures do weaken an army's ability to operate in the field.

Ancient despots usually recruited foreign mercenaries, persons who by their origin or status lacked legitimacy to make political claims. This practice is no longer common. It is certainly unusual to find standing armies composed entirely of foreigners, although there are some interesting exceptions. 'The regular army in the Gulf, which until recently was known as the Trucial Oman Scouts, is composed mainly of Dhofaris, Baluchis and the Bani-Kaab in addition to the Adenis, Persians, Indians and Pakistanis; only one of which can claim local tribe roots'.[26]

A more conventional way to achieve the same result is to concentrate foreigners in the officer corps, a lever not really available to the ancient despotisms where the distinction between officers and ranks was not nearly as sharp or politically significant. In any case, in Latin America, when professional armies were established during the late nineteenth century giving many states their first moments of domestic peace, German and French officers played dominant roles. When those officers were withdrawn, praetorianism ensued. The armies of black Africa were all reliable when whites dominated the officer corps; and when they were replaced, military conspiracies ensued immediately in most countries (for example, Nigeria and Kenya). When Jordan relieved British-born officers from their commands, military unrest materialized for the first time. An insecure government may find special units of foreigners useful too. The elite guards of Palestinians and Libyans saved Uganda's Idi Amin from his army several times.

Foreign mercenaries will always be resented. But in a state where power must be exercised in the name of the people, native soldiers and the public will feel a special anger, humiliation, and fear for policies which reserve important positions for persons who are not members of the people and, therefore, mercenaries have a very limited precarious tenure. The 'news' that the Syrian dictator Za'im was organizing a special corps of Yugoslav Muslims contributed to his downfall.[27] Cuban soldiers saved Congo-Brazzaville from military upheavals several times, but the resentment and hostility their presence created in the end overwhelmed them. The revolt of Arabi in nineteenth-century Egypt came in response to a decision to rely more heavily on Turco-Circassian officers.

A second common practice is to organize the armed forces into units so hostile to one another that a rebellion by one will automatically stimulate a violent reaction in others. The objective is most effectively realized when the individual units are wholly composed of separate ethnic groups which have been traditional enemies in civil society.

> If a prince's body guard is all from one race, then he is ever the prisoner of his body guard and tamely submissive for the reason that the members of one race will be in alliance together making it impossible to use them in holding each other in check.
>
> Mohamud constantly overawed the Hindus by means of the Turks and the Turks by means of the Hindus with the result that both nations submitted to him for fear of the other.[28]

The hatreds excited often cause military disasters, as they did in the 'Middle Period' of the Byzantine Empire.[29] The Seljuk Empire nourished an unending series of blood feuds which eventually destroyed it, and the original military policies of the Ottoman Empire, successor to the Seljuk, suggest that the lesson was not forgotten. The Ottoman standing army, the Janissaries, was originally composed of slaves wholly isolated from their original social context, educated in a new culture and faith to be the Sultan's instruments. For several centuries, they fulfilled their purpose but were finally destroyed when they became unmanageable. In the nineteenth century, the Sultans began to revert to Seljuk practices producing sometimes painful and predictable results.

Among contemporaries, ethnic antagonisms are not always present (for example, much of Latin America, Egypt, Turkey, and Tunisia.) Where they do exist, exploitation may be more difficult because professional ethics and nationalism combine to reduce the government's ability to limit officers to units of a single ethnic character. Sometimes, too, members of one ethnic group may prove so competent that the positions held by them in the officer corps create resentments sufficient to generate a military insurrection; note the fate of the Ibos during Nigeria's first wave of military turbulence in the 1960s.

In those countries of the Middle East, Africa, and Asia where ethnic differences (tribal, confessional, and national) are used, they sometimes do produce an uneasy military peace. The probability of success, in the short run at least, increases when potentially troublesome elements can be confined to the technical services and to the air and naval arms – branches less able to organize or prevent coups. The monarchies of Jordan and Morocco have their deepest support in the Bedouin and tribal populations who dominate infantry and armored units. Bedouins normally are reluctant to join standing armies. King Idris of Libya's strenuous effort to recruit them failed, and his monarchy was overthrown by Colonel Kaddafi depending upon soldiers from urban areas. Recognizing that obstacles in enticing nomadic elements into regular armies could not be overcome, the Saudis have devised a unique solution. The regular army consists of technical and junior services, while the tribesmen constitute a national militia formidable enough to have frustrated several coup attempts.[30] Other states in the Arabian peninsula follow similar practices.

In a striking way the ethnic base which contemporary monarchies of the Arab world have sought has been realized recently in Syria, too, though that state professes radical egalitarian principles. The comparative stability realized since 1963 is partly attributable to the reconstitution of the Syrian army's ethnic base. The rural mountain elements – the Alawi, and to a lesser extent the Druze and Ismaili – now predominate, replacing the majority urban element – the Sunni who had produced so many coups and countercoups after independence that the state nearly disintegrated.[31] Traditionally, urban elements in the Islamic world have had little cohesion and have been difficult to subordinate; in some respects the partial reinvigoration of Syria is reminiscent of patterns which could be observed in some ancient despotisms. The 'Alawi are prisoners of their situation for if military coups become common again the resentful Sunni may have an excellent opportunity to exact a fierce revenge. 'The 'Alawi officer cadre has recognized that its fate is tied to that of Asad. The new elite of Syria, under his leadership, has a guarantee of security and advancement. The 'Alawi officers can anticipate extinction if he is overthrown.'[32]

In the absence of ethnic rivalries to exploit, praetorian governments will cultivate the natural antagonisms between the services. While navies and airforces are in poor positions to execute a coup (because they cannot occupy ground or capture important public officials), if they simply threaten to bomb cities or army posts, conspirators will often withdraw. Conspirators normally depend on negative sentiments toward the government, and even token resistance by military units or civilians may have disproportionate effect because it may reveal how hollow positive support for the conspirators is.

In the ancient despotisms conspiracies could originate from any rank; in the later phases of the praetorian period they often came from the lowest. Contemporary praetorian armies, following the Western practice, divide their forces into two unequal and potentially hostile classes – officers and enlisted men – and a coup, as opposed to a mutiny, organized by enlisted men is rare. Still, every coup requires indifference from the enlisted ranks, at least. Peron of Argentina encouraged enlisted men to organize unions to deal directly with him to redress grievances. More than once they frustrated coups, but the policy, as one might expect, turned too many officers against Peron and the devotion of the ranks had its limits. In Brazil, President Goulart managed to bring about his own overthrow (1964) by soliciting support of the enlisted personnel in the army and navy.[33] In the nineteenth century, Columbia and Ecuador weakened the powers of officers so much that they could not maintain discipline or prevent mass desertions. Trujillo in the Dominican Republic diminished the significance of his officers by more conventional and effective means; he kept them rotating so quickly (none occupied a post for more than three months) that they lacked opportunities to establish appropriate contact with their men!

All governments, praetorian or not, seek to prevent soldiers from taking independent actions which might have political consequences. But the margin of safety is so narrow for insecure governments that they feel compelled to supervise directly most actions, subjecting virtually all conceivable acts to written regulations. Officers themselves may welcome the development since regulations provide protection against actions which might otherwise be questioned: but inevitably the regulations become so cumbersome and absurd that officers feel justified in circumventing them, and the rule-abiding sentiment which every formal organization requires is further undermined.

So victimized by fear have praetorian governments become that some have deliberately sought to destroy the capacities of their armed forces to defend the country against its neighbors, reasoning that weak governments are served better by impotent bodies. At the turn of the century, for example, a British historian found the military policies of the Ottoman Sultan scarcely credible.

> For many years manoeuvers were forbidden, gun practise was discouraged and the discipline suffered [because] of the cruel hardships to which the men were subjected as well as systematic suspicion entertained by the palace towards any officer who ventured to give evidence of superior merit . . . Abdul Hamid feared his fleet more sincerely than his army. Consequently he worked towards its destruction with the same zeal other monarchs have worked towards the perfection of theirs. Millions were squandered on ships which were neither fit nor meant to go to sea . . . The dockyards were encumbered with machines bought at exhorbitant prices to rust unused.[34]

The ultimate sanction government has, is the power to disband the existing army and replace it with a new force. A move in this direction normally produces fierce reactions. In Chile the 'unauthorized' but tolerated efforts of Allende supporters to create a new army (which would 'always' support his government) deeply enraged officers, becoming a key element in making the continent's most reliable army rebel.[35] In very special circumstances, a regular army can be dismantled. Castro was able to establish a new Cuban army because the old one had disintegrated and he already had forces loyal to him. Nyerere accomplished the remarkable feat in Tanzania, because of aid given by British troops and the fact that the army had not really been established for a long time.[36] After many attempts to eliminate them had backfired, the Janissaries were massacred in a brilliant plot in 1826 by Mahmud II.

(3)   VENALITY AND ECONOMIC CONCERNS

(E)nrich the army – nothing else matters.

Emperor Severus

Small bodies of soldiers quartered in trading and manufacturing towns, and seldom removed from those quarters, became themselves tradesmen, artificers and manufacturers. The civil began to predominate over the military character; and the standing armies of Rome gradually degenerated into a corrupt, neglected, and undisciplined militia incapable of resisting . . . attack.

Adam Smith

The donative originated in the custom of Roman generals during the Republic who distributed a share of the plunder to their troops at the conclusion of a successful campaign. The emperors completely disassociated the payment from its original context. Donatives were provided during peace, presumably to relieve the emperors from pressures to pursue more aggressive foreign policies.[37] They were also designed to secure the emperor from domestic political anxieties for they were normally offered at critical moments, that is the decision of the emperor to designate a successor, the accession of a candidate, and the suppression of a particularly dangerous conspiracy.

By divorcing the act from the only circumstances which could have justified or limited it, the emperors completely transformed the act's symbolism and practical import. Soldiers now received special sums of money for turning on their own countrymen. The imperial donatives had nothing to do with *military* achievements; they were given largely in anticipation that soldiers would be tempted to conspire. The irony is that they strengthened the temptation they were designed to destroy, for clearly there was now a vested interest in both successful and unsuccessful conspiracies!

The corruption of the Janissaries initially stemmed from a different but related perversion. The sultans were accustomed to receiving shares of war booty from their soldiers. But the need of the sultans for money grew so great that they began to accept gifts from their soldiers during peace and ultimately sold places in the corps. Commanding officers unsuccessfully resisted the policy knowing full well what the consequences were likely to be.[38]

Governments too insecure or too shortsighted to insist that discipline *continue* to be based on impersonal principles will, whether they want to or not, begin to depend upon links forged by the selfish appetites of soldiers. The gap between government and public grows and simultaneously the capacities of an army to regulate itself for any common purpose is undermined.

Originally, Marx thought that only Spanish civil officials lacked 'what they call public spirit in Europe.'[39] In time, he came to believe that most Spanish soldiers, *even* the worker and peasant conscript, were demonstrating the same selfish concerns – their character being 'indicated by a rebellion of a regiment which not being satisfied with the mere cigarros of Isabel struck for five franc pieces and sausages of Bonaparte, and got them too.' The development could have been predicted. The moral qualities which governments exhibit inevitably influence every rank of the army to the extent that the government depends upon them.[40]

If soldiers qua soldiers cannot find glory through achievement or self-respect through efficiency, their occupation becomes more and more a means to pursue amenities. Thus, on his deathbed, the Roman Emperor Severus, who died from natural causes unlike his predecessors, purportedly whispered the secret of his success to his two eager heirs: 'Stick together and enrich the army – nothing else matters.'

Something else *must* have mattered, because the lavish expenditures of Severus's successors could not prevent them from being overthrown. Yet so often do contemporary praetorian states provide attractive amenities that soldiers themselves are quite likely to believe that the ancient counsel is still paramount. An Egyptian officer reports, for example, that Iraqi officials in 1954 advised him that the secret of government in the Middle East lay in attending to the soldiers' allowances.

> [The Regent] was convinced that the officers were loyal to the throne and to the Hashemite family. He listed the many benefits which the officers enjoyed: they were given villas, their pensions were generous, and they received a full year's salary as a bonus on retirement. He spoke on this subject for half an hour. 'Faruq,' he said, 'treated his officers very badly. That is why you carried out your revolution.'[41]

Still, in the end, the Hashemite dynasty also disappeared in a military coup.

Academics, too, sometimes succumb to the notion that everything a praetorian army does must be paid for. A student of Peru says that '*every* government deposed by a military coup in the twentieth century had reduced the armed forces' share of the national budget'; and, conversely, every government successful in expanding its power by illegal means made a prudent addition to the military budget beforehand. Yet, we should be told, too, that some governments in Peru increased military allowances and were still overthrown, while others decreased them and managed to survive.[42]

Security cannot be purchased in the long run; the Muslim world more than any other concerns itself with allowances, but remains certainly among the most unstable.[43] One wonders how wise a policy of this kind is even in the short run. The fate of Allende is worth pondering. His predecessors successfully resisted demands for larger budgets. Knowing that his tenure would put greater strains on the loyalty of Chile's military, he decided to pay for what he might ask in advance.

> Allende started by openly recognizing the justice of the 'professional demands' which had led to Viaux's 1969 revolt. Throughout his term, Allende constantly sought to meet many of these demands; his government raised military salaries at every rank. These increases were generally more favorable than those applied to equivalent civilian

salary grades, special home construction credit was given to officers along with increasing housing allowances, automobiles and scholarship for military children. Travel opportunities were also increased. After Allende came to power officers in uniform could be seen in the better Santiago restaurants and hotels for the first time in years. Faced with falling copper prices and food shortages, the Allende government confronted a chronic foreign exchange crisis. Yet funds were always produced for new military equipment. The navy received new ships. In September 1972 the government allowed the air force to investigate purchasing new airplanes although it had placed a moratorium on the importation of many categories of capital goods. Between 1970 and 1973 the defense budget rose dramatically despite inflation.[44]

When the armies of Tanzania, Uganda, and Kenya mutined in 1964, only the Ugandan government dealt with the problem as one which could be settled primarily with 'donatives'. Perhaps Obote in Uganda, like Allende in Chile, knew that his policies later would require extra measures of loyalty. Whatever the full explanation for the decision might be, it seems reasonable now to think that he would have been better advised to follow the 'hard-line' policy of Kenya and Tanzania. Their governments still control their armies. But Obote was ousted a few years later by the army's 'candidate', Amin.[45] Once the 'candidate was elected,' the Ugandan army found itself at his mercy – an outcome repeated many times in the Roman Empire.

No one can demonstrate whether 'donatives' will succeed or fail in specific situations; too many other issues are likely to be pertinent. But, clearly, most praetorian governments believe that on balance a 'donative' *at least* provides additional insurance at a cheap cost. In a very important sense, the pressure to provide 'donatives' comes from the *fragmented* nature of the army; the fact is that if only a few resist, coups are likely to be aborted. The government makes a payment to all (which no one can refuse) in the hopes that it will reach a significant few who cannot be identified ahead of time.

All things being equal, the more often donatives are offered, the less effective each becomes in purchasing support; while, at the same time, it also becomes more necessary to offer them and the cumulative consequences become more unbearable for every one.

Military expenditures are the largest item in the budgets of most states, and in a praetorian one where domestic security is always pressing, governments will assume burdens that they cannot meet. The consequences were most vivid in the ancient despotism because they were generally self-contained economic entities, and the wealth they had was wealth they produced or gained in war. Ibn Khaldun notes that the wealth of the despot is greatest before praetorianism begins, but when loyalty must be purchased the supply of money diminishes, and the ruler, against his will, must drastically reduce military expenditures. A century and a half after Severus gave his infamous advice, Rome 'could neither feed her citizens, provide for the upkeep of her administration, nor pay her troops; every year her people were becoming more impoverished and her burdens heavier, while at the same time her forces were less.'[46] In despair, the last emperors devised the cheapest army possible – an ethnic one, barbarians led by their own chiefs 'who had neither the luxury of Roman soldiers, nor the same spirit, nor the same pretension.'[47] The existence of a true international economy in the modern world, where economic aid by nonpraetorian states and investment by foreign firms are always possible, generally prevents contemporary praetorian states from reaching such desperate economic straits; but the military budget problem is still considerable.

The everincreasing demands of soldiers can only be met by strengthening productive capacities. But those who work efficiently, save, and invest, need reasons to do so; and without stable government to guarantee the future, economic energies must be depressed. When wealth makes men personally vulnerable, the prudent will make their money less visible. In the democratic praetorian state they send it abroad, and in the despotism they buried it underground; in either case it is withdrawn from productive use.

To secure funds governments embark on economic policies which ultimately provoke great hostility and general apprehension. The 'easiest' or most painless policy in the short run is one of 'printing money', depreciating coinage, or inflating the economy. Ultimately, dissatisfactions will lead to a policy of redistributing wealth, by expropriations, expenditure reductions, and additional taxes. But both policies have direct and indirect effects on the army exposing soldiers to more antagonism, with the result that they either want a higher price for their services, and/or they become more vulnerable to public indictments. In the Ottoman Empire, military conspiracies often took place in the context of popular riots concerning the cost of living and were generally followed by property redistributions.[48] The sequence of events is still quite commonplace. '[Peruvian officers] are disillusioned with [their] own unpopular police action which has been the means of maintaining the country's anachronistic social and economic status quo.'[49]

Governments everywhere reward supporters unequally. But a policy shaped by principles of equity is one thing; one which shifts always in response to immediate political difficulties is another. Indonesians fighting Malaysian and British troops on the Borneo front in the 1960s were unpaid for six months,[50] and Spanish soldiers who tried to put down Cuban rebellions during the nineteenth century did not receive their salaries for more than a year.[51] Those fighting overseas were not in a position to menace their governments; the comfortable soldiers who stayed at home were. But how long can governments survive such manifest injustices?

No government, moreover, starts afresh; each is burdened by commitments made by many predecessors. In all states, the effort to reduce budget shares involves enormous political resistance because nothing can mobilize the power of entrenched interests faster. In the praetorian state, where the power to say 'no' is always greater than it is in any other kind of state, a reduced military budget is the surest way to generate insurrection.[52]

Frequent changes of government compound the problem. Every new government in a praetorian state will seek to consolidate itself; and that is true regardless of whether it originated in a legal or illegal manner. Compensations have to be given to those you want out of the way, when you lack the desire or an acceptable justification to deal with them by other means. Spain experienced approximately eighty legal and forty-four illegal successions in more than a century, and the cumulative toll on the armed forces was staggering. Early in the twentieth century, she had nearly as many officers as enlisted men, and 141 admirals for two major warships! Throughout most of the nineteenth century, one soldier in a hundred was a general, and the Spanish had nearly six times as many officers per enlisted man as the French army did. The money Spaniards spent for 80,000 soldiers would have subsidized a German force nearly twice as great — a force which would have always been available, and would be much better trained, equipped, and cared for. In 1914, the Rumanian army cost as much as the Spanish did. But it was three times as large, and better equipped and trained.[53]

Spain, furthermore, during the late nineteenth century established two armies, one on duty and the other in retirement. As their inheritance from successive governments accumulates, many Latin American and Middle Eastern states can make the same boast nowadays. Perhaps Spain would have been wise to reduce the legacy; but the soldiers on duty, who had a future to consider, may have thought otherwise, and the discovery of a new use for retirement plans enabled Spain to perfect the bloodless coup d'état — her special contribution to modern praetorian dynamics.[54]

When an officer retires, the Latin American quips, he always conspires. Spanish history of the nineteenth and twentieth centuries provides a dreary list of illustrative examples; the Middle East now is beginning to produce its own inventory. The consolidation of Syria's Baath regime during the 1960s was made much easier because previous governments had retired large numbers of Baath officers who were able and eager to man all critical positions in the regular army.[55]

Two armies are expensive luxuries. In time, Spain found that she could not afford to pay officers on active duty adequate salaries. Lieutenants were forbidden to marry without showing evidence of an independent income or a fiancé who could support them — a circumstance hardly calculated to improve morale.[56]

There were so many officers that finding a job for one on active duty was difficult, especially as only 'loyal' officers could hold several commands simultaneously. Nearly half on regular duty lacked specific assignments. For most, there was ample time, and considerable economic need to take second and third jobs. Spanish governments, like many in a praetorian quandary, encouraged the practice which kept soldiers busy, fed, and out of cafes where everyone talked politics endlessly.

To meet personal expenses, which always multiply during idleness, some took great liberties with military payrolls, filling them with fictitious names and with those too old or too young to serve. Sometimes, the scale of the practice became visible and, hence, the subject of public indignation. In the height of the Moroccan campaign of 1921, 'a sizeable minority of the 20,500 Spanish troops supposedly serving in the Mililla zone were actually away on leave or did not exist except on paper. Berenguer could only find 1,800 military personnel in the town, most of them clerks and supply personnel.'[57]

Similar patterns appear in the despotic praetorian state. On paper, the military forces of the late Roman Empire had twice as many as those in the early empire, but the actual numbers who participated in the late campaigns were one-third as many as those who took the field earlier, which suggests the earlier armies were six times more efficient. In the Ottoman Empire, as the Janissaries enrolled more members their efficiency declined, as did the numbers they could muster for a campaign. One reason was 'that many unqualified persons, either elderly people or children enrolled . . . with the obvious purpose of obtaining pay.'[58]

The 'hardest' item in a praetorian military budget must be allowances for personnel, especially in the higher ranks;[59] while the 'softest' ones will be for a war which may never come. To save money, a large portion of the Spanish military was placed on prolonged leave. There were no funds for maneuvers, training, and adequate logistic support. No wonder, perhaps, that Engels, one of the nineteenth century's most perceptive students of military strategy and tactics, was so appalled by the Spanish performance in Morocco, that he argued that Spanish military capacities had declined from a high point in a much earlier age. 'Superior' equipment simply became *impedimenta*, giving the Spaniards 'a degree of slowness unheard of in . . . warfare'; it took one army sixteen days to move twenty-one miles over a route travelled by another Spanish force of a similar size in one day four centuries before. 'The habit of handling large bodies of troops seems to have *become* quite lost to the Spanish generals.' The troops no longer understood elementary principles of skirmishing; they possessed a 'defensive mentality', even when facing smaller numbers of less well-trained and equipped foes.[60] In virtually every war of the nineteenth and twentieth centuries foreign observers echoed Engels's views.[61]

Similar difficulties troubled the last armies of the Ottoman Empire.[62] For the *first* time in Rome's history, the emperors complain during the third century that their soldiers lack training and adequate equipment. In Latin America, the necessity to cut costs operates in the same way. A foreign officer, who observed them, notes that the armies 'are not built for war and can be expected to experience considerable difficulties in operating away from their garrisons . . . [They] provide a show of force rather than actual fighting potential. It may not be necessary for a tank's guns to be loaded if the noise and mass of the tank is enough to instill fear.'[63] To prevent governments from interfering too much in military affairs, praetorian armies seek promotion procedures inappropriate to the military purpose. Every successful soldier and military theorist since Xenophon has tirelessly emphasized that the officer's character (that is, his fortitude, concern for detail, ability to inspire trust, and capacity to decide quickly in circumstances of great danger), is the critical factor in shaping the fighting qualities of an army. A good promotion policy gives ample scope for the personal judgement necessary to recognize these qualities. But when men who award promotions lack credit, those being judged will want 'objective criteria' applied. Despotic and democratic praetorian armies regularly make excessive claims for seniority; contemporary ones exaggerate the importance of formal schooling and written examinations as well.

In Spain, the seniority principle was embraced early and completely in the Artillery and Engineering Corps, and soldiers exerted constant, sometimes effective, force to expand the principle everywhere else, a pressure which finally exploded in the military syndicalism of the early twentieth century. This curious development, which almost literally turned the Spanish army into a trade union, was a response to a wartime emergency!

Too few members of Spain's enormous officer corps had volunteered for colonial conflicts. To fill gaps, men from the ranks were given battlefield commissions and special promotions were offered to officers in Spain. The policy may have been abused, regular officers may have been 'pathologically' suspicious of government; whatever the reason for military syndicalism, the surge toward it had grave implications. Army officers themselves would not permit military excellence to be recognized, overaged officers held commissions, younger men seethed with discontent, and virtually everyone was demoralized.

Perhaps, the Spanish predilection for syndicalism came 'naturally' for another reason; praetorian armies generally participate in the economy as producers. Quite obviously, a government's economic burden will be eased if soldiers contribute as well as consume wealth, but the policy has, in the past, hastened the deterioration of economic and military capacities – a fact sufficiently important for Adam Smith to note.[64]

The early Roman Empire was wealthy and it encouraged, though it never fully realized, a market economy. As the cost of government rose, it seemed sensible to let soldiers contract services to municipalities. Civilian technicians could not compete with subsidized army specialists, especially as the latter often threw in government materials illegally. The supply of civilian technicians diminished, and dependence on uneconomic military monopolies grew. In the final stages of the empire, Diocletian introduced a military socialism whose products by earlier standards were incredibly shoddy.[65]

In the Ottoman Empire, the Janissaries took up crafts; and artisans in self-defence purchased their way into the corps to pursue their vocations more profitably. Ultimately, the soldiers became so identified with the 'working classes' that one observer likens them to a 'Tammany Hall Association . . . an essential aid and protection for the poorer section.'[66] Yet neither the economy nor the craftsmen themselves could benefit from a policy constructed to enhance the immunities and privileges of a special group.

The circumstances which induced praetorian soldiers in the ancient despotisms to undertake commercial activity still exist, and they are reinforced today by two additional, important considerations. The first is that egalitarian ideologies in the underdeveloped world have encouraged the proliferation of state-managed enterprises, and the latter, in turn, provide suitable alternatives for officers whom governments want to remove from military posts for political reasons. The second is that officers have been encouraged (partly by the writings of American and European academics) to believe that their own military experiences provide them with a special ability, which their civilian counterparts lack, to appreciate the requisites of modern organization and technology. Yet the reasons which explain the soldier's dismal economic record in the ancient world still seem quite applicable. When an advocate of military-managed economies in Latin America tells us that no Argentine government would 'dare oust the military from control' no matter how inefficient they are, one wonders why any one could be confident of the military's capacities.[67] It may still cost less to let a praetorian army lie idle rather than risk putting one to work!

(4) IMPOTENCE

Four brave men who do not know each other will not care to attack a lion. Four less brave, but knowing each other well, sure of their reliability and consequently of mutual aid, will attack resolutely. There is the science of military organization in a nutshell.

Colonel Ardant du Picq, *Battle Studies*

Regardless of the weapon technology available, the effort to sustain, let alone improve, an army's cohesion, and therefore its fighting capacities, never ends. Under the best conditions, when a political order is stable and the government commands the respect and loyalty of its soldiers, this is true. The praetorian state multiplies the obstacles.

The consequences were familiar to traditional political commentators. Ibn Khaldun notes that twelfth-century Arab soldiers *no longer* dug entrenchments to protect their bivouacs, could *no longer* fight in closed formations (which required a more exacting discipline), and that rulers sought Christian and Turkish recruits who were much more amenable to discipline.[68] Montesquieu says that praetorian armies can launch 'incursions' but cannot 'wage war.' He means that they sometimes fight well behind fortifications but they *cannot* sustain offensive actions. I have already described Engels's amazement at the deterioration of Spanish military potentialities.

The relationship between praetorian politics and military capabilities is a subject which soldiers are sensitive to, but which academics virtually ignore. Even the isolated statement like Eliezer Be'eri's interpretation of why the Iraqi army could not resist the British invasion in 1940 is rare.

It is hard to find an explanation for the walk-over victory . . . One reason may have been the excessive politicization of the officer corps. The activism of the officer politicians gave them victories over the politicians . . . and even over rival officers in their own army. But it made the army weaker. They turned the army from a force serving the state into a tool in the struggle for hegemony within the state, and in that way the foundations of both state and army were undermined.[69]

The weakness of praetorian armies does not escape notice. One scholar describes the military records of Latin American armies as 'undistinguished', and another says the Burmese army continually wasted its resources in combat; yet both ignore their findings to emphasize the superior 'organizational rationality' of those armies.[70] Harkabi, alone, seriously discusses the lack of cohesion in Arab armies during the Six Day War. He finds this to be the main cause of their defeats, and attributes it to deficiencies of national character, without touching on the more immediate and visible consequences of praetorianism.[71]

Space precludes a systematic discussion of praetorian capabilities. One would have to develop the notion of what a good army entails first.[72] And one would have to recognize the significance of the fact that those capabilities may wax and wane dramatically depending upon the credibility, durability, purpose, determination, and skill of particular governments. Catastrophic defeat in the Six Day War, and the demoralizing experience in Yemen provided Sadat with justification to move the Egyptian army away from politics, which materially improved its performance in the Yom Kippur War. The relative stability of the 'Alawi regimes in Syria since 1968 provided a similar opportunity.

Still, a few suggestions to supplement earlier comments are pertinent. As a government's physical insecurity and weakness becomes clearer, a series of actions and reactions occur which make officers suspicious and contemptuous not only of that government but of each other as well. Everyone sees additional reasons and opportunities to concentrate on those personal concerns which ultimately subvert the military purpose. General Fazal M. Khan's recollection of why the Pakistani army was so inept in the war against India in 1971 is very much to the point.

> When General Yahya Kahn came into power in March 1969 the armed forces . . . got a spurt of promotions. The number of higher ranks was almost doubled overnight. Such bulk promotions became a topic of *ridicule* even within the army . . . The selection system for officers' promotion was thrown overboard . . . This *capriciousness* naturally resulted in a scramble for promotions . . . Indifferent climbers acquired higher ranks . . . bringing them closer to the President.

While the deterioration was dramatic after the 1969 military takeover, it began when earlier regimes (both civilian and military) tried to prevent their own destruction.

> The appointment of Yahya Khan as C-in-C in 1966 and his out-of-turn promotion had caused considerable upheaval in the senior ranks. [At the same time] the appointment of military governors in the provinces took away a number of . . . highly qualified officers [and their staffs] who should have been in the field. With so many officers busy elsewhere in extra-military duties [the army's] efficiency was seriously affected . . .
>
> Due to the absence of a properly constituted political government

(from 1955 to 1971) the selection and promotion of officers to the higher ranks depended on one man's will. Gradually, the welfare of institutions was sacrificed to the welfare of personalities . . . The higher command had been weakened by retiring experienced officers at a disturbingly fast rate. Those in the higher ranks who showed some independence of outlook were invariably removed from service. Some left in sheer disgust in this *atmosphere of insecurity* and *lack of the right of criticism,* the two most important privileges of an armed forces officer.

Our armed forces, though small in strength, were superior to those in India in tactical doctrines and organizations when the India-China war took place in 1962. We still had the ascendency in these spheres in 1965. *But we had been declining according to the degree of our involvement in making and unmaking regimes.* Gradually, the officer corps, intensely proud of its professionalism, was eroded at its apex into third class politicians and administrators.[73] (my emphasis)

War, soldiers tirelessly reiterate, is preeminently a cooperative activity requiring mutual support. A tank advances because a second exposes itself to provide cover. 'Readiness for a daring mission is predicated on the knowledge that one's audacity is not a desperate adventure. You are sent on a dangerous task not through indifference to your fate but because the operation is necessary and everything will be done to help you or if necessary to rescue you.'[74] The logic of praetorianism, on the other hand, is a logic of distrust, and it is hard to imagine anything which will destroy the morale and fighting capacities of military organization faster.

Mutual support entails trust which, in the first instance, is belief in the *willingness* of others to come to your aid even when they must endure great danger themselves. The soldier who believes himself alone in hazardous circumstances normally surrenders to his fears and fends for himself. The most important instrument in creating confidence is the quality of military leadership – the dispositions of the officers. Pakistani officers, General Khan laments, forgot and abandoned their men. Numerous analysts of the Arab–Israeli wars detail the indifference of the Arab officers to the fate of their charges and their disinclination to take risk – a prudence which ultimately betrayed an extraordinary pre-occupation with self-preservation.[75] The same problems plagued nineteenth- and early twentieth-century Spanish armies; and it generated, as it does now, hatred and contempt from the men toward their leaders.

Trust implies willingness to delegate authority, to allow officers to make decisions freely and group units together in accordance with tactical situations. An atmosphere of distrust militates against this possibility, and the inability to delegate authority is frequently cited as a factor crippling military capabilities in contemporary Arab states, in praetorian Spain, in the Byzantine Empire, and in the praetorian phase of the Ottoman Empire.[76] But sometimes the mistrust is justified. Kassim, in Iraq, was unwilling to let a unit larger than a brigade be placed under a single command. When the Kurds rebelled he had no choice, whereupon a golden opportunity to bring him down was exploited.

To make cooperation fruitful and to make planning pertinent all relevant parties have to be consulted and useful information must be shared. Information, however, concerning the conditions of units can be exploited for personal purposes, and one shares as little reliable information as possible with as few as possible in an atmosphere of intrigue and uncertainty. In the Pakistani GHQ, where officers often were not on 'speaking terms with each other,' the services could not cooperate and units were sent to battle before an understanding of their potentialities was clear and 'without the proper notice required for smooth and deliberate action.'[77]

Conspiracies require deceit, deceit generates distrust, and distrust intensifies the impulse to deceive. Harkabi describes the cumulative effect on the Arab armies in the Six Day War.

> If the channel of communication . . . becomes a channel for exaggerated reports and lies, the situation can lead to catastrophe. All too often each echelon adds an additional measure of false data to the false reports received from its subordinate level. This can create a situation in which the command has no interest in separating truth from falsehood . . . but, on the contrary, may be prepared to accept false reports in order to glorify . . . the exploits of its units. In such a case, none of the levels, including the supreme level, can act from knowledge of the situation. Decisions, therefore, are faulty, subordinate levels are caught in a vicious circle. On the one hand, they know that the command prefers to receive favorable reports – even if this is false boasting – and, responsively they supply them. On the other hand, they cannot trust orders of their command since they know they are based on incorrect data.[78]

While trust initially means confidence in the willingness to help, it can be sustained only if those willing to aid are competent. Competence implies appropriate standards and periods of time committed to mastering and demonstrating mastery of those standards. The praetorian state undermines both possibilities. It compels soldiers to be preoccupied with police and political concerns; it sucks them into a maelstrom of economic activity. Promotion policies of governments reflect their insecurity and extramilitary commitments. If the soldier is to stay within the law, he is likely to press for second-best promotion standards which encourage 'rank-inflation' and 'objective criteria' like 'seniority' and 'written examinations' in lieu of true character and performance evaluations.[79] To be sure, in this last respect, praetorian armies are not distinctive. In all bureaucratic armies this tendency is significant, and sometimes it has disastrous consequences, as the American army in recent years has demonstrated.[80] Still, in praetorian armies these developments are more visible and dangerous because justifying them is easier and the resources available to contain them are fewer.

(5) ONE LAST LEVEL

It is easy to say that the praetorian soldier is too selfish to care. But his predicament is more profound, his life more pathetic. He has become impaled on a system he cannot understand, love, or leave; and he fights it by taking more than he gives – justifying himself by insisting that everyone else does the same thing. But just as he cannot believe what others tell him, he cannot have confidence in his own arguments; and he manifests shame and guilt in peculiar ways. During peace, suicides among Spanish officers were less frequent than in any other European army – which suggests that they took their responsibilities less seriously. But during war, when suicide rates fall, the Spanish rose dramatically to exceed that of any other European force. The meaning of a wasted life was driven home in a vivid fashion.

The praetorian army is a corrupt army; the purposes professed are constantly undermined by its own actions, and members are turned further and further away from it and from themselves. The sources of the problem are the lack of credit in political life and the army's inescapable position as a subordinate and dependent order.

Corruption is manifested on several levels: hypocrisy regarding appropriate standards, and debasement in substituting standards which are hopelessly inadequate – as the passion for 'objective criteria' suggests. More important is the corrosion of human potential. Distrust leads to impotence, despair, and self-contempt; and distrust perverts judgement in unexpected ways.

Skeptical of human capacities, the praetorian soldiers, for example, place extraordinary faith in material objects. Ibn Khaldun tells us that they want big, expensive, and useless weapons. In the early period of the Ottoman Empire, her artillery was the most efficient in Europe; but during the praetorian phase, her cannon grew so large they could not be moved in battle. The Spaniards in the Morocco campaign of the 1920s were immensely proud of their big cannon, feeling that no military move could be taken without them, and employed them so profusely that one Spanish officer in disgust exclaimed that 'cannon would be used to kill flies.'

For the most part my discussion has focused on the obvious. Corruption does mean standards violated and standards debased, and the praetorian army can be discussed in these terms. But corruption also means a perversion and deterioration of the human character, and on this level the action is subtle, morbid, and intensely interesting. It will be said that the perversion of character is not relevant to the subject of contemporary social science, but then one wonders how relevant contemporary social science is to *its* subject.

NOTES

1 Lucian Pye, 'Armies in the process of political modernization,' in J. J. Johnson (ed.), *The Role of the Military in Underdeveloped Countries* (Princeton, NJ: Princeton University Press, 1962), pp. 69-70. Similar views are advanced by virtually all the other contributors to the volume, and by Dankwart Rustow, *Politics and Westernization in the Near East* (Princeton, NJ: Princeton University Press, 1956), Guy Pauker, 'Southeast Asia as a problem area in the next decade, '*World Politics*' vol. 2 (April 1959), pp. 335-45; Daniel Lerner and R. D. Robinson, 'Swords and plowshares: the Turkish army

as a modernizing force' *World Politics,* vol. 13 (October 1960), pp. 513–59, P. J. Vatikiotis, *The Egyptian Army in Politics* (Bloomington, Ind.: Indiana University Press, 1961), Trevor N. Dupuy, 'Burma and its army', *Antioch Review,* vol. 20 (Winter) pp. 60–1, Joseph La Palombara, 'An overview of bureaucracy and political development' in his *Bureaucracy and Political Development* (Princeton, NJ: Princeton University Press, 1963), pp. 3–33, Marion Levi, *Modernization and the Structure of Society* (Princeton, NJ: Princeton University Press, 1968); Morris Janowitz, *The Military in the Political Development of New Nations* (Chicago: University of Chicago Press, 1964); idem, *Military Conflict* (Beverly Hills, Calif.: Sage, 1975); and idem, *Military Institutions and Coercion in Developing Countries* (Chicago: University of Chicago Press, 1977).

2   James S. Coleman and Belmont Brice, Jr, 'The role of the military in sub-Saharan Africa,' in Johnson (ed.), *The Role of the Military,* p. 359. My unpublished doctoral dissertation, 'Praetorianism: Government without Consensus' (University of California, Berkeley: 1960) was, as far as I can tell, the first discordant note in the chorus of general approval of military governments for unenlightened peoples. See also my essay, 'A comparative theory of military and political types' in S. P. Huntington (ed.) *Changing Patterns of Military Politics,* (Glencoe, Ill.: The Free Press, 1962), Samuel Finer's excellent *The Man on Horseback* (London: Pall Mall, 1962), also challenged the existing trend early but on different grounds — differences I discuss in 'The political dimensions of military usurpation,' *Political Science Quarterly,* vol. 83 (1968), pp. 551–72.

3   *Revolution in Spain* (New York: International Publishers, 1939), p. 96.

4   ibid., p. 73.

5   ibid., pp. 55 and 161. The volume consists of articles written at different times. Its view keeps shifting in response to troubling events, and the general trend is toward deeper and deeper pessimism. Predictably, they believed that the revolutionary spirit was more profoundly entrenched in the lower ranks and the praetorian one in the higher levels. Still, Marx's eventual disgust with the selfish pettiness of the rank is unmistakeable, ibid., p. 154.

6   Engels was keenly sensitive to the value of comparative studies of armies and political systems as his 'The armies of Europe' (*Putnam's Monthly,* vol. 6, 1855) illustrates. But despite Marx's letters urging him to do so, Engels never consummated that interest. On the whole, Roger Owen is correct in saying that on this subject Marxist writers have produced very little which is interesting. Soviet writers are inclined to follow Western fashions and speak of the military as a 'modernizing' force, at least when talking about military conspirators sympathetic to the Soviets. See Owen, 'The role of the army in Middle Eastern politics . . .,' *Review of Middle Eastern Studies,* vol. 3 (1978), p. 68, and G. Mirsky, 'Developing countries: the army and society,' *New Times,* vol. 48, (3 December 1969), pp. 15–17.

7   E. Nordlinger, *Soldiers in Politics* (Englewood Cliffs, NJ: Prentice-Hall, 1977).

8   A. Perlmutter, *The Military and Politics in Modern Times* (New Haven, Conn.: Yale University Press, 1978). I had argued that the problems of praetorian governments were fundamentally the same, regardless of whether officials had civilian or military origins, and that in such states the boundaries between civilian and military spheres were largely permeable. The characteristic of praetorian states was not that they produced military governments, but rather that all governments produced lived in fear of military conspiracies.

9   Henry Bienen argues that the concept of praetorianism cannot illuminate the *mutual* interaction of governments and armies because it creates a view of government too weak to shape military patterns. Bienen only has Huntington's discussion of praetorianism in mind, and it differs greatly from mine which Huntington claims as a source for his. Huntington aims to marry two conceptions based on wholly different assumptions – modernization and praetorianism. Consequently, he often uses the term praetorian to mean a strong military regime when, in fact, it should always refer to a set of underlying tensions dividing governments and armies. H. Bienen, 'Military and society in East Africa; thinking again about praetorianism,' *Comparative Politics,* vol. 6 (July 1974), pp. 489–518, W. R. Thompson, 'Regime vulnerability and the military coup,' *Comparative Politics,* vol. 7 (July 1975), pp. 459–80, and A. Perlmutter 'Egypt and the myth of the new middle class,' *Comparative Studies in Society and History* (January 1970), pp. 14–26.

10 Lucian Pye ('The Burmese army . . .,' in Johnson (ed.), *The Role of the Military*, pp. 73–4) ignores Spanish and Latin American experiences because the military has always had 'authoritarian if not reactionary values.' Yet, as the writings of Marx and Engels indicate, the Spanish army once seemed a promising force to astute radicals. A similar story can be told of some early reactions to particular Latin American military coups. Janowitz excludes both experiences because the historical struggles in Spain and Latin America 'have produced political institutions different from those of the new nations.' But the history referred to is one of military conspiracies; on that ground alone it might be relevant. Janowitz is certain that military conspiracies in the new states are a 'transitional phenomena'; *when* 'modernity' is achieved the political role of armies will wither away (Janowitz, op. cit., preface). But until that day comes, we think comparisons could be very useful.

11 'Bureaucracy,' in H. Gerth and C. W. Mill (eds), *From Max Weber* (New York: Oxford University Press, 1946), p. 202. Weber, elsewhere, describes the ancient world as having achieved full rationality only in the military sphere. Clearly, Weber's discussion of the relationship of rationality (or 'modernization') and democracy have not been always understood by many students of military organization who cite him.

12 The Guard's importance, compared to that of other units, originally derives partly from its proximity to Rome. It was the only military force in Italy. Later, other legions asserted themselves but since they were scattered over a huge empire and had to march to Rome to install their candidates, there was time for resistance to develop, producing civil wars sometimes instead of coups d'état. In other early examples (e.g. the Ottoman Empire), the monarch's bodyguard was *the* standing army. Today, as in Rome, a praetorian army usually consists of elite units (normally called Presidential Guards) and regular ones. But the resentment that the privileges of an elite unit generate in a world hostile to the dynastic principle and the different logistical situation make it impossible for Guards to 'represent' the army and, by the same token, make coups by regular units feasible. The chief significance of elite units today seems to be in the prevention, rather than in the making, of coups d'état.

13 The word 'seem' is appropriate because it is hard to imagine unconditional oaths. See my 'The political dimensions of military usurpation'.

14 The nature of the Guard's predicament is symbolically revealed in the aftermath of its first uprising. Those who assassinated Caligula and installed Claudius were then executed by the new emperor, while the Guard itself received additional amenities!

15 Montesquieu, *Considerations on the Causes of the Grandeur and Declension of the Romans*, trans. Jehu Baker (New York: Appleton, 1901), ch. 19.

16 My 'Rome; fides and obsequim, rise and fall,' in J. Pennock and J. Chapman (eds), *Legal and Political Obligation*, Nomos 12 (New York: Atherton Press, 1970), p. 247.

17 For discussions of the Tocqueville and Maine distinction see my dissertation, 'Praetorianism: Government without Consensus,' chs 4 and 6, and the extremely perceptive unpublished one of Herbert Gooch, 'Coup d'Etat; Historical and Ideological Dimensions of the Concept' (University of California, Los Angeles, 1977), esp. ch. 13.

18 My 'The political dimensions of military usurpation' discusses how eighteenth-century commentators saw the 'democratic element' in despotism.

19 No praetorianism is possible when civil and military occupations cannot be distinguished, when the organization of armies conforms to hereditary principles, or when warriors supply their own equipment. In the first case, it becomes impossible to speak of an uprising by soldiers; in the others, the ability of government to organize its army is too circumscribed.

20 The concept of the 'people', of course, is fraught with ambiguity and means different things in various parts of the modern world. In the Middle East, the identity of the people is always in dispute, occasionally referring to the population within existing territorial units, sometimes signifying an Arab nation, and often meaning Islam itself. The confusion only complicates praetorian typologies, since it indicates political expressions can easily transcend borders; witness the history of the United Arab Republic and the mutual intrigues by neighbors in each other's armies during the 'Arab Cold War' of Col. Nasser's era. See Malcolm Kerr, *The Arab Cold War* (London: Oxford University Press, 1971).

21 The considerable interest in praetorianism in the past fifteen years has not yet resulted in useful classifications. The despotic or ancient form is ignored. The analyses of

modern materials speak of the 'institutionalization of praetorianism' – a contradiction in terms. Hardly anyone recognizes that there is a necessary relationship between popular sovereignty and the spread of the phenomena. There is, finally, little interest in attempting to trace the boundaries of praetorian politics in particular states for prolonged periods of time. Cf. S. P. Huntington, *Political Order in Changing Societies* (New Haven, Conn.: Yale University Press, 1968), A. R. Luckham, 'A comparative typology of civil–military relations,' *Government and Opposition,* vol. I (1971), pp. 5–34. E. Feit, *The Armed Bureaucrats* (New York, Boston, Mass.: Houghton Mifflin, 1973), E. Nordlinger, *Soldiers in Politics* (Englewood Cliffs, NJ: Prentice-Hall, 1977) and Perlmutter, *The Military and Politics in Modern Times.*

22   It is also argued that military cohesion is, or can be, converted into political strength. Oddly, the proponents deny themselves tests to gauge military cohesion. Hence, Johnson notes that it 'is easier to create armies than to develop . . . modern . . . civil administrations and political parties,' but the contention is supported only by describing the formal structure of the armies, the formal schooling of its men, and the equipment bought. The same criteria would lead us to believe that other aspects of the state were modern, too. We find it easy to speak of 'paper constitutions'. Is the idea of 'paper armies' inconceivable? (*The Military and Society in Latin America* (Palo Alto, Calif.: Stanford University Press, 1964), pp. 50–1). Academics generally have no interest in what military critics might have to say about the organizational qualities of a particular army. Note, for example, praises for the Egyptian army by social scientists who seem oblivious to very different judgements by soldiers cf., H. Halperin, 'Middle Eastern armies,' in Johnson (ed.), *The Role of the Military,* p. 285, and Vatikiotis, op. cit., p. xiii, with Edgar O'Ballance, *The Sinai Campaign* (London: Faber, 1959), pp. 43–4; and R. Henriques, *One Hundred Hours to Suez* (London: Collins, 1957), pp. 78–9.

23   For a discussion of the effect of repeated conspiracies on a political system as a whole, see my 'Coup d'état: the view of the men firing pistols,' C. J. Friedrich (ed.), *Revolution* (New York: Atherton Press, 1964), pp. 53–74.

24   The conspirator capitalizes more on negative public sentiment than on his own positive assets; unless other factors intervene the disparity between these two dimensions grow in successive coups, though rarely will the conspirators come from the NCO ranks. Too often coups are taken as evidence of an army's strength, instead of illustrations of the argument that *almost* anyone can overthrow a government which everybody else has abandoned! Perhaps the best, certainly the best 'unknown', discussion of military coups appears in Ortega Y. Gasset's *Invertebrate Spain* (London: Allen & Unwin, 1937). In the spring of 1980 the first coup in Liberia's history occurred and was organized by a master-sargeant, Samuel Doe. Presently the information which might help explain this exceptional case is not available.

25   See my 'Political Dimensions'.

26   F. L. Khuri and G. Obermeyer, 'The social bases for military intervention in the Middle East,' C. M. Kelleher (ed.), *Political–Military Systems* (Beverly Hills, Calif.: Sage, 1974), p. 68.

27   Patrick Seale, *The Struggle for Syria: A Study of Post-War Arab Politics, 1945–58* (London: Oxford University Press, 1965), p. 61.

28   Nizam al Mulk, quoted by C. E. Bosworth, 'Ghaznevid military organization,' *Der Islam,* vol. 36 (1960), p. 51.

29   W. E. Kaegi, Jr, 'Patterns of political activity of the armies of the Byzantine Empire,' in M. Janowitz and J. van Doorn (eds), *On Military Intervention,* (Rotterdam: Rotterdam University Press, 1971), p. 19. In the 'early period' (305–610) balancing ethnic elements was less destructive because they (i.e. the Germans and Huns) were foreign mercenaries and as pagans were unable to press political claims.

30   Whether it is appropriate to speak of Jordan, Morocco, Saudi Arabia, etc., as praetorian states is moot, since none has experienced a successful military coup d'état. But all witnessed attempts and the fear of military conspiracy is the distinguishing characteristic of *my* understanding of praetorianism. The practice of recruiting potentially troublesome minorities for the 'weaker' branches is quite common. In Malaysia, a non-praetorian state, non-Malays are in the navy and air force. In Burma, a praetorian state, Karens are concentrated in the air force (from which they have attempted unsuccessful rebellions), while Indians and Eurasians are in the navy. While the ethnicity element in military organizations has received much attention recently, the

studies have not been useful in specifying conditions under which a praetorian government is likely to gain more security. See Cynthia Enloe, 'Issue saliency of military–ethnic connection: some thoughts on Malaysia,' *Comparative Politics*, vol. 10 (1978), pp. 267–85 and her 'The military uses of ethnicity,' *Millennium*, vol. 4 (Winter), pp. 75–6, 220–34, and the 'Symposium on racial and ethnic relations in the armed forces,' *Armed Forces and Society*, vol. 2 (Winter 1976), pp. 227–304, Asaf Hussein, 'Ethnic national identity and praetorianism; Pakistan,' *Asian Survey*, vol. 16 (October 1976), pp. 918–30.

31   The 'Alawi and the Druze have been frequently compared to the Bedouins for their martial qualities and intense group loyalties. But modern academics usually scoff at the notion that some cultures stress military virtues, and the term martial groups appears in our literature as 'martial races.' The consequences are that we find it easy to explain the political reason for the practice of colonial empires staffing their armies with minority ethnic elements from outlying rural areas, while we are inclined to regard the military justification as a smoke-screen.

32   Moshe Ma'oz, 'Alawi military officers in Syrian politics, 1966–74,' in H. Z. Schifferin (ed.), *The Military and State in Modern Asia* (Brunswick, NJ: Transaction Books, 1976), p. 285. For additional bibliography and a most useful discussion of the question, see Alasdair Drysdale, 'The Syrian Armed Forces in National Politics,' Chapter 3 in this volume.

33   Occasionally, conspirators will, for one reason or another, seek to develop support *primarily* among the rank-and-file (e.g. Batista in Cuba and Amin in Uganda).

34   G. F. Abbott, *Turkey in Transition* (London: Arnold, 1906), p. 323. A similar picture is provided by Sir E. Pears, 'Abdulhamid apparently dreaded both in the army and navy . . . a tendency towards improvement of any kind' (*Forty Years in Constantinople*, New York: Appleton, 1916), p. 222). Cf. Kaegi, op. cit., p. 21.

35   A. L. Michaels, 'Background to a coup . . .,' in C. E. Welch (ed.), *Civilian Control of the Military* (Albany, NY: State University of New York Press, 1976), pp. 298–9.

36   Bienen, op. cit.

37   G. R. Watson, *The Roman Soldier* (London: Thames & Hudson, 1969), pp. 108 ff. The Roman army, like virtually all armies prior to the eighteenth century, expected war to produce booty and, thus had a 'vested interest' in new wars.

38   H. Gibb and H. Bowen, *Islamic Society and The West* (London: Oxford University Press, 1950), Vol. 1, pp. 178 ff.

39   *Revolution*, p. 7. The words are those of a nobleman cited to illuminate the peculiarities of Spanish politics.

40   ibid., p. 154. It is not clear whether Marx originally was justified in distinguishing between the attitudes of civil and military appointees or whether 'events' made his initial distinction untenable. In any case, he quickly learned from his mistake.

41   Seale, op. cit., p. 203.

42   Arnold Payne, 'The Peruvian coup d'état of 1962: the overthrow of Manuel Prado,' (Washington, DC: Institute for the Comparative Study of Political Systems, 1968), p. 59. For a better discussion, see Victor Villanueva, *El militarismo en el Peru* (Lima: Empressa Gráfica T. Scheuch, 1962) and J. S. Fitch, *The Military Coup d'Etat as a Political Process, Ecuador: 1948–66* (Baltimore, Md.: Johns Hopkins University Press, 1977). Those who find a notion of praetorianism useful, have a conspicuous tendency to 'overkill' on this issue. Nordlinger (op. cit., p. 78) for example, argues that the 'great majority' of military conspiracies have the enhancement of 'corporate interest' as an object, and that 'since civilian governments jeopardize corporate interests far more than do military governments, we can safely assume that such threats have engendered a higher proportion of coups against civilians.' W. R. Thompson ('Corporate coup-maker and types of regime target,' *Comparative Political Studies*, vol. 12 (January 1980), pp. 485–96), demonstrates that both conclusions are improbable and finds it odd that they are offered. Nordlinger's difficulty, I think, comes from a failure to view the issue in *systemic* terms. A system is praetorian simply if it produces governments which are vulnerable to pressures of this sort, and whether coups actually do enhance amenities most of the time, or not, is irrelevant. The difference between 'civilian' and 'military' governments in a praetorian state also is not likely to be great, though civilians are likely to feel more insecure vis-à-vis the military and, therefore, *more likely* to be lavish!

43   Thompson, op. cit., p. 492.
44   Michaels, 'in Welch (ed.), op. cit., p. 293.
45   Bienen, op. cit.
46   Albert de Broglie, *L'Eglise et l'Empire Romain au IV siècle* (Paris, 1856–66), Vol. 2, p. 229.
47   Montesquieu, op. cit., XVIII.
48   Mary L. Shay, *The Ottoman Empire From 1720 to 1734* (Urbana, Ill.: University of Illinois Press, 1944), p. 31.
49   Richard Patch, 'The Peruvian elections of 1963,' *American University Field Staff Reports,* vol. 10, no. 1 (July 1963), p. 1.
50   *Observer* (26 June 1966).
51   Stanley Payne, *Politics and the Military in Modern Spain* (Stanford, Calif.: Stanford University Press, 1967), pp. 50, 67.
52   The problem must be put into perspective. Praetorian states, characteristically, have highly inflationary economies which, of course, devastate those who live on salaries. There is also a sense in which one thinks of one's present level of remuneration as a right or property, and when 'cut-backs' are demanded they create real feelings of injustice.
53   Payne, op. cit., pp. 87–8 and 99. There is probably no serious effort to compare costs in praetorian and non-praetorian states. S. Andreski's *Parasitism and Subversion* (London: Weidenfeld & Nicolson, 1966) provides statistics to show how much less Mexicans pay for their army since praetorianism has been curbed, compared to that paid by citizens of Latin American praetorian states – a major reason for Mexico's superior rate of economic growth. Sometimes a text will provide an odd interesting comment, like the fact that Argentina in the 1960s had as many generals as the USA did, though its army was one-twentieth the size. The corruption of the Spanish army, of course, was not simply a consequence of praetorianism. A variety of internal pressures can produce a similar phenomenon. 'Rank inflation,' for example, was quite conspicuous in the US forces in 1969, which had more generals and admirals than in World War II, though the forces were then nearly four times as large. Military critics argue that the rank inflation and the extraordinary absence of officers in the middle ranks in Vietnam contributed to demoralization and poor military performances. See the excellent dissertation of Jonathan Balkind on this subject, 'Morale Deterioration in the United States Military' (University of California, Los Angeles: 1978).
54   For a discussion of the development of the concepts necessary to make bloodless usurpations conceivable, see my 'The Political Dimensions of Military Usurpation.'
55   A. I. Dawisha, 'Syria under Assad, 1970–78; the centres of power,' *Government and Opposition,* vol. 13 (1978).
56   Payne, op. cit., p. 124.
57   ibid., p. 168.
58   Abdue K. Rafeq, 'Local forces in Syria in the seventeenth and eighteenth centuries,' in V. J. Parry and M. E. Yapp (eds), *War, Technology and Society in the Middle East* (London: Oxford University Press, 1975), p. 279.
59   Henriques, (op. cit., p. 78) notes that Israelis believe the Egyptian 'officers are too fat, the men too lean.' The Spanish army was even more obviously inadequate; the enlisted ranks rarely had adequate food and clothing rations.
60   *Revolution*, p. 194 (my emphasis).
61   Payne, op. cit., pp. 76, 159–60, 216, 399, 534.
62   Abbott, op. cit., p. 323 and Rafeq, op. cit.
63   Theodore Wyckoff, 'The Role of the military in Latin American politics,' *Western Political Quarterly,* vol. 11 (September 1960). The problem, of course, is partly that the armies are used for police purposes and the police role is very different from the military one.
64   *Wealth of Nations,* bk V, ch. 1 sect. 1.
65   Ferdinand Lot, *The End of the Ancient World* (New York: Barnes & Noble, 1961), pp. 136–7.
66   Gibb and Bowen, op. cit., Vol. I, p. 295.
67   Johnson, *The Military and Society,* p. 130. In the last decade interesting efforts have been made to compare the economic records of military and civilian regimes. Necessarily, the criteria are crude and somewhat unreliable, but the evidence clearly

shows that the early optimism was not warranted. Those who speak of praetorianism (Nordlinger and Huntington) argue, as one might expect, that there must be a difference between military and civilian regimes. Those who have studied the question seriously conclude the difference to be insignificant. Unfortunately, the comparisons are not pertinent to understanding praetorianism, for soldiers will always be 'managing' important parts of the economy regardless of whether the regime is civilian or military. The questions should be: What are the differences between praetorian and non-praetorian forms, between civilian and military sectors of the same economy, and finally between systems which are relatively stable and those which are not? The pertinent literature is reviewed in R. W. Jackman, 'Politicians in uniform; military government and social change in the Third World,' *American Political Science Review*, vol. 70 (December 1976), pp. 1,078–97. The most perceptive discussion of the issues is Jerry L. Weaver, 'Assessing the impact of military rule; alternative approaches,' in P. C. Schmitter (ed.), *Military Rule in Latin America; Function, Consequences and Perspectives* (Beverly Hills, Calif.: Sage, 1971), pp. 58–116.

68 Ibn Khaldun's military facts, David Ayalon tells us, 'prove . . . to be right repeatedly . . .' 'Preliminary remarks on the Mamluk military institution in Islam,' in Parry and Yapp (eds), *War, Technology* op. cit., p. 44.

69 *Army Officers in Arab Politics and Society* (New York: Praeger, 1970), p. 39. Cf. General Leeman von Sanders's discussion of the problem in the late Ottoman Empire, *Five Years in Turkey* (Annapolis, Md: William Wilkins, 1927).

70 Johnson, *The Military and Society*, p. 3 and Pye, 'The army in Burmese politics,' in Johnson, (ed.), *The Role of the Military*, pp. 238–9.

71 Y. Harkabi, 'Basic factors in the Arab collapse during the Six-Day War,' *Orbis*, vol. 11 (Fall 1967), pp. 677–91. For other discussions of praetorian military performances, see W. E. Allen and P. Muratoff, *Caucasian Battlefields* (Cambridge: Cambridge University Press, 1953) and David Zook's works, *The Conduct of the Chaco War* (New York: Bookman Associates, 1961) and *Zarumilla – Maranon; The Ecuador Peru Dispute* (New York: Bookman Associates, 1964).

72 See my 'Military and civil societies: the contemporary significance of a traditional subject in political theory,' *Political Studies*, vol. 12 (June 1964), pp. 178–201.

73 *Pakistan's Crisis in Leadership* (Islamabad, 1973), pp. 151–2, 258. I am indebted to my colleague, Richard Sisson, for suggesting Major-General Khan's book.

74 Harkabi, op. cit., p. 678.

75 O'Ballance, op. cit., Henriques, op. cit., and Harkabi, op. cit.

76 Kaegi, (op. cit., p. 26) states the issue concisely. 'Byzantine emperors never found the appropriate device to give a general sufficient troops and supplies to wage a successful military campaign without at the time risking the possibility that this general might employ these men and materials to seize the imperial throne for himself.'

77 Khan, op. cit., p. 262.

78 Harkabi, op. cit., pp. 687–8.

79 One source of Arab military weakness, General Glubb argues, are proclivities for drawing officers from an urban university context and for substituting schoolroom for military standards. 'Conflict between tradition and modernism in the role of Muslim armies,' *Texan Quarterly*, vol. 9, no. 2 (Summer 1966), pp. 135–48. Be'eri (op. cit., p. 346) says that Arab nationalists complained that Glubb placed 'excessive emphasis on character and past service' in Jordan and 'did not sufficiently value an academic diploma as is customary in the Syrian army.' However, military critics considered the Jordanian army of the time better than the Syrian; and it was certainly more reliable.

In Africa, particularly Nigeria and Uganda, there has been violent strife between those who would carry the seniority principle to unreasonable lengths and those who insist too much on formal schooling requirements. See A. R. Luckham, 'Authority and conflict in the Nigerian army; 1966,' in Morris Janowitz and Jacques van Doorn, *On Military Intervention* (Rotterdam: Rotterdam University Press, 1971), Vol. 2, pp. 203–32, N. Kasfir, 'Civilian participation under military rule in Uganda and Sudan,' in H. Bienen and D. Morell (eds), *Political Participation under Military Regimes*, (Beverly Hills, Calif.: Sage, 1976), pp. 69–70 and J. M. Lee, *African Armies and Civil Order*, (London: Chatto & Windus, 1969), *passim*.

It is interesting to note that military critics of American performance in Vietnam pointed to an unreasonable concern with 'objective criteria' in 'efficiency reports' where significant items are those which can be quantified and where character appraisals (especially initiative and commitment to the troops) are de-emphasized. When 90 percent of the officers receive rating which place them in the upper 10 percent, something must be wrong. See Jon Balkind's excellent PhD dissertation, 'Morale Deterioration in the United States Military,' (University of California, Los Angeles, 1978), pp. 118–19.

80 'Rank inflation' was quite conspicuous in the American forces in 1969 which had more generals and admirals than in World War II, though the military in the earlier period was nearly four times larger. Military critics argue that rank inflation and the extraordinary absence of officers in the middle ranks in Vietnam contributed to demoralization and poor military performances. See Balkind, 'Morale Deterioration,' pp. 115–16 and his 'Lessons from Vietnam; critique of military sociology,' *Journal of Strategic Studies,* vol. I, no. 3 (December 1978), pp. 237–59.

12 The Morphology of Military Regimes

SAMUEL E. FINER

Now that the causes, courses, and immediate consequences of the military coup have been reasonably well established, interest is focusing on the kinds of regime that result from them.[1] From the outset, the literature clearly recognized that it was inadmissible to make a hard and fast dichotomy between civilian and military regimes, and that military regimes (whatever these might be) shaded off by degrees into civilian ones.[2] What was not so clearly recognized was the diversity of regimes which could properly be regarded as 'military', even under a restrictive definition. To classify these is likely to be fruitful in at least three ways: in enabling us to mark off the 'military regime' for purposes of comparison and contrast with other kinds; in furthering our understanding of what military rule entails or implies; and, finally, in certain practical applications one of the most important of which is in the field of development theory. It is now reasonably well established that if regimes are dichotomized into military versus civilian, there is precious little to choose between the developmental performance of the one class as contrasted with the other.[3] Now, this conclusion would be readily explicable if it turned out that military regimes exhibited as much diversity among themselves as civilian regimes.

The classification I offer is not inconsistent with previous schemes, and some of the distinctions made in the past form a constituent part of my analysis, notably those of Nordlinger and Perlmutter, as well as my own earlier efforts.[4] But the present analysis differs radically from all preceding ones I am familiar with, in stemming from one simple brutal and paradoxical question: 'Who governs in a military government?'

At first sight this is curious, indeed paradoxical, since the question invites the retort, that if the government is characterized as 'military', then the military must rule it by definition. To respond, let me set out the bare strategy of my thought. It will then be seen that, far from being otiose, the question leads us further and further down a path to ascertaining where, in a military regime, power really lies.

First of all, it is necessary to establish what regimes can, in some sense or other, be regarded as 'military'. I am now satisfied that this cannot be done in any other way than by successive exclusions until we are left with a core of *candidates* for qualifying as 'military' regimes. Further examination starts with the simple brute question: Do military personnel who in some sense either command and/or represent the armed forces wield supreme executive power? If they do not, then the regime is something less than a military one and conceivably is not a military regime at all. Next, I ask: Even assuming that military personnel do wield supreme executive power, is this power checked or diluted by other governmental agencies such as parties or legislatures? *A fortiori,* in the alternative hypothesis that the military as such do not wield supreme executive power, and if, additionally, whosoever does wield it is checked or directed by political parties or by legislatures, we shall have a regime far removed from those where military personnel wield executive power unchecked and untrammelled by any other political organizations or institutions.

The answers to such questions will establish whether it is the military or civilians who run the central organs of policy formation. But these are not the only site of political power. The bureaucracy, or the political party, for instance, may be colonized by military personnel, who might, therefore, exercise significant power irrespective of whether or not they control the supreme policy-making organs. *A fortiori,* if the military do control those organs, its colonization of party or bureaucracy will add to their power in the polity.

And yet supposing this to be the case; there still remains the further question: What does it *do* with this power? Does it merely control society and economy (or as Perlmutter so picturesquely puts it, merely 'patrol' it),[5] or does it direct it? Does it perhaps even actively administer it?

(1) WHAT KIND OF REGIMES MIGHT QUALIFY AS MILITARY ONES?

At first sight it seems easy enough to define a military regime: it would be the regime that results from a military coup. But, in that case, what about regimes which are constrained and directed by a military that has not overthrown the civilian government, but whose wishes are adopted by it in the sure knowledge that the military is the first and the last resort against domestic violence or insurrection? Or what are we to say about a situation such as France's in 1958, where a General de Gaulle came to power as a direct result of military intervention, but then operated under constitutional restraints and sent the army back to barracks?

The truth is that the class of 'military regimes' embraces a number of distinct subtypes which merge, gradually, into civilian regimes.

Where we choose to draw the line is stipulative. At the 'most civilian' end of the spectrum there exist, for instance, regimes which in law are constitutional and party-competitive, but where the constitutional guarantees are suspended for long periods. Consider, for instance, Sri Lanka, where a state of emergency was maintained for the seven years 1971–7 during which time no less than 18,000 persons were imprisoned.[6]

Next, there is a sizeable group of countries with a constitutionally appointed chief executive or head of state who is, however, exquisitely reliant on the active support of his military forces. Many are, supposedly, 'constitutional monarchies' – Jordan or Morocco, for instance. Some are absolute monarchies like the Sultanate of Oman, or the Emirate of Bahrein. And at least one is the remarkable example of the Philippine

Republic where President Marcos (duly re-elected in 1978) had introduced martial law way back in 1972, and then used its provisions to
suspend Congress, arrest opponents, censor the press, and then, with a
marvellous strategic sense, introduce a totally new constitution duly
approved by popular referendum, whose transitional provisions confirm
him in his role as President, Commander in Chief of the Armed Forces,
and martial law administrator, as well as giving him the additional post of
Prime Minister. Effectively he has been enabled to rule by decree without
challenge by any legislative or judicial tribunal, and to legitimize his
power by calling frequent referenda and rigged elections.

These are indubitably civilian regimes. To mark the military presence,
and the government's extreme reliance on this for their survival, we might
call them the *military-supportive regimes*.

We now come across another subclass of civilian regimes. Here, powerful and self-confident armed forces have intervened from time to time in
the past and will do so again, when they feel it their duty or interest to
'correct' the course that the civilian political forces are steering. A classic
illustration is the pressure exerted by the Turkish army (which had already
intervened in 1960), as a result of which in 1971 the Cabinet had to resign
and make way for one that imposed martial law over most of the country.
This was the way in which the Argentinian military intermittently intervened and withdrew throughout the 1960s. Both countries had 'civilian'
governments; if we wished to draw attention to this military pressure, we
could call them *intermittently indirect-military regimes*.

The next class of regimes is arguably much more 'military' than this. It
combines countries which are headed by civilian governments, who
attain, hold, and exercise power only in consequence of behind-the-
scenes military muscle and pressure. Guatemala, El Salvador, and
Panama provide current examples. We might with some justice call
regimes of this type *indirect-military regimes*.

Only at this point do we reach regimes whose chief executives, at the
very least, and whose entire executive branch, at the very most, are
openly and flagrantly military men who were installed, initially at any
rate, as a result of a coup by the armed forces. Such regimes are prima
facie *military regimes proper*. To put this another way: if any regimes are
to be called military, it will be these rather than the other types already
listed. The question to be asked is whether the military, as such, do in
fact rule in these regimes; and if not, how not. At the moment of writing[7]
there are twenty-nine such regimes. In another three, each the outcome
of a coup, the chief executives are civilians. For reasons explained below
there is a prima facie reason for temporarily including these in the class.
We have then, thirty-two states: Algeria, Argentina, Benin, Brazil,
Burma, Burundi, Central African Republic, Chile, Congo People's
Republic, Egypt, Equatorial Guinea, Ethiopia, Honduras, Indonesia,
Iraq, Libya, Madagascar, Mali, Mauritania, Niger, Pakistan, Paraguay,
Peru, Rwanda, Somalia, Sudan, Syria, Thailand, Togo, Uruguay, Yemen
Arab Republic, and Zaire. (Those with civilian chief executives are Iraq,
Uruguay, and the Central African Republic.)

In parenthesis it is worth noting that when I last undertook a similar

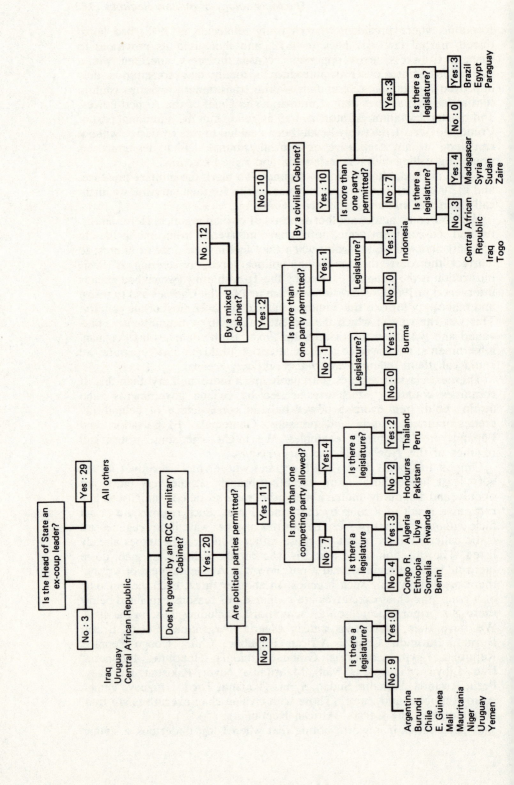

exercise, two years ago, there were forty states on the list. Three have been removed because their current status is provisional: they are Korea, since the assassination of General Park, where it seems that the regime will move toward a controlled competitive-party regime, with the military in support; Chad, in the grip of full-scale civil war; and Uganda, where a civilian government is maintained by a Tanzanian military occupation. Two countries which experienced military coups, Afghanistan and the Comoros Islands, have evolved civilian governments, though they are singularly different. The Afghan regime affects the Marxist–Leninist single-party style, backed by powerful and wholly indispensable military support. The Comoros, once the mercenaries who made the coup withdraw, is a no-party civilian government backed by the local police but with no military support to speak of. And finally, five countries have reverted to a competitive-party pluralist regime – Bangladesh, Ecuador, Ghana, Nigeria, and – after a complicated sequence of coups and countercoups – Bolivia, where the present (provisional) head of state is not a soldier, but is a woman politician.

Though the list was reduced by the foregoing ten states, two new ones have to be added. One is Mauritania, where Colonel Ould Salek deposed and took the place of the former civilian President, Ould Daddah. The other is Equatorial Guinea where the (civilian) tyrant, Macias, was ousted and then executed by his soldier-nephew, Obiang-Nguema, who took over his presidency. Both these coups occurred in 1979.

Now let me briefly recapitulate the strategy of this analysis. I am going to pose three questions in respect to the above mentioned thirty-two states. What is the role of the armed forces *as such* (in contrast to that of the leader they have installed) in governing the country? How does that government relate to the rest of the political system? And how does that system relate to the social and economic life of the country?

(2)   THE FORMAT OF THE MILITARY REGIMES

The entirety of what follows is best pursued by way of the following ALGORITHM (Figure 12.1). It provides a clear and sure guide to the successive stages in our analysis.

What distinguishes these thirty-two regimes from the indirect military regimes or the military-supportive regimes mentioned earlier, is that the chief executive has been installed by virtue of a military coup. As it stands, this statement is true of only twenty-seven of these countries. For the remaining five, it must be modified to read that the heads of state are latter-day selections by the military, subsequent to the original military coup. Thus: in Algeria, President Chadli is the immediate successor to President Boumedienne, in Brazil, General Figuereido is the fourth military President in succession to President Castelo-Branco; in Egypt, President Sadat is the immediate successor to Colonel Nasser; in Iraq, Mr Saddam Hussein is the immediate successor to President Bakr; in the Yemen Arab Republic, Salek is the third in line from the original ex-coupist head of state, his two predecessors having been killed in quick succession.

However, although all thirty-two heads of state are either ex-coup leaders or their militarily selected successors, not all of them are military men. Since the conventional wisdom has been to take the presence of a military ex-coup leader in the chief executive office as tantamount to 'military rule', the presence of a civilian in this office might seem to present a bit of a puzzle. This is easily resolved, however; the conventional wisdom is, quite simply, wrong. Subsequent analysis will show that whether a civilian or a military man occupies the chief executive post after the military coup is not in itself material to the question as to whether the military, as such, rule or not. The three countries with civilian chief executives are the Central African Republic, where Mr Dacko, a politician, was reinstated in office after the armed forces had overthrown Emperor Bokassa; Iraq, where Mr Saddam Hussein took the presidency over from Field Marshal Bakr after an inner convulsion in that country's ruling circles; and Uruguay, where, in 1976, the military chose to instal a civilian, Dr Aparicio Mendez in the presidency, in place of President Bordiguerry. We should be wrong to exclude these three countries at this stage from the category of prima facie military regimes. That is why, in the algorithm, the answers to whether or not the chief executive is a military ex-coup leader, are recombined, to press on to the next question, for this is the critical one. For it asks – whether he be military or civilian – does the chief executive govern with the counsel of a military junta or Cabinet?

This question is the critical one because the installation of a military man as chief executive by way of military coup does not necessarily imply that the armed forces, as a whole, or their senior ranks, or even that group of senior ranks who made the coup, will continue to play a creative part in shaping policy afterward. To anticipate a later suggestion, it is doubtful, for instance, whether the armed forces of Zaire play any significant part in framing high policy under President Mobutu, or whether the Egyptian forces do so under the presidency of Anwar Sadat. We must go on, then, to distinguish two groups of regimes.

In the first group, comprising eighteen countries, the head of state rules by, and through, a group of officers who are 'virtually' representative[8] of the armed forces, as such. In the Latin American countries this body is called the Junta Militar. Elsewhere (as our synoptic table in the appendix shows) it is called by such names as the Revolutionary Council, the Military Administration Council, the Military Committee, the National Policy Council, the National Security Council, and so forth. These bodies are very small. Sometimes they number no more than three persons; this is commonplace in Latin America where the most usual composition is the three service chiefs. The largest is the Dergue in Ethiopia, but this elects a small subcommittee which is the body to exercise effectual power. Thailand has a twenty-three-man council. The median number is eleven or twelve members. These bodies, together with the head of state, exercise supreme power, but appoint Cabinets for the day-to-day work of government. In some cases, these too are military. A large number are 'mixed'; but the greatest number are civilian in make-up. However, from the standpoint of the exercise of supreme power, the composition of the Cabinet is unimportant: in practice, two of the Cabinets are military, six are mixed, and nine are civilian.[9]

To the foregoing eighteen states which rule via the military juntas or councils, we must add two others. Neither in Benin nor Peru do we find a supreme military council but, instead, we find all-military Cabinets, so that the manner of rule is, in practice, identical with the eighteen listed above. We should also note two others where the military component in the mixed Cabinet is very substantial. It forms nearly two-thirds of the Burmese Cabinet, and well over a third of the Indonesian one. As a first hypothesis, one might surmise that in these two states the President makes policy in close, perhaps very close, consultation with the top military leaders, but not necessarily at their behest.

We have now accounted for twenty-two of our initial thirty-two states. This leaves Brazil, the Central African Republic, Egypt, Iraq, Madagascar, Paraguay, Sudan, Syria, Togo, and Zaire. In these countries there are no all-military councils or Cabinets; on the contrary, the Cabinets are predominantly or exclusively civilian. Once again, as a working hypothesis, we might surmise that in these countries supreme executive power is a personal exercise by the head of state and the military play a supportive role, not a creative one. But to help find out, we must turn from the supreme executive council, or Cabinet, and consider two other parts of the central governmental system, namely, the parties and the legislatures.

(a) Parties and legislatures in the military regimes

For two reasons we shall, in fact, be able to ignore the legislatures except in some idiosyncratic cases, and concentrate on the parties. In the first place, a legislature cannot be more autonomous of the executive than the party that controls it, though it may be less so. Secondly, in a one-party state, the legislature is otiose – and a large number of our states are of this kind.

In contrast, the nature of the political party, or parties, is significant. For our inquiry, two dimensions are relevant. The first is, simply, whether the party has a strong or a weak organization. The other, is its freedom from government direction. The two dimensions can be expressed as shown in Figure 12.2.

Parties will be characterized, then, as running along a spectrum from *nominal,* signifying that they are largely paper organizations, to *strong.* They will also be characterized as running along a spectrum of increasing autonomy vis-à-vis the executive branch. *Ancillary,* (from *ancilla,* a maidservant) connotes that the party is wholly subservient to the executive and carries out the tasks allotted to it. *Controlled,* however, suggests that the party has some freedom to select its tasks and mode of operation, but is always subject to the restraints or directions the executive imposes on it. The *symbiotic* party is one having extensive over-lapping membership with the military, so that both have a common ideology, and are regarded as two sides of the same, single coin, sharing a joint way and purpose. Here the party enjoys some good measure of

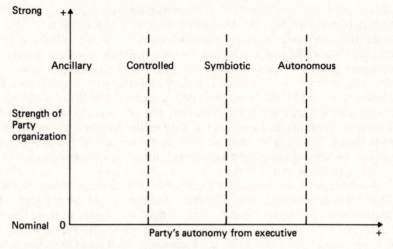

Figure 12.2   *The Party's Autonomy from the Executive*

parity with the military. The *autonomous* party is one that is free to adopt its own policies and determine its own operations.

We can now turn back to the algorithm and start interpreting it from extreme left to extreme right, and it will be seen that, by and large, this corresponds to a spectrum from complete or total military mastery at the left, to a marginal role for it at the extreme right.

First, let us look at the twenty states with supreme military executives, whether these be juntas or Cabinets, and we see straight away that nine of these have neither political parties nor parliaments. They are closed bureaucratic regimes with the military in supreme control. These nine states are not just the hard core of the military regimes; they are the ones that exactly conform to the stereotype of the 'typical' military regime. They are Argentina, Burundi, Chile, Equatorial Guinea, Mali, Mauritania, Niger, Uruguay, and the Yemen Arab Republic.

This leaves us with eleven states which do possess political parties. But seven of these are one-party states, to wit, Algeria, Benin, the Congo Republic, Ethiopia, Libya, Rwanda, and Somalia. (I must confess to some doubts about the status to attribute to Rwanda. Until 1975 it was a military-council type of state, but since that date, references to this body have disappeared. The Cabinet, at the end of 1979, was predominantly civilian, only three of its seventeen members not being civilians. Even so, it is noteworthy that these three soldiers control, respectively, the combined office of President and Prime Minister, the Ministry of the Interior, and the Ministry of Foreign Affairs, so that there can be no doubt that the key functions are held by the armed forces. Despite the lack of contemporary references to a Command Council, I have classified it as still possessing one.) In any event, it is clear enough that the key role is played by the military. What then of the political party? This was formed in 1975, is entitled the Mouvement national pour le développement, and was deliberately designed to try to reduce, or remove, intertribal conflict. The little evidence available suggests that it is a largely nominal artifact, controlled by the executive power.

Of the remaining six, the single, official parties, are all *ancillary,* despite the revolutionary rhetoric that credits some of them – for example, the Benin People's Revolutionary Party or the Parti Congolais de Travail – with a Marxist–Leninist orientation and a 'vanguard' role. In Libya, Benin, and the Congo Republic the organization is weak, perhaps nominal; at the most, it incorporates a narrow political elite. In each case, it is entirely subservient to the executive. This leaves only Ethiopia and Somalia for comment. The Ethiopian Union of Ethiopian Marxist–Leninist Organizations was created in 1977 as an umbrella organization for five groups, two of which subsequently withdrew. The Mengistu Mariam government has made great efforts to establish a grass-roots organization in the form of the *kebeles,* best summarized as local soviets, and his partisans in these *kebeles* launched the official 'red terror' of 1978. But there can be no doubt of the party's purely ancillary and subordinate role to the executive, and its organizational strength can best be described as only 'fair'. Of all the parties in this group, the only one whose organization can be described as even moderately strong is the Somali Socialist Revolutionary Party, founded only in 1976. Its chief task is political indoctrination carried out in the 'national guidance centres' and in the schools and supported by the people's militia known as the *gulwadashaya* (Victory Pioneers), which is an elite corps of young vigilantes. When President Barré proclaimed Somalia a one-party state in June 1976, he dissolved his Supreme Revolutionary Council, but its members automatically became members of the Central Committee of the new party, with President Barré as its Secretary General. Its subservient and ancillary status is beyond any doubt.[10]

Let us summarize: there are twenty states where the executive power is vested in the military by way of a supreme military council or junta, or an all-military Cabinet, and in nine of these there are neither parties nor legislatures. There the military rule untrammelled – and uncamouflaged. And we have now reviewed another seven, where single official parties exist. But these are subservient bodies, artifacts of the executive, and in all but two countries, organizationally feeble, if not quite nominal. They are part ornament, part instrument of the ruling military council and chief executive.[11]

There is still more to come. 'What?' one may cry, 'will the line stretch out e'en to the crack of doom?' Not quite, but we still have to consider those four countries, ruled by military command councils or juntas, where more than one political party exists, and where, in two cases (Thailand and Peru) there is a legislature as well. At first sight, this does look very odd – a supreme military executive coexisting with competing political parties and even, in Thailand and Peru, with an elected legislature. In fact, it is odd (if that is the right word) in only one case, Thailand. The other three paradoxes are readily explicable by a simple formula: each one is a case of a sudden arrest in the process of civilianization. In Pakistan, General Zia, having decided on a policy of constitutionalization in consequence of which he licensed the existence of political parties, took sudden fright at the strength of the one led by the relatives of former President Bhutto (whom he had imprisoned, tried, and refused to save from execution). So, at the moment, parties exist, but electioneering has been halted – hence no legislature, of course. In Honduras, much the same story: the former (military) President General Melgar Castro had, in 1977, licensed parties, with a view to the election of a Constituent Assembly in 1979 (later postponed to 1980). In August 1978, dissension over this and unrelated issues led the Supreme Council of the Armed Forces to depose President General Melgar. The Council did, however, express its intention to carry on with the process of constitutionalization. And there, for the moment, the matter rests. The Peruvian case is similar, but the process of constitutionalization has gone further, parties have been licensed, and the Constituent Assembly elected, but in the meantime the military junta remains.

In short, what we witness in these three cases is not a constitutional variant, but a frozen moment in the transition from military to civilian rule.

This is not true of our final case, Thailand. Its three-year interlude of civilian government (1973–6) was terminated by the coup of October 1976, after which parties were banned and martial law proclaimed. After a second coup, in 1977, the military drafted a new constitution skillfully designed to frustrate civilian efforts to regain power, and its provisions are enough to explain the apparently curious anomaly of a supreme military council as the executive, alongside competitive political parties and a freely elected legislature. The parties are certainly autonomous, although two are led by generals and the largest, the Social Action Party, represents an amalgam of civilian and military interests. Also, the elections were free (although less than 25 percent of eligible electors voted). What renders all this nugatory is the constitution under which (1) the Prime Minister possesses special powers to order the imprisonment, and even the execution without trial, of suspects, in the interests of national security; (2) the appointment of the Prime Minister, motions of censure and no confidence, and the approval of the budget must take place in a joint session of the two Houses of Parliament; but (3) the Senate, of 225 members, as compared with the 301 of the elected lower house, is wholly nominated by the Prime Minister. (Eighty-five percent of his nominees were military personnel.) The legislature is an area where the military–civilian cliques which form the Thai political elite can form combinations against the clique in office and/or legitimate its successor. It can qualify the way the military exercise power, but is incapable of removing them. It is not surprising that after the 1978 elections, three parties with 151 seats, boycotted the lower house in protest.

The Thai case terminates our classification of the twenty states where supreme executive power is vested, not only in a military head of state but a supreme military council, or all-military Cabinet: all, even the apparently 'constitutional' Thai case, are states where the military, as such, exercise supreme governmental power.

We must now turn to those twelve where, below the chief executive, we find Cabinets which are either mixed civilian–military or wholly civilian.

(b) Regimes with Mixed Civilian–Military or All–Civilian Cabinets

Here again, a glance at the algorithm suggests, prima facie, that the regimes will be more military-dominated on the left, and progressively less so as we move to the right. We must start with the two regimes where, although there is no supreme military council or all-military Cabinet, the military have a substantial stake in a mixed Cabinet, namely, Burma and Indonesia. These two regimes appear, at first sight, as somewhat less military-dominated than the twenty regimes so far considered, but more so than those we are about to examine. Is this so?

In Burma, the first point to note is that although the Cabinet is mixed, the military presence is very strong indeed: currently, ten out of seventeen. The second point is that the true strength of this presence is somewhat masked by the nature of the official party, the Lanzin (Burmese Socialist Program Party). From 1962–74 General Ne Win's government was of the military council type. In the meantime, the Supreme Military Council decided to politicize the army, and created the Lanzin Party, with a socialist program for this purpose. In 1964 all parties other than Lanzin were suppressed, in 1972 the members of the Supreme Military Council took off their tunics and became, officially, civilians, and in 1974 a new constitution was introduced which is ostensibly civilian. The Lanzin Party is symbiotic with the military leadership. It was modelled on the Leninist 'vanguard' model, its Chairman is (former) General Ne Win and its Secretary-General is General San Yu. Throughout the country, supporters are encouraged to associate with the party as 'candidate' members, or as 'sympathizers', but full members are carefully selected and correspondingly few. These persons, along with army officers, civil servants, and other leading personnel are trained in Lanzin's ideology and program at the Central School of Political Science, established immediately after the coup in 1963. The symbiotic relationship between the military and the party is attested by the extensive overlap between the two in the higher echelons of government: figures for 1971 show that all the members of its Secretariat, nine out of ten members of its Central Executive Committee, and three-quarters of its Central Affairs Committee and its Central Committee were soldiers.[12] In these circumstances the distinction between the military and the civilian is largely obliterated. And if we took into account at this stage the two other dimensions of a military presence which are to be disclosed later,[13] namely, the military colonization of the bureaucracy, and the extent of interference with the economy, both would indicate a truly gigantic military presence. In brief, the Burmese military, as such, run their country, and there is little to choose between the exclusiveness of their rule and what we have found in the previous twenty, supreme-military-council type of government.

In Indonesia, where the military also play a massive administrative and economic role which resembles that of the Burmese military, the constitutional arrangements suggest that it is less securely and exclusively in control of supreme policy-making than in Burma, and that the President, Suharto, is more independent of it; and this is the case. Indonesia is much more socially and territorially segmented than Burma and its military, too, have a history of extreme factionalism and segmentation, brought under control only within the last decade. A President has to steer a course between civilian 'tendencies' and communities, on the one hand, and the divided armed forces, on the other. He does so by 'managing' the potential civilian opposition (excepting the Communists, who are persecuted, and the students, who are forcibly suppressed) by licencing certain political parties and permitting the existence of an elected House of Representatives. Furthermore, although the Cabinet is predominantly civilian, only nine of its twenty-seven members being soldiers, closer examination shows that the military dominate it, and also the House of Representatives. This consists of 420 deputies, 100 of whom are nominated by the President, 75 percent of them being military. In 1970, furthermore, General Suharto and his military circle founded the GOLKAR 'public sector' Party which incorporates 260 occupational, professional, and functional groups, including the military. Since elections were first held, in 1971, it has always won an overwhelming majority of the seats. In the latest (1978) elections, it took 232 seats compared with the Development Unity Party's (PPP) 99, and the Indonesian Democratic Party's (PDI) 29. If the 100 nominated members are added to the 232 GOLKAR members, the total, 332, forms over 72 percent of the House. Nor should the preponderance of civilians in the twenty-seven-man Cabinet mislead. With the exception of that of the Foreign Minister, held by the hardy perennial Mr Malik, every key post is held by the military: Political and Security Affairs; Welfare; the nondepartmental Agencies; the Interior; Defence and Security; Justice; Information; Religion; and Social Affairs. The outcome is a personal-presidential government operating under tight constraint from the military.

We can now make another shift rightwards on the algorithm, which brings us to the states with all- or largely civilian Cabinets. These fall into two categories: those with a single- or hegemonic-party system, and those with a plurality of parties. The former group comprises three states without legislatures: the Central African Republic, Iraq, and Togo; and four with them, namely Madagascar, Syria, Sudan, and Zaire.

All seven are summarily describable as *presidential*. It is the President who makes policy. The military role is supportive. This does not mean that it is always passive. That would hardly be likely since, in every single case, it is the military who sustain the regime and can make or break it so that winning their support is the first indispensable task of the President. But he has much more latitude in exercising his discretion than in the two previous cases of Indonesia and Burma, and this varies with the nature of the official party which is the best single indicator of the President's freedom of maneuver. Bearing in mind again that the constant is the support of the armed forces, we can use the nature of the party as the variable that discriminates between the different presidential styles. This approach yields us three groups of states: two states with symbiotic parties, namely Iraq and Syria: two states with controlled parties, the Sudan and Madagascar: and three states, the Central African Republic, Togo, and Zaire, where the parties are ancillary – and largely nominal.

In both Iraq and Syria, the Baath Party has emerged from military revolutions as the hegemonic party of the regime, that is, the leader of a 'progressive' Front which includes the Communist parties and sometimes other parties, but which alone is privileged to recruit within the armed forces, to propagandize in schools, and to fill the senior posts in the civil and armed services. In Iraq this party has a narrow popular base: in Syria efforts are being made to recruit in the villages and countryside. Both parties are best seen, however, as tight-knit hierarchical 'vanguard' parties to which the constitution of the two countries accords the leading and core role. At the same time, the provisional constitution of Iraq, and the 1973 popularly approved constitution of Syria accord vast powers to the presidency, including the supreme command of the armed forces, the nomination of all senior and Cabinet appointments, and extensive decree-making authority. Additionally, in each of the two states the President is the General-Secretary of the Baath Party. The current regime in Iraq dates from the 1968 coup that brought Field Marshal Bakr into power, with Saddam Hussein, assistant general-secretary of the Baath as Vice-President, but effectively co-regent. Since that date the Baath has gradually extruded one after another of the leading soldiers from the Command Council, while strengthening its grip over the armed forces by indoctrination, on the one hand, and the enforcement of party discipline, on the other. The 'cold coup' of 1979 which ousted Bakr and made Saddam Hussein President, followed by the latter's bloody purge of the government, has confirmed the dominance of the Baath Party. At its topmost levels, this party is symbiotic with the top levels of the military hierarchy, and it has successfully colonized the more junior ranks. 'The Baath has managed to isolate the army from politics; but the support of the military is essential if the regime is to survive.'[15]

The current Syrian regime is almost coeval with the Iraqi one, dating from 1970. In this year, Hafez Assad, a long-standing Baathist, but a general, ousted President Salah Jadid who headed the civilian wing of the Baath Party, and took over the post of the party's Secretary-General. The result, over a period of ten years, has been neither the ascendancy of the army over the Baath Party, nor the reverse (such as obtains in Iraq), but instead the paramountcy of President Assad himself, with both the party and the armed services acting as supporting and advisory institutions. An Israeli observer could describe the system as a 'fairly popular presidential regime',[16] and a young American specialist in Middle East affairs summarized it in 1978, as 'a presidential system with a powerful institutional sub-system in the form of the Baath party that tended to constrain the President's freedom of manoeuvrability'.[17] That the armed forces played a significant role in policy-making is also in no doubt, but, as the same scholar observes, 'its influences in the policy making process, particularly viz-à-vis the Presidency, must not . . . be exaggerated.'[18] And she concludes: 'the final arbiter of power in Syria is the Chief Executive, President Hafiz Al-Asad.'[19]

In the next pair of states, the Sudan and Madagascar, the President is less constrained by party and military. The official party is a 'controlled' one, an artifact contrived to contain and channel powerful, but conflictual, currents of opinion and harness them to the executive power. Among such currents in the Sudan are the followers of Al-Mahdi who form the Umma, a fundamentalist Islamic party; the former rebels of the southern, black African region; as well as radical student groups in the towns. Until the abortive Communist coup of 1971, the regime was run by a supreme military council: after it, General Numeiri had himself elected President in a referendum, dissolved the Revolutionary Command Council, and formed the Sudan Socialist Union (SSU). Significantly, it was formed from the top down, first its Politburo Executive Committee, and Secretariat (1972), then its Central Committee. In 1977, after surviving three attempted coups, Numeiri embarked on a policy of national reconciliation, in the course of which, both the southern dissidents and the followers of Al-Mahdi were brought into the party. In the 1978 election, the SSU did not itself nominate candidates, merely issuing 'certificates of nonobjection', so that, conjecturally, the elected National Assembly contained some 20 Umma (i.e. Mahdist deputies), 30 National Union, 20 Muslim Brethren, and some 50 independents, as compared with about 130 Sudanese Union deputies. Since then, the President has purged the Political Bureau of the party, reducing it from twenty-seven members to ten, and getting rid of the Umma (Madhist) members. He has also had to rely on the army – and, some reports say, on units of the Egyptian army also – to suppress serious student riots in August 1978.

In Madagascar, the military presence is stronger; the supreme body, the so-called Supreme Revolutionary Council, contains seven military officers out of twenty-two members. Madagascar started its independent life as a civilian regime dominated by the Socialist Party which had emerged under metropolitan French influences as the dominant party in the terminal days of colonial status; and it lapsed into military control, after 1972, when President Tsrinana handed power over to a general. After a period of supreme military-council government, a move back to civilianization began when the composition of this council gave parity to soldiers and civilians, while a new one-party system was envisaged. Formed in March 1976, and called the Avant garde de la révolution malgache (Arema), the party became the leader in a Front National which embraced three other parties. The leftwing Mousima opposition party campaigned but was defeated, and the consequence of the election, in which Arema won 112 seats and its three allies 25 seats between them, was the present arrangement, where ultimate control vests in the predominantly civilian Revolutionary Council, with military participation, a Lt Col. as the new Prime Minister, and General Ratsiraka as the President.

In the three remaining states, presidential rule is highly personalistic. The current regime in the Central African Republic no doubt represents a temporary phase, in which a not-very-powerful or numerous military force, shocked and alarmed beyond forbearance at the murderous excesses of Emperor Bokassa, decided to hand back the presidency to the civilian, David Dacko, the emperor's predecessor. MESAN (Mouvement pour l'évolution sociale de l'afrique noire) played no role whatsoever in the emperor's bloody exercise of power, and no role in the purely military revulsion that resulted in his overthrow. This virtually nominal party is inconsequential in the present phase of the regime which consists, basically, of the personalistic rule of Dacko, via a civilian Cabinet which is headed by a Colonel Bangui.

As to Zaire, observers all concur in the personalistic nature of the regime. 'Mobutu . . . rules through fear rather than through love,' 'Mobutu's dictate has been total', 'he has decisively imposed his image' are only three of the phrases that would be generally accepted by observers of his government.[20] Mobutu is Commander-in-Chief of the armed forces, as well as chief executive, and so far has kept his soldiery loyal. The official party is the Mouvement populaire de la révolution (MPR) whose Permanent Committee of the Politburo (ten persons) he leads. The status of this party can be gauged by the law stating that 'every Zairian becomes a member of the MPR at birth.'[21]

We are left with Togo. President Eyedama came to power and retains it as the representative of the original narrow clique of army officers who assassinated President Olympio in 1963. That murder, and the persistent determination of Olympio's kinsmen to level the score, has rallied the original coup group around Eyedama, and enabled him to pursue his personal presidential policies. The Togolese National Rally (Ralliement du peuple Togoloais – RPT) was founded by Eyedama as the sole national party in 1967, when he took over power. On paper this party appears 'symbiotic': for instance, in 1976 nine members of its sixteen-man Politburo were members of the thirteen-man Cabinet. In practice, as Decalo reports, the 'RPT is still very much a hollow structure – essentially a decentralized organization of Eyedama loyalists with low levels of Ewe participation . . . a tightly controlled ancillary organization . . .'[22] Of the regime itself he writes: 'It is an army clique that is the wielder, arbitrator and guarantor of political power . . . [the regime] is a civilianized military autocracy . . .'[23]

We have now reached the extreme rightward margin of the algorithm. Here are three states, all with ex-coup leaders or their successors in the presidency, ruling through civilian Cabinets in an environment of competing parties and elected legislatures. But we must beware of the misdescription inherent in so curt a summary: the parties compete, but only the officially favored party wins. In Brazil, Egypt, and Paraguay, the key institution is the presidency – the fountain of prerogative power, in supreme command of the armed forces, the police, the ministry, and the bureaucracy. Indubitably, the personality of the President is vastly important in expanding or contracting the influence of the office, and in giving direction to national policy; but so it is in the presidency of the USA. Neither the personal *baraka* or *machismo* of the President makes or breaks the regime, nor that of the High Command. Both make an input varying absolutely and relatively in each of these three countries; but they work within a network of procedures and institutions. True, these are perpetually altered and fiddled in order to suit the President's immediate exigencies, but they serve to domesticate the unmodified personalism that was characteristic of the previous group of the seven one-party states. These three regimes are not personalist, but authoritarian.[24] Lest this be construed as meaning that they are more liberal than the previous group, let it be said most firmly that it does not. The Brazilian regime, as of today, has certainly liberalized itself; but in Paraguay martial law has been in force for the entire twenty-five years of President Stressner's rule, and the pursuit, the arrest, the imprisonment, and torture of political opponents is a commonplace.[25] The Egyptian regime though less barbaric, is equally intolerant of opposition.

The key question remains: In these three authoritarian states, with a civilian institutional framework, does the military, as such, govern or even play a creative part in government? In Paraguay, it does not. The President 'looks after' the army (for which he has an old-fashioned sentimental attachment) and, in turn, it looks after him. His relationship with the ruling Colorado Party, is instrumental, a marriage of reciprocity. 'Paraguay,' comments a distinguished and experienced observer of the Latin American scene, 'is typically governed by the dictatorship of a ranking military officer who shares power with the conservative Colorado party, the bureaucracy, and the army . . .'[26]

Nor does the military any longer play a creative part in Egypt. The executive power in this state is exercised, by President Sadat, in a much more personalist manner than in either Paraguay or Brazil, as witness the President's extraordinary *volte-face* over relationships with Israel. The party system, remodelled a number of times in the last three years is tenuous and not highly influential, any more than the legislature is. Nevertheless, it is through such pliable institutions as these that the President prefers to work. The military plays a cardinal role in support of his policies. Without it, his rule would collapse. But although he consults it, and requires its support, and often the open avowal of such support, it is he who frames policy.

We are left with Brazil, and it is perhaps fitting that the most problematical case should be our last one since we are confronted here with the paradox that the institutionalization of the regime is much more advanced than in the previous two examples – but the creative role of the armed forces is very high also. This role is not visible in the list of summary variables to be found in the Appendix. After the military took power in 1964, the President was nominated by the three service chiefs, and this tradition broke down only in 1979 when the outgoing President (Geisel) nominated General Figueredo (a retired general) as his successor without consulting the military chiefs. The President, who wields vast powers under the various modifications which the military have made to the pre-1964 constitution by their various Institutional Acts, has effectively been appointed by, and held to be, the representative of the armed forces; and these, in their turn, have been led by a group of officers who served together in the Brazilian contingent in World War II, and who have made the Scuola do Guerra a think-tank, as well as a rigorous training ground, for a generation of young, civically educated, and highly interventionist officers. Thus connected to the President, this group has powered the regime so far, acting through its own party (Arena) and limiting, by cunning last-minute alterations to the electoral rule, the opportunities of the licensed opposition party, MDB. President Figueredo, who was by no means the favorite son of this military establishment, has opened up the regime still further than his predecessor, President Geisel. Instead of limiting opposition to one single party, the MDB, opposition parties have now been permitted to form freely. This is interpretable as another of the military establishment's 'dirty tricks', since it is calculated to divide the opposition; and indeed, it has done just this, the former MDB having developed into three competing parties. In addition, the censorship has been lifted and the exiles amnestied. But the official Arena Party still controls the Congress on the President's behalf, and the President still is regarded as 'their man' by the military establishment which operates on him, as of heretofore, behind the scenes. The interplay of President, the top military brass, the very skillful civilian technocrats who head the ministries, and the active and eloquent politicians who make up Congress, is very complex and very subtle. Furthermore, it is always changing. The emphasis has shifted to and from civilian and military on a number of occasions since 1964.[27] In one sense, Brazil is at the very margin of the military regimes. In another, it is in the midst of them.

(3) FURTHER DIMENSIONS OF THE MILITARY PRESENCE

So far we have addressed the question of whether or not it is the military, qua corporate entity, that formulates supreme national policy. Another question is whether it actually administers it, and a further question is whether it merely patrols society or directs it. These questions can be handled in terms of two concepts: military 'colonization' of the bureaucracy, on the one hand; and governmental control of society, on the other.

As to military colonization of the bureaucracy: we have analyzed the military role in our thirty-two polities as being either that of rulers, or as that of support, but we now have a third role – that of acting as a *reservoir of personnel* for key institutions in the state. 'Colonization' will signify that the military have spilled over from the strict armed-service hierarchy into the political parties or the trade unions, the government corporations, or the civil bureaucracy. We have already dealt with its relationship to political parties; for the remainder we can envisage the military establishment as operating either as ruler; as ruler and reservoir; as reservoir and support; or, simply, as support (see Figure 12.3).

Ruler	Ruler-Reservoir	Reservoir-Support	Support

Figure 12.3

The second question, on the scope of government control, can be broadly characterized as being, to begin with, simple supervision or 'patrolling', that is to say, ad hoc reacting to, and correcting, what it perceives as malfunctions. Some governments, however, go further and assume positive continuous direction of national affairs. And, when this is superadded to the role of reservoir, as above, then they go still further: they directly administer the society.

The two concepts can be married, to form a table (see Table 12.1).

Table 12.1 *Military Regimes, by 'Penetration'*

	Ruler Only	Ruler/Reservoir	Reservoir/Support	Support Only
Superintend	Thailand			Egypt[2]
				Zaire
Direct	Nigeria	Brazil		Iraq
	Ghana	Egypt[1]		Syria
Administer		Burma	Indonesia	

[1] Egypt, c. mid-1950s
[2] Egypt, c. mid-1970s

Unfortunately, our information on these matters is patchy. It is not possible to provide an exhaustive catalogue as we have done for the political and constitutional role of the military. What follows is illustrative only. This is why the practice of the military regimes in Ghana and Nigeria, and of Nasserite Egypt have been included, although the first two have recently reverted to civilian rule and the third has evolved away from it.

Thailand, Nigeria, Ghana, and a number of other West African countries are, as we have seen, states in which the military, as such, formulate supreme national policy. They rule – but they rule in different ways. The Thai military supervise or 'patrol', whereas the Nigerian and Ghanaian actively directed a national program. But in none of these three cases did the military themselves administer. This was left to the civil bureaucracy.

In Thailand, the military is almost a 'connection' or 'cousinhood' like English eighteenth-century parties. It is largely interrelated and has inter-married into the Chinese business community which is central to the Thai economy, and into the traditional bureaucracy also. Indeed, it is common for well-born families to place one son in the army and another in the civil service. A distinguished British military observer laughingly recounted to me his experience of meeting 'Generals who were land-owners and politicians, landowners who were politicians and generals and politicians who were generals and landowners.' The Thai civil service is fragmented, and the Thai military elite have acted toward it as politicians rather than as masters: they bargain, negotiate, compromise, and manipulate patronage, but permit the civil servants a wide autonomy in running affairs without exercising day-to-day direction over them. This is not to say that the military plays no 'reservoir' role at all: it does, but it is largely a matter of 'jobs for the boys.' It was estimated, some ten years ago, that over 130 government utilities and enterprises provided lucrative posts for army officers – and for their civilian supporters also. Some 49 of these enterprises (comprising four-fifths of the capital of the total 134 companies, etc.) were administered by the Prime Minister and Defense Office, the Ministry of the Interior, and the Ministry of Commerce, all of which were headed by soldiers.[28]

While something of the kind can be observed in the military regimes of West Africa – and while, too, it is not uncommon there to observe provincial governorships going to the military – the scale is not as great as in Thailand, and the military's reliance on the civil service is very marked. As Zolberg observes,[29] 'governmental bureaucracies continue to be a major instrument of rule,' and Welch confirms that 'army-dominated African governments have worked closely with civil servants . . .'[30] Indeed, a military–bureaucracy symbiosis is one of the salient features of these regimes. Furthermore, the evidence suggests that although the ruling military, definitionally, possessed and exercised a veto power, they were often very much in the hands of their top civil servants. The successive military governments in Nigeria relied heavily on the permanent secretaries of the civil service departments, and although army officers were appointed to public corporations and boards it was left to the civil servants in charge to manage them.[31]

An equally close relationship between army and civil service developed in Ghana during the first phase of military rule (1966–9) and seems to have continued during the second (1972–9).

> During its reign the National Liberation Council presided over an essentially civilian structure: officers of the armed forces filled only a limited number of ministerial and top-regional administrative posts. Apart from those like Major General Nathan Afer, who were appointed ambassadors or High Commissioners, the total of those employed in extra-military roles rarely exceeded twelve in all. The permanent civil service came back into its own and effectively ran the ministries: their opposite numbers in the state corporations benefitted similarly . . .[32]

We can now turn to countries illustrative of the ruler-cum-reservoir class. Burma is a very striking example. It is almost the mirror image of the wheeling-dealing Thai style. The army is a politicized force, professing and trained in Burmese socialism. From the beginning, it loathed the traditional civil service which it regarded as a remnant of colonialism, and vowed to sweep it away.[33] At local levels, down to the rural district committee, the Lanzin Party – which, as we have already seen, is symbiotic with the military – provides the local governor or chairman. Effectively, he is a district commissar. Meanwhile, from 1958, the Military Defence Services Institute expanded, first into joint commercial ventures with Israeli, Japanese, Singapore, and American enterprises, then into the fields of shipping, fishing, exports, banking, bus transportation, hotels, and coal marketing, as each industry was, successively, nationalized. It has established, says one observer, 'a virtual monopoly of the economic activity of the nation . . . The military dominates the governmental bureaucracy. Every major ministry, commission and government corporation is headed by a military man . . .'[34]

Brazil comes nowhere near Burma in this respect; but it has been following the same sort of path, albeit at a considerable remove. There the government has carried out two Five Year Development Plans involving massive investment in industry, energy, education, and health care. Brazil is, nominally, a private enterprise economy, but from personal inquiries it appears that the proportion of civil servants to the adult employed population is some 30 percent. However, these are involved only in the nonagricultural sector, and if the employees in this sector are subtracted, then the proportion of civil servants in the non-agricultural sector approaches 60 percent or more. Private enterprise or not, the economy is 'planned' and subsidized by the national exchequer. The reservoir role of the military is small compared with the vast number of civil servants but for all that, it is noted by a well-informed observer that there has been

extensive, direct penetration . . . by military officers. Always moderately important in specific fields they can now be found scattered throughout the federal and state governments. A recent survey of sixty top administrative posts showed that twenty-eight of them were occupied by high echelon military officers. Some state governments have been virtually militarized . . . [the officers] are chosen by the military hierarchy and from within the ranks for their post, remain in the armed services for career purposes, and often return periodically to field command positions . . .[35]

We can now move on to the class of 'support-cum-reservoir' armies. Its most striking example is Indonesia. For one thing, it had incorporated all the public service associations into its own, officially backed Golkar Party, a party which, together with the military nominees appointed by the President, overwhelmingly controls the legislature. In the administrative sphere, the military have quite overtly claimed for themselves the so-called 'dual function', that is, to steer society. The tasks entailed by this dual function are carried out by the *Karyawan* ('trustees', that is, members of the armed forces on secondment to outside bodies such as ministries, governorships, managers, and the like). It has expanded this function locally as well. Ten years ago, large parts of the 600,000-strong armed forces were working in the rural regions alongside the civil servants whose total numbers in that year amounted only to 700,000. Centrally, its penetration of the civil service began in 1961 when General Suharto began to appoint soldiers to civil service posts. By 1967, they held one in every five of these, and by 1971, to judge by the official *Gazette,* over two-fifths of the named top officials were military men, as were seventeen of the twenty-five provincial governors, and over a half of the heads of the municipalities and districts in the island of Java. At each level of the territorial administration is to be found a 'leadership council' coordinating the civil, military, and police activities and always including a high military officer. And the army's penetration of the economic sphere has been farreaching indeed. It controls the National Planning Council and the Supreme Economic Operation Command. Through *Pertamina* it controls the country's oil industry, through *Berikari* it controls import-export, through *Bulog* it markets rice. This vast economic empire includes large holding companies, industrial and commercial conglomerates, and trading syndicates, as well as individual firms engaged in banking, petroleum and transportation, rubber and tea.[36]

We can end our survey by looking at a state where the regime's style has shifted markedly over time, and that is Egypt. In Table 12.1, this country is shown as Egypt[1] And Egypt[2], and the subscripts refer to dates of, respectively, circa the mid-1950s and the mid-1970s. In June 1954, supreme policy was formulated by the Revolutionary Command Council which consisted of eleven officers, and, under this council, by a Cabinet of nineteen ministers, eight of whom were members of the RCC. Also over 1,000 officers had become ambassadors, provincial governors, managers and directors of economic agencies, and the like. The army was acting both as ruler and reservoir. By June 1974, the RCC no longer existed. The President was an ex-officer, a former member of the original coup-group, but in the Cabinet only one minister was an officer – the Minister of War. Furthermore, in that thirty-man Cabinet, fifteen members bore the title of 'doctor' and another seven that of 'engineer'. And by that time, the outflow and secondment of officers to civilian agencies had ceased. Thus, in twenty years, the Egyptian military moved from the role of ruler-cum-reservoir directorate to that of simple support.[37]

(4) CONCLUSIONS

The conclusions to this chapter can be simply stated. The first is that the terms 'military regime', 'military government', or 'military dictatorship' are terms of art, not scientific categories. The second is that the weight of the military establishment, as such, in the exercise of supreme control over top policy-making can be estimated, and when this is done, the exercise yields four main classes of so-called 'military regimes'. These are the military-junta type, where parties and legislatures have been suppressed – the stereotype of the military regime; the military-junta type with legislatures and parties as simple ancillaries or appurtenances; the personalist-presidential type, where the armies act as a support but do not play an actively creative policy-making role: and, finally, the authoritarian type, where the military are in support of a chief executive who himself is constrained by institutions. The third conclusion is that the weight of the military, qua corporation, must be measured in other dimensions as well, the most notable being its penetration of the civil bureaucracy and its grip of local, as well as central, authority. Where the military have effected great penetration in these areas, as well as

exercising supreme policy-making power, as in Burma, military government is at its height. Where this penetration is great, it helps make up for
the military's extrusion, or part-extrusion, from supreme policy-making –
as in Indonesia. By the same token, the product of these two factors –
symbolically expressible as *supreme policy-making authority* × *penetration
of the bureaucracy* can be exercised over a wide range of socio-economic
activities, as in Burma or Indonesia; or a lesser range, as in Thailand; or,
even less yet, as in Zaire or the Central African Republic. When we talk,
as we do, of military regimes, and so on, we tend to talk loosely,
conflating all these dimensions in our mind simultaneously. We do not
have to do this; it would be wise if we did not do this; and all that has
gone before is an attempt to ensure that in future we do not do this.

NOTES

1 Cf. the somewhat querulous (and yet essentially just) footnote, in E. A. Nordlinger,
   Soldiers in Politics (Englewood Cliffs, NJ: Prentice-Hall, 1977), at p. 110.
2 For one example, of my own original treatment in the 1st edn (1962) of *The Man on
   Horseback* (London: Pall Mall, 1962), ch. 11.
3 Cf. E. A. Nordlinger, 'Soldiers in mufti', *American Political Science Review* (December
   1970); R. D. McKinlay and A. S. Cohan, 'A comparative analysis of the political and
   economic performance of military and civilian regimes: a cross-national aggregate
   study,' *Comparative Politics* (October 1975); and R. W. Jackman, 'Politicians in
   uniform: military governments and social change in the Third World,' *American
   Political Science Review* (December 1976).
4 For my own classification, see *Man on Horseback* (2nd edn, Harmondsworth: Penguin,
   1976) at pp. 149–72 for the first formulation and again at pp. 245–52 for further elaboration. M. Janowitz wrote his *The Military in the Political Development of the New
   Nations* (Chicago: University of Chicago Press) in 1964 (reprinted in *Military
   Institutions and Coercion in the Developing Countries,* Chicago: University of Chicago
   Press, 1977, which does not further elaborate his original, 1964, classification). This
   distinguished (1) authoritarian personal, (2) authoritarian mass-party, (3) democratic-
   competitive, (4) civil–military coalition and (5) military oligarchy (op. cit., pp. 82–3).
   But Janowitz supplies only the haziest criteria for attributing a particular regime to any
   of these categories, nor does he distinguish between different kinds of 'mass parties' or,
   for that matter, different kinds of 'competitive parties.' Nordlinger (*Soldiers in Politics*)
   devotes ch. 4 to 'Officers as governors.' He distinguishes three kinds of executive
   arrangements, namely (1) the predominantly military executive where at least 90
   percent of the Cabinet positions are held by officers, (2) the mixed civilian executive,
   and (3) the exclusively military command council (op. cit., p. 109). In this he appears to
   have based himself somewhat uncritically on McKinlay and Cohan (op. cit.) and he
   does not try, himself, to pursue the classification systematically. He does recognize that
   there are other dimensions to military power than its hold over the executive and
   discusses its relationship to political parties and to the scope of the duties it chooses to
   undertake, but the discussion then wanders off into a discussion of 'style' and the
   classification is not pursued further. A. Perlmutter (*The Military and Politics in Modern
   Times,* New Haven, Conn.: Yale University Press) devotes two chapters to military
   regimes, discerning three types, the arbitrator, the ruler, and the neo-arbitrator types.
   Much detail is supplied, but essentially these three types turn out to be ideal types, and
   nowhere is there systematic pursuit over the whole range of military regimes of the
   structural relationships of the military, as such, with the organs of government, and
   beyond that, with the political parties. The scheme is ambitious and suggestive and
   contains insights, but is not rigorous enough to stand by itself as a satisfactory classification scheme.
5 Perlmutter, op. cit., p. 115.
6 *Amnesty International Report, 1974–5,* pp. 102–3.

7   19 December 1979.
8   In Burke's words, 'virtual representation is that in which there is a communion of interests and a sympathy of feelings and desires between those who act in the name of any description of people, and the people in whose name they act, though the trustees are not actually chosen by them . . .' (Burke, *Letter to Sir Horatio Langrishe*, 1797).
9   The categories are defined thus: the Cabinet is deemed *military* where over two-thirds of its members are military men, *mixed* where the military component is less than two-thirds but greater than one-third of the membership, and *civilian* where the military personnel form less than one-third of the membership.
10 See B. Crozier, *The Soviet Pressure in Somalia* (London: Institute of Conflict Studies, February 1975).
11 In the terms of my *Man on Horseback* classification (*Man on Horseback*. Penguin 2nd edn, pp. 167–9) they are *Direct; quasi-civilianized* military regimes.
12 | 'Friends of the Party' | 763,133 | Percentage military | 0·2% |
    | Candidate members | 260,857 | | 24·3% |
    | Full members | 73,369 | | 57·2% |
    | Delegates to 1st Congress | 824 | | 12·7% |
    | Central Committee | 150 | | 78·7% |
    | Central Affairs Committee | 74 | | 75·7% |
    | Central Executive Committee | 12 | | 91·5% |
    | Secretariat | 4 | | 100·0% |

    (From J. S. Hoadley, *Soldiers and Politics in Southeast Asia* (Cambridge, Mass.: Schenkman, 1975), p. 53.)
    (*Note:* These figures look decidedly odd. Apparently only one-eighth of the *delegates* were soldiers, i.e., 103 persons. Yet 78·7% of the CC, or 118 persons, were soldiers.)
13 See below, pp. 299–300.
14 See J. S. Hoadley, op. cit., ch. 5; Peter Polomka, *Indonesia since Sukarno* (Harmondsworth: Penguin, 1971); N. Notatosünto, *Indonesia: Armed Forces and Society*, in C. M. Kelleher (ed.), *Political Military Systems* (Beverly Hills, Calif.: Sage, 1974). But note Sundhaussen's conclusion that 'The Military is hardly if at all involved in political decision-making.' This, he contends, is done by Suharto who has cleverly played off one group against another to establish himself as *Supremo*. This is a splendid essay on the subject of 'Who Really Governs': U. Sundhaussen, *Decision Making within this Indonesian Military*, in H. Z. Schiffrin (ed.) *Military and State in Modern Asia*. See also the splendid study by C. Crouch, *Military Politics in Indonesia* (Ithaca, NY: Cornell University Press, 1978).
15 G. Lenczowski (ed.), *Political Elites in the Middle East* (Washington, DC: American Enterprise Institute, 1975), p. 112, and see also, pp. 126–7, pp. 146–7. The convulsed process by which the Baath managed to extrude the army from key positions is told in R. D. M. McLaurin, M. Mughisuddin and A. R. Wagner, *Foreign Policy Making in the Middle East* (New York: Praeger, 1977), ch. 4, pp. 116–40. See also Abbas Kelidar, *Iraq: The Search for Stability*, Conflict Studies no. 59 (London: Institute for the Study of Conflict, 1975).
16 A. I. Dawisha, 'Syria under Assad 1970–1978: the centres of power,' *Government and Opposition*, vol. 13, no. 3 (1978), p. 341.
17 ibid., p. 348.
18 ibid., p. 352.
19 ibid., p. 353. For other sources, see R. D. McLaurin, M. Mughisuddin and A. R. Wagner, *Foreign Policy Making in the Middle East* (New York: Praeger, 1977), ch. 6; Lenczewski, op. cit., ch. 6; Moshe Ma'oz, 'Alawi military officers in Syrian politics, 1966–1974,' in H. Z. Schiffrin (ed.), *Military and State in Modern Asia* (Jerusalem: Jerusalem Academic Press, 1976), pp. 277–98.
20 *Africa South of the Sahara* (London: Europa Publications, 1978), p. 975.
21 ibid., p. 992.
22 Decalo, op. cit., p. 118.
23 ibid., p. 119.
24 I follow the distinction made by M. Needler, in, for example, *An Introduction to Latin American Politics* (Englewood Cliffs, NJ: Prentice-Hall, 1977), pp. 135–41.
25 See *Amnesty International Report, 1978* (Amnesty International, London, WC2E 7HF), pp. 133–6.

26 Needler, op. cit., p. 315.
27 See, for instance, my remarks in *Comparative Government* (Harmondsworth: Penguin, 1973), pp. 577–8.
28 C. M. Kelleher (ed.), *Political Military Systems* (Beverly Hills, Calif.: Sage, 1974), p. 11; Hoadley, op. cit., pp. 20–1.
29 A. Zolberg, *Creating Political Order* (Chicago: Rand McNally, 1966), p. 119.
30 C. Welch (ed.), *Soldier and State in Africa* (Evanston, Ill.: Northwestern University Press, 1970), p. 48.
31 W. F. Gutteridge, *Military Regimes in Africa* (London: Methuen, 1975), p. 122.
32 Gutteridge, op. cit., pp. 76–7.
33 For an excellent and detailed account of the evolution of the Burmese civil service and the army's attitude to it, see J. F. Guyot, *Bureaucratic Transformation in Burma*, in R. Braibanti (ed.), *Bureaucratic Systems Emergent from the British Imperial Tradition* (Durham, NC: Duke University Press, 1966), pp. 354–443.
34 Hoadley, op. cit., pp. 46, 58.
35 Cited from P. C. Schmitter, 'The Portugalization of Brazil', in A. Stepan (ed.), *Authoritarian Brazil* (New Haven, Conn.: Yale University Press, 1973), p. 223.
36 For Indonesia, see Hoadley, op. cit.; Kelleher (ed.), op. cit.; Ulf Sundhaussen, 'Decision making in the Indonesian military,' in Schiffrin (ed.), op. cit.; M. Rudner, 'The military in Indonesian development planning, 1969–1974,' ibid.; and R. Kahane, 'The problem of institutionalization of military government: the case of Indonesia, 1965–1974, ibid.
37 See E. Be'eri, 'The changing role of the military in Egyptian politics', in Schiffrin (ed.), op. cit., pp. 269–76.

APPENDIX: A SYNOPTIC TABLE OF REGIMES (1 JANUARY 1980)

Note: Where the military–civilian components of a council or Cabinet are reported, they are given as a fraction, for example, 'Algeria, 8/11', where the numerator (8) represents the number of military personnel, and the denominator (11) represents the total personnel in the organ.)

Name of State	Is an Ex-Coupist Head of State Civilian Military	Is there an RCC?	Is Cabinet Military	Mixed	Civilian	Are there Parties and of What Type?	Does a Parliament Exist?
Algeria	Yes Col. Chadli (1979) (2nd incumbent)	Yes 8/11 (Revolutionary Council)			5/30	Official single (FLN)	Yes
Argentina	Yes Gen. Videla (1976)	Yes 3/3 (Junta Militar)		5/8 (= 62·5%)		No	No
Benin	Yes Maj. Kerekou (1972)	No	16/16 (Executive Council)			Official single (P. de la Revolution Populaire de Benin)	No
Brazil	Yes Gen. Figueredo (4th incumbent)	No			6/22 (= 27%)	Official, hegemonic, licensed opposition parties	Yes
Burma	Yes Ne Win (1962)	No		10/17 (= 59%)		Official single (Burma Socialist Program Party)	Yes (People's Congress)
Burundi	Yes Bagaza (1976)	Yes 30/30 (Supreme Military Council)			3/18 (= 16%)	No	No

Name of State	Is an Ex-Coupist Head of State Civilian Military	Is there an RCC?	Is Cabinet Military	Mixed	Civilian	Are there Parties and of What Type?	Does a Parliament Exist?
Central African Republic	Yes Pat Dacko (1979)				3/7 (= 17%)	Official single (Mouvement d'Evolution Sociale de L'Afrique Noir) = MESAN	No
Chile	Yes Pinochet (1973)	Yes 4/4 (Junta Militar)		6/17 (= 35%)		No	No
Congo People's Republic	Yes Sassounguebo	Yes 11/11 (Military Committee)			1/14 (Council of Ministers)	Official single (Parti Congolais de Travail)	No
Egypt	Yes Sadat (1970)	No				Licensed official plural	Yes
Equatorial Guinea	Yes Obiangnguema	Yes Not available (Revolutionary Military Council)	10/10			No	No
Ethiopia	Yes Haile Mariam (1977)	Yes 80/80 (Provisional Military Administration Council or 'Dergue')			Yes Not available	Official 4-party front (Union of Ethiopian Marxist–Leninist Organization)	No
Honduras	Yes Policarpo Paz Garcia (1978)	Yes 4/4 (Junta Militar)		3/9 (33%)		Licensed plural	No

Name of State	Is an Ex-Coupist Head of State — Civilian	Is an Ex-Coupist Head of State — Military	Is there an RCC?	Is Cabinet — Military	Is Cabinet — Mixed	Is Cabinet — Civilian	Are there Parties and of What Type?	Does a Parliament Exist?
Indonesia		Yes Suharto (1968)	No		9/24 (37%)		Licensed plural	Yes
Iraq	Yes Saddam Hussein (1979)					26/26 (= 100%)	Official single front (National Progressive Front), Baath Hegemony	No
Libya		Yes Ghadaffi (1969)	Yes (General Secretariat of People's Congress)			1/26 (= 4%)	Official single (Arab Socialist Union)	Yes
Madagascar		Yes Ratsiraka (1976)	No Civilian Dominated (7/22) (= Supreme Revolutionary Council)			2/19 (= 11%)	Official single 4-party front, hegemonic official party (Avant-Garde de Révolution Malgache A. Reems)	Yes
Mali		Yes Trauori (1968)	Yes 11/11 (Military Committee of National Liberation)		6/15 (40%)		No	No
Mauritania		Yes Ould Salek (1979)	Yes 13/13 (Military Committee for National Recovery)		7/16 (44%)		No	No

Name of State	Is an Ex-Coupist Head of State Civilian	Military	Is there an RCC?	Is Cabinet Military	Mixed	Civilian	Are there Parties and of What Type?	Does a Parliament Exist?
Niger		Yes Kountche (1974)	Yes Not available (Supreme Military Council)		6/18 (33%)		No	No
Pakistan		Yes Zia (1977)	Yes 4/4 (Military Council)			6/22 (= 27%)	Licensed plural	No
Paraguay		Yes Stroessuer	No			1/4 (9%)	Plural, of which one is official	Yes
Peru		Yes Bermudez (1975)	No	13/15			Plural	Yes
Rwanda		Yes Habyarimana	Yes – at least until 1975			2/14 (14%)	Official single (Mouvement National pour Le Développement = MND)	Yes
Somalia		Yes Siad Barre (1969)	Yes 5/5 (Politburo)			6/22 (27%)	Official single (Somali Revolutionary Party = SRP)	No
Sudan		Yes Numeiri (1969)	No			3/18 (33%)	Official single (Sudanese Socialist Union = SSU)	Yes

Name of State	Is an Ex-Coupist Head of State Civilian Military	Is there an RCC?	Is Cabinet Military	Is Cabinet Mixed	Civilian	Are there Parties and of What Type?	Does a Parliament Exist?
Syria	Yes Assad (1970)	No			2/35 (6%)	Official single front (National Progressive Front) Baath Party hegemonic	Yes
Thailand	Yes Kriangsak (1977)	Yes 23/23 (National Policy Council)			10/35 (29%)	Plural	Yes
Togo	Yes Eyedama (1967)	No			1/18 (6%)	Official single (Rassemblement du Peuple Togolais = RPT)	No
Uruguay	Yes Aparicio Mendez (1976)	Yes 4/6 (National Security Council)		Council of Nation 20/45	1/12 (8%)	No	No
Yemen Arab Republic	Yes Salek (1978) (3rd incumbent)	Yes 4/6 (Presidential Council)			3/15 (20%)	No	No
Zaire	Yes Mobutu (1965)	No			3/27 (= 16%)	Single official (Mouvement Populaire de la Révolution = MPR)	Yes

13 Civil–Military Relations in Socialist Authoritarian and Praetorian States: Prospects and Retrospects

AMOS PERLMUTTER

INTRODUCTION

The political systems, regimes, and orientations examined in this chapter are authoritarian, and praetorian. We examine here the role of the military in two types of authoritarian regimes: the institutionalized and the noninstitutionalized, though this essay will anchor its examination to comparative dynamics of civil–military relations in political systems and regimes which are not institutionalized, whose military institution is prominent both in the realms of politics and policy-making.

I shall offer comparative-theoretical models of civil–military relations in modern authoritarian, noninstitutionalized praetorian regimes whose political dynamics are the outcome of the struggle between political elites and noninstitutionalized social groups in state and society.

We know of three models of contemporary civil–military relations. One, the classical model, the regime dominated by elected politicians coming to power after an exhaustive and elaborative party competitive struggle in an open electorate, and where policy is implemented by subordinate (to politically elected) bureaucratic and military elites.

Two, the Communist model, a regime dominated by a single non-competitive party. Policy is implemented by fiercely competitive party elites and rival subordinate state elites, bureaucracies, and the military.

Three, in the praetorian model where the regime is dominated on the whole by the military, or by a coalition of the military and the bureaucracy, or a coalition of military, civilian politicians and technocratic groups. These military elites (uniformed or nonuniformed) in a praetorian regime innovate political structures and implement policies aiming to dominate the regime.

What is fundamental to the first two models is the subordination of the military to politics. The control of the military is cardinal to these systems. Military intervention is either unthinkable, or intolerable, and at best temporary (China during and after the Cultural Revolution). In the praetorian type, the boundaries between politics and policy are clearly permeable and the nature of the political domination is unstable. Civilian control is not required. Military intervention is what characterizes the nature and structure of the regime and its institutional arrangements.

The most conspicuous difference between models one and two, as against three, is that they are on the whole legitimate, stable, and sustaining political orders, while the praetorian regime, one the whole, is either illegitimate, or unstable.

Legitimacy and stability result from a variety of factors. Above all, from the predominance of an institutionalized political party (or parties) that either serves as a broker(s) for competitive elections of political leaders (the classical type), or as the only vehicle for the selection and election of political leadership and elite mobility (the Bolshevik type). It is distinguished by the presence of institutionalized authority and institutionalized crises. The absence of an institutionalized political party (or parties) system and political structures and institutions invites military intervention – praetorianism. Noninstitutionalized authoritarian regimes are characterized by the inordinate and precarious function of their political structures and, above all, by the relationship between the regime and the military elite.

While the relationship between the regime and the military elite has been stabilized and is institutionalized in the classical competitive party model, the struggle between the regime and the military in some of the socialist models is far from being resolved in a manner and type that would be in the classical case (see Table 13.1). The military's threat for coercion is implicit in this system. In the Communist model, most recently and conspicuously in China, the struggle between the party and the state, and the military intervening between and within the two, sometimes moderating, sometimes exacerbating the relationship demonstrate the different arrangements, priorities, and attitudes in the relationships between civilians and military structures and individuals, that are predominant in the classical model.

Table 13.1 *Types of Regimes and Civil–Military Relations, and Stability*

Types of Regimes	Political Party Cohesion		Regimes' Stability		Viability of Political Structure	
					Civil	Military
Classical	+	+	+	+	+	+
Bolshevik	+	+	+	+	+	+
Praetorian	–	–	–	–	–	–

Thus, dynamics of civil–military relations in authoritarian regimes depend on the interplay between the regimes elites and the military; the processes of institutionalization of each; the relative stability and cohesiveness of each; and the type of political domination each prefers. Organizational explanations, that is, the size of the military, its structure, and organizational format, and skill structure or the social origins of the officer class do not usually stimulate the necessary motivations for military interventions in politics. Also the absence of organizational changes will probably not propel the military into political interventionism. The military intervenes for political and ideological reasons. The military in praetorian conditions is deeply concerned with preventing the seizure of power by its rivals and in consolidating the military intervention (or coup), or in establishing conditions that will not threaten the corporate integrity of its organization. My concern is with the military's *political* motivations explaining military interventionism, other than the narrow and unsatisfactory explanation of the organizational dynamics of the military as the single causal factor for military intervention in politics.

The propensity of military interventions, and especially coup-making in praetorian states, is subtle but in important ways also relates to structural and institutional changes in the military establishment, such as new military doctrines and more professional and foreign training, technical development, management of complex weapon systems.[1] The coup d'état sometimes ensures the stability of the system's structural deficiencies.[2] However, the decision to intervene – improved by enormous organization and technical advancement of the military – is nevertheless *political*. It is clearly connected with the absence of legitimacy and the instability of political institutions and structures. Control over the instruments of violence is an asset only under praetorian conditions. It is neither a sufficient, nor a reasonably good, explanation for the role of the military in politics.

(1)   FACTORS AND ORIENTATIONS CONNECTED WITH THE ROLE OF THE MILITARY INTERVENTIONISM IN NEW STATES

Praetorianism is both a descriptive term and a dynamic explanation for three types of authority relationships. These are (a) the government and the Roman Praetorians, or historical praetorianism; (b) the regime persistently found in societies undergoing change and lacking legitimate political order and support; and (c) a type of civil–military relations prevalent in praetorian regimes. Both Huntington and Perlmutter have linked these latter two: a weak (praetorian) political order produces an interventionist military. The emergence of the military as both an arbiter and a ruler in praetorian, unstable societies is certainly a modern phenomenon. Military intervention, coups, and political rule of the military is linked to conditions, aspirations, orientations, ideologies of the post-1945 world of new states. (I cautiously do not call them modern.) What distinguishes the new states (almost without exception, only India and Israel come to mind) is that they are authoritarian, unstable, politically undeveloped, and structurally noncohesive and, in many cases, nonfunctioning. Most are ruled directly, or indirectly, by the military which, in several cases, is the only institutionalized structure and, in others, is competing for influence and possibly hegemony. The new states are poorly dominated by what I prefer to call *crisis-regimes*, of which the military government, or coalition, is its most conspicuous type. Crisis-regimes are regimes that are maintained mostly during periods of low conflict and mostly emerge in times of crisis, and collapse, or undergo structural changes, during severe crises. Crises in new regimes are multiple: political, economic, ethnic, and social. Crisis-regimes are also established to correct the political mismanagement of institutions and society, or to rule over unmanaged nonmilitary or military regimes. Crisis-regimes are paradoxically of their own creation. They result from high levels of aspirations and expectations that neither the political system nor the social structure can sustain. New states' aspirations arise from deep ideological and intellectual commitments. Most are states where the regimes emerged as a response to anti-colonial and nationalist ideologies, which are the most powerful, motivating factors in the making and unmaking of newly formed regimes. Anti-colonialism, national sovereignty, and national unity are the universal aspirations of new states. These aspirations are also the source of these states' crises, their inability to deal with 'neo' colonialism, to maintain national unity which is disrupted by old historical ethnic and tribal rivalries, and to achieve true independent national and political sovereignty. Thus crises of new states arise from problems linked to their frustrated aspirations, dependency, civil war, and political and structural instability and underdevelopment.

The other motivating force and orientation of new states is the ideology of development. By development, or developmentalism, I mean here an aspiration for a comprehensive process of socio-economic change that includes emphatic attitudinal and institutional alternatives requisite to the creation of a modern productive and industrial system. By development, I also mean modernization, secularization, institutional and structural autonomy and cohesivity, the uses of science and technology to resolve social and economic problems of new states. From urbanization to literacy, from population control to complex industrial development. To meet the aspirations of developmentalism what is necessary is, above all, in my opinion, a political system that is both extractive (resources) and regulative of society, and economy, and population.

The aspirations to expand both extractive and regulative capabilities[3] of new states are responsible for most of its serious crises. The circle is vicious. To extract resources from society you need to expand regulative instruments. To sustain and develop regulative instruments you need the type of society from which you can extract resources. To successfully extract resources you need stable and sustaining regulative instruments or, in the language of modern comparative politics, politically developed structures.

They are, as I alluded to earlier, conspicuous in their absence of developed, institutionalized, and sustaining political structures, institutions and procedures. These regimes, whose orientations are developmental, are shortlived because they dominate weak, regulative instruments.

Political interventionism, military in the case of most, if not all, new states, is an effort (mostly unsuccessful) by the military institution to surrogate for absent or politically underdeveloped regulative instruments.

(2)   STABLE POLITICAL SYSTEMS AND CIVIL–MILITARY RELATIONS

The most significant fact about civil–military relations is the modernity of the concept. It is a post-1789 political problem.[4] Authority in pre-democratic pre-nation state eras and in the pre-bureaucratic state was feudal, mercantilist, and imperial. Political intervention meant the intervention of a tyrant, a dynasty, a feudal lord, or an imperial governor. In other words, politics was the study of the dynamics of rulers and rulership The only type of intervention which was historically legitimate was that of a ruler. The coup d'état is an example. As Herbert Gooch's perceptive study demonstrates, this was chiefly associated with an act of government undertaken by a sovereign.[5] It was not conceived as an illegitimate act. Nor was it a praetorian regime.

The modern age of democracy, constitutionalism, mass authoritarianism, and the nation-state deals with a new sovereign, the 'people'. In modern popular democratic and totalitarian systems, authority relationships between the civilian and military are delineated as clearly as are the discrete structures, functions, and procedures of government, the legislatures, executives, and judiciaries. However, the balance of civil–military relations in modern times is more dependent on the stability or instability of the political order than on affiliation with a ruler, as was the case with the coups d'état and military regimes in the pre-modern age. Just as the political concept of civil–military relations is related to modern nation-states, praetorianism is linked with the two most significant structures and powerful instruments of modern unstable political order – the bureaucracy and the military.

The modernization-mobilization revolution of modern times in states with weak regimes created and enhanced two prominent structures of the classical eighteenth–nineteenth centuries' nation-state, the bureaucracy and the military establishment. The conspicuous growth of the military, as against the relative impoverishment of political parties, pressure groups, organized socio-economic groups and classes, and even an articulated and organized public opinion, characterizes the praetorian syndrome: a weak state, interventionist regime, kaleidoscopic changes in authorities, and permanent and guaranteed insecurity and political illegitimacy.

The purpose of intervention is to accomplish mission impossible – create stability, order, and legitimacy. The goal is to replace a troubled government. Instead, praetorianism begets praetorianism. Nevertheless, the concept of popular sovereignty, the political signpost of the modern age, calls for allegiance to office, not to men, even in praetorian regimes.

The creation of offices, of bureaucracies, and of a state apparatus marks the end of pre-bureaucratic empires and the emergence of the modern bureaucratic state.[6] The state apparatus, constitutionalism, and the procedures of authority, the relationship between separate and functional political structures, brought into focus a new and crucial political relationship between civil–political authorities and bureaucratic and military functions and establishments. The problem was one of constitutional and political responsibility. To whom are the military responsible – the monarch, the executive, to both the executive and the legislature; and what differentiates the governmental bureaucracy from the military, if anything? Is the military establishment another bureaucratic organization of the modern nation-state, or is it a special structure with an esprit, virtue, and a mission orientation? Is the military establishment of the modern nation-state an exclusive corporate and special instrument of the state with special privileges bestowed on it, or is it, once more, a bureaucratic and subservient civil servant structure in mufti?[7] The prevalent exclusivist and corporatist orientations, especially of continental[8] armies, but also of the British aristocratic officer corps, actually *created* the issues of modern civil–military relations.[9] The type of civil–military relations that prevailed in nineteenth-century Europe and America, identified by Huntington as the professional objective type of civil–military relations, was characterized by the distinctions made between the state, the military, and the bureaucracy.[10] Military professionalism, a sense of mission and responsibility to clients distinguished soldiers from some state bureaucrats and politicians in the modern nation-state. The professional model of civil–military relations (Huntington's objective model) is, thus, the product of a stable political regime that dominated the modern nation-state whose supreme legitimacy, in the case of the USA, was 'the people', and in Prussia, 'dynasty'. Both democratic America and authoritarian Prussia shared one fundamental political asset – legitimacy. Unquestionably, the responsibility of the classical professional soldier was not always to the state. In the case of Prussia-Germany, he was responsible to the War Lord and the dynasty,[11] while, in France, the officer, on the whole, accepted republican regimes.[12] The few cases where the French army defied constitutional authority and/or the republican regime, certainly suggests an early form of twentieth-century praetorianism. But there was no inherent conflict between civil–military authorities as long as both structures functioned in the prescribed manner; both the military and the bureaucracy were to defend the government and/or the state. The nation-state, the regime, and the authorities (the government) were legitimate. The military was not inclined to change this arrangement, of which, anyway, they formed a respectable part. Also, political stability and a strong regime could easily, as they did, resist military insurrection, interventionism, and praetorianism. It is the instability of a government that is the crucial factor bearing on civil–military relations. The classical model of military professionalism, linked as it is to an historical place and time – the rise of the modern nation-states in Europe – is an intrinsic part of a stable political structure. Conflict between civilian and military authorities, in the classical model, was not over political supremacy. The civilian supremacy was unquestioned. The conflict between civilian and military authorities in stable authoritative and legitimate political systems has become one over *policy* not power. The military was not expected, nor was it oriented in the classical model, to intervene (except in very exceptional cases) in electoral, representative politics.

Since the function of the military was to defend authority, and not society, it almost always came to the support of the state in suppressing political dissidents, democrats, socialists, and others. The function of the military, to defend stability at home, was almost consistent with its function to defend the state from its external enemies. The function of the military was, therefore, to improve the condition of authority, not to challenge civilian authority. The nineteenth-century military was dedicated to the defense of the sovereign, not popular sovereignty. Military support was expected under stable conditions. Under unstable conditions, the military was expected to support the state, not necessarily the regime; this was the case with the early, but fundamental, praetorianism of Spain in the nineteenth century.[13] The par excellence model of praetorianism was Latin America at the same period. In Spain, the military supported royalty, but refused to support the Republic and challenged republican, democratic, central authority. Intervention is almost guaranteed under conditions of political instability, as was the case of Spain and Latin America in the nineteenth and early twentieth centuries. But what was not studied, nor even identified, were the conflicts that arose between the civilian authorities and the military esablishments.[14]

Historians, sociologists, political theorists, and military strategists were concerned with the analysis of the modern military establishment, the history of warfare and military campaigns, the study of the generalship of the great captains, and with strategy and reform of the military establishment. Few, if any, directed their attention to the conflict between civilian and military authority. Gaetano Mosca was one of the few to analyze the role of standing armies in the making of European civilization, and of the importance of civilian supremacy for the maintenance of European civilization.[15] Carl von Clausewitz, the most illustrious military philosopher of modern times, who demonstrated the symbiotic linkage between war and peace and grand strategy, that is, the combination of policy and military science, failed to perceive the conflict between civilian and military authorities. Clausewitz, who introduced the volatile and impressive political concept of policy as strategy, failed even to identify the conflict between the civilian and the military, even though the essence of his reform was the differentiation of military functions from political ones.

The politics of the reform of the Prussian army, in which Clausewitz was involved, were directly connected with the problems of professionalism, skill, and responsibility – requisites of the classical model of civil–military relations. The absence of attention and interest, theoretical and otherwise, paid to the conflict between civil and military relations stemmed from a corresponding absence of interest in democratic theory and the concept of popular sovereignty. As long as the sovereign's authority and its institutions prevailed, and the military establishment was conceived as an instrument of the sovereign in Anglo-American constitutional theory, (in Prussia, as an organic part of the patrimonial dynasty), then the issue of both constitutionalism – the division of authority – and of democracy – popular sovereignty – were not intellectually necessary to define the sovereign's relations to his instruments.

Only theories of public administration, and of management, defined the scope of analysis of civil–military relations. Additionally, normative theory, so prevalent among political and legal minds in the nineteenth-

and early twentieth-century Europe and America, failed to identify the behavioral and dynamic aspects of politics, thus overlooking the fertile field of civil–military relations. The issue of legitimacy was related to the sovereign's control rather than to popular check. It is interesting in passing that republican theory is embodied in the American Constitution, and the concept of popular sovereignty embodied in its preamble, while Article II of the Constitution that created the President as Commander-in-Chief is not related to democratic, but to popular, sovereignty theory. In other words, the republican requisite embodied in the Commander-in-Chief was embodied in the Constitution in connection with the presidency, not with democratic theory. The civilian supremacy clause demonstrated the Founding Fathers' concern with a popular and constitutional, not monarchical, executive rule.[16] The President was established as Supreme Commander not to solve conflicts of civil–military relations (until so interpreted by the Supreme Court and President Lincoln), or out of concern for the professional integrity of the military, but as a matter of constitutional theory, of the separation of powers, and the division of labor between the three branches of the newly established democratic republic.

The professional military, in the modern nation-state, intervenes in national security and foreign policy. In the second half of the twentieth century, especially among the two superpowers, the military has become, at times, co-equal, (as in the USSR) and a senior partner (in the USA) with civilian and bureaucratic authorities in the formulation and implementation of national security policy. Once again, true to its legacy of clientship, the military's responsibility to sovereign and constitutional authorities was unchallenged. Civil and military relations in the classical model are irrevocably connected with the clear proviso of civilian supremacy and military political responsibility, and significant participation in policy-making.

(3) UNSTABLE POLITICAL SYSTEMS AND CIVIL–MILITARY RELATIONS

The most conspicuous model of civil–military relations in weak regimes or unstable states is the praetorian model.[17] Types of civil–military relations do not necessarily coincide with the classification of political systems into Western, Communist, and developing nations, nor is the classification of civil–military relations divided along an ideological continuum of conservative, liberal, and radical, nor is it a classification anchored in geography. Modern praetorianism is the most conspicuous political arrangement of weak states.

Praetorianism is a type of civil–military relations with high incidence in regimes and states lacking political legitimacy and supportive political structures, groupings, and organized interests. Praetorianism is the mark of the weak and nonlegitimate regime; it is the only type of civil–military relationship prevailing in the weak politics. It is the political system that is continuously patrolled by the military. This type of civil–military relations conforms to F. M. Watkins's classic definition of praetorianism (1933), 'a situation where the military class of a given society exercises independent political power."[18] Praetorianism is, therefore, linked to instability, to the absence of a powerful executive or a reasonably representative legislative authority, and the absence of group consciousness. Above all, it is symptomatic of political decay and the inability to harness and transfer social change into political order.[19]

The praetorian state (where governments are frequently weak) and the praetorian civil–military type are convergent. The modern weak state has become a victim of military interventionism. The modern weak government is characterized as much by a rigid and ineffective executive as it is by lack of instruments and structures to channel political support. Above all, the characteristic of the modern weak states is the *disproportionate* growth of the historical instruments of the classical nation-states, the bureaucracy and the military, over political structures, institutions, and parties. The most powerful instruments of weak states are precisely those structures which traditionally and constitutionally, in the classical model are subservient and instrumental, that is, the military and the bureaucracy. Obversely, the weak government generates, by virtue of its popular institutional impotence, the use of nonpolitical and extrapolitical structures. Those who argue that the administrative state creates legitimacy are misperceiving the praetorian nature of such a state. Legitimacy cannot be secured from the barrel of a gun or from the administrative apparatus. Legitimacy of the modern state can be secured only from the popular organized and representative sovereign – the party system, the interest-group network, the organized articulation system, the media, and, of course, group and collective support. Legitimacy derived from the barrel of the gun that dominates the weak state is passively supported. Thus, praetorianism begets praetorianism. In the weak state and non-legitimate regime the chances are that civil–military relations are skewed in the direction of military domination, if not supremacy. Military corporatism then supersedes professionalism. The only instrument that possesses the instrument of force – the military – has the opportunity, which it often uses, to seize power and turn the classical civil–military arrangement upside down.[20]

Praetorian civil–military relations represent an intense competition for power over the weak state between the two modern and relatively more efficient and institutionalized elite and structures of the praetorian state, the military, and the bureaucracy.[21] The two are supposedly functional and service organizations and are, constitutionally and otherwise, subservient to the state, but this is not the case in the weak states. These civil–military relations are a continuous and unequal struggle for domination between the military and other interests, including weakly organized political groups, on the one hand, and between the military and the bureaucracy, on the other.

In fact, what produces the different types of praetorianism are the kinds of coalitions they create to sustain themselves in power. The coalitions could be with one another, or between the bureaucracy and the military and another political group. Praetorian civil–military relations are clientelistic not regime-oriented. On the whole, the militaries of praetorian states become rather rigid, corporate, noncohesive alliances of ambitious and interventionist officers, bureaucrats, and opportunistic politicians.

The case of Bonapartism is worth mentioning here. Bonapartism was a nineteenth-century concept synonymous with military intervention. What Bonapartism actually represented was republicanism on horseback.[22] Bonapartism was a regime dominated by some type of interventionism, generally military. Although this regime, argues Zeldin, was a truly republican one, that is, subscribing to popular sovereignty, it was, nevertheless, a product of the struggle over the domination of the republic by several political and bureaucratic forces, and in the Bonapartist case was a regime dominated by the military. Bonapartism and the Spanish *Pronunciamiento* regimes are the antecedent of praetorianism: the struggle for domination of a regime that subscribes to the ideology of popular sovereignty, but whose political order is weak or disrupted.

(4) TYPES OF MODERN MILITARY PRAETORIANISM

When we speak of modern military praetorianism, we distinguish between three forms (or subtypes): autocratic, oligarchic, and corporate. Military autocracy is simple military tyranny, unchecked personal authority embodied in a military officer. Military oligarchy is a political system in which executive power is wielded by the few, who are mostly military men. The chief executive is either a former military man who is now a civilian, or a civilian figurehead whose support comes exclusively from the military. Intrinsically, the only difference between the military oligarchy and the military tyranny is the number of rulers involved.

Corporate praetorianism is characterized by a military–civilian fusionist rule. Governmental authority resides in a coalition of military and civilians (bureaucrats, managers, and technocrats) governing with little or no external political control. In the executive, either civilians or officers may be in the majority and the supreme head may be a civilian, who may not even possess military skills. The distinction between oligarchic and praetorianism is derived from socio-economic and political, institutional different conditions. The corporate type, on the whole, is a regime that rules over a relatively developed society, where socio-economic groups are corporatively organized and are linked to the corporative state. The oligarchical type represents a poorly stratified society and the absence, or near absence, of organized autonomous economic interest groups and political articulation and interest aggregation structures.

The corporate praetorian regime makes it costly for society to resist the interests of corporative groups supported by the state and especially the military. Political bargaining is conducted between organized groups where the military either arbitrates or dictates policies. The oligarchical type represents a military more powerful than other organized groups and a bureaucracy with which it allies, the latter either its silent or junior partner. Power becomes dependent solely on the military in oligarchic praetorianism.

Oligarchic corporate praetorian regimes are types which link society with state. It is a product of industrialization and modernization and exists in the Middle Eastern and South American states.[23] Corporate praetorianism is a political system or regime where organizations officially represent 'private' interests and where the range of state activities are wide, managerial, bureaucratic, technocratic, repressive, and efficient.

The corporate (and oligarchic) state is an exclusionary system, that is, one that excludes and restricts the popular sector (urban working classes). The state as authoritarian 'patron of patrons' (the patron of the corporative conglomerate) is arbitrated and stabilized by the military. This is the corporate-praetorian state. It is identified with (1) a weak regime, (2) state penetration into society, (3) corporative structures, (4) the army as a ruler that arbitrates the corporative alliance. The state is praetorian and so is the army. The former is weak, the latter interventionist. It is corporate and authoritarian. Corporate-praetorianism is a political system or regime where the autonomy of the corporative group is dependent on the state. The military being the arbiter of the corporative conglomerate is more autonomous than other corporative structures, in the sense that it is the most persistent interventionist.[24]

The single most important source of political support for the praetorian regime is the military establishment. In the case of praetorian tyranny, only part of the military is necessary for support. In corporate praetorianism additional support can come from such groups as the bureaucracy, the church, labor unions, and the technocracy, but it remains secondary. Clearly, without the support of the military establishment or its major section, no praetorian regime can survive.

As mentioned earlier, the type of political support is the factor that differentiates corporate-oligarchical from tyrannical praetorianism. The tyrannical variety seeks or expects only the support of the military. The corporate-oligarchical seeks to widen its base of support. On the whole, Brazil, Argentina, and Chile, the major states of the corporate-praetorian type, engage in restricted and highly disciplined political mobilization. However, in the area of economic modernization, the corporate and oligarchic types are actively committed to industrialization and economic transformation, although, again, they pursue these goals while restricting the growth of alternative political groups. The praetorian systems in these major South American states and in Peru as well, are committed to agrarian and industrial modernization and even to social and tax reforms. To some extent, this is even true of Nasser's and Sadat's Egypt. Other regimes, however, are less committed to economic modernization.

Modern praetorianism's two most interesting structural political innovations are the military party (a party created by harnessing the popular or radical party to the military regime) and the military executive. Both are auxiliary structures designed to widen the base of political support, help sustain the praetorian regime, and create structures and procedures for regime legitimization. They are not instruments of mobilization.

These two creations are part of the experience of oligarchic praetorianism, which is most prevalent in the Arab Middle East. In the Middle East, the control executive is the Revolutionary Command Council, the instrument of conquest and power; in other words, the executive committee of the coup. Once in power, the RCC assumes different forms, calling itself variously the presidential office, the Cabinet, or council. The motivation in all cases, however, is the same – the continuance of political monopoly. Although the new regime may find a political party or conquerer an established popular party, this party will be kept weak so that the RCC can exclusively dominate the regime. The weak, single-party's function has never been to mobilize the masses, as demonstrated by the history of Ayub's 'basic democracy', or Nasser's semi-bureaucratic-cadre Arab Socialist Union. The function of such groups is clearly to assist the praetorian oligarchy in running the state, whether by dominating the state's elephantine bureaucracy (Egypt), or by subduing traditional opponents and splinter groups (Syria). The Liberation Rally, Nasser's major, nascent, single-party effort, at first was to serve as the junta's chief propaganda vehicle. Primarily occupied with pamphleteering and proselytizing for the Nasserite 'Egyptian revolution' in the countryside and in mosques, it ended in failure in 1954. In propaganda, however, Arab military regimes have been more successful than other praetorians, such as the African regimes.[25]

With the exception of these two innovations – the RCC and the weak, single party – no other parallel and auxiliary structures have been introduced by modern praetorians. In fact, the general inability to institutionalize political structures was closely linked to praetorian oligarchy's failure to institutionalize the military executive and military party. Thus, even the military oligarchies are autocracies that depend on one man's charisma (Nasser), or on the political skills of a Sadat, Asad, or Ghaddafi. The military tyranny of Amin's, Mobutu's and Bokassa's sub-Saharan, African style made no contribution to parallel or auxiliary structures of modern praetorianism, although they introduced considerable refinements in the practices of terror and torture.

(5) THE MILITARY AND THE AUTHORITARIAN COMMUNIST STATE

Without exception, the modern authoritarian state is linked to a large-scale military organization. This is true of both institutionalized and non-institutionalized authoritarian regimes. Thus the special relationship between the party and the army in the highly institutionalized authoritarian regimes are of particular interest to students of authoritarianism.

Unlike the praetorian or the corporative regimes the party-state system represents a web, a network of complex organizations whose relationships to one another are not neutral and isolated, but integrated and, in some cases, are symbiotic. There are times of intervention and episodes of isolated neutrality, but withdrawal to isolated neutrality is relatively brief. The military in the party-state is a senior partner, a major ally of the regime. The party's iron rule necessitates the establishment of hegemony and supremacy over society and state. Thus, unlike praetorianism where the military could set itself as a sole ruler or even as an arbiter among several elites of the regime, in the party–state military intervention means also intervention on behalf of the party against 'Bonapartist' elements among other institutional elites. Most interventions are not military versus party, but a civilian faction (for example, Khrushchev, 1957; Mao Tse-tung, 1966–7) recruiting the military, or part of it, into intra-elite struggles, much as civilian opponents in praetorian regimes recruit military men for a coup coalition. The army, whose institutional autonomy has been increasing, assumes the role ascribed by Kolkowicz as (1) the *protector* of the CPSU's waning legitimacy; (2) the *guardian* of ideological revolutionary heritage of the party; (3) *quasi-revolutionary* agent of Soviet interests in the Third World; (4) *Traditional* defender of the homeland. Thus time sequences of the party–army relationship in the last seven decades of civil–military relations in the USSR demonstrate elements of military dependency and autonomy, of accommodation and collaboration, of expansion with each other in different times. Civil–military relations in the Soviet Union are symbiotic, shaped by important systemic, structural, and ideological parameters of interaction, such as (1) the hegemonial power of the single party; (2) the absence of constitutional means of transfer of power; (3) the presence of security and para-military organizations within, and around, the military establishment; (4) the anti-militaristic traditions of Marxism–Leninism which consider standing professional armies as anti-revolutionary forces and a threat to the revolutionary goals of party hegemony in Communist societies.[26] The military, more than other institutional structure in the USSR, developed special institutional loyalties and relationships to party and state. The professional concept of responsibility and mission and its associative corporate values guarantees the political quiescence of the military, but also its partnership with the party which enhances the military's political role, influence, and privileged position. In the case of China, the party–army symbiosis and dependency are even greater, as is the case of Cuba. In the People's Republic of China, the party–army symbiosis is developed to such an extent that, despite the professionalization of the military since the 1950s, it is still a major political actor in Chinese politics in the 1980s. Again, time sequences in China between 1920 and 1980 will demonstrate periods of dependency and autonomy, eras where there were practically no distinctions between party and army; of involvement, as well as non-involvement, in party affairs. During the Great People's Cultural Revolution, the army demonstrated the political importance of the hyphenated relationship between the most powerful structures of Chinese communism. The military became Mao's mailed fist against the party. It can be assumed that in the absence of the army, the Chinese Communist Party might have been weakened and further fragmented if the military would not be employed as a *political* instrument to fortify the party. The army that was used as an instrument of Mao's purification and the return to pristine communism was also used by his successors to restore the order in both party and state!

Rather than withdrawing at the end of GPCR, the military consolidated its political position and strengthened its domination over regional power structures. This coincided with the reconstruction of the party.[27]

The limited disengagement of the military from politics demonstrates that the post-GPCR upheaval is, as yet, not completely settled and the military still serves as the revolution's praetorian guard (sometimes represented by party, and other times by army). The military in China plays, and will continue to play, a role in the politics of leadership succession as it did in the USSR in the past and is expected to do in the future. The military will almost certainly have considerable input in the next political leadership struggle in the USSR. The era of withdrawal coincides with a relative era of party stability, the eras of intervention are linked to political crises in Communist systems. The most prominent crisis management and conflict resolution is accomplished within the confines of the party by both the army and the party.

The case of Cuba certainly demonstrates the symbiotic, almost organic, relationship between army and party.[28] The armed forces in Cuba began as the 'Politico-Military Vanguard' of the Revolution, and gave birth to the new Communist Party in the early 1960s. If the Chinese Revolution was born in the bosom of the People's Liberation Army the Cuban Revolution is a progeny of the army. The army predates the party, and the National Chinese Communist Party apparatus was too weak to fully subordinate the military to party authority.

The military in Communist systems is Janus faced, the guarantor of the party civilian regime, and the protector of party hegemony which also implies intervention into party affairs during hegemonial crises within the party. In Romania, according to Kenneth Jowitt,[29] the relationship between the party and the army is conflictual and necessary. Both party and army are assigned heroic roles. In Romania, conflict is resolved by the party leader Ceausescu, whose role is similar to Lenin and Stalin in the USSR. This was also true of Mao, Ho and Kim Il Sung. The leader subordinates the heroism of party and the army. Reconciliation of party–army conflicts in the USSR has been routinized by the Politburo, the arbiter of the system and the surrogate for the maximum leader. The leader – Stalin, Ceausescu, Kim, Mao, Tito, and Ho – reconciles the army at the expense of its institutional autonomy. In the USSR, the relationship is more complex, especially in the absence of the maximum leader since Stalin. In the era of today's collective leadership, the military certainly enjoys greater institutional autonomy. The leader and the collective leadership represent the final arbiters of hegemony, heroics, and supremacy in party–state Communist systems. In Yugoslavia, the military never ceased to be part of Tito's party-state. Yet Tito's disappearance may create conditions for a collective leadership that would probably change the relationship between the party and army only to reiterate the principle of partnership and cooperation, and protecting the party-state.

Authoritarian regimes and the military's special relationship has been analyzed thus far in terms of symbiotic and conflictual relationship. The next question to be posed is, could authoritarian party-state regimes survive without the military? My answer is negative. The function of the military in the party-state is to protect the party's hegemony, supremacy, and heroics even when that conflicts with its self-image and institutional autonomy. In fact, without the military, I presume the reign of the party-state might come to an end.

Party-states, at least Communist ones, have always been more interested in policy results than in formal procedures. Thus the 'rules of the game' (that is, procedures) for resolving serious policy conflicts tend to be implicit, vague, and highly flexible. 'Winning' within the party is usually (but not always – for example, Mao) decisive. But 'winning' within the party is generally a process governed first and foremost by the dictum: 'By any means necessary.' This lack of reliance on procedures is derived from from ideology and from the very fact of party hegemony – that is, no other center of power is autonomous enough to challenge the legitimacy of the party on procedural grounds. To the extent that the symbiotic, party–army relationship exists, with the army enforcing party hegemony, winning a policy conflict in the party *is* winning.

But, if we move away from the symbiosis (that is, remove the army or assume its neutrality), what is the result? A losing faction within the party may refuse to surrender – that is, may carry the struggle into other arenas with no fear of military retribution – for example, Mao's appeal to the masses at the outset of the Cultural Revolution. What they would actually be doing, of course, is challenging the hegemony of the party – hence the very essence of the party-state.

In sum: the absence of the military removes a key restraint on intra-elite conflicts which may challenge party hegemony. This is more likely when the procedures for resolving intra-party conflict are poorly developed and often ignored. The absence of an institutionalized and autonomous military could not only create intra-party conflicts, but also *systemic*, structural, and the ideological parameters of the party-state. It augurs an implicit threat to the party's revolutionary goals, and an explicit threat to the party's coercive and participatory functions. Since the military would not be just dissolved extra- and intra-party elites, it could generate structural and societal conflict that the party itself could no longer sustain. Contrary to theorists who warn against military coercive and participatory functions as a threat to the party, the opposite would be true, that is, in the absence of the military, the party will be subject to more serious intra- and extra-party coercive and societal threats. In contradistinction to praetorian armies, which often threaten authority, legitimacy, and order, the Soviet military heavily contributes to political, economic, and party development in the USSR, above all the party's security and its commitments to foreign and defense policies. Party–army relationships, I concur with Kolkowicz, are certainly not purchased without conflict nor is the military unaware of the dangers to its own if the party-state collapses.[30]

The case of China and Cuba are conspicuous demonstrations of the primary role that the military plays in institutionalizing the party; and, in China, in an effort to reform both party and state. The military, in fact, is the hyphen that buckles the party to state without which single-party authoritarianism could not be sustained. Colton warns of the dangers of the army's role as a participatory mobilization vehicle.[31] In my view, the military's participation in Communist politics in fact is the *normal* and *natural* state of affairs in the party-state system. As a guardian of the heroic party, of ideology, and as a potential coercive instrument, the army in the party-state is ipso facto political, and politically oriented. The degree of tolerance of military participation in Soviet, Chinese, Cuban, and Yugoslavian politics is high by virtue of its own definition as the guardian of the Communist Constitution. Military intervention is considered a positive, and sometimes welcome, political act in authoritarian regimes, but it is taken at the initiative of the party elites. Certainly it is so in praetorian and corporative states.

For the theoretical disappearance of the military in the party-state is a step toward praetorianism. The army in the party-state guarantees the regime from the praetorian syndrome prevalent and characteristic of the noninstitutionalized regime and state. 'A more appropriate approach,' Colton writes, 'often is to orient the analysis toward military *participation* in politics rather than the process of civilian control over the military.'[32] Yet, contrary to Colton's assumption, the higher the scope of military participation in the party-state, the more safe the regime.

The conflict between army and party in the party-state system enhances the political power of both institutions and the stability of the regime. The military's institutional and societal goals and values are congruent with the party. Yet their internal values may not be convergent, as is the case with large-scale, complex organizations. Here, the bureaucratic model is useful to analyze the relationship between powerful converging and conflicting, complex organizations like the party and army in Communist systems. Yet, as Colton writes, 'in comparative perspective, the Party-Army relationship has been remarkably free of direct conflict, and the safest prediction is that such confrontation will be avoided in the future.'[33] Odom correctly identifies the consensual (in contradiction to Kolkowicz and Colton) aspects of party–army relationships. Their alignments are horizontal. The military is an administrative arm of the party. Divisions over military policy are not civil–military but intra-party factional divisions. The extent of interlocking between party and army, according to Odom, is underestimated by Kolkowicz–Colton. The military–party relationship is symbiotic. They share to a considerable extent the same values, even if their roles are clearly differentiated. Political values are not necessarily identical with political roles. In short, 'the military [in the USSR] is first and foremost a political institution.'[34]

In a civil war, the military 'would reinvent the party or one very similar.'[35] The army in the party-state identifies its values with that of the party. The military in the authoritarian state is dependent on the central system – the party. The party exclusivity and hegemonial aspirations depends on the military in legitimizing the party-state, but leaves the military a considerable role and input into stabilizing and maintaining modern authoritarianism. Some would also argue that the tight relationships between the two could also disintegrate and fragment. Certainly it could, but it is not a very likely prospect in an institutionalized authoritarian political system. It would not be too vigorous to argue that by institutionalized authoritarianism, we also mean the party-state system where the military buckles the party. The military in modern authoritarian states is a central political and bureaucratic structure, endowed with political and sometimes considerable executive power. The most interesting political development of party-state systems is that the linkage between two authoritarian and competing structures enhances political stability, modifying each other's excessive behavior and routinizing the dependency on one another. No other political system will (democratic) or could (praetorian) tolerate this type of relationship between the central instrument of political control and the military establishment.

(6) IDEOLOGY, ORGANIZATION AND PRAETORIANISM

The failure of reformists, praetorians, and other noninstitutionalized authoritarianism is connected with the failure to either successfully emulate or adopt the political structures of institutionalized authoritarianism, the single party, and the ideological machinery. The success of authoritarianism in the Bolshevik model is connected with the linkage between ideology and organization.[36] The former becomes the organizational weapon and the latter the oil of the organizational machinery.

The single, ideological, and 'totalitarian' party and its auxiliary instruments, and the propaganda-ideological networks become necessary to sustain developmental authoritarianism. The cases of Egypt and Peru clearly demonstrate that the failure of the reformist has to do with the ideology and organization:[37] Nasser and his free officers corps opted for an Egyptian revolution to be carried out and implemented by the military. After a decade of failure, Nasser hesitantly opted to establish this time a political, rather than bureaucratic, instrument to lift the revolution in the form of the Arab Socialist Union (ASU) (1962). It was designed to separate the military from the machinery of reform, and the reform from the administrative structures. Again, he failed. Nasser was not fully committed to an experiment – the ASU – that could wrest political power away from himself, but he would not have been dissatisfied to see the ASU wrest political power away from the military establishment. Thus, Nasser failed to establish an organization imbued with a revolutionary ideology (as the ASU was supposed to serve), and instead used the nationalist and pan-Arabist ideology to make his praetorian and authoritarian rule more effective, not the revolution.[38] Ideology, in this case, did not buttress the revolutionary organization; it made authoritarianism more effective. 'The fact that the military – and generally *only* the military – made final key decisions in their private closed quarters, "hermetically sealed" from potentially important civilian output.'[39]

(7) THE GOVERNING OF PRAETORIAN STATES: THE FUTURE OF PRAETORIANISM

In the last two decades we have witnessed the emergence of few praetorian states that are relatively effective or enduring. Unquestionably, the most stable of the unstable types are the corporate-praetorians.

The cases of Brazil since 1966, Argentina since 1966, Peru after 1970, and Chile since 1973 demonstrate that the praetorian regimes that represent a coalition of modern groups and structures – military, bureaucracy, technocrats, industrialists, and union managers – stand a better chance for political longevity, not necessarily for legitimacy. No praetorian-organized and dominated coalition, however authoritarian, repressive, and 'efficient', could transfer political assets into political legitimacy. What is guaranteed is more stable order, but the price is stagnation of social dynamics.

The cases of Egypt, Syria, Iraq demonstrate that long-term military rule by military organizations (and those few states have the most powerful military organizations next to Israel in the Middle East), or the moderniz-ation revolution (Egypt, Syria, Iraq, and Iran are supreme examples of military modernization), changed the nature and structure of the regime, the political control over society. The military intervention in politics, voluntary or coercive, is a product of the ideological, secular, and devel-opmental aspirations of the latter, as it is of other modernizing groups, parties, and rulers. The praetorian syndrome is an ongoing process until the regulative structures will finally dominate the extractive motivations.

In sub-Saharan Africa, we have witnessed the rise of more praetorian tyrannies: Uganda, the Central African Republic, Chad, and Togo. In each, we have witnessed the emergence of tyrants whose chief motivation is to stay in power and eliminate and annihilate opposition within the military and outside it. We clearly witness Decalo's model prevail: that several African armies are noncohesive, tribal, nonWesternized, non-professional, and personalist; that they are as corrupt and inefficient as the civilian regimes they have replaced; that recruitment and promotion is not based on skill or merit, but on personal idiosyncracies of tyrants; tribal connections; that the military is neither interested in, nor capable of, raising the momentum of modernization-mobilization; that grievances are not corporate but personalist, and that competing ambitions are of greater value than so-called national aspirations; that army rule is corrupt (at least not less than former civilian rule) and economic development policy is bankrupt; and that personal, not political, institutionalization is of the utmost concern for the competing, ruthless and venal officers; and that the hallmark of praetorianism – instability – reigns. Here corporate fragmentation, personal strife, instability, and authoritarian rule are indeed high.[40]

Nor does the subscribing to popular sovereignty ipso facto render corporate praetorianism into a popular and legitimate political system. Various recent studies on the political dynamics of actual oligarchic and corporate praetorian regimes – Nigeria, Peru, Brazil, Indonesia, Egypt, Syria and Iraq, Burma, and Thailand[41] – demonstrate that the essentials of praetorianism are inherent in their political order: instability, illegiti-macy, absence of collective group action, of representation of effective political parties and interest groups, and, above all, inability to close the gap between the aspirations and the realities of popular sovereignty. A coalition between the military and bureaucracy, as is the case of corporate and oligarchic praetorianism (Brazil, Argentina, Egypt,

Burma, Thailand) helps sustain the regime but not to legitimize it, or for that matter to stabilize society, order, and politics. In fact, one major purpose of all praetorian types is to harness social change and political dynamics. The difference between one praetorian regime and another is just the scope and level of effective manipulation of temporary order and social discontent, dissent, and alienation. The prospects for praetorianism today are:

(a)   More praetorian regimes, states, and militaries. The World Coup Zone[42] is increasing, as is the number of more unstable political orders, some states are without even a semblance of order and/or stability, and some regimes are only passing affairs.

(b)   The rapid increase of new nations and mini-states which are inherently unstable enhances praetorianism. This is especially true of sub-Saharan Africa as well as the new (and old) Arab states extending from the Persian Gulf along the Arabian peninsula, over the Red Sea to the Horn of Africa.

(c)   The breakdown of some of the precarious, federated new states and the deeply rooted conflict within multiethnic states (Lebanon, Malaysia, Ethiopia, Chad, Congo Kinshasa, Pakistan, Nigeria (1966–9), Sudan (1966–70), Iraq to 1973) contributes heavily to instability of the political order. Some of the above could not control revolution among ethnic populations and eventually became praetorian. The penetration of weak states into one another also contributes to praetorianism and to instability of new states, for example, the PLO into Jordan and Lebanon; Uganda into Tanzania and Kenya; the UAR, during Nasser's time, into South Arabia; and India into Pakistan. The revolutions of black people in Southern Africa certainly guarantees more praetorian regimes. The rise of ethnic nationalities in Central Asia and the Persian Gulf ensures more instability and praetorianism.

(d)   The futility on the part of several new states of aspiring to adopt a revolutionary ideology and, at the same time, a stable system of politics also ensures praetorianism. The founding father's aspirations to adopt democracy, socialism and, in my view, also vulgar Marxism (Angola, Mozambique, South Yemen, Ethiopia) will have been dismal failures and only lead to disappointment, recrimination, massacre, and racination. I predict that the fate of the so-called Marxist South Arabian states of the PDRY, North Yemen, and Somalia will be similar to the 'democratic' and 'socialist' experiments of Egypt, Syria, and Iraq – more praetorianisms, this time under a Marxist and liberal guise. The dilution of ideology buttressed by the rise of ethnicity and religious fundamentalism in Central Asia, and the Arabian Peninsula and the Persian Gulf will produce a greater Coup Zone, more praetorian states, more unstable regimes, and greater internal and regional international conflict.

Praetorianism is an incomplete political system. The praetorian and oligarchic tyrannies may not disappear and the corporate praetorian regimes will survive, not by virtue of consensual political order of societal satisfaction, but by the brute use of a sophisticated, highly technological military force combined with bureaucratic corporative organizations that will substitute order for chaos, but at the same time reduce the quality of life, and achieve strictly coercive legitimacy and ruthless political order.

In the case of the Communist systems, the rule of the military will increase, and the military establishment will become a pillar of the party's cohesiveness and political order. The symbiosis of party–army will, of course, have serious implications for the foreign and international policy of the Communist systems.

NOTES

1　See John Samuel Fitch, *The Military Coup d'État as a Political Process: Ecuador 1948–66* (Baltimore, Md.: Johns Hopkins University Press, 1977) pp. 11–13.
2　Alfred Stepan, *The State and Society: Peru in Comparative Perspective* (Princeton, NJ: Princeton University Press, 1978).
3　I freely have borrowed the concepts 'extractive' and 'regulative' from A. James Gregor, 'Italian Fascism: A Case Study in Mass Mobilization, Developmental Dictatorship' (unpublished manuscript, University of California, Berkeley, Calif., 1977).
4　Amos Perlmutter, *The Military in Modern Times* (New Haven, Conn.: Yale University Press, 1977).
5　Herbert Gooch, 'Coup d'Etat: Historical and Ideological Dimension of the Concept,' (PhD, University of California, Los Angeles, Calif.,1977), p. 293.
6　S. N. Eisenstadt, *The Political System of Empires* (Glencoe, Ill.: The Free Press, 1963).
7　Some of the above are analysed in S. P. Huntington, *The Soldiers and the State* (Cambridge, Mass.: Harvard University Press, 1957). See also, Max Weber, *Economy and Society*, ed. G. Roth and C. Wittich (New York: Bedmmaters Press), Vol. 3, pp. 1,006–71. Martin Kitchen, *The German Army Officer Corps, 1890–1914* (Oxford: Clarendon Press, 1968).
8　Perlmutter, *The Military in Modern Times*.
9　G. Harris-Jenkins, *The Army in Victorian Society* (London: Routledge & Kegan Paul, 1977).
10　Huntington, op. cit.
11　Kitchen, op. cit.; F. L. Carsten, *The Reichswehr and Politics, 1918–1933* (Oxford: Clarendon Press, 1966).
12　D. Ralston, *The Army of the Republic* (Cambridge, Mass.: MIT Press, 1967).
13　Perlmutter, *The Military in Modern Times*, ch. 6, pp. 166–204; R. Carr, *Spain* (Oxford: Clarendon Press, 1966), E. Christiansen, *The Origins of Military Power in Spain* (London: Oxford University Press, 1967).
14　D. C. Rapoport, 'Praetorianism: Government without Consensus' (PhD, University of California, Berkeley, Calif., 1959).
15　Gaetano Mossa, *The Ruling Class*, ed. and rev. Arthur Livingstone (New York: McGraw-Hill, 1939), pp. 222–43.
16　Rapoport, 'Praetorianism'.
17　For an elaborate theoretical disquisition on praetorianism see Perlmutter, op. cit., pp. 89–114.
18　Quoted in Perlmutter, *The Military in Modern Times*, p. 89.
19　S. P. Huntington, *Political Order in Changing Societies* (New Haven, Conn.: Yale University Press, 1968).
20　Perlmutter, *The Military in Modern Times*, p. 93.
21　R. Dowse, 'The military and political development,' in Colin Leys (ed.), *Politics and Change in Developing Countries* (London: Cambridge University Press, 1959), p. 227.
22　Theodore Zeldin, *France 1848–1945* (Oxford: Clarendon Press, 1974), Vol. I, pp. 504–5.
23　On corporatist, authoritarian-bureaucratic, praetorian-corporative and populist-corporatism in Latin America see Guillermo O'Donnell, *Modernization and Bureaucratic-*

Authoritarianism (Berkeley, Calif.: Institute of International Studies, 1973); James Malloy (ed.), *Authoritarianism and Corporatism in Latin America* (Pittsburgh, Pa: University of Pittsburgh Press, 1977) – see especially the essays by Malloy, O'Donnell, Kaufman, Skidmore, Mericle, and Dietz; and Phillipe Schmitter, 'The Portugalization of Brazil,' in Aldred Stepan (ed.), *Authoritarian Brazil* (New Haven, Conn.: Yale University Press, 1973). See also Peter Cleves, *Bureaucratic Politics and Administration in Chile*, (Berkeley, Calif.: University of California Press, 1974); Fitch, op. cit.; Susan Kaufman Purcell, *The Mexican Profit Sharing Decision* (Berkeley, Calif.: University of California Press, 1975); Kenneth Erickson, *Corporatism in Brazil* (Berkeley, Calif.: University of California Press, 1977).

24   O'Donnell's model in *Modernization*, op. cit., pp. 113–14.
25   For the literature on military praetorianism in the Middle East, see Eliezer Be'eri, *Army Officers in Arab Politics and Society* (New York: Praeger, 1971); P. J. Vatikiotis, *The Egyptian Army in Politics* (Bloomington, Ind.: University of Indiana Press, 1966); R. Hrair Dekmejian, *Egypt Under Nasir* (Albany, NY: State University of New York Press, 1971); A. Perlmutter, *Egypt, the Praetorian State* (New Brunswick: Transaction, 1974); and Raymond Baker, *Egypt's Uncertain Revolution under Nasser and Sadat* (Cambridge, Mass.: Harvard University Press, 1978).
26   Roman Kolkowicz, 'The future of civil–military relations in socialist countries: the Soviet Union', paper to conference on civil–military relations in socialist and modernizing societies, Center for International and Strategic Studies, UCLA, Santa Barbara 17–19 May 1979, p. 14.
27   I am grateful to Ellis Joffe's incisive commentary and his paper during the Santa Barbara conference. See Ellis Joffe, 'The military as a political actor in China,' p. 20.
28   Here I have found the pioneer work of my colleague William LeoGrande enlightening. See his seminal pieces: 'The politics of revolutionary development: civil–military relations in Cuba,' *Journal of Strategic Studies*, vol. 1 (3 December 1978), pp. 260–95; 'The case of Cuba,' in Dale Herspring and Ivan Volgyes (eds), *Civil–Military Relations in Communist Countries* (Boulder, Colo.: Westview Press), pp. 201–18.
29   Kenneth Jowitt comments on Alex Alexiev, 'Party–military relations in Eastern Europe: the case of Romania,' paper to Santa Barbara conference. See chapter 9 of present volume.
30   See Kolkowicz, op. cit., pp. 14–17.
31   See Timothy Colton, *Commissars, Commanders and Civilian Authority* (Cambridge, Mass.: Harvard University Press, 1979), pp. 231–49.
32   Colton, op. cit., p. 232.
33   ibid., p. 43.
34   William I. Odom 'The party–military connection: a critique,' in Dale Herspring and Ivan Volgyes (eds), op. cit., pp. 25–52, quote p. 212.
35   ibid., p. 48.
36   For extensive analysis on ideology and organization see Philip Selznik, *The Organization Weapon* (Glencoe, Ill.: The Free Press, 1962); Franz Schurmann, *Ideology and Organization in Communist China* (Berkeley, Calif.: University of California, 1966); Amos Perlmutter, 'Ideology and Organization: The Socialist-Zionist Movement, unpublished PhD, University of California, Berkeley, Calif., 1957).
37   For Egypt, see Baker, *Egypt's Uncertain Revolution*; Perlmutter, *Egypt,*; Dekmejian, op. cit.; and P. J. Vatikiotis, *Nasser and His Generation* (London: Croom Helm, 1979). For Peru see Stepan, op. cit. and A. Lowenthal (ed.), *The Peruvian Experiment* (Princeton, NJ: Princeton University Press, 1975).
38   Baker's analysis of Egypt's 'Uncertain Revolution' is an excellent exposition of the Nasserists' dilemma (op. cit., pp. 88–131).
39   Cynthia McClintock, 'The ambiguity of Peru's third way: costs and benefits,' *Workshop on the 'Peruvian Experiment Reconsidered'* (Washington, DC: The Wilson Center, November 1978), pp. 9–11.
40   The finest study demonstrating the corruption of authoritarian and praetorian military rule in Africa is Samuel Decalo's *Coups and Army Rule in Africa: Studies in Military Style* (New Haven, Conn.: Yale University Press, 1976). See especially pp. 5–39 and pp. 231–55. See also S. Andreski, *African Predicament* (London: Joseph, 1968).
41   Henry Bienen, 'Nigeria,' in Abraham Lowenthal (ed.), *Peru* (Princeton, NJ: Princeton University Press, 1976); Perlmutter, *Egypt*; Dekmejian, op. cit.; Alfred Stepan, *The*

Military in Politics: Brazil (Princeton, NJ: Princeton University Press, 1971); Stepan, *The State and Society*; Moshe Lissak, *Military and Modernization in Burma and Thailand* (Chicago: Russell Sage, 1976); John Maynard, 'A Comparison of Military Elite Role Perceptions in Indonesia and the Philippines' PhD, The American University, 1976), pp. 117–51.

42 On Coup Zone see William Thompson, 'Explanation of the Coup d'état' (PhD, University of Washington, 1972), pp. 10–21.

Notes on the Editors and Contributors

Alex Alexiev is a Staff Member at the RAND Corporation. He is a specialist on Soviet and East European affairs and is coauthor of *East European Military Establishments*.

Richard H. Dekmejian is a Professor at State University of New York at Binghamton, and has published two books on the politics of the Middle East: *Egypt Under Nasser: A Study in Political Dynamics* and *Patterns of Leadership: Egypt, Israel, Lebanon*. In progress is a work on Sadat's Egypt.

Samuel E. Finer is Gladstone Professor of Government and Public Administration and Fellow of All Souls, Oxford. He has published *Man on Horseback* and numerous articles on military affairs. His other publications deal with British Government and Comparative Politics.

Daniel Horowitz is a Senior Lecturer at the Hebrew University of Jerusalem. He is coauthor of *The Israeli Army* and *Origins of the Israeli Polity* and has also written a monograph on Israeli defense strategy 'Israeli Concept of Defensible Borders'. He was recently appointed Director of the Leonard Davis Institute for International Relations at the Hebrew University of Jerusalem.

Ellis Joffe is Professor in Chinese Studies and International Relations at the Hebrew University of Jerusalem. He is author of *Party and Army: Professionalism and Political Control in the Chinese Officers Corps, 1949-1964* and many articles on Chinese military affairs.

A. Ross Johnson is a senior social scientist at the RAND Corporation, Santa Monica, California. He currently leads research projects dealing with Yugoslavia and Eastern Europe. He has published two books on Yugoslavia: *The Transformation of Communist Ideology: The Yugoslav Case, 1945-1953* and *Yugoslavia: In the Twilight of Tito*, along with articles on Yugoslav military and political affairs.

Fuad I. Khuri is Professor of Social Anthropology at the American University in Beirut. He is the author of *From Village to Suburb: Order and Change in Greater Beirut* and has contributed numerous articles to such journals as the *Middle East Journal, Human Organization*, and *Africa*.

Roman Kolkowicz is Professor and Director of the Center for International and Strategic Affairs, UCLA. He has published *The Soviet Military and the Communist Party* and has also written on Soviet foreign and defense policies and on arms control and strategic issues. He is currently researching a study on the roles of defense intellectuals in the USA and USSR.

Andrzej Korbonski is Professor and Chairman of the Department of Political Science at the University of California, Los Angeles. He is the author of *The Politics of Socialist Agriculture in Poland 1945-1960*, and has written on various aspects of East European politics and economics.

Amos Perlmutter is a Professor at the American University, Washington, DC. His publications include *Politics and the Military in Israel, 1967-1977; Military and Politics in Modern Times*, and *Egypt and the Praetorian State*. He is editor of *The Journal of Strategic Studies*.

David C. Rapoport is Professor of Political Science at University of California, Los Angeles. His main interest is theory and his most recent publication is *Moses, Charisma and Covenant*. He has published *Assassination and Terrorism* and several articles on military conspiracies and institutions.

Sarah Meiklejohn Terry is Assistant Professor of Political Science at Tufts University and an Associate of the Russian Research Center at Harvard University. A specialist in Polish affairs, Dr Terry has published a number of articles on the domestic and external politics of Eastern Europe, and has just completed a major study of the origin of the Oder-Neisse boundary during World War II.

Index

activism
  and hegemonial systems 236
Afghanistan 285
Africa
  and Soviet expansionism 121
  see also individual countries
Agranat Commission 92
Albania
  anti-Soviet position 201
Algeria 13, 288, 305
  military intervention 14
Amin, I. 259, 260
Amir, Marshal 34, 35
anti-Semitism
  in Poland 168, 169, 170
Antonescu, Marshal 210
Arab-Israeli War 1967 16, 33, 34–5, 66, 270, 272
Arab Socialist Union 33, 34, 40, 321, 326
  reorganization 38
Argentina 288, 305, 320, 326
armaments
  and Soviet expansionism 121, 249
  in Yugoslavia 184
  industry in Romania 214
  see also nuclear weapons
Armed Forces of Yugoslavia
  territorial defense forces 185–6
army
  and praetorianism 252–6, 272–3
  antagonistic ethnic minority units 259
  discipline 262
  donatives 262–4
  functions 315–6
  Gulf 258
  Spanish 266–7
  see also army officers; soldiers
army officers
  and leadership 271
  and political decision-making 91, 220
  capabilities 130, 269, 272
  control of strategic government posts 32–3, 190
  early retirement schemes 86, 94–5, 185
  education of 115
  foreign 258–9
  geographical origins 59–62, 182, 198
  military syndicalism 268
  Perlmutter classification 28, 30
  privileges 23, 44, 70
  social origins 10, 18–19, 21, 84
Army Mutual Assistance Association 44
Asad, Hafiz al- 68–9, 70–1
  personal guard 70
assassination
  in Syria 72

Ataturk, M. K. P. 13, 20, 41–2, 48
Augustus 253, 254, 255
authoritarian regimes 310–11 and
  military interventionism 312–13, 321–6

Barré, President 289
Ba'th Party 65–71, 293
Ben-Gurion 91
Benin 288, 289, 305
'Bonapartism' 47, 319
Brandt-Gomulka Treaty 176
Brazil 296, 300, 305, 320, 326
Brezhnev, L. I. 133, 135, 241, 248
  and the military 245
bureaucracy
  and civil–military relations 314–15
  and elitism 19
  and Soviet Communist Party 109–10, 238–9
Burma 291, 299–300, 305
Burundi 288, 305

Ceasescu, I. 204
Cebesoy, A. F. 41
Central African Republic 286, 292, 293, 294–5, 306, 326
Chad 285, 327
charisma 35, 41, 48, 118, 130–1, 321
Ch'en Tsai-tao 147–8
Chile 261, 263–4, 288, 306, 320, 326
China
  civil–military relations 322
  Cultural Revolution 144–5, 148
  'gang of four' 151, 154
  Great Leap Forward 142, 143
  Military Control Committee 104–1, 146
  new Party Committees 149–50
  relationship with Romania 215
  relationship with Soviet Union 146, 151
  relationship with Yugoslavia 186
  Revolutionary Committees 145
civil defense
  in Romania 213
  in Soviet Union 114
civil–military models 232
  classification 13
  Institutional Conflict Model 200
  Institutional Congruence Model 200
  Participation Model 200–1
civil–military relations
  classical model 310, 311
  Communist model 310, 311, 321–6
  in China 140–3, 322
  in Eastern Europe 199–201
  in Egypt 30–40
  in Israel 77–99
  in Poland 161–2, 166–73

in Romania 204–6, 217–20, 221–2, 323
in Soviet Union 109–35, 200, 232, 233–5,
   237–49, 322
in Syria 65–72
in Turkey 40–9
in Yugoslavia 186–93, 323
Praetorian model 310–11
research orientations 2–4, 232–3
Welch basic schema 28, 29
coalition governments
in Turkey 45
colonialism
and military models 12–13, 14
communist system
and role of Soviet military 109–35, 322
in Poland 162–4, 173, 176
in Romania 216–17, 323
in Yugoslavia 181–4, 190–1, 197, 323
organization in China 140–1, 149–50,
   155– 6
versus military desiderata 203
see also hegemonial systems
Comoros Islands 285
comparativists
and research orientations 2
conformity tactics 18, 21
Congo Republic 288, 289, 306
'constitutional monarchies' 282
consumerism
in Soviet Union 247, 249
corruption
and praetorianism 273
coups d'etats 254, 256–8, 260, 285–6
bloodless 266
in Latin America 260–1
in the Middle East, 11, 16, 19, 30, 42–4,
   46, 57–8, 63, 65
in Romania 209–10
in Thailand 290
crisis-regimes 312–13
Cuba 261, 323
Cultural Revolution
Chinese 144–6, 148
Cyprus
Turkish invasion 45, 46
Czechoslovakia 170, 184

Dayan, M. 86, 89, 90, 91, 92, 93
decision-making
and military influence 91, 116, 146–7, 155–
   6, 160–1, 170
importance of communication 272
defense expenditure 264–5
in Israel 95
in Romania 214
in Soviet Union 115, 120
in Syria 70
in Yugoslavia 184
defense policy
in Israel 77–80, 82–4, 87, 88–9, 91, 93–4

in Romania 213–14
in Soviet Union 124–6
in Yugoslavia 185–6
Demirel, S. 43–4, 45, 46
despotism 255, 256
détente 121, 124, 125, 133, 249
developmentalism 313
diplomatic exchange
and Arab-Israeli relations 92
and Romanian foreign relations 215
domatives
to soldiers 262–4

Eaglets Programs
in Soviet Union 113
Eastern Europe
political relationships and the military
   201–3, 221
see also individual countries
Ecevit, B. 45, 46
economic development
and the military 95–6, 114–15, 124, 239
in Romania 204
in Yugoslavia 184
Polish difficulties 171, 172
projects and military support 17, 67–8, 219
Edhem, C. 41
education
influence on military training 64
Soviet military network of 112, 115
Syrian expenditure 68
Egypt 13, 20, 320, 321, 326, 327
civil–military relations 30–40, 296, 301, 306
coup d'etat 1952 30
relationship with Syria 63
relationship with USA 39
relationship with USSR 36
War 1967 33, 34–5, 270
War 1973 37
elitism
and military regimes 18–19, 22–3, 161
Engels, 252
and praetorianism 253
Equatorial Guinea 288, 306
Eshkol, L. 89, 90, 91
Ethiopia 288, 289, 306
ethnic minorities
and military cohesiveness 47
and stability 260
influence on Syrian coups 57–62, 73
influence on Syrian military regimes 52–7,
   63–4, 70–2
in separate army units 259
Europe
influence on military models 12, 13

factionalism
in Syria 68–9
Fawzi, M. 32, 35, 37
France

and colonial Syria 52–7

Gaddafi, Colonel 260
Ghana 298, 299
Gierek, J. 168, 169–70, 171, 172
Gomulka, W. 165, 166, 167, 168, 169
Gośnjak, I. 187
government departments
  functions of 90
  military control of strategic posts 32–3, 200
government systems
  and military regimes 281–2, 285–301
  see also coalition government; civil-military
    relations
Gürsel, C. 42, 43

hegemonial political systems
  definition of 235–7
  problems of civil–military relations 232–3
Honduras 290, 306
Hua 254–5
Hungary 170, 201

ideological strategies
  and Israeli national security policy 82–3
  and Syrian Army 69
  competing 147
  of communist parties 119, 132, 206–7,
    216–17
independence
  and military models 14
Indonesia 291–2, 300–1, 307
Inönü, I. 41
instability
  and ethnic minority differences 259–60, 328
  and praetorian regimes 311, 318
  in Poland 172–3
  in Syria 62
  in Turkey 44
intelligence information
  and communication 272
  and defense planning 92
Iran
  nationalism 20
Iraq 13, 269, 271, 286, 292, 293, 307, 327
  Shawwaf attempted coup 16
Islamic fundamentalism 71–2
Israel 13
  Arab-Israeli conflict 88, 92
  military identity 14
  military organization 89
  national security policy 77–80, 82–4, 87,
    88–9, 91, 97–8
  October 1973 War 80, 85, 89, 92
  relationship with Syria 92
  Six-Day War 1967 90, 93–4, 168, 270
Israel Defense Service Law 81, 83
Israeli Defense Forces
  image 84–5
  military doctrine 93–4

Jadid, S. 68–9
Jaruzelski, General 168
Jordan 13, 260
  foreign army officers 258
  tribal based military 15, 16
Junta Militar 286, 287, 301
Justice Party (Turkey) 43–4

Karabekir, K. 41
Khalil, M. 40
Khrushchev, N. 115, 122–3, 124, 125, 133,
  135, 243, 244–5
kinship
  and military regimes 22
Kissinger, H. 37
Knesset 91
Korea 285
Korutürk, F. 45, 46
Kosygin, A. 133

Lasswell, H. 78–9
Latin America
  coups d'etats 260–1
  types of military regime 283, 286
  see also individual countries
leadership
  and army confidence 271
  and charisma 35, 118
  in Soviet Union 118–19, 122–3, 125–6,
    129–31, 239
  weakness in Egypt 32, 34, 37
Lebanon 13
  Ahdab coup 15
  civil war 71
Libya 260, 288, 307
Lin Piao 143, 144, 148, 150, 152
Lo Jui-ch'ing 144, 151

Madagascar 292, 293, 294, 307
Malenkov, G. 122, 123, 124, 133
Mali 288, 307
Mao Tse-tung 142, 143, 150, 233
Marcos, President 283
Marx, K. 252, 262
  and praetorianism 253
mass-mobilization
  and support in Syrian politics 67–8
Mauritania 288, 307
Meir, G. 90
Menderes, A. 42
mercenaries 258–9
Middle East
  and Soviet expansionism 121
  civil–military relations 27
  Gulf regular army 258
  military regimes 9–21
  see also individual countries
military doctrine 93–4
military identity 14
  in Poland 174–5

in Soviet Union 234
military intervention
    in China 139, 145–50
    in Soviet Union 127–8
    in Syria 52, 65–72
    in Turkey 40, 42, 44–6, 49, 283
    types 16–17, 282–5, 311–12
military models
    in the Middle East 12–17
    see also civil–military models
military professionalism 12
    and political decision-making 91, 315
    and political involvements 142, 143, 151–2
    in Eastern Europe 201
military regimes
    and modernization 17–18, 162, 177
    and political pressure 92–3
    chief executives 285–7
    classification of 281–2
    ideologies 17–21
    in Eastern Europe 201–3, 208–11
    in the Middle East 10–17, 49
    in Poland 162–6
    in Soviet Union 111–13
    types of 282–302, 305–9
military service
    in Israel 81, 83
    in Soviet Union 113–14
military technology 22–4
military training
    for Romanian youth 218
    see also military service
minority cultures
    and military models 14–15, 47
    see also ethnic minorities
Moczar, 167, 168, 169–70, 171
'modernization'
    and military regimes 18, 23–4, 162, 177,
        232, 240
    see also economic development; political
        development
Morocco 13
    and minorities dominated military 15, 260
Mubarak, H. 38

Nagib, M. 30, 31
Nasser, Abd al- 10, 30, 32, 34–5, 38, 48
Nassif, Al-Laithi 36
nationalism
    Arab 17, 20
    Chinese 141, 147
    Israeli 98
    Polish 167–8
    Romanian 205–7, 218, 221
    Soviet 131, 132
    Turkish 41–2
    Yugoslav 187, 188, 191
National Unity Committee (Turkey) 42
NATO
    relationship with Romania 21

Niger 288, 308
Nigeria 259, 298, 299
nuclear weapons 90, 133

Obote, M. 264
officer-technocrats 33
Ozaydinli, I. 45

Pahlavi, R. S. 13, 20
Pakistan 13, 270–1, 289–90, 308
Paraguay 296, 308
participation
    and Israeli society 82–4, 98
    and Polish military 160–1, 170–3, 175
    civil–military model 200–1, 324–5
P'eng Teh-Luai 142, 143
People's Liberation Army (China) 139
    factionalism in 148–9, 154
    organization 140–1
    political ascent 144, 146–7
    relationship with the Party 142, 143, 145–
        53, 156
    role of 140, 155
    role in Cultural Revolution 144–6
People's Liberation Army (Yugoslavia)
        181–2
Peres, S. 90
Perlmutter, A. classification of military
        officers 28, 30
Peru 289, 308, 326
Philipine Republic 282–3
Poland
    de-Stalinization 164–5
    economic problems 171, 172
    image of military 174
    industrial unrest 171–2
    Partisan movement 167–8
    relationship with Soviet Union 161, 166–7,
        172, 174
    relationship with West Germany 176
    role of the military 160–1, 177
    Sovietization of military 162–4
political development
    and role of the military 160–2
    in Soviet Union 239–40
    influence of army officers 94–5
    projects and military influence 17, 18
political systems
    and civil–military relations 314–17
    and the 'new states' 312–13
    see also authoritarian regimes; hegemonial
        political systems, praetorianism
power
    and army officers 23
    and minority groups 14–15
    Arab-Israeli balance 80
praetorianism
    and civil–military relations 317–19, 325
    and military capabilities 269–72
    as corruption 273

concept 253–6
  definition 253, 312, 317–18
  democratic 255–6
  despotic 255, 256, 260
  exploitation of natural antagonisms 259–60
  future of 326–9
  in Egypt 31–5
  modern military 319–21
  vulnerability of 257–8, 260–1
presidential government systems 292–7

Rabin, Y. 91
radicalism
  in China 153–4
Red Guards
  role in Cultural Revolution 145–6
Republican People's Party (Turkey) 41
reserve systems
  Israeli 80–1, 86
rioting
  in Egypt 38, 39
  in Poland 168, 169
Rokossovsky, Marshal 162, 164
Roman Republic
  and praetorianism 253–5, 267, 268
Romania 170, 174, 323
  independent drive 204
  international relations 204, 215
  nationalism 206–7, 218, 221
  reestablishment of military roles 208–11
  relationship with Soviet Union 204
Rwanda 288, 308

Sadat, A. 35–7, 38–40, 48
Sadiq, M. 36
Salim, M. 38
Saudi Arabia 13, 16
sectarianism
  in Syria 71
Sharett, M. 90, 91, 93
Shazli, S. 37, 39
Sidqi, A. 32
Six-Day War *see* Arab-Israeli War
social change
  and the military 3, 9, 17–18, 19–20
  in Eastern Europe 170
social class
  and army officers 18–19, 22–3, 46
  conflict 44
social development
  in Syria 68
social mobility
  military as outlet for 21, 22, 84
social planning
  in Soviet Union 237–8
social science theory
  and civil–military relations research 1–4
sociologists
  research orientations 2

soldiers
  and coups d'etats 256–8
  dependency 254–5
  ethnic origins 53–6
  remuneration 263, 265
  see also army officers
Somalia 288, 289, 308
Sovietologists
  research orientation 2
Soviet Union *see* Union of Soviet Socialist Republics
Spain
  praetorian army 252, 253, 266–7, 268, 273, 316
Spychalski, General 165, 166, 168
Sri Lanka 282
Stalin, J. 113, 122–3, 131, 133, 135, 241, 243
  and the military 244
  conflict with Tito 183
  Five Year Plans 114
Sudan 292, 293, 294, 308
suicide 273
Sünay, C. 43
Supreme Military Council (Turkey) 42–3
Switzerland 78
Syria 13, 21, 292, 293, 309, 327
  and Lebanese civil war 70, 71
  and minorities-dominated military 15, 17, 52–73, 260
  coups 22, 57–8, 63, 65, 68, 69, 73
  defense expenditure 70
  merger with Egypt 63
  relationship with Israel 92
  rural-to-urban migration 23
  social and economic development 67–8
Syrian Social Nationalist Party 61

takeovers *see* coups d'etats; military intervention
Tanzania 261, 264
Thailand 286, 289, 298, 299, 309
  military regime 290
Third World
  and military exports 120
  and Soviet expansionism 121, 241
'threat potential'
  and research orientation 3, 231
Tito, J. 181, 183, 188, 189
Togo 292, 293, 295, 309, 327
totalitarianism
  decline of 110, 117, 128, 159
tribe
  based armies 16
  definition 15
Tunisia 13
Turkey 13
  attempted coups 43, 46
  May 1960 coup 42–4
  role of military in politics 40–8
tyranny 319, 320, 321, 327

Uganda 259, 264, 285, 327
Union of Soviet Socialist Republics
  changing pattern of leadership 110–11,
    116–17, 129–31, 242–3
  expansionist policies 120–2, 238, 241, 243
    248
  political relationships with Eastern Europe
    202–3
  relationship with China 146, 247
  relationship with Egypt 36
  relationship with Poland 161, 166–7
  relationship with Romania 204
  relationship with Yugoslavia 183, 184–5
  roles of military 126, 130, 322
  security forces 239
  size of military establishment 113, 120
  systemic priorities 237–8
United States of America
  relationship with Egypt 39
  relationship with Yugoslavia 186
  sovereignty theory and the Constitution
    317
Urgülü, S. H. 43
Uraguay 286, 288, 309

values
  and the military 13, 19, 21, 246, 247
  and Romanian society 217–18
  and Soviet society 110
  civilian versus military 78–80, 203, 325

war *see* Arab-Israeli War; World War II
Welch, C.
  schema of civilian-military relations 28–9
West Germany
  relationship with Poland 176
women

military service in Israel 81, 83
Workers' Defense Committee 172
World Coup Zone 328
World War II
  Romanian participation 209–10

Yadinm, Y. 81
Yemen 13, 288, 309
Young Pioneers (Romania) 218
Young Pioneers Programs (Soviet Union)
  113
Yugoslav People's Army
  development 181–2
  nationalism in 188, 191
  organization 182, 185, 187
  'Partisan commanders' 193
  proportional national representation 187,
    192
  roles 183–4, 185, 186–93, 194
  see also Armed Forces of Yugoslavia
Yugoslavia 323
  effects of invasion of Czechoslovakia 184–
    5, 186
  reform programs 188
  regional self-affirmation 187
  relationship with China 186
  relationship with USSR 183, 184–5, 186,
    201
  relationship with USA 186
  total national defense system 185–6, 194
  veterans organization 190
  see also Yugoslav People's Army

Zaire 292, 293, 295, 309
ZboWiD 166, 168
Zhukov, Marshal 124, 125, 245
Zionism 82–3, 88

Publications of the Center for International and Strategic Affairs, UCLA

William Potter (ed.), *Verification and SALT: The Challenge of Strategic Deception* (Westview, 1980)

Bennett Ramberg, *Destruction of Nuclear Energy Facilities in War: The Problem and Implications* (Lexington Books, 1980)

Paul Jabber, *Not by War Alone: The Politics of Arms Control in the Middle East* (University of California Press, 1981)

William Potter, *Nuclear Power and Nonproliferation: An Interdisciplinary Perspective* (Oelgeschlager, Gunn, & Hain, 1981)

Steven L. Spiegel (ed.), *The Middle East and the Western Alliance* (Allen & Unwin, 1982)